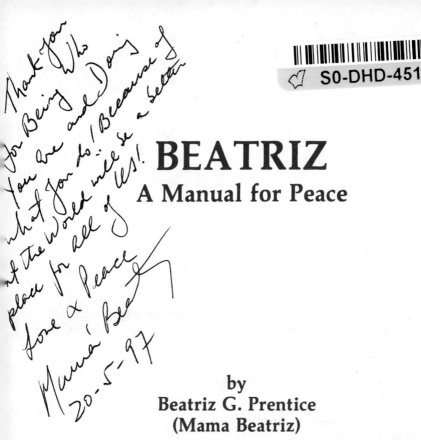

Thank you
for Being Who
You are and Doing
what you do! Because of
the world will be a better
place for all of US!.
Love & Peace
Mama Bea
20-5-97

BEATRIZ
A Manual for Peace

by
Beatriz G. Prentice
(Mama Beatriz)

Published by World Purpose Foundation

Distributed by Coleman Publishing
99 Milbar Blvd.
Farmingdale, N.Y. 11735

Published by:
  World Purpose Foundation
  140 University Ave., Ste. 4
  Palo Alto, California 94301

Other Books by the Author

Porque Quiero Al Mundo, an anthology of verse
  (in Spanish)

First printing 1984
Printed in the United States of America

Library of Congress Cataloging in Publication Data

Prentice, Beatriz G., 1941-
  Beatriz: a manual for peace.

  Includes index.
  1. Prentice, Beatriz G., 1941-   . 2. United States — Biography.
3. Interpersonal relations. 4. Conduct of life. 5. Success.
I. Title.
CT275.P834A33   973.92'092'4   83-51579
ISBN 0-915485-10-9

CONTENTS

To my children:
The Nations of Planet Earth

FOREWORD

Beatriz, who never, ever, thought of writing a book herself, and flatly refused to work on her English, "because it isn't important," has now, suddenly, written a book . . . in English. She did not plan it; she was impelled and instructed from within. I was sent to her — to edit that book — by something far beyond my comprehension.

The reader deserves some comment on the organization of the book. The first five chapters examine the same forty years in Beatriz's life, along five different themes: Sex, Money, Food, Mind and Feelings. Within these chapters, anecdotes illustrate her applications of Divine Laws. As the pieces of a jigsaw puzzle are all needed to complete the picture, so also a reading of all five autobiographical chapters is essential to cover the first 40 years' span.

A rough chronology is attempted, which the reader may better understand by reference to the Chronology Chart printed between the first two chapters. But it should be remembered that, as in describing a landscape viewed from a helicopter, the sequence of presentation is quite arbitrary, particularly in the Chapter on Feelings. Therefore, bridges between episodes have in many cases not even been attempted, and in others are most tenuous.

The Sixth chapter is a purely chronological account of some of the "Experience" which Beatriz had from Spring to September 1981.

Chapter Seven presents the theories, Laws and logic distilled from her entire life's experience and confirmed and integrated by The Experience.

Throughout the autobiographical first five chapters, which have been my editing responsibility, I have attempted to retain the language and flavor of

Beatriz herself. We have worked very closely on these. I cannot speak for the text and organization of the remaining two, since I have not seen them in the original.

To say that this is a remarkable book by a remarkable woman, is a gross understatement. The word "remarkable" has become hackneyed and no longer conveys its old import. But the reader will see for himself/herself . . . And if he/she will **dare** to put into test-practice even just some of the Laws here illustrated, the power of this message will uplift the quality of his/her life, and the lives of those around, to a level previously undreamed. I know what some of this application has done for me!

Palo Alto,
May 1983
MCH

ACKNOWLEDGEMENTS

I would like to thank, from the bottom of my heart, the tide of people who left my shore. They made it possible for the next tide to come in. Both, therefore, have been instrumental in bringing this book about.

My heartfelt thanks go to Karel Edith, who had to put up with my peculiar writing, as: No **He, She** or **It** in front of a verb . . . or **ed** at the end of it . . . never mind about having verb agreements . . . ! But far more important she gave me moral support as I was still writing the first draft.

The final version of Book I was the triumph of MCH who worked with me up to 14 hours a day, and believe me, even though our hearts were open to each other, to work with me was no picnic! There is no way I can ever pay this human being, except to say, "She is a Saint." Hers was a labor of love!

I'd like to express my gratitude to Mike Patton who sat with me and edited Book II for 8 hours at a time after working a shift of 8 to 10 hours on his regular job. He told me once: "At first I thought, 'This lady has cracked, but then I tried to see where the seams would have been glued if you had cracked. It was then that I realized there were no cracks, you had never broken down, you had just grown." His was another labor of love!

Mr. Saadi Klotz is responsible for the editing of Book III. I must say this Book was so easy . . . ! I just gave the manuscript to him and bingo! It came back done.

Finally, I'd like to give my thanks:

To feminine Peggy Blackshaw and courageous Kathryn Reeder who tirelessly typed this manuscript, who sat at my table and shared their lives with me. Another labor of love!

To sweet Shirley who paused to proofread the chapters in the midst of her busy life.

To Timothy E., Sura, James Fetler, Al Young, Mary Jane Moffat, Bathsheva, Margaret and Connie for constructive criticism.

To Allan P. for much help with photocopies and his personal writings.

To American Copy Service, of Palo Alto, for truly helping, at a time of need, with much needed paper.

To Delmer Israel Business Machine Center for selling me a typewriter when I went and said, "I don't have any money, I am going to write a book, I need a typewriter," and they graciously said, "Take one," and when I paid them, 5 months later, they charged no interest!

To Andrea who, when I had nothing and said, "I am going to write," opened her house, her fridge and her purse to me and Robert.

To Robert Prentice who not only gave his artistic skills in the creation of the duck illustrations, but also patiently gave up his time with me so I could complete the book.

Each door closed or opened as I needed it. To ALL, the ones who closed their doors to me, and to those who opened them, to ALL, Thank YOU! I could not have done it without ALL of you.

PROLOGUE

A dream is a reality in its seed.

I have spent my life showing people how they could realize their dreams. Most people do not want to be shown how they can do it, because then they would have to get up and do something, or to dream a new dream, about which they could again say, "I wish but I can't."

Now my dear world, it is not different. You do have a dream, it is Peace. And you keep saying, "I wish but I can't."

Excuses! Excuses!

You Can and we Will, because I have come to show the way. My father was right. I acted as if saying, "I am here. I have come," when I was an infant. It is true: I have come. Finally, after 40 years of inner working for the few, I begin my next 80 years working for Mankind.

You Want Me White

By Alfonsina Storni
(Translated by Beatriz G. Prentice)

You want me alb
made of sea foam,
made of mother-of-pearl.
To be lilywhite
Above all, chaste.
Of tenuous perfume and
Closed corolla.

Not even a moon ray
has entered me,
Not even a daisy could
call herself my sister
You want me niveous,
You want me white,
You want me alb.

You who have drunk from
every cup you found,
Your lips are purple
from fruits and honeys.
You, who by
celebrating at
Bacchus' banquet
have become fleshless.

You that in the garden
Black from deceit
Dress in red
run amok;
You who still have
your skeleton intact
from which miracles
I do not know.
You want me pure.
(God forgive you)
You want me chaste.
(God forgive you)
You want me alb!

x

Flee towards the forest;
Race to the mountain;
Purify your mouth;
Live in a cave;
Touch with your hands
the wet soil;
Nourish your body
with bitter roots;
Find drink from the rocks;
Sleep over hoarfrost
Renew your tissues
with salt and water;

Wake up at dawn
and speak with the birds
And when your flesh
has been turned
and when you have
reclaimed your soul
which in all the bedrooms
has been tangled
THEN, good man,
Demand me white,
Demand me niveous,
Demand me chaste.

BOOK ONE
BEATRIZ

CHAPTER 1
GOD OF SEX

My sexual life started a long time ago. I am now 40, but when I was two years old my father would take me for walks and show me flower buds. He showed me how they grew and the differences in size, shape, color and species. The walks were lazy and I remember the feel of spring in the air. I can still relive the looking, observing, touching of all those different buds, smelling all those scents . . . My eyes were curious, my little hands needed to touch, my nose wanted to smell . . . and many times I just had to eat one of them! Roses: I remember eating petals of roses. Father encouraged me to touch, to smell, to explore . . . basically to Be.

As I grew older he showed me the chickens and their eggs. Those moments waiting before a glass case to watch the chick break the shell, are still vivid.

My father watched me.

I knew even then, he enjoyed looking at me while I was transfixed, marveling at what I saw as a new and miraculous event. He smiled approvingly at my innocence. All those experiences, and more, were the seeds of my sexual life.

When I was about seven he took me to see horses courting. What a delight! I can hear his voice, "Now Beatriz look at the mane floating in the air. Look how one neck curves over the other, they are caressing. See how they run, how they play?" Hours were spent looking at the horses: sometimes quietly, sometimes with papa making sure I observed every detail.

He was very pleased with me. I guess I responded as he wanted: inquisitive and happy to be there with him, making him feel important. Time and again I told him he knew everything about everything. At that, he would laugh and reply, "One day you will say I do not know anything. Later you will start to discover that I know some things. Finally, when I am no longer with you, you will remember me as someone who knew quite a bit." It was all true! I did say all those things, which only shows how normal I can be!

Back then, in the forties, he was constantly saying how sad it was that parents take care of their children so well in many ways, love them so much, and yet leave them alone, unguided in a matter as important as sex. He swore he would never do such harm to his children, and he did not. Every day sex was openly discussed at the table, dinner or lunch. Father would say, "If one is hungry one goes to the fridge. If one wants sex, one makes love." Thus for me, sex and food were always associated. Making love was presented as a natural appetite, a natural urge that could be satisfied. I was shown that it is something beautiful, that purifies, that cleanses and brings light.

I was only too well aware that these concepts were not held by the world at large. I knew how differently he was bringing me up, and this knowledge made me love him more. It showed his courage, and that he knew how to stand apart from the crowd. I had something very solid to which to look up. He was not just talking about great men, he was **Being** one. By taking risks, he was an example to me. I was truly aware of all this as a child. Yet, I felt he was not my father, rather, I was his mother.

My sexual education also included personal examples. If Father and Mother had any sexual problems, these were discussed at the table. Some people talk about the logistics of car pools at the table. In my parents' home, sex, politics and religion were the mealtime subjects. I observed how to deal with these problems. And to observe the struggles between my parents was very beneficial for me. He had little time for her, sexual or total. She wanted him more. I also saw how they accommodated each other.

However, maybe it was not beneficial for my sister, Ana Maria. She would get up from the table, when she was about twelve, and say it was all "silly." I can't speak for her.

Not many people have a view of the sexual life of their parents. Parents are somehow asexual. By the time I was five, Ana Maria and I always knew when they were going to make love. The foreplay at the table was obvious, as was the closing of doors, the running to bathrooms. It was funny. We tried to guess how many condoms tonight. The following morning one of us would check the night table to find out how many were missing.

Children in those days were told they were brought by a stork or left in a cabbage patch. Don't laugh; it is true! But my father, after lessons with flowers, then chickens and horses, taught me about human beings. Using encyclopedias, he showed me how babies are born. Homosexuality was also discussed and we looked at pictures of men sitting on each other's laps. Sure, they were fully dressed, but remember, this was 1947-48-49.

The more he explained to me, the prouder I was of him. But the outside world was cruel. Home was good, warm, where I felt loved, understood and protected. Outside it was hard.

I attended a Catholic boarding school. One day when I was four I walked onto the patio of the school and stretched my arms out to play ring-around-the-roses, or something of the sort. No one would hold my hand. In shock, I asked why. Someone answered, "I like you. I want to play with you, but I can't because my mother says you are evil." (**I wish** . . . **but I can't** . . .) How? Why?

The next time I was home, I ran to Father and told him what had happened.

He went to the nuns. They said the parents had told them that their little girls were not to play with Beatriz because she was evil. What evil had I done? I had told the girls how children were born. It was true. All the girls would get together in the bathroom and tell incredible stories of where they came from. I could not believe my ears! In all innocence I told them these were not true and that my father had told me and shown me pictures of how children were born. I also told them that this was why women got fat before a baby comes. To these parents this knowledge made me evil.

Father explained to me that those parents were lying to their children. He did not want to lie to me because he felt it was wrong. He said that to live by what one believes sometimes brings sorrow and misunderstanding, but that I should be proud to know within myself that I had parents who were honest with me.

This incident made me decide to live to prove myself to be a Christ, a saint. **I will** live to prove THERE IS NO EVIL! THERE IS ONLY GOOD! **Even if** I am the only person who thinks so!

And so, little by little, my sexuality grew.

I turned twelve. Oh, how I looked! I was as developed as a mature, sophisticated, 19 year old.

Suddenly Father realized what he had done: I was ready to act on the theories he had taught me. He became frightened. Because of this he turned on me and said, "Well, all I have taught you is good, but you can't just make love to justify your sexual urges as easily as going to the 'fridge to satisfy your physical hunger. Society is not ready."

Oh, what pain I felt! My hero had let me down! How could he change his tune after so many years? I had been so very proud of him for his daring. I had imagined that I would never have sex before marriage. I would have conducted myself as society expected me to live. That was going to be my gift to him, for his courage to be different: because he dared to live differently! And now he had turned on me, like a pancake flipping in mid-air.

From "**I will** . . . (live freely) **even if** . . . (society says no)" to "**If** . . . (society is ready), **then I will** . . . (live freely)."

I could not take the pain I felt at the falling of my hero. My respect for him was gone. I thought, "I am going to show him. I am going to make him live the consequences of his teachings and actions. He will regret it. Oh, Daddy, how can you change a principle? How could you be so **scared?!**"

3

Before this he and I had been very close and physical. He would take me places, to sculpture exhibitions, to Palermo to see outdoor ballets and to El Colón. But all of this stopped. I missed this closeness and did not understand why it stopped. "What did I do? Why is he not available like before? Why doesn't he touch me any more?" The only contact that remained was on Sunday afternoon, when we would lie down together to listen to opera, and on Saturday nights to listen to the theater on the radio. All the rest was gone.

By then I had boy friends. At twelve I had a boy friend 28 years old. I could not relate to younger men and boys. They were not interesting to me. I entered high school. All the girls were talking on and on about boys and movie actors. I could not bring myself to join in these conversations. My preoccupations were Religions, God and three questions: Who am I? What am I? Why am I? These are the same questions that had haunted me since I was five. I wanted to be part of the group but I was too grown up. They did not understand.

After a while they decided to invite me to a party, but I had to bring a boy friend. I brought Enrique. I was 13 years old at the time; he was then 29 and we had been going together for a year. He was dressed like a God. He wore a hat and had a moustache: an incredible Adonis.

The girls were amazed, stunned. I was with this man, and what a man, according to them. And, our relationship was a year old and I had said nothing about it! I had not known there was anything to say. They had thought I knew nothing about men. Instead, I had a man.

After that party everyone at school thought I was great. I became very popular, a heroine. It was all strange to me. Why was it so important to talk about my relationship? Why was it so extraordinary that he was 16 years older than me? This was exactly the age difference between my father and mother. Why did they make such a fuss? I did not understand.

The girls decided I had wanted to keep it a secret. That thought had never crossed my mind. As with so many events in my life, others interpreted it in a different way than I did. A lot of conversations with my friends are due to this difference in views. They tell me I don't want to face one thing or another. They tell me how I really feel. They are not correct. Maybe this is because I feel and act so differently.

What stands out in my mind about Enrique is how romantic our relationship continued for the three years from when I was

4

12 until I was 15. It was nice. We went to parties, came home late at night, and used to rent horse-drawn carriages. He bought me flowers, little ones, like violets or a white jasmine ... so aromatic that thinking of them still brings the aroma back to me, and he would say that the jasmine did not smell as sweetly as I did. He said I spread unsmellable odors, deep and sweet, the kind that carried one's soul. I believed every word. I always believed every word anyone told me, if what they said was positive.

We dreamed we were going to marry and he would buy a house. We used to neck a lot, even on the porch of my home. I used to get very excited and let him touch me anywhere. We never did go to bed. We broke up when I felt he no longer needed me. We did not fight. We remained friends.

During the years I went with Enrique, there was another man on my mind. (I always went out with lots of men at the same time.) Hector was the platonic one. I loved him dearly and wanted him to love me. He did, but alas, it was as a sister, a friend. It all seems childish now; my pain was real then.

We are nothing more nor less than what we think. I created a fantasy of patiently suffering and waiting years for him.

Hector would get married and be very happy. He would have two children. His wife would die (talk about melodrama!) and I would eagerly and willingly raise his children and thus become part of his life.

He would not be aware of me and would go out with women while I stayed home and took care of his children. I would suffer in silence.

The years would go by and the children would grow into their 20's, healthy spiritually, emotionally and physically. After all those years of service, he could no longer ignore me. He would finally ask me to marry him.

I was very happy with the whole fantasy — happy to wait, happy to give for years. I believe this was played out many years later with my husband.

Hector had other girls with whom he had sex. I could not understand why he would go with them, women whom I thought at the time were beneath me, and yet would not have sex with me. I did not yet know we are all One, that no one is higher or lower.

Hector and I were friends. We met every morning and took the train together, I to school and he to work. At lunch time we ate together and then would go to see "Dibujos Animados"(cartoons). In Buenos Aires there were theatres where you could see cartoons all day long. After that I had

English Classes. Later we sometimes met the rest of the "barra" (Enrique and Raul) at "Confiteria Richmond" on Florida Street and went bowling. We called ourselves the Three Musketeers and D'Artagnan. Then we'd catch the 7:10 train home.

A month after Enrique and I broke up, another guy appeared. Jorge was not attractive, in fact, he was ugly. On our first date I wore a white dress with Swiss dots and round scoop neckline edged with a black ribbon. We went to see "Three Coins in a Fountain." We sat in the last row of the balcony and necked like crazy. My hat kept coming off. In those days I was always properly and neatly dressed: black shoes, black purse, white gloves and hat.

Later he propositioned me and I said "Yes." How could a good Human Being refuse? I am the one who grew up with a father who taught free love and associated food and sex. Can you deny another Human Being such a basic thing as a piece of bread or a cup of soup? Of course not! You can go to the market and select vegetables. This one yes and that one no. But Human Beings, no. Human Beings can't be selected! I truly felt that whoever came to me came from God, was God-manifested. I could not say "No." So Jorge pushed for sex, and at age 15, on June 27, 1956, we went to bed.

The circumstances building up to it were hilarious. My friend Gladys was going to bed with her boyfriend. Although I hate to admit that anything I do is influenced by someone else, I think this had something to do with my going to bed with Jorge. The four of us talked and talked for hours. Should I do it or not? Why? After deciding to go ahead, the next problem was: where? Finally, Gladys found an apartment, the one she and her boyfriend used.

After the decision was made, it all seemed very natural. I did not feel ashamed. I did not feel uncomfortable nor did I feel daring. I did not feel I was sneaking since I had discussed it with my mother. When it happened, I did not feel pain nor did I bleed. Not everything I had been told held true for me. I was happy. I had an orgasm that first time. My sexual life started beautifully and it seems to have also ended beautifully.

Jorge however was a bit disappointed. He told me he had expected me to suffer. He thought that I would scream with pain or at least cry. Instead I moaned with pleasure. I enjoyed it. For neither of us was it what we had fantasized or been told to expect.

Mother had told me sex was to be enjoyed. I had a long preparation for it, yet the physical aspects did not seem to match what I had been told. Later, I talked with Mother and she found out for me that a few women do not experience pain. I was one of those few.

We had a few months of love. We made love everywhere. Once his brother caught us in their parents' house. It was awful. To put this into historical perspective: this was taking place in 1956 in Argentina, a Latin culture. Not too neat! Good girls did not go to bed with boys! But we even made love on the grass in the back garden of his parents' house! The possibility that we would be caught was exciting.

My parents had a bedroom in the back of the house. We used that too, until one day my mother discovered us. As always, she was understanding. But she said, "If it was your father, he would kill you." I think it had to do with respecting the honor of the house.

I was just going with my feelings, being true to what I felt. I saw nothing wrong with loving, nothing wrong with expressing at all levels what I felt was good and pure. I did not want to feel one way and act a different way. That seemed to be hypocrisy. I did not want to play games!

There was a way the boys used to discover the "good" girls and the "bad." They would take us to "El Maipo," a theatre like the "Folies Bergere." The women who laughed at the dirty jokes were with their husbands. The women who did not laugh were supposedly single and "good" girls. They were not supposed to understand this type of joke. I laughed like crazy. I was not going to play that game even though I did not like dirty jokes.

On the street one day, I met Elvirita, a close friend from childhood boarding school days. We had not seen each other since we were about nine.

The following Sunday we went to Mass at our old school to visit the nuns. Afterwards, we decided to go to lunch, but Elvirita wanted to make a day of it by also going to the movies. We counted our money and found we did not have enough for both projects.

As we were walking on Lavalle Street talking about this, a very distinguished man voiced the most delicate, gentlemanly, compliment about "beautiful eyes." Since I thought Elvirita was a truly beautiful woman, I turned towards her happily and said, "Congratulations!"

The man stopped when he realized I thought the compliment was for Elvirita and said, "Oh no! It is for the brunette!"

I was surprised and pleased.

In the middle of all this, Elvirita, who is quick as they come, whispered, "Make him pay for lunch."

I looked at her and then decided, "Why not?" It was a challenge to do something I had never done before, and at the same time provide what someone else wanted.

I stopped to look at a picture of Clark Gable on the window of a theatre we were passing and said to Elvirita, "What would I not do for that man . . ." I was talking about Clark Gable, but hoping to attract the gentleman.

He did notice, and coming over, asked, "What would you do for that gentleman?"

"I don't know," I replied.

"Are you thinking of going to the movies?" he asked.

Before I could register the question, Elvirita replied, "No, we are thinking of going to lunch."

He took us to a beautiful restaurant where he was obviously known by every waiter. We were treated royally. It was a strange and dreadful experience. He would not talk; I hated silences. So I tried to make conversation:

"What's your name?"

"Roberto."

"Do you work?"

"Yes."

"Where?"

"Downtown."

"Do you work for yourself?"

"No."

"Do you work for a private firm?"

"No."

"Oh, exactly for whom **do** you work?"

"The Government."

It was horrible — like pulling teeth. Each answer was as close to a monosyllable as possible. But in this way we discovered he was a lawyer and the director of La Caja de Jubilaciones (Social Security). I did not believe him.

Also, why had he invited us to lunch? He obviously did not want to talk and was a shy man. I did not understand how he had had the guts to voice that "piropo" (polite compliment).

Finally, the lunch was finished. We were glad, or at least I was glad! Elvirita and I went to the movies and afterwards had tea. It was a full day. I thought about that man a few times. He seemed so strange to me. He asked for nothing. He just invited us to lunch, and it was a pleasure, and went on his way.

Jorge worked as a cashier. He took money from the company and lost it gambling. He was desperate and told me about it.

Of course I, Beatriz, must solve this problem. I felt that my purpose in life was to solve problems, anybody's problems, whether or not they asked me for help. If you had a problem, I had a problem. And when I had a problem, I had to act on it, to solve it.

So Jorge needed money and I felt I had to get it. As I was thinking about it, I remembered that strange man who had taken Elvirita and me to lunch. I would go and ask him for the money. I would tell him that my friend needed it. Why not? What could I lose? (**I will** . . . **even if** . . .)

The more I thought about this incredible idea, the more I thought it had possibilities. I did not believe that he was who he had said he was. I thought that I would go and ask for the Director of La Caja de Jubilaciones and someone else would come out of the office. I would apologize and leave, feeling that I had tried my very best. But I had to take action on each idea (Thought, Desire, Action).

As is the case for most people, my scenarios never work. However, the end result for me is that I get exactly what I want most of the time. I did not know this then, nor till last year.

Well, surprise, the Director was indeed the gentleman who had taken us out to lunch! He ushered me into a very impressive office. I could not believe it. I wanted to die. I was here and had to tell him why I had come. It was hard! But I was in love and Jorge needed help. I told him I needed money, the equivalent of $2,000, for a friend who was in trouble. This was the truth, but he did not believe a word I was saying. (It had never occurred to me that he, or anyone else, would consider that I would ask for myself!)

Without a word, he got up, went to the safe, took out $2,000 in cash, and gave it to me saying, "I hope this will help your friend. It is a gift!" He showed me the door, said it was a pleasure seeing me again, and goodbye.

I was in 7th Heaven! I had solved the problem . . . But what a strange person! He had given me an incredible amount of money even though he did not believe me, and had asked nothing in return. I could not understand it. But I was so happy I had the money for Jorge, that I sang at the top of my lungs while walking along 9 de Julio, the widest street in Buenos Aires.

That was our first problem and how I solved it. Later Jorge came back with the same problem. This time, I went to Mother. She loaned him the money, since she was worried that his mother would find out. She spoke with him and he promised not to do it again. He looked very contrite, but he did it again.

Then Mother said this was the last time she would bail him out. She gave him her engagement ring to pawn. In this way he could put the money back immediately and redeem the ring as soon as possible.

Well, time went by and he did not bring the ring back. Soon Father noticed that Mother was not wearing her ring.

He asked, "Where is your engagement ring?"

Mother replied with vague answers like "Somewhere."
Father started to insist on knowing where the ring was.

It developed into the most painful situation I had ever experienced. Father would come home at 6 pm and ask the question, "Where is your ring?"

Mother would refuse to answer.

Father would hit her every day.

She still would not respond.

To watch my father hit my mother was terrible. I wanted to tell him, but Mother said, "What the right hand does, the left must not know." I was **not** to tell him.

Every day she was being hit harder and harder. She started to get bruises. Father was going blind with rage and Mother was more determined to maintain silence. I tried to convince her otherwise. She kept saying that for Father to understand, she would have to explain all the circumstances. That would expose Jorge, and one does not do that. The Divine Law of Sacredness requires that a gift to someone or to God be made sacred by silence. She would keep her peace no matter what the consequences (**I will** . . . **even if** . . .). This continued for quite a while.

At first I begged Jorge to get the ring. Then I just asked for the pawn ticket so that I could redeem it myself. I had no luck on either account.

At last a friend asked me, "Beatriz, do you know what Jorge is saying about your mother?"

"No. What?"

"Well, he is saying that your mother wants to marry you off so badly that she gave him her engagement ring. He is showing everyone the pawn ticket."

Oh, God! I could not believe my ears . . . Every day my mother was being hit because of her silence to protect him: a thief, worse, a worm. In return, he was spreading lies about her. This was too much. This human being was not a Human Being. I had always said that you could do anything to me and I would not react, but do not touch those I love. I felt rage . . . and a sense of purpose.

Again I had a problem to solve. My reasoning was that when you find a rotten apple, you take it out of the barrel, otherwise it will spoil all the others. Clearly here was a rotten apple. How could anyone be so mean to someone who had been as noble as my mother had been for him? I had told him mother's situation. He had seen the marks. How could he do this? My anguish grew. I felt I needed to protect the World . . . I always thought in such global terms. For sure the world would be a better place without him. What would he do next? Whom would he hurt next? No, he will not hurt anyone else! (**I will** . . . (protect the world), **even if** . . (I have to go to jail)!)

The morning after my decision I got up at 5 am with Father, on the pretext of making his mate-tea. Sometimes I would do this to say, "I love you." I would make the mate while he shaved, and then sit on the toilet seat serving it while his face was still covered with cream. Sometimes we talked, sometimes just commented on how awful the mate was, how badly I made it, and that I did not yet have the technique. He would drink it, appreciating the fact that I had gotten up to do this just for him.

That morning, while he shaved, I took his keys and opened the safe that was in his wardrobe. I took his revolver and put it in my closet. That evening I went to see Jorge.

We met on a dark street. I asked him for the pawn ticket. He refused. I asked him if it was true he had been saying things about my mother.

"Yes. I believe all of it. Why else would she be so nice to me?"

Oh! This was the man I went to bed with! The man I loved! This man knew nothing about kindness. He had no concept of the pleasure of doing something for someone else with no ulterior motive, no strings attached. A person like this loose in the world would do a lot more harm than good. I felt justified!

At point blank range, I shot twice, wounding him in the chest. Incredibly, the bullets went right through without causing serious damage.

He looked at me, not quite believing what had happened.

I was calm. I had thought it through. Feeling, "Mission Accomplished," I turned and walked home.

Father saw me come in and, as if he had ESP, went to the safe. "The revolver is gone," he said.

"Yes, I know. Here it is." I handed it to him.

"What did you do?"

"I shot Jorge," I said calmly, quite sure of myself.

He did not believe me, laughed and looked at me. We sat down together to watch T.V.

About half an hour later the police rang the bell. Father went to the door, saw the police, and, stunned white as a sheet of paper, turned to me and blurted, "You did it."

"Yes," I responded, "I told you."

We had to go to the police station. He was in dazed despair and asked the officer, "What shall I do with her?" and me, "How could you do that to me?" He was feeling sorry for himself instead of being aware of how much pain I must have felt to do something like that, especially since at that time I was a vegetarian and believed in non-violence. I felt that if I could not kill a cow, I should not eat its meat. My hero was Ghandi. Yet calmly and with forethought I had shot a man. It had to do with making the World a better place for all of us. Truly.

That night when we returned from the police station, my friend Gladys was there. While Father tried to get a lawyer for me, we all listened to him talking on the phone.

"Hello, . . . This is Mr. . . . I am calling because my little girl just shot a man." Gladys, Mother and I looked at each other. To hear him describe me as a little girl in the same breath in which he said that I had shot a man, was incredible. We broke into uncontrollable laughter.

Father finished the call. He was furious. "This is certainly not a laughing matter. Have you gone mad or something?"

We repeated to him what he had said. He too realized the absurdity and laughed suddenly. "We should have cameras in this crazy house. Dramas and laughs are constantly jumbled together. If we filmed what went on no one would believe it — they'd think the writer had a great imagination."

Later I had to go to La Plata to present myself to be judged by a "Tribunal de Menores" (Juvenile Court). Father took me but Mother stayed home, sad and nervous that she might not see me for a while. At the court I entered a room alone. Three men sat at a big desk and while I was there two or three others came and went very casually. Apparently the three were judges.

As always, I had no fear. So I just started talking to them about my favorite subjects: Gandhi, non-violence; peace; the laws; the conditions of the jails and the rampant homosexuality that existed in them, the rights prisoners should have and the **spirit** of the law. These were not subjects about which people usually talked, or were even aware! I paced up and down and monologued for two or three hours.

Finally they called in my father, looked at him and said, "We know what your daughter has done; but there is such a thing as the "spirit of the law" about which your daughter has so wisely spoken. In this case, if we follow the letter of the law we would not be following the spirit of it: to protect society from harmful elements. By following the letter of the law we would not only **not** be protecting society, we would be harming it. We are sure your daughter will one day sit here as a Judge or make an enormous contribution to the world. Congratulations, you have a remarkable young woman on your hands."

When we returned home Mother looked worried and Father finally exploded. "She can get away with murder! They congratulate me on our daughter! Do you understand this? She can do anything!"

"Are you out of your mind? Would you have wanted them to convict her? Aren't you happy with the outcome?" said Mother, as she hugged me, her whole face wet with tears pouring from her eyes like water from a faucet.

I was just glad it was over. I never felt I had done anything wrong. I never considered for a second that anything bad would happen to me. That feeling of security made me act naturally, and was what saved me from an otherwise grim path.

Thus my first affair ended. I had no feelings of any kind left for Jorge.

Enrique, the one who wore hats, was now 32 years old. He came over to tell me how disappointed he was in me. I thought he was going to talk about my shooting someone, and ask how I could reconcile that with my views on non-violence. But no. Again the scene in my imagination did not take place.

He wanted to tell me he had told Jorge he could neck with me but not "sack me," as he delicately put it. Jorge had made a bet, and the day before, had collected on that bet.

So now I discovered that my love had wanted me just to win a bet! That hurt was only resolved a few years ago in a Sex workshop conducted by Stan Dale. I said once to Stan, "With the excuse of sex, you bring them by the rows and heal their souls."

Sometime later, while watching a program on T.V. about the economy of the country, I saw that strange man who had given me the gift of so much money. I sat and listened. On T.V. he was sure of himself, so unlike the man at lunch. He knew what he was talking about. But the thing that impressed me most was his humanity. He was talking about the economy as numbers, statistics, etc., yet one could feel, sense, see, that he never forgot that he was talking about people. He obviously wanted to be of service, to help these people.

The following day I called him at his office and said I wanted to see him. We had tea at the "Confiteria Ideal," a tea house. I, of course, talked. He did not. I told him how impressed I was with the program and about how his humanity came through. I told him I wanted to be a friend of someone with such high principles. He smiled, feeling flattered, but did not want any part of me. I was sad, but determined to be his friend. He intrigued me.

Not much later he appeared on another T.V. program. Somehow the date of his birthday was mentioned. I had to wait for two or three weeks. That day I bought a tie, called him, made a date at "Confiteria Ideal" and wished him Happy Birthday. This time I knew I had him. He was touched.

From that day we met once a week for tea and talk. He talked about Lisandro de la Torre. I started to read about Lisandro de la Torre. Soon we were meeting twice a week, and before my sixteenth birthday we were lovers. Neither he nor I had planned it. He was 52 years old and I fifteen. Yet, it was so comfortable. We could talk. I spent much time with him. That was the beginning of a love affair that lasted seven years, until I left Argentina. It was 1956.

About that time the book *Lolita*, by Vladimir Nabokov, came out in Buenos Aires. Everyone was talking about how scandalous it was. The press made such a fuss!

I could not understand what the fuss was all about. She was supposed to be my age and the man in his forties. I was going with Roberto in his fifties. What was so strange about that? A person has no age, the body does! When people talked about the book in front of us, we'd look at each other knowingly and secretly laugh.

I believe that in many ways he took the place of Father, who had stopped taking me places when I was twelve. I had missed that. Now I had Roberto.

We went out for dinner on Saturday nights. I felt good, important. We would go with his friends, ambassadors, congressmen, lawyers, etc. The conversation was stimulating, the food fantastic. We would talk until 2 or 3 in the morning about politics, world situations and religion. I felt I was learning how governments work, how things are done behind the scenes. Very young I realized that what really happens in the government and what is reported, do not necessarily match. It felt good to be on the inside. What I did not know then, was that all this was going to be of great value to me!

We would go home to our apartment, our love nest. This was the apartment he had used when he was single. Ah! I forgot to mention that he was married . . . ! Small detail. It never interfered. I saw more of him than his wife did.

. . . we would arrive home on Corrientes Street near Maipu at 3 o'clock Saturday morning, make love and fall asleep.

Sunday was great. We would breakfast in the neighborhood where we were going to see the soccer game. We sat at a table someplace, slumming and doing the crossword puzzles. Actually, **he** did them. I could not guess a single word, even if the description was "Big grey animal with a long trunk." That was not because I am not intelligent. I have always considered myself very intelligent. But in a test my mind does not function. I guess subconsciously I knew that some day I would have to take a test, and would fail.

Later we would walk around the neighborhood, meet the friends of the night before, or others, and go to the stadium. I truly enjoyed myself. I did not understand soccer. I still don't. To me the spectacle is the people: how they stand up, scream, become so passionate. All these serious men, who the night before had been discussing literature and politics, now passionately yelled their heads off as very much a part of the masses. That is something I do not know how to do, even today. I can't be caught up in any mass force, perhaps because of my need to retain self-control.

Over a period of time, I painted our apartment, sewed a cover for the bed, made cushions, and bought dishes and glasses. I was making the place a home, my first home of my own. My sign is Cancer. I started to give luncheons and dinners there. Since I did not know how to cook, I just ordered everything. I knew how to put it together.

What was Roberto to me? Everything: father, friend, teacher, confidant, lover. Now I can look back on those seven years and see how he prepared me for my future life's work. He taught me about politics, governments, international relationships. He gave me the opportunity to meet and see people at different levels: not just as so-and-so the ambassador, but as so-and-so the ambassador, who could talk intellectually and also scream his head off at a soccer game, a Human Being. He taught me to see things in perspective. Of course, Father had taught me not to bow down to authority, to question and disobey when appropriate, even if **he** was the authority. It was a natural progression from that to Roberto.

I used to tell Roberto, "I am leaving home, I will stay in the apartment." This would be at 10 in the morning.

"Yes, of course," he would say, listening to my complaints about how badly I felt about whatever. But by 7 p.m. he would manage to make me feel happy and very diplomatically send me home, with phrases such as: "I would feel so much better if I knew you were with your parents tonight. I can't bear the thought of you all alone in this apartment." Thus I went home. I never ran away.

These were incredibly exciting times, like when he decided to run for Congress. There were members of the party who wanted him to run. Over dinner this was discussed. There were about six of us. I said nothing for a change, just observing the others and how they were trying to get him to run. Dinner as usual was great. Prosciutto with Melon, Canelloni a la Rossini, and more, plus good wine, coffee and Spanish cognac. But what topped it all for me was that when we were leaving, they took me aside and said, "We did what we can. Now it is in your hands." Oh, how powerful I felt! Yes, it was in my hands. I knew I could give Roberto the confidence he needed to make the 'yes' decision.

He had studied law later in life than was usual in Argentina, with the idea of entering politics. Now was the time — just what he had been working for for so long; and now he was scared. I lifted his spirit so that he himself could see the horizon and say, "Yes . . . I can do it."

With this decision made, the organizing began. I traveled to hear him make speeches and I did postering. That was fun! In certain parts of Buenos Aires, there were key walls each political party postered nightly. It was unbelievable! Each morning those walls would be proclaiming a different party. The trick was to be the last one putting up posters — so that they would be there all the next day — and yet do it while it was still dark, since all those posters were covering signs saying "Prohibido Fijar Carteles," or "Posters Prohibited."

How needed, how useful, I felt! and how especially nice it felt that all of his friends had accepted me! His colleagues, office personnel, and now people from the Party. We were a couple. No official function passed without me being present.

There were sad times too. One campaign took all his money. That was horrible, not because he found himself without money, but because he fell into the hands of his wife who had money. She helped him . . . but there were strings attached. He had less time for himself and me.

When he was sworn in at the Congress, his wife, not I, was in the official place. I cried a lot. But that was later; now I was accepted. All his camp were aware of my place in his life.

I do not want to give the impression that my love affair with Roberto was a monogamous one on either side. He knew I was going out with other men. He kept telling me not to say anything about our affair as no one could, or would, understand it.

I kept saying that the man I chose to marry would not only understand, but would appreciate that who I am at the moment he falls in love with me is the result of all that I have experienced. If he loves me, he must love Roberto, because Roberto is a big part and factor in who I am as a woman.

Roberto kept saying I was crazy, that would never happen, and that I was just too young to know. People have told me that all my life. Now, at forty, I think back and see they were wrong. I did find the person I was seeking. But the search took eight years and over 600 men.

What do I mean: 600 men? Just that. Why?

Well, let's see. If you worked as a doctor, would you say, "I'll doctor this many people, but not more," or, "I'll cure all those people who are short, and fat, but not the ones who are slim and tall?"

No you wouldn't. Why not? Because you are Love, therefore you express yourself to All people by giving through the skill you have learned, Medicine.

If you worked as a dancer, would you say, "I will dance in front of only Anglo-Saxon audiences?"

No, you wouldn't. Why not? Because you are Love, therefore you express yourself to All people, by giving through the skill you have developed, Dancing.

If you worked as a cabinet maker, would you say, "I will make cabinets for only red-haired people?"

No, you wouldn't. Why not? Because you are Love, therefore you express yourself to All people, by giving through the skill you have learned, Carpentry.

If I worked as a spiritual person, could I say, "I'll love this person but not that person?" or "I'll love that mind and heart, but not that body?" or, ". . . this heart, but not this mind?"

No, I couldn't. Why not? Because I was Love, therefore I expressed myself to All people by giving through all the three energies I knew (Mental, Emotional and Physical), until the three would grow to be One — Spirit — governed by the Law of Three in One. Therefore, I had no choice but to give myself totally, completely, until I learned to blend the three energies into one, and thus became able to give to All people through the skill I had learned, Spiritual integration.

Between my 15th and my 19th years my life was a roller coaster. I was looking, searching desperately for someone who would love me for myself. I was a very beautiful young woman: attractive, intelligent, with a silver tongue. I had big breasts, so every head would turn as I walked down the street. I talked with every man or woman who came near me. I talked about peace, non-violence, politics, religion, about Lanza del Vasto and about Gandhi.

Later I talked about Roberto and me: what we felt for each other. This would open them up and they would talk about subjects they would never discuss with anyone else, secret thoughts, secret happenings. Each time this happened I felt very close to them and that they also felt close to me. In a matter of hours, days, or weeks we would end up in bed. To me it was a natural way to give all of me at every level.

The surprise came each time when the person walked away. I felt used; but that did not stop me. I felt it was one of the purposes of my life to be of service. If that meant to be used, so be it. Some of them came to be cleansed. Some of them just needed to throw up, mentally and emotionally, and then continue on their roads with a better feeling about themselves. The more it happened, the more desperate I became.

I began to realize that being beautiful did not help; I felt that no one looked beyond my body. I wanted my soul to be loved. In desperation I went crying to the best plastic surgeon in Buenos

Aires, and asked him to take off all my breasts. He realized I was serious and operated on me. But he only took off three-quarters of them. I felt cheated then. I am happy today.

My mother thought I was crazy. "People want more breasts. You do not want them."

"No . . . ! They are in the way. Men do not see me . . . **Me** . . . My soul."

I asked Roberto, "Why do the men walk away?"

He responded, "Because they can't accept that you are a decent Human Being, a good girl, a family-oriented person who knows how to give but does not know how to play games and have a lover. Don't you understand that the world is not ready for you? Good girls do not go to bed with a man if they want to marry him. Even if they have lovers, good girls do not admit it."

"Why do you want to complicate things?" He was asking me to keep quiet. I could not. I did a thing because I thought it good, and therefore should be able to tell the world. Under no circumstances could I do something and keep it quiet.

Thus I kept trying, day after day, week after week. I met men year after year in cafeterias, on the street, in department stores, anywhere. Each time I believed that this person understood. Each time I was devastated that he did not. I tried again and again to make myself more clear to them. I was searching for unconditional love, which would go beyond judgmentalness, jealousy, possessiveness; I wanted someone big enough to understand the truth. I did not want a relationship based on a lie.

With each encounter with a man, I felt, "This is it." To me, each individual was perfect and it never occurred to me to transfer my previous disappointment from one person to the next. Why should I? I was obeying the Divine Law of the Here and Now. This was a different person! Why should I not trust him? I felt I had to trust until that person proved unworthy of my trust. I felt no one ever did; I still feel that way. I may be naive, but I would rather be thought of as naive, than to live not trusting. They just did not understand me.

I was very well aware of how to use my Female energy. I attracted to me, never initiated.

Some of the men remained with me on and off for years. Antonio was one of these. He had come to visit his niece, my friend Sarita. She and I and some other girls all went for a drink with Hector, Raul and Antonio. Antonio was 48 or so. Hector dared me. "You can't get the old man, Beatriz."

I looked at him. "Oh no?" I thought (challenge!), "Don't tell Beatriz she can't do something!" Seemingly I did nothing, but my eyes knew how to talk. I looked and looked. Antonio was after me in no time at all. When we shook hands to say goodbye, he gave me his telephone number. I showed it to Hector. I had won the bet.

What Hector never knew is that I did call Antonio, and we went out. He wanted to see more of me so I suggested he invite Sarita, her parents and me to Comodoro Rivadavia, where he lived. He did. That trip to Comodoro Rivadavia started a relationship which lasted until I left Argentina at age 22. He never believed I would leave.

Whenever he came to Buenos Aires, he called me and we spent time together. When he came to have an operation, he did not even let his family know, but I went to the hospital and spent time with him. I took flowers and chocolates. I was then sixteen.

Antonio had a lot of money and through him I became aware I could do a lot more for people. He insisted on buying me things. I refused, but said I would take the money. With it I bought clothes for the poor. Every Sunday I gave clothes to people in a Villa Miseria, a very poor ghetto.

Roberto would ask, "Why can't you be like everyone else?"

I would respond, "Would you love me if I were?"

"No."

Once I knew men were willing to give me money, I could not just ignore that piece of knowledge. Another Divine Law says: New Knowledge Must Be Applied. If one knows and feels, one must act, as long as one does not harm anyone. I wanted to get as much money as I could to use for the benefit of others. I would talk it over with Mother. She continually responded, "Beatriz, each Human Being must walk a brand new road called Life. The one thing you must ask yourself is, 'Am I doing this for me or for someone else? Is this selfish or not?' Constantly check your intentions. If you can look yourself in the mirror, if you feel at peace with yourself, then, even if what you do is outrageously different, go with it. We only have to account to God."

One day at a party I must have talked so much about books that someone asked if I had read a particular one. I said no. He encouraged me to buy it. The next day I started to look for it. Every place I went they told me they did not have it. Finally, I said to a salesman, "I have looked for this book for a month and no one seems to have it." With compassion in his voice the man asked, "Do you know what type of book you are looking for?"

"No," I replied. "Someone recommended it to me."

"Well," he said, "I do not think you will find it, it's a pornographic book."

I turned red, blue, yellow, all colors. They had played a joke on me! I did not realize what that episode was all about until just a few years ago. I must have bored them to tears and this was their way of getting back at me. They probably laughed, thinking of me looking so seriously for that book.

The telephone lines in Argentina were not very good. One week we received several calls from the same person, although he was dialing a different number. He liked my voice and I liked his. We started to call each other every day and talk for hours. On the phone we said, wished for, and expressed things that we would not have expressed face to face.

He said that one of his fantasies was to go to bed with two women. One of the things I mentioned was that although I had gone to bed with lots of men I had never gone to bed with a woman. I asked "Why not do it?"

Mother was around while I was talking to him and I spoke with her about the possibility. (She was my best friend; I kept no secrets from her.) To me this is the way of life: if there is something I can't share, I should not think it. If I **can** think it, I can say it. If I can say it, I can do it. An action starts in the MIND. THOUGHT IS ACTION.

I thought about why I wanted to go to bed with another woman. Why is it bad? Why can't I express what I feel for a woman in the same way I express what I feel for a man? Aren't they both Human Beings? A Being has no sex, only a **body** has. Do I have to allow society to tell me how much I should share myself with someone else? I felt this was wrong! It meant I was not allowing myself to be totally giving at all levels. It was imposing restrictions. I did not like that.

I told Mother how I felt.

She said, "Beatriz, you know I do not judge you. The heroines I brought you up with were George Sand, Colette, Alfonsina Storni, and Gabriella Mistral. I would not have talked to you about these women since your childhood if I thought they were wrong.

"However, I am frightened for you. Society is not ready for you, and it can be cruel. You are very young now. In a few years you will be married and have a home. Later, say 15 years from now, the woman you go to bed with today may appear and blackmail you. It could destroy everything you'd worked for."

She was right, especially for a Latin culture in 1958. Once she had given me the reason why I should not do it, I knew I wanted to — and why. I would neither **act**, nor worse, **not act**, from Fear of what could happen. I would make my decisions out of strength (Love), not weakness (Fear). I must conduct my life honestly, openly and fearlessly.

She did then what very few human beings are capable of doing, even from love. Despite her own preferences otherwise, she offered to go to bed with me herself. "They will have to kill me to get this information out of me," she said. Out of the deepest love, to protect her headstrong child, a noble woman did what I know myself incapable of doing. She set no boundaries, no limits, no conditions, **ever**, on her Love. She did not judge, she loved. How can I express my gratitude for being the recipient of such love? (Maybe by helping make this world a better place!)

All went well. I was accustomed to thinking of my parents as sexual beings, so the idea of having sex with my mother did not seem mind-boggling to me. But it is one thing to believe something, to think it, and another to live through it! This is a lesson I have had to learn over and over. The living, creating of my Being through experience, the forming of who I AM, is different from my mental image of life.

So the episode had unexpected consequences: afterwards I could not concentrate at school. The doctor said I had "surmanage," whatever that is. I could not read or study because pictures of Mother and me in bed kept jumping onto the pages of my books. My heart was full of love for her, knowing well why she had done it. My emotions were in turmoil. "How come I am not mature enough? How come I do not feel well?" I asked myself. "Am I judging?"

I never told her. I didn't want her to know how I felt. It was my responsibility. I wished I was the type of person who places responsibility outside of herself; but I knew only too well that action starts and finishes with oneself. This event touched something very deep in me.

Years later I realized that part of the problem was that I **was** judging, myself. She made me aware of how small I was. I could not love with such capacity, with that type of giving, with so strong a feeling of protectiveness towards my offspring. I am a mother now, and I **know** I am not as noble as she.

Not long after, I started to wind down my incredible search for love, though I still thought I could find Love in other people or through loving other people.

My parents rented a room to a young man. He lived upstairs and had a private entrance. He was handsome and had light brown hair and big expressive green eyes. We liked each other very much. He would not say what he did except that twice a week he went to a place where all they said was "Om." At that time I had no idea what "Om" was, nor why he was saying it. I did know it was the most important thing in his life and that he was an extraordinary person. Neither work, nor me, nor anything else, would keep him from going there.

He was proper. Sometimes I would prepare a breakfast tray

with coffee, croissants warm from the bakery, a flower and a napkin, and with a smile, take it to his room. We fell in love and were planning to get married. In fact, we looked at a new housing development. I wanted to be with him. I waited a lot of time on weekends — which was when he worked — for him to be free to be with me. He said he was celibate and would save himself for marriage. I accepted it but did not understand.

When we broke up, he spoke with Father. He told Father he was not going to marry me and that he had been a gentleman and felt my father should know that. He said he had had lots of opportunities. I had wanted sex but he felt it was wrong. He was portraying himself as some kind of saint because he was doing just what **he** thought correct.

I looked at my father, expecting him to defend me. Father looked at the young man with knowing eyes, as if he really understood how difficult it must have been for him to resist making love to me, and that it was wrong for me to express myself like that! He said **nothing** in my defense.

I felt betrayed. This was my father, who had brought me up to Be and express myself no matter what the cost? Didn't he know it was hard for me **not** to express myself at **all** levels? Why should I suppress the outcome of pure feelings, of spiritual union? Why would a piece of paper make it OK? What hypocrisy!

Why didn't Father speak up? Did he agree with this man who obviously thought little of me for feeling and expressing my sexuality honestly? Oh! This man deserved one of those girls who play innocent with the man they want to marry, but play around with anyone else and then have themselves sewn up so the husband believes he got the only virgin in town. How repulsive! What a bunch of lies! I will not live like that!

Father, oh, Father, why didn't you defend me . . . ? Why didn't you say you understood what he went through, but felt proud of my honesty, my risk taking, my stamina to remain true to myself regardless of what I might lose!?

So this platonic love affair ended with pain, which passed, like everything in life.

I fell in love with a married man. He had two children. I bought gifts for the children. He told me his wife found out and tried to commit suicide. He said he was going to divorce her anyway. We got engaged in October. Christmas came and he was supposed to visit me. He did not. I waited for a few days. I thought, "He will come for New Year's," He didn't.

Then suddenly I sat down in a chair and stopped speaking. I did nothing but sleep, get up, and eat. My mother bathed me, powdered me, changed my nightgown, massaged me. All the time she told me how much she loved me.

At the end of three months, as suddenly as I had become catatonic, I snapped out of it. Mother never took me to the doctor. Later I asked her why, and she said that she knew me. She knew the shock was too much and I needed to go into hiding. When I was healed I would come out, provided I felt love out there to which to come. That was why she made a point of constantly telling me how much she loved me.

During that time of catatonia, my feelings were strange. I clearly remember sleeping, eating, sitting, everything. But I also remember that I felt as if I was not in that body. That **body** was doing all those functions; I was someplace else.

When I came back I felt an incredible understanding for the man. People tried to tell me what a worm he had been, but I knew he had acted the best way he could. That is all any of us can ask of another. He felt trapped. He had bonds with that woman and those children. Divorce in those days in Argentina (even today) was almost impossible. He was torn. He probably knew he could not tell me his decision face to face — a normal human reaction. The pain was all gone, but the purging was done at a level which I did not quite understand. It certainly was not conscious.

The outcome was good: I had no bitter feelings towards him, and that is what is important. I do not want to carry bad feelings. They impede one's traveling through life on this magnificent planet Earth. I always felt one must travel light, and to me "light" did not mean things, but rather light within!

Also I had learned to avoid going to bed with married men; I did not want to cause pain.

This ended my search for love in Argentina.

When I was 22 I left Argentina and moved to Canada. In Toronto I met a lady who was very kind to me. Her son, Allan, would pick me up to take me to their house for dinner.

One day when Allan came to pick me up, he looked up the stairs at me as I was coming down. I felt a chill up my back, as if I had just been completely undressed, and someone had looked right through me. I asked, "What happened? Why did you look at me like that?"

He responded, "I did not look at you."

With that chill I became aware of the union of our two energies, our real meeting.

After dinner, his mother suggested he take me to see the beautiful Christmas decorations around Toronto. When we were in the car, I decided we were **not** going to have one of those usual incredibly boring conversations. So I asked him, "What does God mean to you?"

He looked surprised. "Do you really want to know?"

"Yes," I replied, since this had been my question to every man. "I want to know." For me, everything depended on that answer.

Well! He gave me an answer that lasted four hours! How can I express what I felt? After having searched for so long! Finally I had found someone who gave me an answer about God which showed me the depth and breadth of an incredible mind! This was a mind I knew belonged to the world.

I knew he was emotionally stuck. I also knew I could unstick him. Only through being emotionally free could that extraordinary mind bear fruit, and my job would be to help him to Become free. I saw my marriage to him as that job. I knew I could not go where he would go then.

Here was someone I could tell about Roberto and about shooting a man, someone who would understand! not forgive, not overlook. Here was someone who would recognize that I was the sum of all my experience. If he loved me, he had to love all the components: my totality; and he did. What joy!

We were married on March 26, 1965.

Here was a virgin man who wanted an experienced woman. Here was an experienced woman looking for a virgin man. He was so hungry for sex, there was nothing he did not want to try. And, of course, I was free enough to go along with it. Sex was perfect. Always free. Never the same. For 16 years of marriage our sexual life was like a dream.

We continued our established practice of writing letters, now back and forth, even though we were living together. Here are just a few:

Hamilton, Canada
June 15, 1965

My Angel:

You just left; I went to bed to read. The whole house has your smell. Oh . . . how I wanted you . . . ! Remember? We were talking . . . having breakfast; you had your hair done . . . you looked so handsome! You were thinking . . . you said, about me. You found a girl soft (fat) intelligent (skinny) or something like that, you said. Whatever it was, I had a wonderful feeling listening to you . . . I wish I could create something new to be able to love you more and more deeply if that is possible. I enjoy so much just looking at you . . . kissing you . . . having you inside me . . . When you sleep you look so peaceful, just like a child. Sometimes you act like one too, and I wish you could find in me in these moments, love and peace.

24

This house, or any other wherever we are, is full of you — your voice so tender, deep and full of love, answering my "God bless you, Allan," with your, "and you, Sweetheart." You carrying my cup of coffee to my place, as if I could not do it myself . . . you waiting on me, making coffee or doing all these little things you do . . . Honey!! I do not know if we are different or not but who cares anyway? I know one thing: I love you. You are the only thing that counts in my life, I wish to be your slave, your rug, your blanket, your wife, your friend. I wish to be air so I could be in your lungs inside you and be vital and important . . . Oh . . . the whole world is you for me. I do not enjoy a thing without you. You are in my mind so much and I want you so badly . . . I love you all, your nose, your cheeks, your lips so sensual and warm, your tongue — that works so well all over me, making me feel cold and hot — Oh — so hot! Your neck with all your strange noises . . . your chest and stomach that I enjoy to kiss and your penis. Oh your penis: little and soft, and sweet and friendly and hard and big and hungry of my hole: your bottom: round and nice; your legs . . . all . . . all of you. I love you . . . you never forget that . . . !!!!

Beatriz

On my birthday he gave me this note:

Hamilton, Canada
June 24, 1965

My dearest, darling Beatriz:

As you sit behind me now — talking of nudism, cross because I am laughing, and thinking about the freedom of Canada — I love you. You throw me a kiss — I love you. There may be nothing to go with this because there is no money — but I love you, I love you, I love **you.**

Allan

I replied:

Hamilton, Canada
June 24, 1965

Darling, my love:

There is nothing more important than your thoughts . . . I do not need gifts, you know that . . . I need you!! Your love . . . !! I could not be happier today!! . . .

Thanks a lot for the wonderful card.

Your pussy-cat
Beatriz

I discovered that he masturbated. I approached him to talk about it, but he was reluctant. However, he always conveniently "forgot" the cloth he used, so I knew each time, and that he **did** want me to know. Why else would a person leave the evidence? I tried to make him feel it was OK to masturbate and that what I did not like was that he could not share it with me. Years later Stan Dale freed him from this shyness.

In 16 years the only bad time was one whole year of not making love at all, followed by another during which it was very rare. Our time schedules were incompatible. Well . . . that was rough on me. Now it all seems like a dream, but then I attempted suicide. I was desperate. I wanted to make love with him. I loved him. Since I had married him, I had not looked at another man. I still had no eyes for anyone else. My cup was full. I put myself 100% into whatever I do, and the whatever was him.

Nor did it occur to me to masturbate. Since fifteen, I had always had a lover, so touching myself did not cross my mind.

To me, "making love" has always been associated with love and spirit. Three times our bedroom became light, pure light as if the room light had come on. God was present. The union lived; the souls were one; the room shone. The first time I was scared, rather, surprised. I thought someone had entered the room and turned on the light. I stopped. We stopped. We looked at each other and knew we were making love in the presence of God.

Given these intense feelings of mine about Sex and God, I could not understand my feelings during that year of enforced celibacy. I learned what people meant when they talked about making love like an animal. I felt like an animal. Never in the years before, with any man, had I felt dirty. Now, a married woman, I felt cheap, a savage.

I could not understand then that I looked for the depth and therefore had to experience **Heaven** and **Hell**. The animal coming out of me was Hell! I wanted to master my feelings with my mind, but the animal in me was bigger than myself!

After a year, we made love. Our son, Robert, was the result. **Allan** suggested that we name our child after Roberto, since he had been an important person in my life and Roberto and I had not had children. Roberto had been a good Human Being, and we should tell our son about him. It had not even occurred to me! Once more I had proof of how extraordinary a Being I had married. How many people are big enough to do that? I knew I had found a diamond; of this I was well aware.

When Robert was about three weeks old he was giving me love, and my little brother Freddy (who lived with us) also loved me dearly, but I still found it was not enough. I felt desperate! Cornered! But above all, I felt evil! I loved my husband; I could not think of being alive without him. He was my life.

I am and was an independent woman. I have always been self-sufficient, so it could **not** be said, "Here is a poor unliberated woman in love and helpless, dependent on her husband." That simply was not true.

I was horrified by the sexual animal I had encountered in myself. It wanted something and I could not appease it. I became resentful of anything that might interfere with making love. If neighbors came over to chat I found myself thinking, "What if Allan comes home and he wants to make love now and they are here?" I resented them being there because maybe . . . maybe . . . Love making had resumed, but so very rarely and sporadically!

In desperation I reached out to Allan with this letter:

> Stanford University
> Stanford, California
> July 30, 1972

Dearest Allan:

I have told you not once but a hundred times I love you . . . !! But now I'm afraid. I am getting lost between roles . . . The mummy of Freddy and Robert, the housekeeper, the social person, the friend to people, and somehow I can't find the lover . . . that one who could make your heart beat faster, the one you would want to come home for faster.

The one who is pretty and I don't know what. Maybe you can help me to find her, maybe you can tell me what are the things you love in me, or what turns you on. I don't know and it is disconcerting. I love you!!!! every day more and more. Hope we can keep together, not just loving but together growing, getting to know each other more and more. So little does one know anyone else! So little does one know oneself!!

> *Love,*
> *Beatriz*

How do I get out of being controlled by the animal? That I did not know . . . until one day I looked at my child when he needed changing, and for a second I thought, "What if Allan walks in and wants to make love. You can't because of this child." I experienced resentment of my own child! I was horrified that the animal in me could even exist, and now, it seemed to possess my mind. At that I knew I preferred to die rather than feel like that. I saw no other alternative. I did not consider having sex with another man; I did not think of masturbation; nor was divorce an option. My life was with Allan until I finished my job or not at all. How melodramatic! . . . Nevertheless, my true feelings.

When Robert was four months old, I attempted to commit suicide while my father was visiting us. He remained with us for another seven months.

After my father left in June, I gave Allan an ultimatum that he must change his limbo status at Stanford by October, or I would leave him. In October 1973, when Allan had not yet taken any decisive action, I moved out of our apartment on the Stanford University Campus. I took an apartment in Palo Alto with my brother Freddy, aged 13, and Robert, now 15 months.

At the time I felt my sexual needs very strongly and could not understand why my friends would not help me. Yes . . . I expected them to go to bed with me! I needed it. Again the scenario did not work. I found that people set limits which I did not understand. To me this need was as basic as food! One always gives food to a hungry person. I realized my release could not come through them. So it came through sneaking with Allan!

While we were separated for six months, we dated and made love to each other, avoiding being seen together. We did not tell most of our friends. I needed support from my friends and if they knew about it they would have removed their support.

From the experience with the animal in me, I realized several things. The first was that I was a "Good woman." I had preferred to die rather than sleep with someone not my husband. Although all those years I had behaved as I wanted and as I felt was right, the judgment of society that I was "no good" had left its mark. At 31, I "proved" to myself through my attempted suicide that I **am** good, since only the "good" choose to die rather than think of committing adultery. That discovery let me feel free again to go to bed with anyone, if my intention was not for me, but for my husband Allan.

My second realization was the horror of feeling dependent upon another individual. This brought two results. For myself, I realized I did not want to be sexually dependent on another human being ever again. So I decided to masturbate. I didn't feel right about it, but I needed the independence. I would make love to Allan when we felt like it, and if I wanted to make love and he was not in the mood or not available, I could satisfy myself.

I found masturbation did relieve the pressure. The problem, as I see it now, was not between us, but in each one of us.

Something bothered me about masturbating, but I could not figure out what it was until 1979, when I finally realized that my sexual satisfaction comes from the blending of energies, a feeling of communion. By masturbating, I was meeting only myself, and therefore had no feeling of communion; so the sacred aspect was missing. After this realization I stopped masturbating and did not miss it.

As I recognized my feelings of dependence, I became aware of Allan's predicament. If I — who knew other men, and did not now desire other men — felt like this, what was Allan feeling? He was a true prisoner. He did not know **how** to approach another woman. If I died he would bury himself in his computers and books, unable to approach a woman — wanting to, but not doing so. I knew I had to teach him.

Allan had come a long way since we were married. But even though we were lovers, we were never a couple. I had always felt like his mother instead of his wife. When a child is **ready**, the mother goes out and finds other children with whom her child can play. A mother knows it does not matter how much she loves that child, her love alone is not sufficient. The child needs other children, the outside world.

I felt it was time for Allan to explore other relationships. For many years I had brought the world to him through parties and dinners at home, where he could participate even if only for 5 minutes. Then he would flee to the bathroom. Now he was able to sit through a whole meal with other people. He was **ready** to explore the outside world. He had gone to bed only with me. He needed to experience, to know others. Only experienced knowledge brings freedom.

Once a week I went to Stanford University for group therapy. We discussed this thoroughly. They kept asking if I realized what I was doing, that I could lose him. As things stood, he would never, ever move away from me.

Of course I knew! Again, as in the case of sex with another woman, when they gave me the reason **not** to do it, I knew I **wanted** to do it. I would never act — or worse, not act — from Fear of what could happen. I would make my decision out of strength (Love), not weakness (Fear). I must conduct my life honestly, openly and fearlessly.

The actions of my life have never been based on what I want for me, what is good for **me**. These questions never occur to me. If, from my helping Allan, he freely chose to leave me: so be it. If not, all the better. My job was to free Allan so that he could become what he was meant to be. I only thought of what he needed, what was best for him. Therefore, I could not refuse to help him because of fear of losing him. (None of the fearful, "**If you . . . then I . . .**" for me! Rather, "**I will . . . even if . . .**") After

I had thought it through, I knew what I had to do.

I answered an ad in the . . . newspaper: "Couple looking for another couple." I felt strange yet I had to do it. I phoned and spoke with the man. His name was Allan too, so we talked of that, then of other things.

We met at their very fashionable house in San Francisco. He had a Porsche. The meeting was strained. They suggested we go to the houseboat of their friend in Sausalito. The friend was away so they thought we would be able to enjoy the boat and the hot tub by ourselves.

Well . . . other friends of their friend had the same idea, so the boat was full of people, each expecting to have the boat to himself/herself. The night was perfect: the weather warm, the sky clear, the air fresh. The hot tub was outside on the deck, filled with bay water. The boat was designed for sex: beds everywhere, dimmed lights, a huge mirror above the master bed, vibrators of different shapes connected to the walls. This was a place where sexual parties and workshops were conducted.

I could see in Allan's eyes how much he wanted to touch other women and how restrained he was. Since I now knew beyond any doubt that I did not want to go to bed with any other man, I felt I could do so as necessary for Allan's development. Nothing teaches like example, so I went to bed with the other Allan. I did not like it. I was not interested; but I wanted Allan to feel if Beatriz does it, I can too. (Permission was granted.)

While I was in bed with the other Allan, a woman came in and joined us. I realized she was a giving person: she knew how to give sex, not as an animal. I asked her if she would go to bed with my husband. She said, "Yes."

Then I went and talked with Allan. I wanted him to make some move, but I did not want him to find rejection. If he did, his confidence could be seriously damaged.

The evening ended and he had gone to bed with M. He had had his first taste of the outside world. He was excited about it. He wanted more . . .

On the radio I heard a man named Stan Dale. I knew he knew and understood sex. He went further: he saw how sex and feelings are connected.

I found out there was to be a three-day seminar in Santa Rosa. We went. There were 200 people in a huge room. Stan Dale stood at the front and talked and encouraged people to share. I shared a great deal. I wanted Allan to share too. I did not think he would, but I was hoping. Stan is magnetic. He actually got Allan to stand up in front of all those people and say something! I knew then that Allan was on his way.

The last night of that seminar something happened that changed our lives for the next few years. After dinner there was a dance. Allan invited a lady to dance. I saw him dancing and I could not believe it. He was in love!

"I felt," he said, "like I should have felt when I was 16, at school dances ... the ones I never went to ... the dances I never danced."

I was happy for him — he was picking up his life where he had left it off — and grateful to that woman. She was satisfying a need impossible for me to satisfy: she was blond, petite, very Anglo-Saxon — everything Allan always wanted. I am short, dark, plump and very Latin looking!

They made a date. I got his clothes ready. Allan came home from work early to rest, to have time to bathe, to buy a rose for her. They would meet by the sea. Oh, how exciting for him! I enjoyed seeing him organize his time so well! I was proud of him.

I was waiting at home ready to hear all he had to say. He was flying high, in love. Love-making with her was beautiful!

Allan's birthday was soon after that. I organized a birthday dinner in San Francisco, where she and her husband would come. Her husband had made me feel he was interested in me. It all seemed to fit nicely.

We sat at a table with all our "square" friends and this couple who had had an "open relationship" for quite a few years. I guess this meeting had to do with my need to integrate. Whatever I do, everyone has to be able to know. If I need to keep something "secret" it means to me that I should not do it. Since I was doing something good, I could tell all my friends about it.

This was now all the more relevant to me since I had kept my sexual meetings with Allan secret during our separation. I had become aware of how and why secrecy is born.

After that dinner, we invited her to come to our home. I made a beautiful dinner and had the fire lit. After supper Allan and I gave her a massage. She looked beautiful lying there by the fire. The massage got more erotic and before long she and I were one. I loved her truly, not because I was hot and not because my satisfaction with Allan had diminished, but because this Human Being was giving Allan — the man I love — something I could not. I was grateful.

She loved to make love.

She and Allan were a match: they both enjoy making love for hours, like some people enjoy playing tennis for hours. I never could. For me sex was never for sex's sake.

It was very late. We went to bed, the three of us. And again they were at it. I could not believe it! Allan turned to me and made love to me again. Then he turned to her to be with her again. We got up in the morning and she said something beautiful: "I thought I was coming to f---; I feel I am leaving a church." I was radiant. Yes! That is what sex is for me: a union of souls, an expression of deep love that only knows how to give to the other. She did feel my love, my giving. I had wanted it all to be sacred! The most sacred place is my body, my temple where God resides: through it its works are shown. I had succeeded in making the experience a sacrament!

The next day Allan wrote me this letter:

Palo Alto, California
January 14, 1976

Be advised by these presents that the undersigned wishes you to know that he has the most cordial, felicitous feelings for you personally.

I want your body!
Allan

(I kept talking about all our experiences with our friends. They said nothing. By now they had learned to expect **anything** from Beatriz.)

A month or two later she and her husband invited us to their home for a beautiful dinner. Theirs was obviously a home. The house was cozy. It was well organized, neat, with a place for everything! We ate, talked, and sat by the fire.

We divided. She and Allan stayed in the living room and made love there. Her husband and I went to the next room where we could hear them while we talked. He realized I loved Allan dearly. He loved her too. They had known each other since they were 15 or 16 years old, and now were in their mid-forties. Lots of years together! He was not really interested in having an "open relationship," but he wanted **her**.

I spoke of Allan and how intelligent he was, how the world would know about him, of his contributions which I knew would be big and important. He thought I liked to dream. I could see he thought. "This is the talk of a woman in love." How wrong! I can love a Human Being and see that person is short of brains. One thing has nothing to do with the other.

Anyhow, we stayed and slept there, but Allan and I together and she and her husband. Very strange. We drove back in the morning. Allan was talkative, happy, I was delighted to see him happy.

We went to other workshops led by Stan Dale: smaller ones, where the sharing was not only verbal, but physical as well. The energy of this man is fantastic. He seemed to know that he was turning people on to their own divinity. He was making people aware of themselves, of their own power; teaching people to risk; showing them that "Life is simple, but not easy," as he says. I am forever grateful to this man who dared to Be. That is the fundamental question for **all** of us: to Be ourselves or not. Through these sexual workshops I started to see how very different my life had been. I saw how much pain people carried within themselves because of misinformation received from parents, wrong messages. I saw I carried pain within, but mine was self-inflicted. I chose my pain. In each workshop I became more aware how consistent it was that when everyone was going any place, I was coming from it . . . or, if all were coming, I seemed to be going. In each, Allan asked more for what he wanted.

The next workshop was held at Harbin Springs, a lodge in the hills of Northern California. The weekend started on a Friday evening around 6 pm. About 50 of us all gathered and got acquainted in a dining room where snacks were provided. By now some faces were familiar, so we started to feel we were among friends.

Deep things were shared. I found it very easy to talk about sex because of my background, but realized it was not so easy for most people. Once they shared, they felt they had given an important part of themselves, they felt vulnerable. I was not able to experience that feeling of vulnerability. I always talk with people about their deep and difficult subjects, and because of this, people always confide in me. My life has been one big workshop. I never expressed my own deep feelings, which are about God and Peace, until now in this book.

The place had a hot spring and after each of us had shared his/her first sexual encounter, we went to the spring. The night was cold; the air crisp, the water hot. The feeling that first night was restrained, guarded.

The next morning we ate a magnificent breakfast cooked by "Dancing Shoes," a delightful man who lived on the premises. Food was vegetarian and of top quality. The price of the workshop was ridiculously low, just enough to cover the food. What was happening there was a labor of love. It certainly was not a moneymaking operation.

As the weekend progressed, the love energy was felt, seen. Faces became more open. People seemed more relaxed. At the ending Sunday night, people felt so close they wanted to keep in touch.

A party was organized to follow after, like a reunion. People started to see each other, to do other things together. It became the community of Stan Dale workshoppers. There was warmth. There was support for truly painful situations. There was healing.

Allan became more unblocked with each workshop. Each was very positive for him.

At the very beginning of the first workshop I had shared my desire: Time with Allan. He was now able to approach some of the women he wanted. I felt he had realized it was not sex he wanted, as much as an emotional closeness. My happiness increased as I saw him doing more and more of what he wanted to do, to Be the person he wanted to Be, **even though** he still was not giving to **me** of himself. (I felt what he gave me came from his sense of obligation.)

Through Stan, I heard of a community called "W.F." I went alone.

It was at the home of a professional man in a "good" neighborhood of Palo Alto. His family includes children, who, though not present, were aware of what was happening. There was a beautiful swimming pool and a hot tub. I met interesting people, including a minister and a very religious Mormon man. They shared their pain with sex, their search, the conflicts they felt among religion, sex, their feelings and their spouses. When I got home I told Allan I felt we should go.

Their parties were held in the homes of various families, but the same people always came, so we all got to know each other well.

I knew I attended these parties not only for Allan, but also for myself. There I could — for the first time — feel I was a good person and still say "no." If I refused sex with someone, I was not depriving that person, because there were so many other available partners. It was as if you said to your guest at a banquet, "Eat, but not of this dish." No one would starve. That was truly important to me: by refusing I was not being a mean Human Being, nor denying anything basic, and was still living the Law of Harmlessness. I was learning to say "no," yet while I was learning I didn't hurt anyone. So I used those parties to practice. I felt OK. As I learned, I lost weight. I did not need to carry all that protection around to keep men at a distance. I could be sexy and slim because I had learned to say "no." It felt fantastic!

One party was in a house with an incredible view, a table full of food (each person brought something), people making love everywhere (in two's, three's or more) — and I wasn't doing anything.

A lady sat quietly doing stitchery.

I went over to say "Hello." I knew her. We talked about her not wanting to stay home alone. She had felt like being with friends, but had this little picture to finish for her granddaughter for Christmas . . . I wondered if her daughter would ever know that gift had been partially made in the middle of an orgy!

I was aware of the good feeling the place had: there was no pressure to make love: I was doing nothing, the grandma was sewing, at one time or another everyone else was making love. In between, some sat talking of movies. Each person was freely doing what he/she wanted to do.

We got more and more involved. At our last party I felt Allan wanted me to participate, to have sex with another man. I decided to give Allan what I felt he wanted from me.

We were in a room with maybe ten other people. In one corner three men were talking. Clothes were over in another corner. Chairs, a table with glasses and wine filled a third.

Allan was with two women who were fondling him. He was obviously enjoying what was happening. I found myself with a woman who was with a man. I knew him. We started to talk, all nude. We were close to Allan. I could see him, feel him.

The woman started to touch me and I did not move, except to give a sign it was OK. In a minute both of them were caressing me on my back. I turned, wanting to see Allan's face. I saw how much he wanted to see me with that man. I decided, "OK, I'll do it."

I closed my eyes and tried to enjoy their hands. They were light and suave like velvet. There was no doubt he was a good lover. A part of me was saying "No," yet I kept seeing Allan's face. I fixed his face in my mind. With the thought that I love him and could and would do anything for him, I abandoned myself completely.

I was able to finish, to have an orgasm with this man and woman, through his manipulation. Allan was looking at me, as were the two women with him and the woman and man working on me. I did it! The effort, the concentration and the love that I felt for Allan, to be able to do that, was inexplicable! I knew I had broken a barrier bigger than I had ever imagined.

When we drove home I spoke about it in the car. I felt I had finished doing something for him; I wanted him to be happy, to love me. I wanted him to say, "There is no one like you."

But I got something quite unexpected. He said, "Yes, I did see you finish with that man. You have no idea how happy, how relieved, it makes me! You always said I was the only man you wanted, I was the only person who could satisfy you. Well, now I know someone else can satisfy you, and I am relieved. I felt a burden each time you said it to me. I don't want to have to bear that burden alone."

All of a sudden my very soul broke. I began to bleed. The one thing I perceived that Allan was giving me at that time was the sexual communion. And now I discover he felt it a burden and had wanted to be relieved!

That I felt no one would or could satisfy me like he did, was **a burden!** Something broke that I knew was irreparable.

In March 1979 Allan expressed to a whole workshop group, that the best thing that had happened to him was being married to me. He had always sent cards that told me, "I love you." But they were private. This was the first **public** statement from Allan. (He had never before even so much as **introduced me** to anyone!) Suddenly it all seemed worthwhile. I was thrilled! This was more than I could have imagined!

In that workshop I became aware that everyone was trying to open up, to have "open relationships." They were dealing with jealousy, possessiveness, etc., none of which I had ever experienced. No one had ever been jealous or possessive about me, nor had I ever felt jealous or possessive. I heard what people said.

All of a sudden it came over me: I had **never** had a "**closed** relationship!" Jorge and Roberto had overlapped. I shared Roberto with his wife, and he shared me with all the other men with whom I went. Although Allan and I had been "faithful" to each other, there had never been any possessiveness or jealousy. I understood now, after so many years, that I longed for what other people seemed to want to get out of: I wanted to be treated like "You are mine." I knew perfectly well that no one can possess another Human Being. Yet, people do give these messages even if they are ridiculous and unloving. I wanted someone to act as if I were his possession. I was only too well aware that whoever felt like that was like a rhinestone. I was already in possession of a rare diamond. Yet, there was the feeling.

Meanwhile, Allan had learned: to relate to other women, to phone them, to buy flowers for them, to date; to organize his time to be able to work and come home to rest and also play racquetball, sing in operettas, . . . in other words LIVE. I felt so good . . . so proud . . . so satisfied! It was as if a mother, having spent years on her child, finally saw him ready to fly the nest. She would not want him not to fly, not to use every tool she had given him.

In this area I can't take all the credit. I feel I prepared the soil. Stan, Helen, and all those incredible people who shared themselves in all those extraordinary sexual workshops, who opened themselves up and dared to feel vulnerable, were really responsible for a growth, a maturing, that now started, will have no end.

Now that Allan's emotional unblocking was done, I felt I wanted to receive freely-given unqualified love.

I am a person of action: once I discover a problem I seek its solution. In that last workshop I had realized I wanted to feel wanted, so, at the next opportunity I let my feelings be known.

It happened in a resort in the mountains of central California. We were sharing. I put it out for the group that I wanted someone to see **me** sometimes.

The group dissolved and we started to play. We got eight people together, lifted another in the air and rocked gently. Then we put the person down. I helped rock quite a few people; later I just sat aside and watched.

John saw me and said, "You seemed to enjoy what you were doing."

"Yes," I said, "It was fun."

"Would you like to be rocked?" he asked.

"Oh . . . yes!" I answered.

He looked at me quietly for a few minutes and then asked, "Will you do it?"

"I do not know."

He looked at me again, remaining quiet for a few minutes more. Then he asked, "Will you ask for it?" as if he had found the right question.

"No," I answered.

He got up and gathered eight people. They lifted me gently, rocked me for a while, and then set me down on the floor. I started to cry. I cried like I had not done in years. This man had entered my heart.

John was in. There was nothing I could do about it. For the first time since childhood, someone had stopped and looked at me, seen what I needed, and taken the trouble to get it for me. I had received! Never had I had that feeling. No one was ever even aware I needed or wanted anything. I had always seemed so self-sufficient! Of course I had been surrounded by love, and people had given me physical things. But no one had taken the time and trouble to look and see what **I needed**. Oh! I was touched.

We met at the hot tub later. The night was crisp. It was the New Year's weekend. December in California. The stars were all out, just like light bulbs beaming down saying, "Hello Beatriz, we too are aware you exist." The water of the hot tub was inviting. We talked and began to kiss. It was a beautiful night. We separated and I went to sleep.

In the morning I woke up expecting he would appear any minute and give me a cup of coffee. He did not. I sent Robert to look for him. Robert could not find him. I got up anxious to see him. As fast as he had come, he was gone. I was disappointed.

Time went by.

I went to the mountains again in February. He was there! We felt good together again. John was a giver. I had never encountered people who were givers. Maybe I had been so busy giving I'd left no room for anyone to give to me, nor had I allowed relationships with those who did not need **from** me. The fact is, John was the first person from whom I had experienced receiving. It felt wonderful. I wanted more . . . more.

This weekend in February, we danced. Oh! He could dance like an angel! We moved together to the rhythm of the music as if we were one. I had not danced in a long time and I love dancing. Again, like lightning, he disappeared: he was gone the following morning. I decided he did not really like me.

A month and a half later, John called me at my house to invite me out for dinner. I could not believe it.

He came; Allan was there. Of course Allan knew all about him. There was nothing I would not share with Allan. My motto has been, if one can think a thought, one must be able to share it or do it! If a thought should not be told or done, then it should not be thought. Thought is Action. Thought is Creation. For me, that's how it always has been.

Anyhow, he came in, said "Hello" to Allan and gave me a flower. We left for dinner. It was an elegant restaurant which served fish. We were talking and a waitress came to ask for our order. He knew the priorities and said, "Please come back later."

What a gift! I am sure he thinks nothing of it, but he was saying, "You count for me. What you have to say is more important. Let that food order be second." I had always been second . . . or third . . . or fourth . . . We could order later, now we had to continue; he was in control; the outside world would not be allowed to intrude.

After dinner we went to his house. The following day I wrote:

April 26, 1979

I never thought I could feel like this. I always talk about being spiritual and union, but I have never turned to God in thankfulness with all my heart as I am doing now. The feeling that someone really takes me into account, sees me, tries to make me feel at ease in his house! He was aware I was not very comfortable, and did everything in his power to soothe me. I am not accustomed to being given to like this, to being with someone who really cares and is aware of me. He talks and my heart melts away. How can someone get into my heart so swiftly, so sweetly? I don't want him to leave.

One evening at the lodge in the mountains, he was lying by the fire and all the women were surrounding him. I did not want to be just one more, and left.

I can't function . . . my head is in the clouds . . . my whole life is replaying what he said, how he said it and how he looked. I am experiencing such a tender being, so loving, so giving . . . so sweet I want to drink and drink. I feel so thirsty! . . . I can't have enough of him!

While I was listening about his wounded knee, he thought he was boring me. I felt wonderful that he would take the time to tell me every detail. I was there with him. How could he bore me? He gives pearls and does not know it. I guess we all are like this. I can't imagine what he sees in me, or why he would want to be with me.

As I write my heart pains . . . Why? Did I think little of myself? No, I know that is not true.

I asked, "What about us going to Spain together?"

He could have said "Yes" in many ways: "If I can arrange it, sure," or, "Let me think about it, it sounds nice." But no, he just poured out, "I'll make it a reality for you. Somehow I can take off, at least for a few weeks." His first thought was to give it to me; the second was to arrange what needs arranging; and then he thought of Robert. I wonder if he ever will know how great, how big a person he really is . . . Even if we never go to Spain together, he has already given me this gift.

At the restaurant he said it was an honor and a privilege to know me. It is funny, that is what I feel now for him.

I guess that is why I turned to God this morning and said, "Thank you God, for bringing this man into my life. I am asking you, God, for love, mercy and the healing of his wounds."

He deserves all the happiness in the world. I would like to be able to give it to him, but he has lots of worlds, fragmented like he says, but lots of them. I unite, integrate. That is the only way I know how to function.

But now, I seem to be flying high, very high . . . dreaming about walking the beaches of Spain, making castles in the sand, sleeping on the beach, dancing. How he dances! How he moves! It's so easy to tune my energy to resonate with his! If he leads I just follow . . . what a switch!

He squeezed the lemon on the fish for me. His manner, his voice were so soft, so loving . . . I want to feel helpless . . . I want him to feed me, to take care of me. I want him to be the one who leads. I am the one who makes decisions, and I am so tired of it! I want to call it quits. He makes me feel beautiful, feminine. I feel like playing cat and mouse and feel I will love it all the way. We move so well together . . . so far . . .

I wanted John to be part of my life, to come have dinner, be part of the family. He resisted. Finally, he came for dinner, but remained very distant. By the end of the evening all was changed, we said goodbyes very lovingly.

I waited for his call. It did not come. I became more and more anxious. Finally I called him early one morning. He told me we should not see each other again.

I was destroyed. We felt well with each other, so why? I ran to the house of a friend. She was about to go to work, but she gave me her shoulder for crying. Later this letter came:

> *Palo Alto, California*
> *May 29, 1979*
>
> *Dear Beatriz:*
>
> *. . . in the few short weeks we have known each other, each of us has recognized value in the other.*
>
> *I have resisted your wish to integrate me more fully into your life and this has caused you pain — for that I am sorry. Only more pain will ensue for both of us if we do not stop now finally and totally.*
>
> *I know the strength of your character and your ability to integrate your experiences into your life of growth. Take what you have gained and integrate that into your life with Allan and Robert. You offer a great deal to each other.*
>
> *Be gentle when you think of me, be kind and loving to Allan and Robert who love you so well.*
>
> *John*

I knew he did not want to be responsible for any break-up. And I saw I could not make him understand it was time for me to move on from Allan anyway.

I realized that while I had wanted one who would want me and be jealous of me, I had attracted him. At the same time, I knew I could not have an open relationship with a husband and a closed relationship with a lover . . . Not unless I could lie, and that I never do.

I was desperate. I wanted him; I wanted to feel. I wanted someone who knew how to give, someone who would show me he **wanted to be with me.** I felt like a dishrag.

Allan was wonderful. He was supportive. **My husband** was saying, "The pains that humans inflict on each other because they are afraid to love!" He understood only too well why poor John was withdrawing.

Yet, I would have loved Allan not to understand so well. I would have preferred him to be mad at John for hurting me, or at me for wanting John.

But no, that would not be Allan. He would take neither side. He just saw and understood both with his head, as if all this had nothing to do with him.

My heart was torn. I felt deeply for someone other than Allan. That was a shock to me.

As planned, my son Robert and I went to Europe in July 1979. We had put the down payment on a house, to which we planned to return after two months. Things happened to change that.

The flight to Europe was fine, but I could only feel my pain. I had dreamed about a trip to Europe since I was fifteen, and now I was going there, feeling terribly depressed. Our destination was first Copenhagen for nine days — to see a dear friend (from Canada days) — and then Spain for the rest of the two months.

The more hours away from home, the more clearly it came to me that my leaving was the end of an era. The words of Allan as I left for Europe kept repeating in my ears, "Now we will be able to have parties at **our** . . . house."

NO! I knew how he felt. If he did anything, he had no problem about letting Robert know.

But Robert was only eight years old. **No**, I did not want Robert involved in the sex parties. I knew Allan needed them, they were good for him, had already helped him to get out, to grow, to Be. I did not care how many other families had parties at their homes, how many other children were aware and part of all this. I did not think it right for Robert.

That was the first time I had ever even thought of saying "No" to Allan. I had married a person who had finally tested me to my limit. I could give no more.

"My rights end where and when the rights of the next person begin." If I continued giving to Allan I would involve another Being, Robert. That Being would have **no** choice. No! I can't do it. I can't.

Then I allowed myself to feel the terrible bleeding, as Allan's other words came to my mind: "It is good to know you can finish with another man. It was such a burden." Burden, burden!

Later, on the Costa del Sol, alone with my child, — the only adult alone or just with a child on the whole beach — I started to think. Why isn't Allan with us? I had begged him to come. Now, finally, I had to face the inevitable, the painful truth: the job was done and Allan had **not** chosen me.

I had said to him, "When you are free you will fly where I can't go." I had known when we married, it would only be to a certain point, and I would not get to enjoy the harvest of my efforts. Well, now was that point, he was free: he knew how to call people, was unblocked, could Be. By Being, he would find himself and therefore God.

I had to accept that those two hours of free, complete and full (mental, emotional, physical and spiritual) love I had always wanted with Allan, would never come. This was no longer because he was afraid and **could not** give them to me, as years before, but because now that he **knew how** to give, he **chose** not to give freely of himself to me.

Beatriz looks at Allan

ONLY BY CHOICE ⟵ DOES NOT GIVE ⟶ HAS NO CHOICE

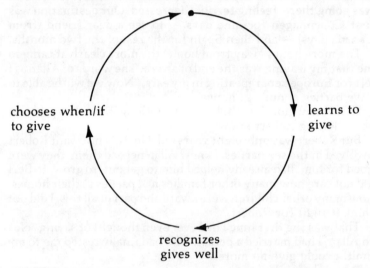

chooses when/if
to give

learns to
give

recognizes
gives well

I wanted action. I knew Allan's sense of obligation would not allow him to ever leave me; but I would never, ever get his time. Since my job was accomplished, he would be all right. He had not chosen me, therefore I should move on. I sent a telegram asking for a divorce. It was August 16, 1979.

During the two days before, I had sat on the beach thinking it all through. I had written a list of what I wanted in a man.

I was fully aware my cup was not full anymore. I had extra time, extra energy, no job requiring all of my Being. It felt as when someone working in an office suddenly realizes half the day is empty. On a job, we want to work and need to expend the energy required. When done, I would leave.

My marriage was a spiritual job, and that job was done. He was free. **He** was in control. I did not decide, he did. I wanted him to be free, and once free, to choose me. He did not. I had to leave the finished marriage job as I would the finished office job.

Crazy? By risking I have always won.

I sent the telegram from Spain in the morning. That afternoon I thought, "I am free; I am no longer a married woman." So that evening I went dancing.

I had it all figured out in my head. I would go into a discotheque, look for a corner, and sit quietly there. I had never before gone to a discotheque. I had never entered a bar alone in my life.

My knees were trembling. I went in and looked around as I had planned. That's as far as it got. My eyes stopped at a man sitting at the bar. He was like a magnet. I found myself sitting next to that man, absolutely sure that he liked me. I took a cigarette; he lit it. He did not speak. I started to think, "Maybe I am crazy." I decided to see what was what.

I took my glass and sat elsewhere. If he was interested he would turn to look at me. So I sat where he had to turn 180 degrees to see me. He did! I knew it! But that was all he did. I left.

I found myself looking for him all over the place. The second evening Robert and I wanted to sit at an outdoor cafe, but all the tables were occupied. He was there. He got up and invited us to sit with him and his son. We did. We talked about which beach we went to during the day. He told me he went to Burriana. I told him I went to the other one.

The following day I went to Burriana. I looked for him all day, fruitlessly. I was feeling like a fool. "I don't know this man! Why am I doing this?" Anyhow, I knew if I went to the cafe that night he would be there.

I went with Robert and sure enough, there he was. Again the tables were full and he invited us to sit with him.

I discovered he had spent the day looking for me at the beach where I'd said I went. I didn't tell him I was looking for him on the beach where he'd said he went! I said Robert wanted to go to the **pedalos** (pedal-operated boats) and they are only at Burriana. That was true: The pedalos could only be rented there. But Robert wanted it because I suggested it, and I suggested it because I wanted to see him. Of course, I said none of this.

Anyhow, he invited me to go dancing. I said I could not because I had to go home, give Robert dinner, put him to bed, etc.

He looked at me, put his firm, wide hand on my arm and said, "Go and do whatever you need to do. If it takes you 1 hour, 2, 3, 5, 10, 24, I will be here waiting for you."

These words were a miracle! I was the one who had waited . . . 14 years for **two hours** of full, free and unqualified love from Allan. And here this angel came and told me the exact words I needed to hear: "**I will** wait **even if** it takes you 24 hours."

I went flying!

We went dancing. We could not talk with each other very well. He spoke French, a bit of English and a bit of Spanish. I spoke Spanish and English. We managed. He commented that dancing is a universal language. I felt his Being. We could look at each other and understand each other. We knew how to read each other. It was so strange!

At 2 o'clock in the morning we were necking on the bench by the Mediterranean, looking at the moon. He said things in my ear which I could not understand. He was speaking in French! All of a sudden we looked at each other and realized we did not know each other's names! We both laughed, he throwing back his head in a frank roar, as both of us realized names were a small detail, nothing important.

That is how the romance with Jose started.

We walked the all-white streets of Nerja, the small Spanish town where we were staying. We walked together well. He did not need to adjust to me nor I to him. We passed a bakery at 3:30 in the morning. The smell of freshly-made bread innundated the street. He wanted to share it with me. He had smelled that before.

We spent three idyllic days going to the beach, lying by the Mediterranean, having lunch on the waterfront, dinner with the kids, dancing or movies in the evening.

He had to go home. He told me he would come back by horse or by foot in ten days. "Please wait for me, wait. Promise me."

I was an observer. How strange to receive all this attention. I was not yet accustomed to it, although I did know I was a nice person.

The first few of those ten days were spent reliving the previous few days. Could it be true that he had fallen in love with me? Could the feeling that he expressed be real? I remembered how fast love for John had arisen in me, how I had felt. I concluded that if it had happened to me then, it was possible it had happened to Jose.

I wanted to make him feel welcome. I put an ad in the paper saying, "Welcome Jose, Stephan (adopted son) and boat." I ordered two roses. He did feel welcome.

I did not know his vacation had been finished. He had gone to Belgium to get more time, just to be with me. He gave me the most precious thing any human being can give me, his Time. We had one ideal month. He spent every minute with me.

Near Nerja there are some of the most beautiful caves in the world. Once a year the National Ballet of Spain comes to them to perform. One of the many things we did, was to go to this Ballet. A Garcia Lorca piece was presented. To be in the womb of the earth while listening to great music, seeing the dance, the lights, the energy of the place and the people, is an experience everyone should have! I hope one day someone will show this spectacular place in a movie which will be shown all over the world!

Jose wanted to learn how I thought, how I felt, everything about me. We ate lunch and dinner at one table, he, Stephan, Robert and I. We were a family. **Finally**, after 14 years of marriage and with a child 8 years old, I had a family! I had longed for one. He was thinking about Robert, trying to give to him, and thinking about me. I had a hard time finding out what **he** wanted. Each one of us was thinking about the other, Perfection Itself!

He asked me to marry him. He had so much feeling! I had swum in Allan's mind. I could analyze every particle, go deeper and deeper . . . cut an idea in a million pieces. With Jose . . . I could swim in feelings, get lost to the point where my mind did not function. He told me something and all seemed right. I was under his spell. It took me a week away from him to be able to realize, "Hey . . . wait a minute, I am being had . . . !" or "What he said is faulty logic. It is not like that!" It frightened me to know I could be so gullible. Allan warned me, and I responded:

Nerja, Spain
November 2, 1979

Dear Allan:

 . . . *You asked me (over the phone) to have my eyes open! I have no idea what that means! I know that I feel well when (Jose) is with me, and I know it is because he demonstrates that he wants to be with me. I know he feels proud to have me at his side, and I love that feeling. That is all I really know . . .*

Beatriz

We made love. I realized very early I did not care much if we ever made love. I got emotional satisfaction. He healed each wound I had. It was as if he was a doctor and knew what was wrong with me. He healed each bleeding sore.

I didn't care for sex with him. I felt sex could never be as good with anyone else as it had been with Allan.

After a month he left, two days after my husband arrived in Spain.

Allan had received my telegram and been stunned. He **said** he did not want the divorce. I knew he **did** want it, but didn't know how to let go. If he were free he would not come back. I decided I had not asked him to come to Spain at this time, so I didn't have to sit and hear him complaining, "You take energy from me." It was especially painful to hear that since he had written me in

45

1969, "We can help each other I know, because we have strength for each other."

So I flew to Brussels to see Jose. I spent a week and discovered he was a skilled laborer. (Much later I learned he had won a substantial lottery some time before meeting me.) He seemed unsure of himself in Belgium.

People looked at us as if saying "What are you doing with this man?" I felt angry. "How dare they! Can't they see who he is! Can't people see his gentleness, his generosity, his thoughtfulness, his trust in the goodness of people. Even if they can't, why do they judge?"

He wanted to know if I could accept him for what he was. Of course, silly man! "What you do for a living is not who you are!" I know he didn't believe it.

Each time Jose was gone to Brussels, he wrote me loving letters. Here is a sample.

Bruxelles (Belgium)
November 2, 1979

My dear:

  . . . I hope that the time to be apart will be a short one, because the days without you are a very difficult test. I need your presence in my life. Beatriz, I am all the time in your heart and in your spirit . . . I love you and hope to see you next week.

Thousand kisses your
Jose

I spent a year in Spain with Robert. Jose phoned twice a week. He opened a bank account for us. We were able to eat and dress because of him. We lived in one of his apartments but continued very close to Pilar and Manolo, the people with whom we had lived our first two months in Nerja.

He would stop in jewelry stores and ask me what I wanted. He wanted to give me the world! I mentioned that I felt lost without a car. He rented one and gave me the key the following day. I felt loved, cared for.

He was proud of me. He thought I was beautiful. He felt I was a jewel he wanted to show the world. "Look. It's mine." Oh, I knew I was not his, I do not belong to any Human Being; I belong to God. Yet, I felt so good! So whole!

One night as a way of saying, "Good night," he said, "I love you Beatriz." His voice was so deep, it told me of such a tenderness, a softness that I was frightened.

I waited for him to fall asleep and then got up. I looked at the stars and asked, "Please God, please don't let me ever hurt this man." I was crying, full of love, remembering his voice.

He realized I was not in bed, got up and came to get me. He took my hand, took me to bed, forced me to look at him and said, "Don't ever cry alone, don't ever do that again! You are not alone, not anymore. When you are here and I am in Belgium, you call me or send a telegram. Here you wake me. You are not alone."

As long as I live I will remember those words, that feeling. I placed myself under his arm and fell asleep. I felt protected, my physical body lost in his, not aware of where my body ended and his began. For that whole night we were one. That feeling of well-being remained with me for a whole year.

Christmas came and Robert and I went to Brussels at Jose's invitation. We had a beautiful Christmas. We bought a tree and had nice presents. Jose gave me a beautiful fur coat. We ate good food. We went dancing.

Robert and I went to Denmark to receive the New Year 1980 with my dear friend K. This trip was also part of Jose's Christmas gift to us. From Denmark I called Jose and asked him to join us.

He did, and told me we could not get married. I was sad. But I knew something in the relationship was missing: we could not communicate on a mental level.

I left Brussels saying goodbye lovingly. Two weeks later I received this letter:

> Bruxelles, Belgium
> January 15, 1980

My dear:

> I love you and I can't live without you. When I saw you leave with Robert at the airport my heart closed and I was in despair as if a part of me was sick, and it is only now that I am capable of seeing that my life is with you. I feel very badly about all the pain I gave you at the end of the year. Please forgive me.

> Wait for me Beatriz . . . a little time . . . a long time . . . I do not know. I will go the U.S. in May with you, for 15 days, to see and live your life near you. You write me a letter telling me how you want to organize it so that everything will be OK. I believe that my life is with you, and I am now sure that you are the woman of my life. I love you for all my life.

> Your Jose
> Je t'aime

He came to Spain in February to talk about a little girl, his dreams of **our** little girl.

I had gotten a vaginal infection during Christmas in Brussels and realized he had gone to bed with another woman. I was furious. I told him not to lie to me, I could understand anything, everything, but please don't lie. Finally he admitted it. We fought. We made up. We dressed up, he in his tuxedo, I in a long black dress, went to a good restaurant, had a great dinner and went dancing. It was a splendid night!

He went back to Brussels.

Robert really loved him. He expected Robert to behave, to eat properly. Robert wanted to do his best for him, for Jose to be proud of him. Jose acted as if he felt he was Robert's father.

March came. Jose had an accident. He sent me a letter informing me that he was on sick leave from work. I called and asked if I should immediately go to him. I saw him in my mind with a broken leg, not going to work, staying home. I thought I could help.

He said, "Yes. I will meet you at the airport."

Thinking he was not feeling well I said, "I will take a taxi."

I got to the apartment and found he was not there. Obviously he did not need me there. I knew he really was going with someone else, but could not think of an excuse for keeping me in Spain. He had behaved badly towards me. He was trying to keep two women going, and thought I did not realize it! I was sure he was with the other woman (I was correct).

So I decided to talk with his adopted son, see how Stephan was feeling, and try to find out if Jose was leading this undisciplined life all the time. The boy confirmed that Jose was burning the candle at both ends, and drinking and gambling.

We talked. I could see the poor child was afraid to express his own feelings. His grandmother had died about a year before and then his mother, Jose's wife, just a few days before we had first met. These had been the two closest people to him. Jose had entered his heart only a year before, and now was acting this way. The child was afraid to say anything that might alienate the only person he perceived he had left.

When Jose returned I made them sit down and talk to each other. The boy felt better after expressing his feelings and I could see Jose was glad to know how his behavior had affected his son. When all was smooth and clear we went to the movies to see "Kramer vs. Kramer."

As we left the movie Jose and I looked at each other and both knew I had to go back to the States to see what would happen with Allan. Maybe this time away had made Allan wake up to the fact he was a father. We both hoped so and felt I had to go back to see.

Back at the apartment, I was feeling badly because I knew he was juggling his time between me and another woman. Jose made a joke I did not take well. He jokingly, sternly, ordered me, "Put your coat on and let's go to dinner."

I looked and said, "You hold the coat for me."

He said he would not.

"I'll go without it."

He said, "I'm not going out in the cold with you while you're not wearing a coat."

"I'm not going then."

They left for dinner. I left before they returned.

I spent the night in a hotel and returned to Spain the following day. Yet every night I could only sleep by placing myself in the bed just like the night he had told me I was not alone. I needed to again feel that security, even though I knew it was unreal. It gave me comfort.

Meanwhile my correspondence with Allan continued. On March 20th, 1980 I had written him:

. . . I received the letter which has the "SEX pictures." I am so far away from sex that it really repulses me to see them. How strange! So next time please don't send things connected with sex; I am not interested anymore . . .

Beatriz

Clearly I had begun to wean myself from sex. He had responded.

Palo Alto, California
April 1, 1980

Dear Beatriz:

I'm up to here with all this crap about "no sex." If that's what you feel, then perhaps we're beating a dead horse . . .

Nerja, Spain
April 19, 1980

Dear Allan:

I am sorry you are "up to here with all this crap about 'no sex'!" You said you understand how hard it must have been for me to see you free. How wrong you are! That made me happy, that brought satisfaction to me. What was hard was something else.

I thought I was an example, for 14 years, of what Love is. To be there for you. To allow you to enter my Being whenever you wanted. To never hide from you, not even a thought. To ask for what I wanted. I was hoping you would someday do the same.

What I asked, were not big ti ings . . . things of every day: . . . to
go to bed together, to get up together, . . . to have the hope or the
illusion every day, that at a certain hour you would come (home), and
this thought could give me the strength during the day, (which) I
needed to keep going among people who are uncaring and apathetic.
But that hour never arrived; that was the pain, Allan. The pain
appeared here in Nerja, the pain drowned for many, many years. But
God seems to give to one exactly what one needs . . .

Beatriz

Meanwhile his own involvement with sex-centered activities
had deepened. He wrote his mother:

April 9, 1980

Dear Mom:

. . . Last weekend I took another great leap (forward?). I had been
invited to participate in making some films for the National Sex
Forum in San Francisco. So Friday night we met there and discussed
the project after a hearty buffet dinner. They showed a few of their
films — one was a beautiful film of a man giving a massage on a
table in a patio surrounded by an oval of tall slender trees. The
sensitivity of the work — both subjects and cameramen — was
delicious. The upshot of it all is that I agreed to participate!

So Saturday, a group of us gathered in a sunlit apartment in Twin
Peaks (S.F.) and lovingly made love to each other while X took about
two hours of video tape. I'm in a sex movie! The tapes — after they
are edited — will be used for sex education. I met a marvelous
woman, who is very much into liberation — men's and women's. She
harangued me into promising to start a men's support group in this
area. We stayed up all night talking and talking and talking and
greeted the dawn of Easter. She reminds me a great deal of Beatriz —
I really am attracted to intense women . . .

Bless you all
Allan

At the end of April Jose showed up in Spain. He was distant.
He stayed three days. He had come to make up, but it took him
until the last day to come close to me. I just enjoyed him. I knew
we were saying goodbye, that he would go. But I wanted to drink
every minute. I wanted to feel his feelings; look into his eyes;
read what he wanted and give it to him for whatever little time
he was there.
He left "forever." I stayed.

Robert had his first communion at the end of May. Jose had
known about it. Like a miracle he came again, to see Robert. Jose

made Robert feel he was in heaven. Jose understood feelings. He was a master of them. He could play with them.

I also felt as if in heaven, because my child was taking his first communion and Jose was there, the father of my child. Oh, I know he was not physically Robert's father, but we are not the children of our parents. Certainly Robert is not the son of his blood father. Jose had given Robert so very much! He had paid attention to him. He had worried about if Robert had clothes or not when winter came. He was the one who thought of what Robert needed. Jose would write about his feelings years later:

Bruxelles, Belgium
October 2, 1982

Dear Beatriz and Robertito:

I have received your letter of . . . especially the few words from Robertito. I was really touched. I hope that a son like him will keep a heart clean and upright, as I could foresee when I met him. I wish I had a son like him. All the time we spent together I esteemed him mine. Tell him that . . .

Love . . .
Jose

I will never forget. When a person does something for your child, you do not forget.

After the communion we said our "last" "Goodbyes."

As we had decided in Brussels after seeing "Kramer vs. Kramer," Robert and I went back to California. The first week back was fine. Then again I did not have Allan. He was not there at all. Not for me, not for Robert.

I cried. I prayed. I prayed so hard Jose called me and asked, "What's the matter Beatriz?" He knew. He knew! He told me he was coming. He had to see me.

He came and stayed three weeks. I absorbed him again. He was different. I was living in the house with Allan, Robert, Freddy, Jose and a friend who came with Jose.

Allan and I were sleeping in the Master bedroom. Jose kept telling me he could not go to bed with me because he would not do that to Allan. I kept saying that Allan would not care. He had not come all the way from Europe not to touch me!

To celebrate his coming we all went to a Moroccan Restaurant and had a great dinner. During dessert I asked Allan if Jose could sleep with me that night. In other words, I was asking him to get out of his own bed.

Allan looked at me and said, "I was wondering if you would ask me. Yes."

I turned to Jose and said, "I want you to sleep with me tonight."
He said, "No."
I put on a sad face.
He said, "Why so sad?"
I replied, "How would you feel if you had a great dinner and no dessert?"
He laughed. "Oh, well, I didn't know I was depriving you of dessert." So he changed his mind and slept with me.

During the next twenty days Allan and Jose played musical beds. Jose felt very uncomfortable. As a traditional man he could not understand what was happening. He felt that Allan loved me and that I loved Allan. Freddy tried to explain to Jose that Allan was giving me to him. Allan knows he does not own any human being. I know I loved them both. Jose again asked me to marry him.

We went to a psychic. We wanted to see if what we felt was right. I felt I had to let go of Allan for **Allan's sake**, but was confused because I had a good reason **of my own** to let go. I wanted confirmation of my belief I was doing it not for me but for him. I wanted to know what was best for Allan. I also wanted to know if I could help Jose. Was he my next spiritual job?

The answers came: It is right to let Allan go.

Jose needs your energy, but he will do it alone!

I wanted to know about Robert and Stephan. I felt I could not help Stephan.

The answer came: Jose could help Stephan, not I.

We all felt we had received the confirmation we had sought, and left happy.

It was hard for me to accept that what I **wanted** to do was what I **must** do. This was especially true since my entire life I have done what I **must**, never what I **wanted** at first, but **making** it what I wanted. In this case, "must" and "want" coincided. I was finally aligned with the cosmos.

Finally, Jose left at the end of July. I felt fine. I was left with so much of him. Later, I began to feel very alone again.

On August 4th, 1980, Jose committed himself to a mental hospital. He had lost his job. He had led such a life during the previous year, with booze, women and gambling, that he had ended up shaking like a leaf. Now, with no money left, his "friends" were also gone. I wanted him to feel that he was not alone. I wrote every day and phoned him every other day. I wanted him to feel I would not change, even if all the circumstances since we'd met had changed. He wrote telling me there were 2,000 patients and six doctors. My worry increased.

In December I flew to Luxembourg. I wanted to take him to

the States, where I thought he would get better care. I talked with his doctors and therapists and realized he had gone there because he **chose** to be there. He was actually curing himself, intuitively doing what was necessary.

The therapist told me she was angry because I was giving him too much. She thought I wanted to get him out for myself.

I explained I just wanted what was best for him, even if it meant letting go. I thought now that he was poor and sick no one of his so-called "friends" would be there, so I wanted him to feel I was there. I was willing to take care of him for life. I did not want or need sex. I just wanted to be near him and take care of him, if he would let me.

He asked me to release him from his promise to marry me. Repeatedly he said, "I am not good for you."

The therapist kept saying he was reaching too high.

And I kept telling him that there is nothing too high or too low. "Don't let anyone tell you you are not good enough! It is not true!" So I left.

He did not come to say goodbye at the airport. He wrote me a letter immediately afterward:

Ettelbruk, Luxembourg
December, 1980

Dear Beatriz:

I will never forgive myself for not seeing you off at the airport, but I could not stand it, I was so nervous.

. . . And you, how are you sweetheart? I have thought a lot about you since you left and I miss you. I know that you are thinking about me too. But life is that way. In any case, if you believe in your fate, sooner or later we will be reunited for more bliss. I talked about you with Mrs. Heinen (his therapist). She found you extraordinary . . .

All my tenderness,
Jose

On Christmas he called to say, "Thank you for everything." He had asked me to keep writing, so I did, but I told him that maybe he would be better off with another woman. I took a chance. I knew he was proud. I was hoping he would tell me no, or . . . go and find himself another woman and let me know he had done it. I wanted him to show me that his love for me was bigger than his pride. His pride won.

In April Jose wrote to inform me that he had another woman and was going to marry her. I had let go of Jose, January 22nd, 1981.

My divorce hearing was January 28th, 1981; I had already let go of Allan in December, before going to see Jose in the hospital.

In between, Allan and I had sex for the last time. It happened in January, 1981 when Allan stopped by the house. As he was leaving, I held his hand and, moved by something which came from within, said: "Let's go and make love."

He looked a bit confused; he was going with Ann.

I said, "Well, we're still married!"

He looked at me, laughed and followed me to the bedroom. We made love, as always, so easy and free. But this time I saw a big white eagle. At first its wings were heavy, awkward, not graceful at all. But then it just took off flying beautifully, going up and up. I began to cry and cry. Allan was surprised since he knew it was the first time in my life I cried while making love. I told him what I had seen and felt. "I've done it, I've done it! He will fly high!" I took the eagle to be Allan, since he is a Scorpio, and when evolved, the Scorpio becomes an eagle. It was such a strong feeling. "I've done it, he is free, he'll fly!"

I stayed home for the whole month of February. I had wanted to serve Jose without sex, and now it looked as though God had taken the sex drive away from me. I had really enjoyed sex. I was a sexual being and had always recognized that part of me. Now I could masturbate or use a vibrator and I felt nothing. I was not frustrated, in fact it was nice. Yet I kept talking to God and saying, "I hope it is not forever. I hope you give it back to me. I don't mind serving mankind, but at this expense?" Ha! Ha! Yes, this is how I talk with God. Two years and a half have gone by and I still feel nothing.

Thus was concluded my search with the God of Sex, the search that had taken me to the center of myself through giving freely and consistently at all levels: sexually, emotionally, intellectually. By directing my spirit outward to manifest itself through all, I had arrived at the center of myself.

CHRONOLOGY

1941	June	Beatriz born in Buenos Aires, Argentina.
1945	End	Decides: "I'll prove there is No Evil."
1956	Spring	Meets Roberto.
1959	Jan	Freddy born in Buenos Aires.
1960	End	Catatonic cleansing.
1964	Feb	Leaves Argentina - arrives in Toronto, Canada
1965	March 26	Marriage in Toronto to Allan Prentice.
	Aug	Visits Argentina with Allan.
1967	June	Mother dies. Allan graduates from McMaster University.
1968	Sept	Move to Columbia University, New York.
1969	Sept	Move to Stanford University, California.
	Fall	Accepts "social limits."
1970	Dec	Freddy arrives in Stanford.
1972	July 9	Robert born in Redwood City, California.
	Sept	Father arrives in Stanford.
	Nov	Attempts suicide.
1973	June	Father leaves and returns to Buenos Aires.
	Oct	Separation from Allan.
1974	March	Re-unites with Allan. Buy house on Emerson Street, Palo Alto, California.
1975	Dec	Sex exploration begins, Sausalito, California.
1977	July	Father dies. Allan sings in opera, "H.M.S. Pinafore."
1978		Returns to old ways: "no limits."
1979	July	Visits Europe — Denmark, Spain.
	Aug 16	Sends telegram asking for divorce. Beatriz Free. Meets Jose.
1980	June	Returns to Palo Alto.
	Aug	Beatriz and Allan file for divorce.
	Oct	Allan moves out of house on Emerson Street.
	Dec 4	Asks Allan: "Do you still want me?" Lets go of Allan.
	Dec 6-13	Trip to Luxembourg to see Jose.
1981	Jan 22	Lets go of Jose.
	Spring	Start of Experience, Palo Alto.
	Aug 6	Arrives in Argentina.
	Sept	In Miami, Florida.
	Sept-Oct.	In Spain. End of Experience, Nerja.
	Nov	Return to Palo Alto.
	Dec 4	Lets go physically of Robert. Robert goes to Argentina.
	Dec 5	Begins to write this book.
	Sept	Completes first draft. Conclusion: "There is No Evil."
1982	Oct-	Edits book.
1983	Sept	

CHAPTER 2
GOD OF MONEY

One of the many things taught by my father was how to handle money. He used to sit me at the table with Mother and treat us alike. If you knew Mother, you would understand. According to world standards, you could not find a more irresponsible person about money. Father used to say, "Your mother is like a chicken. The chicken is the only animal that spreads out with its feet instead of gathering in. Your mother is like that."

We would sit there, he with a piece of paper and pencil at hand. "Now, what do you want this month, Beatriz?" I would give my incredible list. He'd listen, then turn to Mother. "Now, what do you want this month?" She would give her list. He would explode. Why? Well, according to him, Mother was supposed to take care of the money, to be the financial administrator of the household. He was only supposed to go out and earn it. But . . . she knew nothing about how to distribute it. So he was in the unspeakable position of having to do a "woman's job." There would be loud voices, etc., and then he would try to calm down and give an imaginary number. The number was the amount we could spend that month.

Then he would turn to me, "We have just so much. You want all this. Good! Now, if you get all that, you will only be able to eat Monday, Wednesday, Friday and Sunday. You will have to skip Tuesday, Thursday and Saturday." He never told me, "You can't have what you want." He just made me realize you may have to pay a price to get what you want. So I would consider the alternatives, and tailor my list. We would finally agree on my eating every day and not complaining if one day I ate something I did not like. This was in exchange for sometimes the whole list, sometimes parts of it. Around that table I learned to negotiate and to accept that one can't have the whole cake and eat it too. Yet, it didn't mean to lose. It meant all parties can win.

As I grew I realized sometimes he told me "no" when there was money to buy what I wanted. That learning was hard. I wanted a reasonable reason, like, "There is no money." Instead, I got, "Yes, there is money, but no, you can't have it."

"Why?" I would ask sadly.

"Because life will tell you 'no' many times. It is better if you learn to accept a 'no' now." I am very glad for this training from Father.

I got trained, but what I learned was that "no money" did not mean "not doing." It meant using your head. It meant being

57

creative. It meant doing without, to be able to do what you wanted.

Father worked very hard. He did make an awful lot of money. There was never enough. But the money was not spent on us. Mother had a heart bigger than life. She would bring people in, help them get started, and off they went, sometimes taking with them more than what was intended.

There was always someone who needed more than we did! Here is a simple story: Mother made a cake. She cooked very well but she did not bake well. This time the cake came out fine. I entered the kitchen and saw the last piece of cake. I had not eaten any. I said, as she was giving the last piece to a neighbor, "Mama, I didn't taste it." She ignored my request, and gave the last piece to the girl.

When the girl left, she turned to me and said, "I know you will be with me tomorrow; you will eat. I do not know if she will eat tomorrow." Now the lesson was obvious: You must give to others even if you sometimes have to take from your own. In fact, there are no "own." The world is our "own."

Looking back, the whole thing does not make sense. We were not poor. We were not talking about someone who would not eat tomorrow. That girl was the daughter of a general who lived on the first floor of our apartment house. The daughter of a general would not starve. That is how every opportunity was used to teach me. There was a reality within a reality. And that invisible reality, it seemed to me, was the real one.

There were high times and there were low times. They trained me to know quality, yet not to think that anything below it was unacceptable to have or wear. No. If you can, buy the best. If you can't, buy the best that you can afford. The best never meant the most expensive. It meant quality, and quality never meant a brand name.

I had a grandmother who always gave money to me and to my sister. She always gave the same amount to each of us, to show that she didn't make any distinction between us, that she was fair. The fact is, she did make distinctions in how she treated us.

Father said Charity and Gifts are two things that must come out of one's own pocket. I knew I could go and ask for a toy, a movie, all sorts of things, except that which I most wanted. What gave me the greatest pleasure was to give, gifts for people and charity at school.

I grew up in a boarding school. There was a little black boy doll made of metal. When you put money in it, it nodded its head to say "thank you." I loved to do that. But that was charity, so I could not ask for it. The two things I enjoyed most had to come from the money they gave me. I never felt I could spend that money for me. You can say that since it gave me pleasure, I was spending the money on myself. Yes, but . . . I wanted some material things too. My choice was to give myself the invisible. My satisfaction came from doing what I felt was right. The Divine Law of "One in All" is fulfilled when **wants** and **shoulds** are the same. Thus the person is aligned.

The money from the black boy piggy bank went to Africa. We could adopt a child by giving a certain amount. I wanted to do that! I saved a long time . . . and got a Certificate for it. I gave him a name, Hector Alexander. I still have the Certificate. I followed him in my mind for a long time.

Then came birthdays. In January was my sister's birthday; I saved for her. In February was my grandmother's. March was that of a friend of mine. June was Father's Day. July was my mother's birthday, September my father's. Each month there was a gift and every day at school that little box pulled me towards the people the nuns told me needed more than we did.

Yes, I did want to buy a candy for myself. Yes, I wanted to squander the money. But, I felt I had a job to do. I had to use that money for others. Unconsciously, I already knew what money is for. Divine Law says that "Money Belongs to All." That is how I felt.

My sister received lots more money than I did. She received from every corner. She spent it all on herself. I remember how I used to wish I could be like her. She would enjoy all that money, buy whatever her heart desired, and then when a birthday came she managed always to write a poem, a letter, something that made everyone melt away.

Her gift was always more appreciated than mine. Hers came from within. Mine was bought. I knew I could not write. I still can't, I just have something to say. That is different. She could write. No one ever paid attention to the fact that I saved for the gifts. I had to plan ahead. The lack of recognition did not stop me from continuing on the path. I felt I was right. I felt I had to keep giving even if no one ever recognized it. Even as a child, it was already important to me that I had to "feel right." I "felt right," so no change of the path was necessary. This attitude has continued all my life.

Even then the Law was clear to me. "Love Is A Gift." No recognition is necessary. I felt grateful, the person could refuse my gift! That was scary. So the thing was to keep acting givingly, and hope they would not refuse my gift (Love).

My father used to send me to make bank deposits for him. I was so small I could just barely reach the window by stretching my arms and standing on my toes. The teller knew that when this little hand showed up it was Mr. Caprotta's daughter. He was behind a barred window, in a big, very impressive, marble bank. To me it was all familiar, friendly and loving. The teller sometimes had a sweet to give me. I was the only child around. In the late 1940's not everyone had a bank account in Argentina, . . . Never mind a child doing deposits. But in this simple manner I got acquainted with banks and what they do and why they exist. Father was a good teacher.

When I was 12 years old, Father had a setback. He had always trusted his partner. He had left blank signed checks and his partner cashed out all the money. He was wiped out. That episode was good for me.

Mother said, "I hope you learned."

Father responded, "Yes, I did. I will never trust that man again."

He did not say, "I will not trust again," nor, "I will be careful next time."

It was clear to me: Why should the next person pay for what the last one did? Trust was to be kept until THAT PERSON betrayed it. This I applied in all human relationships.

Again we were all at that famous table. Father called for a family quorum. I was eleven, my sister eight.

Father: We have a problem. We have no money.

Mother: (almost hysterical) You'll have to get a job.

Father: Don't be stupid! I can't ever work for anyone else.

Mother: We have two girls to feed.

Father: Let's not argue.

Mother: I can't see what all this talk is good for.

Father: It is good for seeing alternatives. It is good because I want suggestions. It is good because I want to know what we have.

Mother: Don't you understand, we have nothing.

Father: One always has something.

Mother: Like what? This apartment that we rent?

Father: See, you've got it! That is precisely what we have. An apartment we rent. It has an excellent location. Now what we will do is to put an ad in the paper saying: "Exchange apartment for a house." I will mortgage the house and have capital again. I will start all over again. Yes, that's it!

Mother: Are you out of your mind? You mean to tell me you want to buy a house when we're wiped out?

Father: Yes. I'll trade the "key" to this apartment for a house in the suburbs of Buenos Aires. There is someone, just one person out of 8 million, who needs to live downtown and is willing to give up a house for that privilege. I've got the location, he has the house. Fair trade. We both will win. Divine Law: "Everybody must win."

He put the ad in the paper and it worked! Someone was willing to do it. We moved to Ramos Mejia. He did mortgage the house and he was in business again.

The whole episode of losing everything was very dramatic. My mother crying, my father, the eternal teacher, teaching me by his example. He looked to see what we had, to see how to come out on top. He did not allow circumstances to defeat him, nor to make him do something he did not want to do (work for someone else). An incredible man! That is how I learned from him to gather and deal with money.

From Mother I learned to give it away, to spend it for others.

From Grandmother Belly I learned to use envelopes and budget it carefully. Every month she filled different envelopes for light, telephone, taxes, food, Ana Maria and Beatriz, etc. I saw them when she gave me money. It came from the envelope with my name on it.

By the time I was 15 I had a good idea that money was a tool, to be used for a purpose. It was not something that I could believe would make me happy.

By age 16, I realized there were a lot of poor people. I started to notice "Villas Miserias." This was the same time I discovered men wanted to give me the world, as mentioned in the chapter "God of Sex." I wanted them to buy things for the poor instead of me, but I saw they were not willing to do so. I knew money was for all, so I just took the money, happily went to Gath & Chaves and bought clothes for little children, and sheets and towels. On Sundays I went to the Villas and gave the clothes and linens away. I felt so good!

I did not want to wait until I "grew up" to help. I knew the time was now, when I saw the need, when I became aware of it. Having seen, I felt, I thought, I acted. Law: "Here and Now." It could not be wrong to help. It could not be wrong to serve by giving myself completely to someone and being a "Robin Hood." (I did not yet know the story of Robin Hood!)

There is something more. I had no concept of "wrong," or "bad." I felt we were mirrors, who simply saw what we were. I knew myself to be light; therefore I would only encounter light. I guess another way of putting it is: I had not eaten from the Tree of Good and Evil, but from the Tree of Life.

God is everywhere. My actions were not right according to the society or morality of the time and place. But actions are to be judged by **intentions** and only between the person and God. I knew myself to be a Human Being. As such, my job was to BE. I was meant to feel and follow that which I felt within. Therefore I did not pay attention to what **society thought, felt or said.**

As long as I could get up in the morning, look at myself in the mirror, and feel each day I was more giving, more generous, and more understanding, I could go on. I felt I was on the right track. The faces of the children, the tears of the mothers when I went on Sundays, were telling me it was right. The tables with white cloths in those rooms where the floor was clean swept dirt, told me it was right.

This went on for a couple of years. Then I started to work, and by then the money was needed at home. By then I was 18 years old and had gone through big changes. By then I only had my salary.

I dealt with my salary in a simple way. When I got a check, I divided it into envelopes to pay the bills at home and put aside bus fare for me. I still had an account at Gath & Chaves which I used for clothes and Roberto paid. When I needed money for movies, I asked Roberto. So basically I did not use my salary for me. I did not think the money was mine because I was working for it.

On my first job I worked with a lawyer. I learned to do Corporations (an involved legal procedure for the creation of corporations). This was not part of my job but I realized it was a money-making operation.

I left that job and took another. There I learned the money market. It was exciting. To me it was the development of intuition. You read the papers, read between the lines, and decided on a strategy of selling and buying dollars. There was a lot of gut feeling in it, not just knowing the market.

At the same time, I convinced Roberto we also should do Corporations. We did, and made quite a bit of money. It was perfect timing since my father had had an accident and could not work, and for a while we could not even take money from the bank. It never occurred to me I was young and therefore could not earn as much as he did. It never occurred to me that my mother could solve the problem. Father was incapacitated; Freddy, my brother, was 1 year old; we needed money and that was my problem.

I worked hard. During the day at Continental, in the evening twice a week at the studio preparing the work for the secretary for the next day. As the situation got worse I felt I should go to another country where we could all be in a better financial position. For example, Freddy was going to school and the bus would come to the door to pick him up. It never occurred to me to reduce expenses, that this was unnecessary. But it did occur to me that in another place where no one knew us, we would not need a bus to come to the door. So I decided I would leave the country.

I put to work the "Divine Law of Money." First I decided what I needed to do. The job that needs doing can't be for oneself but must be for others. (What the business world translates as, "Find a Need and Fill It"). After that is clear in me, then I start talking with everyone about my project. (Utilizing the power of the WORD) (advertising). My decision was to arrive in Canada on the first of March. I was going by myself and from there I would send for all the rest of the family. I was 21 at the time. We all agreed it was what we all wanted. I told people I was going to arrive on March 1st.

People asked, "How are you going?" "With what money are you going?" I said I did not know. What I DID know, was that on March 1st I would be in Canada. People smiled. They did not believe me.

March 17, 1964

My dear friend Beatriz:

. . . I was speaking with Valenciano when the postman arrived with your letter. You cannot imagine how happy we were when we found out you had arrived in Canada. It looks as though you were right with that incredible confidence you had that everything was going to go well. Sincerely, I believed you could not bring this about. I am very happy and I envy you, and I wish you the best of luck with all my heart . . .

Juan Berria

I kept on talking and Father started to get worried. January was here, I did not have a penny with which to go and I kept talking about the first of March.

At the end of January, my father talked with my mother one night. I heard him from my bedroom. He thought I should be taken to a psychiatrist, that the pressure of the situation was getting to me, and I was obviously losing sight of reality. Reality is that which one **sees**. The facts HE saw were: the end of January and no money; no plan nor clear way to get it; yet I kept insisting on the March 1st date as firmly as if I had all the money in my pocket.

I knew I did not have it. Yet I knew the Law. Whatever I needed would be provided if my motives were pure. I knew they were. The money would appear. How? I did not know.

Well . . . on February 9th I took the train to go home from work as usual. A man sat down next to me. He looked at me, his eyes big, bright, and happy, and said, "Beatriz, how are you? What have you been doing? Such a long time! I am so glad to see you!" I looked at him, surprised. Obviously this man liked me a lot. But who was he? I could not remember him! He realized, and told me we had gone to high school together. He was the poet, the guy of whom every one had made fun, until I put a stop to it. I had "protected" him right through, and he was eternally grateful. He had never forgotten me, I was so good, etc. I heard it all. I believe him. It was his life, why should he lie? I did not remember being the protector, but . . . it must have happened.

We began to talk, and he told me he was getting married in June. He was very happy. I told him my story: "The first of March I'll be arriving in Canada. By the way, I do not have any money, so if you know anyone who is willing to lend me the money, I'll pay interest. Please let me know. Here is my telephone number." I said that to everyone with whom I spoke.

Two days later the phone rang. "Hello, Beatriz."

"Yes . . ."

"Remember me? . . . the poet?"

"OH! . . . Hello!"

"Well, I'm calling because I started to think: I owe you so much and I have this money in the bank that I will not need until June, when I get married. So, if you think you can give it back by then, it is yours."

I knew it! I knew it! It materialized! I knew my intentions were pure . . . The Law at work! "Of course I can use it!" I did not know how I would pay it back, but again I checked my intentions with myself. If what I was doing was truly selfless, the money would appear again when the time came to return it, just as it had appeared now.

I said I would return it on time.

After that it all happened like a miracle. A lady I just met, told me she was a seamstress, came to my house, sat at the sewing machine, and sewed a whole wardrobe for me, for free. She came out of nowhere, worked for 8 or 10 days, and sent me off.

The 29th of February of 1964 I arrived in Toronto. It was a leap year, so I did arrive on March 1st.

The money was enough for a few things: part of the ticket, baggage, etc. But to enter Canada I needed to have $500 cash to pass Immigration. I knew it. I did not have $500, but only $50. I also was supposed to have a return ticket. Again I checked my intention: "Beatriz, are you here for yourself or for your family?" "Yes, for my family." Then I knew it was all right.

I walked into the Immigration office at the airport. The officer asked me if I had $500.

I looked at him offended. How dare he ask me, how dare he question me about such a thing! I threw my purse at him. "Look for yourself . . ." My eyes fixed on his, daring him . . .

He looked surprised, said, "No, no it's all right!" He did not open my purse; he did not make me show the money I did not have. I did not lie. I did not respond to his question. My knees were trembling! I could hardly walk out of there. But I did, like a queen, well dressed, straight back, as if I owned the world! I did!

There are more ways to make a budget bigger than to acquire more money. Utilizing my knowledge of human nature got me through. Therefore, my budget was bigger by this.

I got a job taking care of a child. The child was six months old, so I did not need much English. I got the job two days after I arrived and sent the money back as promised.

Of the $125 a month I received, I sent home $110 or $115. I lived with a family. I had clothes and food and everyone was a delight. They took me everywhere, so I truly enjoyed that country from day one.

After a few months, when I got a work permit, I started to work in a department store. I kept sending money home, but now I had to begin buying clothes for me. Again the question: "Do I stop sending money and spend it on me, or do I keep sending it and charge the clothes. Again, am I doing this for me? Am I doing this for them?" Once the **intention** was clear within me, I charged what I needed, knowing the money would appear. I did not know how.

The money did appear. I got married and the bills got paid. At that point I felt I could not continue sending money. Since I was married now, I could not involve someone else. I stopped as mother had requested. Here are excerpts from her letters:

Buenos Aires
March 9, 1964

Our dearest Beatriz:

Today finally we received your letter. We were all worried that you may have been caught by white slavers. You were so beautiful when you left, that it would not be strange for them to have an eye for you.

I am happy to see your letter full of optimism. Father was happy to hear that you will be able to send 190,000 pesos.

Take care of the child for now, and send 1,500 pesos to pay for Ana Maria's English classes . . .

tu madre Bertha

Buenos Aires
March 18, 1964

My dearest Beatriz:

. . . Well we have received the check, I hope to be able to cash it, because instead of "Bertha" it says "Bartha." It comes at the right moment because I had to buy shoes for Ana and books. She got an F because she does not have them . . .

Bertha

Buenos Aires
June 5, 1964

Dear Betun:

. . . what happiness your letter gave me, that you tell me that you consider me your motor. I want to thank you, thank you my beautiful little daughter, you have no idea how much strength your words gave me. Do you think that within two years we will all be together? You ask me to tell you my dreams. The one and only dream right now is to see you again and to be there, even if I have to work. Please Beatriz, if you find a good man and you love him, please, please accept him and don't think of us, because you have to build your life and I do not want you to refuse anyone because of us.

Chau Mama

Buenos Aires
July 29, 1964

My very dear Beatriz:

. . . I am anxious to be there to be able to work, because here I cannot . . .

Chau Mama

Buenos Aires
August 31, 1964

Dear Betty:

. . . I do not know how we are going to go there, since the government does not allow us to take money out of the country . . . I hope that they cancel this new law of not taking money out, so that I can be with you, this is the dream of us all . . .

Carinos Mama

My dear Beatriz:

. . . They will still not allow us to take the money out. We will not go.

Mama

Dear Beatriz:

. . . Don't worry about sending money, God willing, we will manage. Very soon the apartment house that Father is building will be finished and we will be able to rent it . . .

Mama

In the letter of November Mother says, they are not coming. In her letter of June 5, 1964, she said, "If you find a good man, don't refuse him." That was my release. They would not come. The apartment house was built. Their economic situation was more or less solved. I was free. I needed a new job. I decided then, I'll marry. I decided on December 5, 1964. I said I will be married in March. March 26, 1965 I got married.

After each sacrifice I found myself happier than before. Since I could not believe it, I wrote Father telling him I felt funny about it. Since I had left Argentina because of them, I thought I was sacrificing, but I had ended up happier than before. He replied:

Buenos Aires
24 June 1964

Dear daughter Beatriz:

Today is your birthday. I remember how and when you were born. I remember how, since you were a little tiny baby, you acted as if saying, "Look at me, I am Here, I have come." I do not know why there are beings like you on Earth. But I have seen you attack each single project, and I have seen you succeed at each. But above all I have seen you succeed without hurting anyone, which is what counts. Do not feel badly because you are happier there than here. You deserve to be happy . . .

Papa

Allan and I decided we would go to Argentina. I wanted my parents to know Allan. Here again was a project: no money for the next intention. I had quit my job to move to a new city. There was only Allan's salary from which to pay bills and save money to go. We ate rice for six months, went to Argentina and arrived starved. Then we ate like pigs and gained weight. We had a great trip!

When we returned to Toronto from our visit to Argentina, we lived in an apartment house. A few months after we moved in, the position of manager opened up and we took it.

The building was sold and the new owner sent out a letter informing us the rent would be raised for all the tenants. As soon as I saw the increase I realized the new owner could not have all the pieces of the puzzle when he made the decision. Therefore, I called and explained to him that the majority of the tenants were elderly and such an increase would be a hardship for them: Moving would be horrible for them. They had lived there for many years; that was their home and they expected to die there.

I offered to see if I could negotiate something which would be satisfactory to all parties. I asked how much he really needed to cover his obligations. He said he did not want to hurt anyone, and as long as he did not lose money and could cover his expenses he would not raise the rent to the elderly, but would raise the rent on each apartment when it became available. He was saying: "I'll wait for them to die."

I spoke privately with each tenant, telling them the owner was a kind man who did not want to hurt anyone , but needed to raise $ . . . to cover his expenses. Would they please each decide if and how much the rent could be increased?

One of the tenants said, "I sincerely can't afford one cent more."

Another told me he could afford an increase of $ . . ., which was less than the proposed one.

The last person asked if the owner had all the money he needed to cover the mortgage. I explained the situation to her and said, "No." Then she said, "I want this to be confidential. I'll pay my share plus the increase of all the others who can't afford it. I can. They can't. Please, Mrs. Prentice, don't tell anyone. They have been my friends for years. I don't want them to treat me differently. They do not know I have money."

Problem solved . . . in a humane manner: All winners. The owner had his money; he was happy. The tenants did not need to move. And the person who had the means was delighted she could use her money in a meaningful way. I was in 7th heaven!

Good negotiation means everyone is a winner. My armor was the Truth, plus my Faith that each person would do his/her very best. They did!

To me dreams are realities. A dream is a reality in its seed. If one can dream of something, for sure one can do it. So when my husband said, "It would be nice to study at Columbia University," I immediately decided he would. He sounded as if it was a dream, something impossible, far, far from his reach. I had no concept of wanting something and not getting it, so I decided I would give it to him!

Again I started to talk, this time about Allan going to Columbia University. I put the date in my mind. People again asked the traditional questions and I gave my usual answers:

"Columbia is a private University, isn't it?"

"Yes," I replied.

"Doesn't it cost a lot?"

"Yes."

"Well then, how are you going to go? Do you have any savings?"

"No."

Again, mysteriously, out of nowhere, a friend came at 12 o'clock at night and invited me to go to New York with him. I was so glad to go to New York!

We went shopping at New York Macy's. He bought me a mink hat! He felt proud of me, of how I dressed, of how I looked! It made me feel so good! It was especially a good feeling since I knew Allan felt the opposite about me.

While in New York, I went to Columbia and talked to Mr. Trump. He looked very amused that I would be inquiring for my husband, and he tried to explain that it was very difficult to get in. I told him my husband would, he was brilliant. He looked like people always do: "There she is dreaming, in love, not seeing reality . . ." I can love and see that a man is an idiot. I can love and see that a man has a brilliant mind. A person is not his mind. Why should I have to believe someone is brilliant to love him, if he is not?

Anyhow, I assured him Allan would get in. If there was only one place, he would get in. We said good-bye.

I took the admission papers home. Allan filled them out. They included a requirement to write a piece. I knew that, based on his work, he would get in. He did.

We arrived in New York. I had gotten a job by mail from Toronto, and so started to work the second day I was in New York.

The University cost money. I do not need to say how much . . . Allan signed a waiver for September, October, November and December. He was worried. He kept saying, "How are you going to do it?" I did not know. By December we had to pay. I knew that by then he would have shown who he was and they would not want him to leave. I was counting on it.

I went and talked with the professors and told them Allan was going to stop studying for lack of money. They said he was one of their better students. "He can't quit." So they generously worked on his behalf and secured a grant for him. He finished and graduated from Columbia University.

I knew the money would appear. It was the Law at work. I did not want it for me. Not even as prestige! The intentions are what makes the Law work or not! I was working to bring about the dream of someone else. To me it was clear: Conscious, unselfish giving always produces gain.

I worked at Columbia University all that year. I got quite a few raises, which was unusual, yet the money seemed to fly. My sister Ana Maria wanted to study. I sent $1,500 to her in Argentina.

Allan got sick. He called me one day and said he could not make a certain phone call. He told me he had gone to the subway and was thinking of how it would feel to jump onto the tracks. I realized he needed help. I got in touch with Dr. Cott, an outstanding psychiatrist. He was doing orthomolecular medicine. In 1968 vitamin therapy was not yet a popular medical practice. He saw Allan and diagnosed him as schizophrenic. I was shocked. He explained it was all biochemical, just like when people who have diabetes need insulin; if they take it, they are balanced and lead perfectly normal lives; so Allan could lead a normal life if the chemistry balance of the body was corrected. It made sense to me. It certainly made a lot more sense than giving him Valium or keeping him in a hospital.

Allan started to go once a month to see Dr. Cott, once a week to see a psychologist, and twice a week to Schizophrenics Anonymous at Fordham University. He also took vitamins. It all added up to money. That therapy helped him a great deal and enabled him to finish the year at Columbia.

He was accepted at Stanford University. The Ford Foundation gave him a grant to work toward his Ph.D. It was enough for us to live on.

I started to work at Stanford and found myself with extra money. I decided to send for Freddy, my brother. He was 11 years and 11 months old and could still pay half fare. I felt his was an ideal age to travel. I had thought of going to Europe myself, but again asked: "Was money to be used for oneself or for others?" I decided to use it for him. I could probably go to Europe later, and he could only come half fare now.

This decision was to change my life. I had invited Freddy to come for his summer vacation. He came and stayed until grown up. I could not have been happier. As always when I give a gift, the winner is not just the other person; I win also. He brought much love with him, and much happiness to my life.

My father asked me to keep him. Allan and I did, of course. This put me in the position of needing to make a financial decision. I was working from 3 to 12 p.m., perfect hours since

Allan was a night person. We were up until 5 a.m., went to bed together and got up at noon or 1 p.m. By 3 p.m. I was at work again. With Freddy there I knew I would have to change my schedule and that would change my life.

Since I had to make a big decision, I went camping for 15 days, all alone, in an almost empty redwood park. I slept for four days and then walked and thought. It was March.

A trailer arrived and parked just next to me. The only people there were the couple with the trailer and me. Why did they park next to me? The Force sent them! I was able to talk with them. The lady was a warm human being who knew how to give.

I was there because I knew I had to decide between Freddy and my marriage, and between Freddy's needs and my job, which I liked. In other words, among priorities. I knew what the world would say: "Keep the job, the kid will adjust." I needed to know what came from within myself, what answers were true to me.

They came. I had to quit my job and be home for Freddy. My energy was needed, not money. Not only would we have less money, one less salary, but instead of two people, now we would be three.

The other issue was: who needed me more at the time? I decided Freddy did. He would need help to adapt to a new country and language. I had to adjust my schedule to his. It meant going to bed earlier, like 9 or 10 o'clock at night instead of five in the morning, and getting up early to send him off to school. I had to know I was strong enough to do it. It meant I would never be in bed at the same time as Allan. I knew he would not move one finger to change his life, so it meant the end of my sexual life. I was not wrong.

With me not working and one more person, we needed something to balance our finances. Again I thought, "If what you are doing is not because you Beatriz don't want to work, but because Freddy needs it, something will happen." As usual, it did. As soon as I resigned my job at Stanford, the job of manager opened up at the place we were renting. We took it. Now we did not need to pay rent. The budget was balanced! There is more than one way to skin a cat! . . . or balance a budget.

A year later I got pregnant as the result of the first time in the whole year that Allan and I made love!

The invasion of Cambodia came and the campuses were in fever. As a consequence, the Ford Foundation cut money from the campuses. Allan's grant was cut off.

So I was pregnant and we had no income! I had waited seven years of marriage for the right time to be pregnant. Since I had made this pregnancy sacred by doing it as a gift to Allan, I knew something would show up. October 21, 1969 I wrote my sister:

Dear Ana:

. . . I am thinking of having a child these days. I am suffering because I feel the time to be a mother has passed for me. The years have gone by and I have used my love for others and now I don't feel I want to work for my child. But I believe I must have it soon. Allan is finally ready. He is reading Natural Childbirth, *and keeps talking about how the child will behave, etc. I truly believe, my time has passed . . .*

Love, Beatriz

Allan meanwhile was writing to a friend:

Palo Alto, California
18 January 1970

Dear Sam and Susan:

. . . Beatriz has finally put away her white gloves to devote herself to home-making, and hopefully motherness. She is in the process of becoming impregnable, complicated by an I.U.D. embedded in the wall of the uterus, thereby necessitating a minor operation. But fatherhood looms and we're both looking forward to it all with great anticipation . . .

Peace and love is our hope and prayer for you in 1970 and the years ahead,

Allan Prentice

Of course I never told him, or anyone else, for that matter. You don't go around talking about the sacrifices you make. You do them, that is all. Why am I speaking now? Because now I know I am not the doer. I did not do it. It came through me, like everything else, for a purpose.

Since I knew my intentions to be pure, I knew all would be well. I decided I would put up an ad at Stanford offering my services to take care of a small child. I felt that would keep me home when Freddy came home from school. I put the ad up one afternoon.

That same evening, while we were having dinner and I was telling Allan what I had done, and how I hoped to solve the problem of his grant cut, the door bell rang.

A lady who lived in our apartment complex had just gotten a job and was wondering if I would be interested in taking care of her child! There is only one energy. Put what you need out there in the universe and Bingo, it comes! I'm sure I looked stunned!

We were just talking about it! I had just put up the ad! We were talking with Allan about how he can just **think** of something and bring it to himself, and I needed to **do** something, even if it is a small gesture. Well, there was the solution at our door! As it turned out, the lady had not seen the notice on the bulletin board.

That baby became my baby! I loved her. It was hard to remember I was not her mother. That lady made a beautiful shower for me. I needed things so it was all welcome. Everything was new and pretty. But I was so involved with "my baby" and so unaware of "my pregnancy" that when I entered the house and saw everything prepared for the shower, I said in my head, "Oh, it is a shower. I wonder who is having a baby." Talk about in the Here and Now! It never occurred to me it was for me; I kept forgetting I was pregnant. They could not believe I would be so casual until they found out I did not realize it was for me! Then we all laughed!

Robert came and by then we had moved to the campus. Allan got a job at the University earning minimum wage. Stretching the money was quite something! When you don't have money there are two things you can do. Either you believe you don't have any and therefore can't do anything, or you decide what you **want** to do and find out **how** to do it without money. I always chose the latter.

There were two things we liked: movies and getting together with other people. So Allan took over an International Movie series and we sat and pored over the books to choose the movies we wanted to see. We worked at organizing the series. We did not pay to see the films.

I started to cook and we got together with some people every Sunday. These were warm evenings . . . I would buy meat, barbecue it, make a salad, baked potatoes and fruit. The University supplied the cash; I supplied the womanpower. The students paid just to reimburse the cost, (really cheap!) and all had a grand time.

When my son was born my father came and stayed with us for almost a year. We were living at Escondido Village, Stanford University. That is a beautiful place. We were broke.

Father decided he would help the budget by picking edible wild plants all over Palo Alto. We ate them as salads through the whole year.

Before he left he told me, "Well, the experiment worked!"

"What?" I said. "You mean to tell me you fed us all these different foods and you did not know if they were good or not?"

He said to me, "I decided that if I was not repelled by the smell or the taste it was OK. But what I want to tell you Beatriz is that

73

this is the last piece of information I have for you. Now you know you can eat wherever you are. You'll not go hungry." ("You will always have food . . . .")

"There he goes again," I thought! But doesn't this man realize the situation. I am married to a man who is doing his Ph.D. Can he see my future? Why is he saying I have to know I can eat from the wild wherever I am? It was just as crazy as when he took me to hear Billy Graham and kept telling me, "Remember, you will need a good interpreter, that is all. You can go and speak all over the world. Remember!" I was not a public person. I just loved whoever was near me: my family, my friends, whoever I met. Besides my escapades in the bathroom talking about Peace when my pain was too much, it never occurred to me I might become a public person.

So dealing with money was not always working in a job to have cash income. Spirit is a creative principle. When one is being creative about it, one is using Spirit. This was not cash, but it gave us the entertainment and salads we wanted, without cash. So it was part of a budget! Creating money is not always creating green or multicolored paper!

Allan and I separated when Robert was 15 months old (October, 1973). I needed to decide if I would go to work or if I would stay with my child. That was simple; I knew I had to stay with Robert and Freddy. So I went on welfare. I got a lot of pressure! I was in a University environment, where the women's movement was brainwashing everyone. I knew myself strong. I did not need to get a job to tell myself I was worth something. "I" was not what I did. I was a Human Being.

The other heavy pressure came with statements like: "Your child will grow up to be a welfare child." It sounded awful. I looked inside of myself. What do I feel? Not what society tells me, not what the women's movement tells me. What do I think my job is right now? Is it more important to feel important in the eyes of the world? In my own eyes? . . . or to be there for Robert and Freddy and give them what only I can give them?

Welfare was not enough. I too had to lie. I got a babysitting job taking care of two children in their home, and did not report it. In this way I could be with the boys. Between welfare and the job, I was OK. I did not like having to lie. But if I declared what I earned it would have been discounted from the welfare check. Then I would be back to zero, working and with the same amount as if I did not work: not enough to live on.

My separation lasted 6 months. Allan was able to let go of the University and get a regular job.

While I was on welfare something happened which made me realize I was at the mercy of the apartment owner. Within three months he had raised the rent twice. The increase was phenomenal. He actually was proposing to give me the money back, and just wanted the figures on the books. He was trying to sell the property and the price would depend on the income from it. It was clear what was happening, but in the meantime I was treated unfairly. There was nothing I could do to protect myself. I decided **no more**! I decided I would own my own house.

Allan started to work. We decided we were not finished with each other. I said we would buy a house.

I had just finished being on welfare, and now I said we needed a house, in Palo Alto, no less! People looked at me with incredulous eyes.

So again the circus started. First, they told me, you need to save for the down payment. Then you buy in the boondocks. And then eventually you will be able to buy in Palo Alto. Who wants to do that?

Again I thought. Do I want this for me personally, or for the kids? The experience of going from apartment to apartment and seeing the pain in Freddy's face had been hard. Some apartments would not rent to small children; Robert was 15 months old. Others who would take little children, would not accept teenagers; Freddy was 15 years old. His face was sad and mad. Why would people not want him?

So I knew we needed a house they could feel was their own place, where no one could raise the rent and force us to move, where no one could decide the boys were the wrong age.

I went to see a realtor. He asked me how much money I had. Since I did not have any, and I knew he would not take the time to show me the houses if he knew, I reminded him his job was to show me houses. He did. After a while we found one I figured I could support even on welfare, without Allan, if necessary. I decided that was our house.

Again the realtor asked how much we had. I told him to get me an 80% loan. It was work for him. He made inquiries at several places. He finally secured a loan. Now we were at the end of the road. "Well Beatriz, how much do you have?"

"Just one month's salary."

He looked rather incredulous.

I said, "I guess we need a second mortgage."

He looked at me, "You are incredible!"

But he turned around and asked his own mother for the second mortgage. That is how I bought the house. I did not save for the down payment; I did not move to a neighborhood I did not want to live in. I decided what I needed and **checked my intentions.** Sure my motives were pure, I went right ahead knowing that it would be fine. It was.

Now I had the house. But how many women on welfare go through an ordeal like I went through? I knew I wanted to do something about that. I got involved with a group of women who wanted to start The First Savings and Loan for Women. I thought it was a great opportunity. I organized a meeting. I talked to groups. Finally, I thought, women on welfare will have an institution to which they can turn to buy their own homes. I felt if at least 5% of the mortgages were given to people who normally did not qualify, it would be good. At least it was a beginning.

As I became more involved, the eyes of the industry were turning to see what would come out of it. The fear of failure broke in, and the **sure** way to success is **not** to try something new. Then I realized that the talk was of giving loans to professional women who, because of discrimination, were turned down at other institutions. To tell the truth, I did not have much compassion for professional women who needed to go to two or three institutions to obtain a loan. I felt compassion for the women who would not even apply to one, because they knew they would not even be considered, while at the same time they were paying rent which covered the payments of someone else's mortgage. I realized I was wasting my time. I resigned.

We had nothing but a house, not even a car. In California to live without a car is not difficult, it is simply impossible. I am saying this because in so many places a car is a luxury. Not in California.

I decided I had to find one for free. I went to look at bulletin boards on the Stanford Campus. The first one I looked at had the ad: "The use of a car for one quarter in exchange for taking care of a dog." I knew that ad was for me! It was!

I took care of a remarkable dog. Animals have a way of expressing the being of their owners. This one was no different. She was as brilliant as her owner, and played the same tricks as the son played: she loved to escape. Her owner was Nobel Laureate Professor Arthur L. Schawlow.

Mrs. Schawlow came and looked at my house. She wanted to be sure the place was secure so the dog could not escape. She knew the dog! She saw and decided Chienne, the dog, would be safe there.

Chienne had ideas of her own. She hit her head against the wooden fence until she made a space big enough to escape. We blocked it. Then she dug a hole in the ground under the fence and escaped. We blocked it with rocks. I decided I would leave her in the living room while I was out. I came back and found the sofa eaten up. She was an effective communicator! Then I decided there was nothing else to eat, so I left her in the living room again. When I returned I found she had chewed the wood on the frame of the door.

That was that; I decided I would take her with me in the car. I left her, being careful to leave windows open enough for air, etc. She ate the dashboard (made of foam). I could not believe it! I decided to lock her up in the front yard. It took her two days to learn to open the gate. I never saw such a resourceful creature in my life. We should learn from Chienne! People try to tell me humans are smarter than animals. How pretentious we are! . . . Always needing to put others below us to feel ourselves important! How sad!

At that point I told Chienne, "You win." She could do whatever she wanted, since I could not hold her. Then she just sat on the front lawn and waited for us. She became a part of the family.

Mr. and Mrs. Schawlow and their children all came to pick Chienne up. It was painful to give her back. I thought that I would never do that again. I kept seeing her in every room. She was loving, gentle; she just loved her freedom. I guess I identified with her. Don't put me in a box! Don't tell me what to do! I'll do what I see fit! And if you let me be free, see how good I am? I'll just wait patiently for you to come! I too waited patiently for God to come!

Anyhow, again money had come in a different way. I did not go and spend what I did not have. I did not charge, in the society of charge accounts. I just acquired what I needed by different means. By the end of that time I had been able to save enough for a car. We also refinanced the house and paid off the second mortgage.

A dear friend decided to buy a house. I went with him to see several houses. He decided to buy in another town but asked me to go with him and see one he liked. Then he asked me to negotiate the contract for him. I loved it. I loved negotiations. I loved to arrive at the point where every one is happy with the transaction. To me business is another expression of the Divine Force, so, unless everyone is a winner, there is no good deal. If everyone is a winner, it shows the Divine Law at work.

I spent time with him, not just that day. It never occurred to me I would be paid, but the Universe always provides appropriate payment for all energy spent.

As I was doing the negotiating, the realtor realized I knew quite a bit about the market and thought I should look at a property which was a good investment. I did. Two hours later I made an offer on it. Again, I put very little down. Allan was not earning enough for us to have a house in Palo Alto, to say nothing about a second house. But here it was.

I said I believe in everyone a winner. Here is the transaction: The owner wanted, let's say, $30,000. I offered $33,000 and asked him to leave $2,500 in escrow to build a garage. So in reality the seller was getting $30,500, $500 more than the asking price. He probably had thought he was going to get less than the asking price anyway. He was happy he got his price plus $500. Then I asked for a 90% loan on the $33,000, which is $29,700. The result was I had to come up with $800 to arrive at $30,500. The rental payments covered the mortgage plus $5 or $10. The realtor was so happy she offered to find the tenants for the house for me, at no cost. The tenants were extraordinary people. They saw me as a friend. They invited me to their gigs, and I went.

This transaction was in the good old days of 1976. But even then people did not go buying houses for $800. I won; the seller won. The realtor was happy. The tenants felt I was a friend, not a landlord. Everyone involved won. To me that is good business. At the time I could have done this over and over again, if making money was what I was all about. But that did not interest me.

I sold that house two years later and made $19,000 on the $800, a good investment, I'd say. The tenants did not need to move. The neighbor bought the house, happy because the property was so close to him. My realtor was so delighted with my dealing that she called me and said, "Beatriz, I am calling to say it has been a great pleasure doing business with you. I have been working as a realtor for a while now, and I can't say this very often. Thank you." My heart was overflowing ... Who says business is cold? Who says making money needs to be inhuman? I knew it! I proved it! Not just as a young woman in Argentina, but as a mature woman in North America.

Allan was working. He too had a different way of looking at money. He was learning at his job; he felt it was a miracle he was earning a salary. As far as he was concerned, as long as he was learning, he should be the one to pay the company. Nevertheless, he would not stay in a job where he was not learning. Now, that is a different point of view if I ever saw one!

I knew he was doing well. I felt he should have an increase in salary. I knew he would never ask for it because of his feeling about learning. Although we did not need it, I felt if his salary did not represent the quality of his work, he was being cheated. I knew people judge, in whatever field, according to the salary.

So I went to his office, talked with his boss and negotiated an increase in salary based on Allan's performance. Basically I put it on their consciences. If they truly felt Allan did not merit a raise, they should not give it to him. But if they looked at his work,

78

there was no way they could say, in fairness, he did not merit it. Allan was a person who could perform superbly on the job. But he did not have the skills necessary to defend himself, to get what was fair for himself. I started from that point of view, showing that because he did not have the skills to negotiate, I was doing it for him. These were not skills he needed for the job. Therefore, the lack of them should not count against him. They gave him a raise, even though he was too weak to ask for it himself.

Later, Allan learned to negotiate and did it on the job. He did so very successfully, as part of his job. By then I felt Allan deserved another raise. I told him he should ask for it, now that he knew how to negotiate. He had proven it to them. He told me, "I know how to do it, I have learned the skills. I have used them, but they are not skills I want or like to use, so you go please, and negotiate for me."

I went again, but this time out of strength. I was negotiating for someone who was strong enough to be different. How many people send their wives to negotiate their raises? You have to be strong yourself!

I could negotiate knowing that as long as it was fair, I could present a reality that, although unusual, would be accepted and admired. As always, what society did, did not matter. Each of us must find his own path. Each of us opens a new road by using his own creative force for the benefit of all. Yes, a raise was a benefit to all. The Company had the opportunity to look at this raise in a new and very different way. I was giving them the opportunity not only to be fair, but also unique: to depart from established procedures. I was not playing games such as, "If you don't give me what I want I will leave;" or "I have another offer." No! No threats of any type! Just the truth presented to them, not even by the person employed, but by someone else who could say, "Look at this performance and look at your consciences, and tell me if what I say is not true." I trust that people are fair, that people are not there to "take" me. I knew the Law: "We are Mirrors; We get back according to what we put in." I knew I was being fair and trusting and I could only get fairness back. I did.

These two salary negotiations appear to be the same action, but since they are from two different intentions, there is one result based on weakness, and the other based on strength.

With the money from the sale of the second house, the raise, our house, and getting a friend to invest with us, I decided I would buy "my dream house."

I went to the lawyer; the papers were drawn. The money matters were taken care of; the house found; the down payment was given. All was done with love and humanity. All the outside was taken care of.

Yet, I knew this deal would not go through. Nothing was indicating the contrary, yet I knew. At the time, I needed new checks from the Bank of America. My friend Andrea asked me if I had put the new address on them. I said, "No." I did not elaborate for her. I knew deep down. This was the first deal that was for me, just because I always wanted a lovely house. I was not doing it for anyone else. It was My Will not Thy Will. I was about to not follow the Law.

I left for Europe and while there realized I needed time away from home to be alone. Since I had made all the financial arrangements, did not want to invest one more minute of my time in money matters, and felt I had no right to bother anyone else for me, I had only one choice: to let the $20,000 down payment go.

This correspondence with Allan ensued:

Nerja, Spain
August 10, 1979

Dear Allan:

I am thinking that maybe you could buy the new house and rent Robert's room and the other room upstairs for $200 each, giving you $400, or rent the whole house, or let it go. I want to stay, I am not going back, I just want to find a way to stay here. If there is no other way, I want to sell the house. (I felt I would need $600 a month.)

I feel I want to explore who I am for a while, and what I want. I am surprising myself with the realization of how little I really have changed . . .

Beatriz

Note: This letter shows a very important formula:

I said:

"I want to stay, I am not going back" even if we have to "sell the house," which means:

I will . . . even if . . .

STRENGTH = the power of my action is **in Me.**

WEAKNESS = the power of my action is **conditional upon outside circumstances.**

I did **not** say:

"If I find a way to stay, then I will stay," which means:

If . . . then I will . . .

Remember these formulae. They are very important. They show the difference between acting from Strength and acting from Weakness, in absolutely any circumstances in life: for me, for a company, for a town, for a country! The first formula (strength) leads to Peace, the second (weakness) to War!

80

Dear Beatriz:

. . . Of course you may have the $600 a month and we will not buy the house. I have in fact been thinking of that since the prospect for the future of real estate and the economy are questionable in the long run and I'd rather have a house that cost me $42,000 and is worth $120,000 today than one that cost a quarter of a million and I lose money. But that's really not the point — just noise in my head — It is more important for us to use the money we have now to do something now — to live, to travel, to enjoy it. Even though tightening the belt and investing in property may be a good ethic, it is not as good as loving, living and being happy with what we have already.

I will tell our friend tomorrow that we are backing out of the house and discuss the matter with Russ (lawyer) to see what we can salvage . . .

P.S. . . . if I didn't say it before, let me say it now: It is becoming clear to me that I need the time too. I will send you $600/month at least. I'll arrange to come over for two weeks in late September, perhaps sooner if I can figure out how.

Love and peace,
Allan

The news that we were willing to let go of $20,000 created the most incredible reaction of anger among some of our friends. Allan and I were in accord, yet a friend talked to Allan against me. It is very painful for some people to observe people acting with an economic freedom they do not feel for themselves. To observe the non-attachment to money, the use of money as a tool for self-knowledge, that we displayed, was so unfamiliar to them, that they could not understand it.

Palo Alto, California
October 18, 1979
Dear Beatriz:

. . . News about a friend: He feels that you have created a situation and expect others to deal with the dirty work — I don't feel that is true, although I do feel a lot of pressure myself. It's part of what I'm dealing with, and I'll have to work it out . . .

Allan

Norja, Spain
November 2, 1979
Dear Allan:

. . . What you tell me about our friend, about how he feels about me, does not surprise me. He is quick to judge! For 14 years I dealt with the dirty work; now you finally are ready for it. It's not only fair, but an opportunity for you, as you said yourself . . .

Beatriz

As it turned out, my friend the lawyer felt there was no need to let the money go, and worked to get it back, along with Andrea, good old dependable Andrea!

In this Allan and I were always clear: what comes first, comes first, and money is never first. Money is a tool, a good one at that. But the tool can't get in the way of the job. The job is knowing oneself. I can use money, as I have shown before, as a tool to test myself, to prove myself, to know myself. But money remains a tool. If once I forget that, I could become trapped.

The decision to stay in Europe was based on a real feeling of: "I have lost my soul. I need to recapture it. I need time alone to do this."

Europe was terribly expensive, and I had my son with me. For all practical purposes my decision to stay was crazy. I had let go of the only cash I had. The amount of money Allan could send me was not enough. I knew I did not have enough money, but I also knew the Law. I was staying to find my God within, deeper than I knew Him at that moment. I was not staying because it was nice, or fun. And I was staying even though I saw no clear way to pay for it. I only needed to know my intentions clearly, not to fool myself, that they were pure. Then the door or doors would open and my survival be taken care of.

Allan sent money to me in Europe in October. It arrived in February. What he could send me was certainly not enough at the time. Like a miracle I had met a man who was generosity itself. He opened an account for me after he had known me one month. He wanted to feel I had whatever I needed. I told him at the time that Allan was going to send me money, therefore I would not need anything. He did not want to hear of it. Thank God he did not. His was the money I had until Allan's money arrived in February. And Allan's money was not enough for a whole year, only half a year.

The point of all this is that by using spiritual Laws, things work out. When I decided to stay the money was not there. Knowing how the Law works, I was not worried. Now if you have an apple in your hand and you decide to open your fingers, you "know," you don't "hope," the apple will fall. It abides by the Law of Gravity. Just as there are laws below, so there are Laws above. I live by them. They work.

I realized that the job with Allan was finished. I knew I was a Human Being and had another job to do. That job was to know myself. I was to know myself through service to others. I could do no more for Allan. I still loved him, but I had finished my service. So I asked for a divorce.

When I returned to California, we went to a lawyer. I told the lawyer she was going to see a divorce like she had never seen

82

before. She looked at me and said she had been a lawyer for many years and she had seen everything. Since I know that whatever one does is a reflection of oneself, I could not imagine us having a divorce other than a very creative one. To me it was a happy conclusion. I had accomplished what I had set out to do.
The money talk came. The lawyer asked Allan how much he made. Allan said $2,000 take-home.
So she said, "What about $1,000 for Beatriz."
He said, "Yes."
I looked at her and said, "The question is how much does he think is fair to give?"
She looked at me a bit angrily. After all, she was the lawyer and trying to get a good deal for me. She did not ask the question.
The next time we met, Allan said he was thinking about the amount and felt $1,250 would be appropriate.
Again I asked the lawyer the question. She looked at me. This time she put the question to Allan. Allan said he felt $1,500 was fair.
She looked at us and broke into a big laugh. "Well, I have seen negotiations in divorces, but never going up, initiated by the person who has to pay!"
I looked at her and said, "I told you you were in for a surprise. You just did not believe me." By now I am accustomed to being disbelieved.
During the negotiations I applied the Law and trusted that Allan would be fair, just as I had trusted his Company would be fair to him. Some people may say, "You took a risk and won." No! No risk. I **knew** that if I trusted in my heart, if it was not a ploy, if I was not doing it to win, but to give the other person the opportunity to be fair, it certainly would have a good outcome. I knew what I had put into that marriage. We are mirrors, we get back only what we put in, just like from a bank account. I knew ours was a divorce of love. He wrote to me:

April 1, 1980

Dear Beatriz:

. . . As far as I'm concerned, you can have the house or anything else I have if you want it or need it. (That feels good but scary to write). Please remember that, whatever happens, I am who I am, and I love you, respect you, and want to do what I can to help you be happy.

Love,
Allan

I knew only good could come back to me. It did.
My divorce was settled. I knew how much money I would have for at least the next four years. I wanted to feel economically

secure for years to come. I started to think about what I could do, what my options were. The first thought that came to my mind was to sue. My child had been born at a hospital and I had signed a paper stating that he should not be circumcised. Not only had I put a big "X" in the corresponding box, but I also wrote a big "NO," next to the box. I had seen that the nursery was full of boys. I said to my husband, "Robert will be circumcised!" He said, "No! Impossible, we signed, etc."

I said, "Look, they have lots of work. They will see his Anglo-Saxon name and never imagine we said "NO." If he had a Latin name they would check."

He did not believe me.

Sure enough. The doctor came with his tail between his legs because they had done precisely what I had predicted. When the doctor told me what had happened I started to laugh. He could not quite believe my reaction. I explained that I had told my husband what was going to happen. He wanted to know if we would sue. I told him everyone makes mistakes. Suing would get me money but it would not reverse what had happened, so let's forget about it. He wanted to know if my husband would feel the same way. I assured him he would.

After eight years and a divorce, I thought I could sue and it would be a sure case. I would win and keep the money to be secure. As I thought about it and checked my motives (intentions) I realized that it would be an action out of fear. I had acted all my life out of trust, love, not fear, knowing the Law and applying it. Yes, I could get the money. Yes, it would be substantial. But my actions must come out of trust, out of love. I could not sue out of Love, but only out of Fear. Therefore, suing was not an option for me.

I wanted an action which would tell me, "You are special." I felt sad and insecure. I needed someone. I called Toronto and asked Estherelka Kaplan to come. She had been a dear friend for years and years. She was busy. She was/is the wife of the Canadian Attorney General and has three children. Her life was full. Furthermore, the Queen Mother was going to Canada and she had extra work to do. President and Mrs. Ronald Reagan were also going to Canada, and she also had a part in that.

Her response to my call was, "Let me clear my calendar. I will fly down there for a few days." She was acting her word written to me:

Mexico
February 21, 1966

. . . Your phone call the day the baby was born was one of the most beautiful gestures I have ever known anyone to do. My mother came into my room in tears and realized then that you are a very special person indeed . . .

Love, Esther

We are mirrors . . . she saw me special, she is special, so very special! We see that which we are!

She came. We cried, ate, shopped; we were together. We felt each other's humanity. We decided I would contact a realtor in New York and start to invest in a few deals. I could have a good bank account in two or three years ($500,000). She left.

Because of her, thanks to the love she gave me, I could again see the road perfectly clearly. I knew how the deals could be made and I knew I could generate that much money in that period of time. It would be enough to keep me comfortable for years to come.

Again I looked inside myself. Was this the way? Yes, I did not have a lot of money. Yes, Esther did have a lot. But, this money did not give her, or anyone else who had money whom I knew, the answers I had been looking for all my life. Then I knew: No, that is not an option for me. I could not take that road. I was looking for something more than security. I was looking for somewhere to put my energy, my purpose in the Universe. So I let the offer and the whole idea go.

I thought a great deal about money then and realized not only that Money is a tool to be used for the good of all, as I have used it, but that where one opens one's purse, is an open statement of where one's heart is. In other words, if you notice where money is allocated, it tells you where the heart of the person or nation really is! Do I love my family? Where do I spend money? In jewels, furs, expensive clothes for myself, or do I spend it on them?

Do I fear in my heart? Where does the money go? In security gadgets, alarm systems, iron bars for windows? In building my bank account?

At this point I had a settlement that would allow me to keep Robert without going to work. I had a house in which I could live. All money matters were taken care of. And I knew that my purpose could not be found in a bigger checking account, nor my security. Now that I could see my way through I could create a decision, since I could freely choose one road or another.

How did I make money a sacrament? By offering it as a gift. I did not expect the little black box to thank me. I was happy doing it. That was my reward.

My family needed, I gave. I did not expect something in return. I was happy doing it. That was my reward.

Allan asked me to help him study. I worked. I spent the money on him, Ana Maria, Freddy. I was happy doing that. That was my reward.

By offering what I was doing as a gift, I made each action sacred. Thus my life was not just sacred in bed. It was sacred every day: each time I bought something, each time I shopped at the market, each month when I distributed the money. It always went to others, not to me. By this process I made each action a sacrament.

I live in my temple. I worship by following the Law. The Law is to Love. Love is Giving. Spirit gives. Matter takes.

CHAPTER 3
GOD OF FOOD

God as Food is so well known that I have little to say. My process, as for everyone who has struggled with food, was a hard road.

I grew up in Argentina in the forties and fifties. Like everyone else in the country, my mother and father were very much into food. The table was the center of the household. Talking, fighting, laughing and singing mostly took place around a table. Great care and thought went into what we ate. By the first of December each year, the conversation gravitated to the menu we would have for Christmas. For days, each person thought about what she or he wanted and tried to persuade Mother or Father to include this or that dish. Father and Mother tried to convince us of their choices because we all had to agree.

Sundays were spent around food from morning until night. First, there was the cooking. By noon we would be sitting around drinking vermouth with cheese, shrimp, snails, etc. Then there were the famous cold cuts from Belly, my grandmother. Her arrival was something to see! Every Sunday she would get out of the taxi with a tray filled with cold cuts in one hand and in the other 10 to 12 balloons of all colors for us and all the other children in the apartment building. Thus she was teaching me that the family unit was larger than Father, Mother and we, her grandchildren. The whole apartment building would feel her visit. Everyone knew her and expected her! She created a family, a world. No wonder I always thought in global terms!

Every Sunday my father argued with her about the enormous amount of food she had brought. (He always used her given name.) It went like this:

Father: Guillermina, I wish you would not bring so much; we all eat too much of this first course and then we can't eat and appreciate the rest of the meal.

Belly: You do not need to eat too much. You can serve as much or as little as you wish. Whatever is left over you all can eat tomorrow.

Father: Tomorrow? There's enough for a whole week!

And so went the conversation at lunch. I don't want to give the impression that the meals were boring. They never were. Father and Mother were incredibly interesting characters, so not just mealtime, but life, was active and certainly eventful. What I do want to express is that food was very important and, for me, connected with love.

Food was not just something one ate. Father was an epicure. He trained us. We not only ate the food, but we were supposed to tell him what ingredients the dish contained. Thus I learned to distinguish different spices and cooking methods! He felt that eating was an art! On the other hand, although Mother was a great cook, she would swallow anything! She did not take the time to savor each morsel, especially if it was sweet.

Once, to tease her, Ana Maria and I bought three real chocolates filled with salt and pepper at a joke store. We placed them inside a box of chocolates. We laughed thinking of how surprised Mother would be when she ate them.

We were the ones who were surprised. She didn't even notice them!

Father said, "I told you she is an ostrich!" (an animal well known to Argentinians for its omnivorous taste).

Every morning, before Father went to work, Mother would ask what he wanted for lunch that day. While he was working, he was thinking, anticipating his lunch. Sometimes the needed ingredients were not available at the market. Those days there was trouble. He would be furious. He had told her what he wanted. He had thought about it, and now he was terribly disappointed, like a child from whom someone has taken a toy! She would try to make him understand that she had gone early to market, had done her best, and it was not her fault. After a while he would calm down. Thus thought was not just put into planning, making and eating food, but obviously into anticipating it as well.

The whole atmosphere was food. How to cook it, how to smell it, how to eat it (yes, how to chew it) and how to distinguish each flavor, were all very important. Love was expressed through food. Wherever I went, people offered food. To go visiting meant sitting around, eating, from morning to night. We started with vermouth, then lunch until two or three in the afternoon, then coffee with cognac till four. At four-thirty the table would be set for tea, which lasted until six-thirty or so. We just sat talking, eating, laughing, constantly eating.

As I grew up, I started to go out with men. Dinners, restaurants, candles, dancing at restaurants — all expressed love.

Since I always felt chubby, I always had to control my eating. I did not want to be fat like Mother and Father, not too big.

As a teen-ager, I made the first change in my eating habits for noncosmetic reasons. I decided to become a vegetarian. As a great admirer of Gandhi, I discovered vegetarianism. If I had the

88

courage to kill a cow, I had the right to eat it. But since I knew I could not kill a cow, I felt I could not eat meat. This was in the fifties in Argentina, the beef country. I made my announcement. The world trembled! No one knew what to feed me. Mother decided that since I was on such a "weird" diet, she would feed me rice, potatoes and noodles. Needless to say, after a year I was very sick.

She said, "What do you expect? A person can't live without meat! Who ever heard of not eating meat?"

I was amazed that such an intelligent person could be so set on certain ideas. On the other hand, it had never occurred to me to go to the kitchen and make myself a salad, or pick up a piece of fruit, or cut a piece of cheese for myself! It never crossed my mind that I did not need to be dependent on Mother's cooking or the maid's, nor that I had two hands with which I could prepare food. Thus, my first attempt at changing my eating habits failed.

The diet failed, but the principle on which the diet was based has remained with me. I should not ask someone else to do something I cannot do. I could not kill the cow; therefore, I should not eat it. This has been a guiding principle in my life. If I ask you or anyone else for something, I **can** do it myself, otherwise I shut up.

Since I have always had a weight problem, I was — and am — on a permanent diet. This dieting has become a way of life for me. In this way I learned the nature of overweight, which is learning to differentiate between one's body and one's Being. Then came learning to control the body's desires. You, Beatriz, are not your body!

My second dietary change was when I emigrated to Toronto, Canada, at age 22. There I was served eggs and bacon for breakfast instead of my normal cup of coffee and croissants with butter and jam. For lunch I was served cottage cheese, toast and fruit, instead of an 8 ounce steak with salad, a glass of wine, fruit, coffee and liqueur. This was a very drastic change in my eating pattern. The experts say that eating habits are among the most difficult patterns to change. I had moved to a new country and was living with people from a culture different from the one in which I had grown up. I felt that learning to eat like them was part of becoming part of that new country.

Little by little I became accustomed to the change. A year later, when I married Allan, I did not know how to cook. So I served salads, fruit cocktails, canned soup and cold cuts.

My weight was getting out of hand, so I went to see Dr. Shannoff, who put me on a diet. Instead of losing weight, I continued to gain. Dr. Shannoff decided to show me that it was lack of will power that kept me from losing weight. He said if I were in a hospital, on controlled intake, I would lose weight. Oh, I was mad! I knew anyone could accuse me of many things — people can always find something — but lack of will power was **not** one of them. So I entered the hospital. What I encountered and learned there was something I had never dreamt.

At first I continued to gain weight even in the hospital. Dr. Shannoff kept cutting my intake until I was down to 300 calories a day. For the first time in my life I experienced intense hunger. As I grew up I was told we have an animal just under our skin. Now in the hospital I met that animal. How I suffered! I thought, "I cannot possibly feel like this — so hungry that I feel like doing anything for a morsel of food!" The war was on between me and that animal. The animal would creep in, wanting to eat, smell, taste, and I would say, "No. It can't be that I feel like this! I am civilized. I am a Human Being. I am in control and I **choose** to be here and not eat — I can be calm."

The feelings continued, especially when my hospital roommate's family brought her hot steak and stuffed zucchini, fresh home-grown tomatoes sliced with olive oil and oregano, stuffed green peppers, etc. Never in my life have I cheated. So I knew I would not eat anything the hospital did not serve me. But I could not control my mind! A great beast inside me wanted to kill, to steal, to fight, to sneak — to do anything — for a piece of apple or toast. Oh, the power of that beast! My anguish was great.

"I, Beatriz, am in control. I am not going to eat! How can I be Human and feel like this? I don't care what I feel, I will not give in to you, beast. You will not be stronger than I am! I am stronger!" But the feeling was there.

The month crawled by and my heart felt hurt. Oh, so hurt. "Is this monster me? Is this who I am? I will fight you! You will see, I will win! You can scream for the toast all you want, but I will give you only what I have decided!"

Through this experience I had a glimpse of the hunger due to war or poverty, and also the fight to overcome drugs. Food is like a drug. I knew I had chosen the starvation and I knew I could go home and end that torment. Yet, once I met my animal, I needed to bring it to submission. I did it. The job was monumental. It took from June 1965 till 1981 for me to conclude that it was just as satisfying for me to eat as not to eat and that it was I who made these decisions on a daily basis.

After being in the hospital for one month, I had lost seven pounds. I kept the weight off for a year, then went back into the hospital for another month, keeping that weight off for a whole year also.

Dr. Shannoff told me, "Well, Mrs. Prentice, if you are ever put in a concentration camp, you will be the last to die." We laughed. I was glad he finally realized that it was not lack of will, that my weight had little to do with what he thought determined it. A few years earlier, I had become aware that my weight had nothing to do with my food intake. The first month Father was in the hospital I had been worried, thinking he would die. I had lived on nothing but black coffee without sugar, and yet had gained 20 pounds.

During my hospitalization, my other need was sex. With it came the realization that when one is in a hospital, doctors and nurses expect you to leave your sexuality at the front desk, to conveniently put it away with all your personal belongings. The reality is different. I was outraged that they felt they could pull aside the curtains around a person's bed without permission. What if I was meditating, or masturbating? The funny thing is that I did not then meditate or masturbate! But what if . . . ?

This experience taught me we treat each other in a manner that contributes to our disintegration instead of helping us to integrate. I refused to be treated like that. I wrote Dr. Shannoff a letter telling him I wanted him to acknowledge me as a person, not as a chart. He made a bit of fun of it, but, after that, when he stopped by my bed, he held my hand and looked at me, the whole of me, not just the chart. When I was treated as a whole person, my sexual needs disappeared. Nothing works like integration!

After that first experience of hunger at the hospital, many others followed, but each time the animal was weaker. By August 1980 I was able to eat every other day with no fight. One week in December 1980 I ate only one meal and had no thought about eating food! The importance of this was not the length of time — in the past I had fasted much longer — but that this time I actually bought food gifts, and did not even mentally savor them. The animal did not fight me.

In the mid-sixties Canada hosted a World's Fair in Montreal. Practically every country in the world was represented. Since Allan was working as a journalist, we had a press pass and didn't need to wait hours and hours in line to enter each pavilion. Therefore, we were able to see the whole Fair in the two days we were there.

We were there early in the morning till late into the night. We **ate** our way through it.

Oh! Did I feel one with the world!

To have tea served by you, Russia, with your beautiful samovars; jam, instead of sugar; and your special gentle service!

To eat snails, with melting butter and lots of garlic, like only you, France, can prepare them!

To sip white wine while eating cheese fondue by candlelight . . . only you, Switzerland.

To see your multicolor buffet, my dear Denmark, how artistic you are!

As I was enjoying it all, I kept thinking, "And you did all this just for me, your Mommy? Thank you, thank you. You know I am working for you; that is why you let me go right in, without having to wait a minute . . . thank you." And I kept eating, laughing, enjoying. We never had a better time than when we were with all of you!

I should have gained 50 pounds, yet I didn't. If I could not travel to visit each of my children, at least I could sit and eat with each one of you. I wanted to have communion with you, and what could be a better way than by enjoying your food and wine, and laughing as if we were already a big happy family?

Oh! I played that time! I was not a Mommy those two days. Because of you, my children, I became a child myself. What pleasure I had!

Allan and I moved to New York, where he became a graduate student at Columbia University and I worked. He needed medical treatment which cost $100 a month. I was earning $400 a month, so about one quarter of my salary was spent on treatment.

Since Allan was studying journalism, he needed to buy *Newsweek*, *Time*, *The New York Times*, and *The Christian Science Monitor*, all the important publications for a journalist. This also ate into the budget. And since he was studying, I felt he should eat well. It never occurred to me we could **both** eat less. Therefore, I just did not eat. The fasting training took place, I thought at the time, for practical reasons: to make the budget go further.

Years later, Allan said resentfully, "I never asked you to do that for me." True. I just gave. I was young and I loved; so, if he needed, I provided. To not eat was natural but very difficult! I did not know then the extraordinary by-product of that attitude: the taming of my beast, the getting to my center and finding God within, my I AM, my Peace, my Happiness!

Later we moved to California. Allan had a fellowship at Stanford and I worked at Bechtel International Center, so we had plenty of money. What did I do the first month we had extra money? I sent for Freddy, my brother, to come and spend his summer vacation with us. That decision was to change my life. Freddy arrived on December 23rd and was supposed to stay until March.

We were putting his bags into the car for Disneyland when Father called from Argentina to ask us to keep Freddy. We did.

Freddy was 12 years old, a time when a boy looks at his peers and establishes his identity. I knew he would not be able to recognize values or unspoken clues. He was going to need help. It was easy for me to decide between his needs and a salary. The job had to go.

With less money and one more person, I started to fast once a week. I was entertaining every week or two to encourage Allan to relate to people on a social level. If he could not socialize in the world, I was going to bring that world to him. He would sit at the table for a few minutes at the beginning, then flee to the bathroom. By the time we were at Stanford, he could sit among the guests for a while — not all the way through dinner, but I could see progress. Therefore, I could not stop the dinners. I could be without food, but he could not exist without people (love).

Later, when Allan's fellowship was cancelled and we became managers of the apartment building in which we lived, we earned free rent. But what about food? Taking care of someone else's child provided some cash, but by then I was pregnant! Fasting became a way of life for me — once a week, twice, three times a week. No one noticed. I was proud of that! No one asked me to do it. I just felt that Allan and Freddy needed food, and my presence was more important than any money I could bring by going to work. It took courage and strength to resist going back to work, in the middle of the women's movement, in a university crowd that wanted to brainwash everyone into believing in earning as THE means to self-expression (as if only through earning money does one have value); at the same time I was so very hungry.

With all this starvation you must have an impression of a slim lady, skinny like Gandhi. Not a chance! It did not matter what I ate, I was still overweight. I tried different diets and lost a lot, only to regain it without eating, as when my father was injured. I went from 220 pounds to 150 on the Stillman diet. It worked, but only once. A diet never worked for me more than once.

I lost weight with injections. I swear by them. Actually what I swear by is the warmth I received from Dr. Stevens and his staff. They treated me like the intelligent Human Being that I am. They did not assume I had no will power. They did not behave as if I did not know who I was or what my problem was. They just helped me with moral support and their daily smiles, to cope with my life. As I purposefully directed my spiritual energy in the direction that it had to go, the weight just left me. When I lost control of my spiritual energy, the weight came back; it did not matter what I ate.

Someday someone will make a scientific study of how consciousness and weight relate to each other, and discover the real cause of overweight. To me, a tendency toward excess weight is the greatest exercise for a Being who needs to Become. Will Power is needed to lose it, and then to keep it off or start all over again.

But it is not simply the control of the intake of food. The important thing is to control the spiritual energy day by day, the thoughts minute by minute, and to eliminate frustrations second by second. All that is difficult. But it is at this invisible level at which one must deal with the problem. The tendency is always to treat the visible. We keep ignoring the fact that everything that we see is but a manifestation of the invisible. Any problem must be solved at its base, at the invisible spirit level. We must acknowledge cause, not consequence.

Finally Allan and I "made it." We had a salary, a house, and a car that could go forward and backward! (You laugh? Have you ever tried to drive a car without a reverse? In San Francisco? And park it? You have to have faith! I did. I parked it.)

Now it would seem, I finally could eat. No. Now I decided to again change my eating pattern, this time for spiritual reasons. Again, I put myself consciously through torture. The torture was not the diet this time but that I would cook for others and just sit at the table with them and not eat. It was hard! But I felt it was good for me. Of course, it would have been easy to keep away from food altogether, not to give dinners, not to go to my friend Sean's wonderful dinners. But I wanted to tame that animal within me. I wanted to be able to sit, enjoy, say "no" to myself, and feel I had won. My success was never measured by the loss of weight. I was dealing with another discipline.

I could not quite explain it to people. It is usually easy for me to explain things by speaking in terms that people understand, so I tried. But the only one who did understand was Allan.

I doubt that any of us can really understand anything another talks about. Things happen at so many levels all at once, and our crude, linear way of communicating is so inadequate! How can we expect people to understand us? As we evolve and hook ourselves to Higher Consciousness, we will be able to communicate at a better level.

I was trying not only to tame my beast, but to separate food from love! I was very aware that since childhood, food and love had been connected for me. I could not imagine enjoying anyone's company without also eating. One went out for tea, dinner, lunch, breakfast, snack, or whatever, but one always ate. That was part of the fun, part of the enjoyment of friends and the expression of love. When my child was born, I knew I did not want him to associate food and love. So when I wanted to express love, I read to him or sang songs or made a fire in the fireplace or set up candles and cuddled with him looking at the flames.

When Robert was two years old, Allan and I decided to change our diet for spiritual reasons. That was in 1974. We stopped eating any red meat, salt, sugar and grains of any type. I almost entirely stopped cooking. We ate lots of raw vegetables, cheese, yogurt, fruits, nuts and juices.

This change was also not an easy one for me. We now had the money to go to restaurants, but we had to find ones where we could eat fresh vegetables, fish or omelets. Our menu was restricted. Yet I felt I was regaining the strength I had had as a single woman.

At some point I became very weak about continuing this discipline because I felt I was doing it for myself. I felt I was breaking the Law: "Find a Need Outside of Oneself and Fill It." The action must be taken to fill a need, and as a consequence of filling the need, there is a profit (benefit) for oneself **and** others. Not only in business is the Law clear! I could not see how doing something for myself could achieve good results. The **Intention** had to be for others. It would have violated the Law of "Living for Something Higher than Oneself." That was not me! I always did things for others!

Like a miracle, Freddy, his friend Mark, and I went to the movie *Phantom India* by Louis Malle. It was very depressing to see how people lived, or rather how they died, from starvation, and how lepers are isolated. Freddy asked, "Why look at this? We can't do anything about it."

Something came from the bottom of myself: "You are wrong, there is a lot you can do. **You can reduce your own Greed.** This inhumanity occurs because there is Greed in the world. If you reduce your so called **needs**, the Greed in the world will be reduced by that much. This will help these people. We all affect one another." (What I did not know then is that Greed exists because of Fear, and Fear because of Pain. The bottom line is Pain.)

As I spoke, I realized I had found the larger context "why" for reducing my food needs. I could understand things only in terms of part of a whole. Finally, I was working for the world! I felt I had found a way to contribute. This diet **was** spiritual! I could see cause and consequence, the visible and invisible, the inner and outer. I was delighted.

Once this new way of eating became well established, my weight remained very constant at 155-165 pounds. My family were all very big people. My sister now weighs over 300 pounds. I have weighed 220 pounds and gone up and down 70 pounds at a time.

One of the by-products of my learning about this God, Food, was to see how people treated me as my weight went up or down. The most remarkable instance was at Stanford when I was leading discussion groups. The participants seemed to perceive intelligence as an inverse function of weight. I used to tell Allan it seemed that when I lost weight, they thought I gained in brain power, and I lost my brains while gaining weight. I would always say the same things, but the responses to my opinions were completely different.

After we filed for divorce and Allan moved out, I had lots of people coming to the house. Thank God! I needed them! But I was feeding them. Meanwhile, I was calling Jose (the man I had met in Spain the previous year) in Europe every other day (and sending him cards every day), so he would feel loved and cared for and recuperate. (He had lost his job and had entered a hospital in a state of depression.) This meant enormous food and telephone bills. To balance the budget during these months I hardly ate.

Finally, I borrowed money from my friend Silver (good old Silver!) to visit Jose in Europe. I took along vitamin pills but no money for food. I was strong while speaking to Jose's doctors. I changed time zones, walked, did not eat, and **never** for one second, thought of eating food! The beast was tame! At last it knew who was in control! During my experience (Chapter 6) I could not eat anything except fruit, and very little of that, yet I was truly satisfied. That was the only time in my life I could actually **sit at a table** where an extraordinary **paella** was served and know my **addiction** to food was gone. I said, "I don't want to eat it, I want fruit," and meant every word — not because of diet, discipline, or control, but just from Being free and natural, because I was being fed by the only source there is: Love! What a delight!

Thus I finally learned why I had chosen this body and family. If one has to exercise will, there is nothing like a weight challenge to do it. Once one loses the weight, of course, one puts it back on again to exercise one's will losing it again! Did Rubinstein express himself through one concert, and never again? No, of course not. Similarly, one expresses oneself through one's body by using one's will again and again. As the energy becomes better channelized, the weight becomes steady. When I gain weight, I am gathering energy in me for work to be done. As the work is at its end, the weight gradually comes off.

So, it is not at the food intake level that one steadies one's weight, but at the mental, spiritual, and emotional levels. When one balances the invisible three, Bingo! the weight stays off!... until the next level is achieved and energy is again needed to do new work.

Can anything be solved at a level other than the invisible? No. We must go to the Cause. And Cause is always invisible. When the Cause is solved, the visible consequence is modified or cured.

CHAPTER 4
GOD OF MIND

I was born into a politically and intellectually free-thinking and permissive household. I was encouraged to read, discuss and argue ideas as an equal with the grownups.

There is a story Father and Mother told many times which shows how early this training took hold of me. We were having dinner, an important one for my father. An architect was there to decide if he would give my father a building contract. They were talking.

Apparently I decided to speak, contradicting the architect. My father, in no uncertain terms, told me to shut up. I did. The next morning I got up at dawn when I heard Father shaving in the bathroom.

I confronted him, "Daddy, you always told me I should say what I think to anyone, on any occasion. You told me I should never consider if I would win or lose by speaking my mind. Isn't this true?"

Father: "Yes, it is."

"Well, I think you owe me an apology."

Father: "For what?"

"Yesterday with the architect. You asked me to shut up."

Father: (making a face trying to remember) "Oh ... I'm terribly sorry."

He ran to the bedroom holding his laughter, told Mother what had happened, and said, "She was right, I had to apologize. You should have seen her! So straight. So serious. So sure. I felt like a heel. So funny!" I was three-and-a-half years old.

I don't remember the incident myself. They told it many times and said that showed who I was. Mentally I had examined what I knew and come to a conclusion different from what the architect was saying. To me the next step was action, to voice my contradiction. Thinking was action. Thinking was evaluating and doing something about it.

I went to a Catholic **jardin des infantes** (nursery school) in Tandil when I was two-and-a-half years old. My mother was pregnant with my sister and did not feel very well. She thought both of us would benefit if I was with other children and she could be by herself part of the day.

Near the end of my first year of nursery school, I must have done something and a nun scolded me in front of the whole class. I climbed on top of the desk and, while the nun was writing on the blackboard, I broke a ruler on her head.

98

The nuns called my mother and told her, "She is an incorrigible child."

How can anyone be an "incorrigible" at age three-and-a-half? Mother asked me what had happened. I told her I did something wrong. I should have been reprimanded, but privately. Instead, the nun did it in front of the whole class and embarrassed me. I got angry.

My mother saw that the nuns wanted me out. Before they could close the door in her face, she took me out, saying, "I think Beatriz is right. I don't want my child in this school."

That is another part of my history that I know about but don't remember. In this case also, I thought about what the nun did, and took action. Thought is Action.

What I do remember is being taken to Plaza de Mayo and Mother yelling against Peron. The police would ask, "Don't you feel ashamed? You have a child. Go home."

She would yell even more. "I am screaming because I **do** have children. I would rather see them dead than to live in a country without freedom. Take them, kill them. I don't want them to learn to live on their knees!"

Mind was clearly to be used to direct action, not just for mental exercise.

I began to read. I studied how to recite poems in public. Mother spent hours teaching me how to express each word, how to stand, how to walk to the platform.

She wanted me not only to **know** poetry, but to **feel** it, **express** it, **project** it. She would say, "Your mind has to touch the minds of others. Give the subject life."

These were the only occasions my mother raised her hand against me. As she taught me, she lost her patience and struck me several times because I did not quite express the poem. Mind, ideas, were something I had to bring to life. I had to give them force, bring their spirit out. I learned. I am today an effective speaker, glad of the training.

I began school and wanted to learn. Because I was a good student, by the time I was six I was teaching the 7-year-olds a religion class once a week.

There was a feeling I had to control them. I did not want them to get out of hand. I had to speak to them, teach them religion. That was an important subject for me. I was applying my mind especially to studying religions.

My father was a Protestant. I was in a Catholic school. When I arrived home each Sunday, Father wanted to know what I had learned on the subject of religion. After he had heard, he would say, "Now, on Monday you get up in class and say, 'the Bible says so and so.' " Week after week I carried the argument back and forth between my father and the school.

Finally, I became worried. A nun found me crying, "Why?" she asked.

"Because my father will not go to Heaven because he is not a Catholic!"

She looked at me with incredible love and said, "Come with me."

She took me to a classroom. "Stand here in front of the room and look at that picture in the back of the room. Look at it. See it? Now, move here, to this end. Now here, to this side; now, as far as you can. Now, as near as you can. Did you notice anything?"

"Yes," I said.

"What?"

"It looks different from different places."

"Well? But you know it is the same picture. It looks different from each different place you stand. The same with your father. He just sees it differently. He is looking at the same picture. Don't worry. He too will go to Heaven."

I was so glad and relieved! I have never forgotten that lesson.

Each time a person spoke to me, I remembered it was only the location which was different, and I tried to place myself mentally next to the person to see what that person was seeing.

I

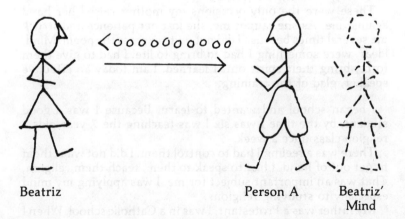

Beatriz   Person A   Beatriz' Mind

100

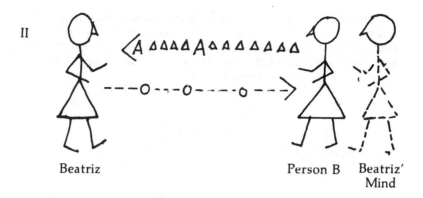

II

Beatriz   Person B   Beatriz' Mind

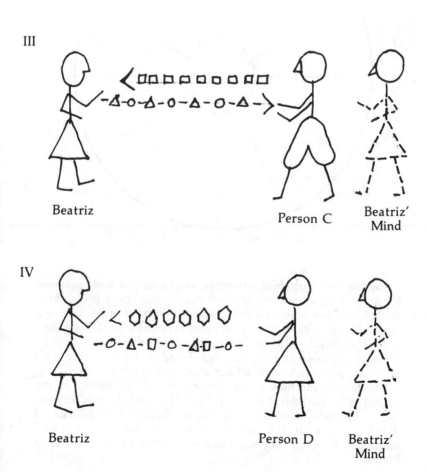

III

Beatriz   Person C   Beatriz' Mind

IV

Beatriz   Person D   Beatriz' Mind

Each person showed me, through arguments, what he saw. I put myself in his shoes, saw what he was saying (showing), and made it my own. As I did this, my breadth of view grew, until I saw the whole. I learned from each person. I made the complete puzzle with the pieces from all of them.

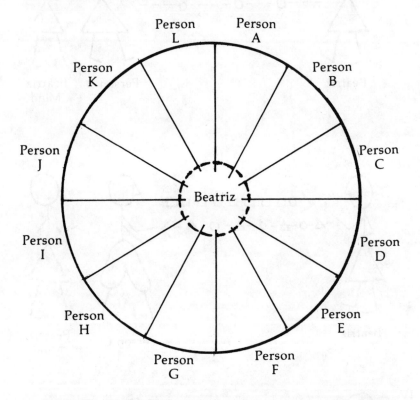

I was a studious child, attentive and careful, a good planner, hard working in school, learned easily, and could lead others well. I was the teacher's pet. I wanted to be number one and worked hard to be. Sometimes it was very hard. But I disciplined myself so well I could sit and study when others went to play.

I was the object of vicious lies. I had to learn to live with criticism. My mother's teaching was very helpful.

She taught me **how** to use my mind to be of service to my higher self. She did it in this way: I would come to her sad, crying, hurt. "Mommy, someone said this or that, and it's horrible. I didn't say or do it. Why do the girls accuse me of something I didn't do? Why do they say I said something I didn't say? I got blamed."

(We all have gone through that! But I was lucky enough to have a mother who guided me to use my mind to apply the Law.) She would say, "Beatriz, let's look at this. I know you are hurt. Let's put feelings aside. Let's see, . . . is this true?"

"No!"

"Good," she'd say. "Then you have a clear conscience. Now, we don't know why they said it, but there must be a reason. One possibility is that life is giving you the opportunity to transcend what you feel, through looking inside yourself. You know you can't be ashamed, because you've not done what they say you did. Of course, if you had done it, you could look at it differently. As it stands, you should thank them, because those who perpetrated a false rumor gave you the opportunity to get to know yourself a bit better. Now you can look at a situation that otherwise you would not have examined.

"We don't even know if it was an intentionally false rumor. Maybe someone just heard it wrong and told it as she heard it. It all **could** have been innocent, no one trying to hurt."

With this attitude she taught me to trust, to put distance between feelings and mind, and **how** to use my mind to change my feelings if what I felt would not lead to peace. She taught me to look hard until right thinking brought peace within. She was teaching the Divine Law: "Mind Is Objective." Mind is the software of a computer (the hardware is the brain). I, the Being, use my mind to do something with the information received and arrive at the only conclusion possible: understanding for all, trust, and thus peace within.

With Father it was different. He taught me to argue. Day after day at the table he would start a topic of conversation, one day saying white, the next black. The first day he demonstrated the point was white. The following day he equally demonstrated the point was black.

I wanted to do it to him, but he would not let me. He'd say, "I taught you that. Don't play it with me."

After years, I caught on. I would argue then on the train going to high school. In this way, practicing public speaking, I started such good debates the people on the train would applaud whichever side was winning. It was fun. It was exciting. I was full of energy afterwards. The subjects were the ones which had always been my favorites: philosophy, politics, theology and sex.

I started to cut classes just to discuss, to argue, with other girls and boys of my age. Later I discovered they were cutting classes because they did not like those classes. I was staying out of school to learn: to argue, to try to clarify, to challenge whomever came my way, and see, hear and feel what they said. After a while the high school kids were not enough challenge for me.

103

Later I became friends with the principal. We used to cut school together. He would come to my class or send his secretary and we would go to a cafe to talk for hours. I never thought I was not learning. Neither did I think of him as an authority figure. When I was about 14 years old, President Juan Peron decided that any student who did not go to school on a certain date would have a double absence recorded. The chosen date was a religious holiday on which we never went to school. He wanted to get back at the Church. For me it was perfectly reasonable to go to school. But two absences when we would miss only one day was unfair, unjust. With this feeling that it was unjust, I had no alternative but to organize a strike. Patsy Mendez Paz and I organized it. It was successful. I had felt the unjustice, Thought about it, and Acted.

All the pupils were asked to bring a letter saying that they were sick that day. I could not do that. Neither did I feel I could get my father to write me a letter saying I thought I should not go, since he knew the probable consequences. So I arranged for Father to sign a blank piece of paper and on it I copied the letter that Patsy's father had written. He was a political man who had been in jail fighting against Peron. As a consequence of these two letters we were expelled from all the public schools of Argentina. But Peron was ousted, so we were "saved by the bell."

I changed to another high school where there were three great teachers. One was a math teacher who had served many years in the Army. We used to go for walks after class and talk. I think he was interested in me. Nothing ever happened, but we had very stimulating conversations.

The director, Mr. Preluker, was another great one. He was an atheist. I was also, at that time. After years teaching religion as a child in a Catholic school, after praying every minute with my mind, keeping mental tally of how many prayers I said to try to win a doll, and studying or talking, all at the same time . . . I had become an atheist.

In my teens I examined **all** my beliefs. I found I believed in God because I had been **taught** to do so. I felt most people believed in God because they were afraid of death. Since I had no fear of death, I decided not to believe in God. Later, I found within **myself** a knowledge that God IS.

The third high school great was the psychology teacher who invited a few students to her house on Saturday morning. We would read Pablo Neruda (Chilean Nobel Laureate in Literature) or Merleau-Ponty (French writer) and discuss for hours and hours.

Roberto was in the Partido Democrata Progresista. The founder was Lisandro de la Torre, who was also an atheist.

But to me what was most amazing at that stage, was this scenario: I would think and come out with a whole theory, feel so proud of myself that I would tell it, and to my surprise, someone would invariable say, "I see you have been reading Nietzche or Schopenhauer or whomever." My balloon would burst. I was so proud that it was **my** theory! To discover someone had already thought of it made me quite ashamed! I wanted to developed **new** theories!

I never quite said then that such and such was **my** theory. That took growing up, maturing, becoming more sure of myself: to tell I thought this or that, even when people told me so and so had thought of it before me.

This has never changed either, just as no one quite believing me about what I am going to do. It took me years to feel that even if I never brought a new thought to the world, I should feel proud that my thoughts came from within me, and not just from reading. Of course this was when I still thought Mind was a God.

Father used to talk to me as a child about the process of the mind and how to govern one's thoughts. He used to say, "It's just like learning a habit. It is just as easy to learn to be clean as to be dirty. So be clean. You'll be clean while you are under my roof. Of course you can be dirty when you have your own house."

He used concrete examples to show me how the mind works. He'd say, "First comes the thought: 'I could steal.' If you don't censor it, it comes back as 'I may not get caught.' If you don't censor that, then: 'What could I steal if I did?'

"Before you know it, you feel comfortable within your mind with the idea of stealing. Once that occurs, doing it is easy. Once the thought is allowed to get hold, to grow, to bring about a desire, the action follows." (Thought, Desire, Action) He was teaching me how to govern my mind, how to be Master of it and not let it be my Master.

He would show how it goes in the other direction in the same way.

First thought: I like this person I see.

Then: Really, she seems to be very nice, I would like to get to know her.

Next: I wonder how I can get to meet her?

I will inquire if any of my friends know her?

I will get introduced to her.

Finally:

Now that I have been introduced, I'll invite her to a movie.

The process is the same: Thought, Desire, Action. My mind does not judge the content of my thoughts, I do.

As I started to go out with men, I saw that I gave myself completely: emotionally, intellectually and physically. Each time I could see I was used and discarded.

At this point, my feelings said, "You hurt, Beatriz."

My mind was inquiring, "Why?"

The answer was: Because you gave and the other person not only didn't give to you, but didn't even understand or trust you.

Question: What can you do?

Answer: You have a choice not to trust, in other words, not to give completely next time. To hide. Not to show yourself completely to the next person.

Question: Is that what you Beatriz, want to do: not trust, not give, just because others do not understand?

Answer: No. They do not understand, but I DO understand why they walk away. They are afraid, their pain is greater than mine.

Should Einstein stop his research because the world does not understand? I can't keep loving that human being who left me, but **I can** love the next one who comes to me. I want to keep being who I am (Light, Love), giving myself completely over and over, until someone comes along who does understand.

Question: Should you change your behavior? This is what the world tells you, Beatriz. Can they all be wrong?

Answer: I do not know if the world is wrong or right. I do know I can't allow the next person who enters my life to pay for the last person who left my life. I will not change because I **do** understand them.

Thus, I never gave my power away. My behavior was not dependent on the behavior of any other human being. **They can do what they want. I will love. I will give. I will care. I will understand them.** My mind was indispensable. Without it, I could not have loved as passionately, as steadily, as freely. Thus I fulfilled the Law: "Love One Another."

Miss Boland, my English teacher in my last year in Argentina, knew the results of this use of my mind.

Quilmes, Argentina
March 19, 1965

My dear Beatricita:

I cannot tell you how happy I am that you are getting married. Tell Allan that I think he is a lucky man to have found a sweet, sensible, understanding girl like you and that I am sure you will make him a wonderful wife . . .

Love from
Juana Boland

My mind had thoughts I did not see as good or bad. Neither do I view people as good or bad. Thoughts just ARE. People just ARE. To me thoughts are like seeds. If you take care of them, they will grow and manifest. A thought that is positive or negative will manifest whichever it is. The other will remain unmanifested. But that does **not** mean it doesn't exist.

That is why I could see and accept myself when I shot Jorge. I did not see myself as a non-violent person, nor as a violent one. I could not be just one or the other, I was both. One cannot exist without the other. But I do have a CHOICE upon which to act.

I view it like this: My body has two sides, one left side and one right side. I could not exist as Beatriz with only a right side. I need my right and left sides to be alive. In explanations it may be convenient to divide myself. But that is only for convenience. I should not believe there is a division in me; there is not.

When I see people my mind does not see them as bad, regardless of what they have done. If they have just killed hundreds of people, I only see their incredible fear, their incredible pain. How much pain must a Human Being feel to hurt another Being?! How little Love am I putting out into the world for the world to be still starved for it! I know I only hurt others when I am in pain.

It was always very funny for me to observe how people can look at other people and judge them as violent when a hand is raised, or a gun shot, and yet pretend they are non-violent when **they** say, "I am not taking you to the party," or, "you'll not go to the party," and then watch you cry for a whole day: as if emotional violence were less violent! As if words were less powerful than a gun!

We were having dinner one day and someone gave Allan a very difficult puzzle to solve. I was amused because I knew Allan could solve it quickly. Years later the person told me he had searched for a long time for this difficult puzzle, and that it had taken him a whole month to figure it out. He was amazed to see Allan solve it in 20 minutes.

He wanted to prove to me Allan was not as intelligent as I kept saying.

Here we have a classic example of intellectual violence. All that time and effort was spent **to show someone** up as less intelligent! If this is not violence . . . what is! As always when people tried to be violent with me, it back-fired.

I knew Allan could do it because Allan does not use the intellect alone. He uses intuition as well. He looked at it, put it down next to his plate and continued eating. He allowed his subconscious to do the work, and after a few minutes looked at it again, **knowing** the answer would surface to him, without any effort! Intuition goes to a "Central Library" and brings out any information we want, **when** we want it, **if** we want it.

There is a reasoning logical mind, but there is an intuitive mind as well. When you work with the two in an integrated way, it looks as if you are brilliant. It is not brilliance; it is working with the whole. Most people are handicapped because they refuse to trust that part of themselves which they call "flaky." But that "flaky" part of us, when we learn to use it, provides the difference between intelligence and brilliance.

Thus they are using half of their minds, therefore **appearing** less intelligent. They are not less intelligent; they CHOOSE to be.

I have experienced intellectual violence too, when I heard, "I went to graduate school because I certainly didn't want to be a secretary," said as if to be a secretary is the lowest intellectual monster there is.

We allow ourselves to be brainwashed into evaluating people strictly on the basis of mind. What things pain makes us do! We are very creative at rationalizing our own violent actions. We pretend that because we don't shoot anyone, because we send money to Amnesty International, we are peaceful and have no animal to tame! We humans can be funny creatures!

I have no compulsion against saying, "I don't know." I said it so often people thought, "Beatriz has a good heart, but I'm not sure she has a good mind." I don't need to go around demonstrating my brain power, it's not very important! I do need to go around demonstrating myself (Love). That is very important to me.

By the time my son Robert was two years old, I recognized that he was brilliant, but full of hate. I kept talking to God, "Why didn't you send me a retarded child with a heart, instead of a great mind without a heart? Dear God, is Robert going to be one of those people who can apply information and create an atomic bomb? One of those people who have decided to make the intellect, the head, the deciding factor for them, instead of the heart? My dear God what good is this great brain going to be for him, if he has no eyes in his heart? What good can he produce in this world if he does not have the ability to SEE where and how information can be applied for the benefit of mankind? Give me the strength I need to develop his heart."

When Robert was seven, Allan expressed his hope:

Nerja, Spain
September 2, 1979
5 a.m.

. . . the peace I feel in my heart can be transmitted to Robert and he will settle down from his hatred of all that does not go his way . . .

Allan

108

and Robert himself was aware:

Nerja, Spain
October 9, 1979
Dear Allan:

. . . Robert says that now that he has the (toy) gun you bought he is able to get rid of his hate. Maybe he is right.

Beatriz

That year in Spain awakened Robert's heart. Three years later he wrote:

Palo Alto, California
4th Grade
Miss Forest, 1982

Builders and Wreckers

Wreckers either destroy somebody's property or they destroy someone's feelings. If I had a choice between having someone destroy my house or my feelings, I'd rather have destroyed my house. A builder can create things with their own hands or can give confidence to others and make them feel better. Either way they both spread. For example: if someone calls you names you feel bad and call someone else a name and so on. But one can stop that by being nice back.

Robert Prentice -
9 years old

Now he can see. His mind will be usefully directed, now that it has been taught to listen to his heart.

We are coming of age and learning at great leaps. I experienced emotional violence for a while in my marriage, but I decided, "No one can make me miserable if I don't let him. You don't want to go to a movie, I'll go without you. You don't want to live, I will. You don't take a vacation, Freddy and I will. You want to hide, I will not. You will not be violent with me, I will not let you!" My mind provided my protection.

As I started to deal with money and to feel the power of my mind applied to bringing about a deal, I felt the exhilaration of the power of the WORD. I could talk a businessman into buying what I had to offer. I knew what I was selling was of little value. I sold it anyway.

It was Father who did not judge me and had patience with me then. The whole process took a few months, but it was decisive. I was coming home happy because I had stuck some poor unsuspecting man, trapped him with my words! I was proud! I was young and using an ability I had — as I am using it now. But then it was used in the opposite direction.

109

Father looked at me. "You feel proud, eh? Maybe we should call all those people to whom you sold so successfully, and invite them for dinner?"

I realized I wanted to hide from them; I would die of embarrassment if I saw them again. Then I knew I was not proud at all of what I was doing.

Father did not make me feel I had done wrong. He showed me how to use my feelings about my actions to choose consciously what I wanted to manifest, what I wanted to Become. This was learning to **Be**, training to **Become**.

I was not a person who lied to make a sale, because I did not feel good about it afterwards. So, by doing it, I learned this was not a behavior I wanted to continue. It was neither good nor bad. It just was. I had a choice of what to manifest and I chose to manifest the behavior that made me feel better about who I was, knowing full well that I was capable of the other, since I had done it.

That is how I used my mind sometimes. By the time I left Argentina, I had acquired the "I am" of the thief, the prostitute, the businessman, the con man, the healer, etc. The one "I am" I felt I did not have, was the "I am" of the homemaker.

I asked every man I met, what God meant to him. I was looking for a particular mind, a deep one that had been used to think about what God is and is not. Mind and God were together for me even then, though I did not know how they went together. When I met Allan, I asked what he thought of God. He showed me the depth of his mind in his answer. I married him because of that answer. It was a well thought-out decision.

Roberto Rois
Congressman of the Nation

Miss Beatriz Caprotta
TORONTO (Canada)

Buenos Aires, Argentina
March 22nd, 1965

Enchanting Beatriz:

. . . Congratulations, because I have no doubt of your choice. In spite of your few years, the kilometers you have travelled are many. I am absolutely sure this is not the decision of the "Craziness of Youth," but a well thought out and meditated step . . .

Kisses to the bride,
Rois

One of the things Father, Mother and Grandmother constantly harped on was that we must leave a road behind us, for others to walk on. I believed it. I was involved at age 15 or 16 with the Youth Hostels. Several of us worked hard to bring the First Youth Hostel Association to Argentina.

Since I felt every woman in my family had accomplished a lot, I felt I could not leave until I had done my part. When I got to be the first woman voice in the money market, I felt I had done it. After I arrived in Toronto I had a lot of problems with Immigration. I decided I would do something so that no one who came after me from Latin America would find themselves without help. I didn't know anyone. I had no idea how it was to be done. (**I will do** . . . **even if** . . .) I just decided I would do it.

As always, first the idea. Then I opened the telephone directory at random, as I always opened some book to find any answer I needed in books. Bingo! A South American Boutique. The next day I went there. The lady was from Europe, but she had lived in Argentina for a few years and now she was operating this business. I told her my idea and that I felt an Association would be nice to have, to help newcomers. She looked at me, opened a drawer and brought out some files saying, "Here are the names and addresses of my clients, about 200."

In no time at all, the First Latin American Association was formed. A miracle! But my life has been one of miracles! What I did not know at the time, is that the roads I and all of us have to build, are spiritual roads. A blueprint of the **way of thinking** which can lead mankind to Peace.

When my husband decided to study, and since he wrote to me asking for help, I went ahead full blast to bring that wish into being, even though I felt it was a crutch.

Hamilton, Canada
January 13, 1965

My dear Beatriz:

. . . I am considering the question of returning to University very seriously. You're partly right when you say I need it as a crutch. But there is the feeling in me — right or wrong — that what I will be called upon to do next will require all the learning and studying power I can muster. And God knows I need all the help I can get, especially where somewhat uninteresting subjects are concerned . . .

I love you,
Allan

I was living: "Thy Will Be Done." As always, I gained enormously by so doing.

When Allan entered the University, a whole new world

111

opened up for me. It was a meeting of minds. I would swim in three of the great Universities of North America: McMaster, Columbia and Stanford. But along with remarkable minds, I was to meet the emotional vacuum in which many students found themselves. I was to meet all sorts of ideas, new and old, and be excited to see what one could do with them. I was to meet students with money, brains and knowledge, doing nothing, with no purpose behind their knowledge. They drifted from idea to idea, or just accumulated knowledge likea sponge absorbs water, becoming full of it. As they learned, some of them just kept the knowledge; fruits did not come. They felt pain from the lack of release. (Thinking, Feeling, NO Action). I felt their pain.

I saw their degrees, their knowledge, as freedom. Yet, it was not freedom for them. I felt if I had it I could do so very much! Yet, I did not go for it. For knowledge for myself, I went inside. But I went to work for my husband, so he could get his degree.

It is not totally true I got knowledge only from inside myself. It was a combination. I read; I listened; and I looked inside myself. "Understanding" comes from what one knows through one's own mind. "Belief" is through faith in others. "Knowledge" was only of what I had lived, experienced, made part of me, even beyond my own mind. But when I got beyond, then and only then, I found out I didn't have knowledge of anything. I was nothing. That was later. Now I was still trying to feel more, to see more, to hear more, as if the answers were on the outside.

In this search, I met some remarkable men, including three at Columbia University. In the Journalism Department I met Professor Fred W. Friendly, Edward R. Murrow Professor of Journalism. He had traveled widely as a correspondent in World War II, had produced NBC news and worked with Edward R. Murrow to produce the widely acclaimed "I can Hear it Now," "Hear it Now" (CBS radio), "See it Now" (CBS TV) and "Small World" (CBS TV) broadcasts. He had been the president of CBS News, an author, and TV adviser to the Ford Foundation, among other things. He brought the most impressive experience to the school. But I was impressed not with his experience, but with his humanity. He worked very hard to give the best of himself to the students, and to bring in the best speakers he could find. He exposed them to everything they would need to be top press people. He tried to tell them how lucky they were, how much he would have liked to attend a university like the one in which he was teaching.

He took us to his home and shared his family with us. It was a home filled with mementos and eight children, at that time. He was not just a giant physically and a giant in his field, but also a giant human being, who could give at home and at school. One could feel his energy spreading about as he walked. He did not hide his assurance about that which he knew, and his vulnerability about that of which he felt unsure. I admired him for this, and because he was able to just BE big and small, strong and weak. Although he could have hidden behind his position, he did not.

I had the opportunity to meet the Publisher of the *New York Times*, Mr. Arthur O. Sulzberger. He spoke to us about how the *Times* allocated space. He told us Latin America was an important continent then, in 1969, and that Africa was soon to become very important. He explained the paper was giving space to Africa to educate the public.

I heard that reasoning, amazed! I waited for one of the students to question him. No one did. I never shut up; I do not know how. So I had to ask, "Why, if the newspaper is a vehicle of today, don't you give space now to Latin America, which in your own words is the continent of today, instead of to Africa, when it isn't important yet?"

He looked at me and said, "That's a good question."

"Don't let him get away with such an answer," I was screaming inside, "You'll be the reporters, not I." But no one asked further.

Still, I was glad to have seen and heard him. He gave me firsthand knowledge of the workings of one of the world's greatest newspapers. I felt excitement to be aware of it, and could see his commitment to service. He felt it was important to let people know what is going on in the world. Excellence was important to him. He was a doer! I admire people who bring about results. Through action I learn. Whether the results are bad or good is irrelevant. I do not understand that division. The learning is what I understand.

The third remarkable man was Professor John Hohenberg, Administrator of the Pulitzer Prizes and Secretary of the Advisory Board, editor, scholar, political writer, world traveler, author and winner of many prizes. He taught so much and so well that it spilled over. I wrote him a letter to thank him because I felt Allan had learned so much from him. He answered:

New York
May 1, 1969

Dear Mrs. Prentice:

I am most grateful to you for your most welcome note, but really it is I who have gained through having worked with your husband. He is a man of great talent, and like many talented people, needs confidence in himself to go on with his writing. You, more than anyone else, have given this to him and made his year at Columbia a success. My best wishes and my prayers go to both of you.

Sincerely,
John Hohenberg

113

I went to see him later and we talked. He was an incredible man! Full of energy, full of accomplishments, yet, big enough to recognize a student as someone bigger than himself. He said, "I write. Allan is a writer. Some of us write because we have something to say, others are just born writers. Allan is one of those." At that time he was the Secretary of the Advisory Board of the Pulitzer Prize Committee.

I knew he was right. I knew Allan was a writer, a great one at that. People always laughed at me. "Where are his books? What did he write? Is he famous?" I can look at a seed and see a rose, or a potato. I do not need to see the fruit to recognize the seed. It is all there: a great plant, a great rose, an incredible fragrance. If it is never planted, if it never grows, if it never has flowers, it is not any less a rose seed. It just has not grown yet. He too could see! Not only did he see Allan, he clearly saw my role. He saw I was giving Allan confidence. I knew it. How else can we help anyone? How else can we heal?

I loved and love this man because he is big enough to see and not feel threatened, and because he can recognize talent and announce it. For that, one must be big within, loving, without fear.

His contacts with the U.N. made the year a very exciting one for the students and me. He had access to places, people and events few people have. My warm spot for the press, and rare inner knowledge, accented this for me.

One day, Professor Hohenberg sent Allan and another student to cover a political rally. They went independently and came back at the same time. Each one wrote the story as he saw it. I was curious to see each story. I got the surprise of my life when I read Allan's story and that of the other student. Both had gone to the same event. You would never know by reading the two stories. How can two people write so differently?

I realized we bring a lot with us to any event. What takes place is never really the issue. People would say, "This story is not true. I was there. So and so did not say this."

Actually, the people just heard such and such. It was not changed by any editor, nor by the policy of the paper. Yet the editor gets blamed for changing the story. The difference is the result of two different people writing up the event, with all their best intentions to be accurate, fair and objective.

How can one leave his consciousness home and be able to report? How can one not take his own eyes? One can only see with his own eyes, hear with his own ears, think with his own brains. How can they or I be objective? What is it to be objective?

I guess I am trying to say that when anyone writes about this book, either good or bad, right or left . . . divisions, divisions again! I do understand. We write that which we see. The whole, the part, the near, the far, and each is the truth as each of us assesses it, just as I saw the picture at the end of the classroom when a small child. I knew from my teen years with Roberto that what I saw from the inside was different from what was reported. But now I knew **why** it was different.

While traveling to Stanford, California in 1969 Allan and I stopped in Sacramento to visit Mr. and Mrs. George Onoda, the parents of my friend Eleanor, whom we had met in New York. The visit gave me the strength to face a new place, life style and self.

Mr. Onoda spoke about the Japanese, who had earned more decorations during the Second World War than any other group. He spoke with pride of how honorable all the Japanese had been, of the love that led them to earn these honors.

I knew through Eleanor that they had spent time in a concentration camp, during World War II. Yet, her father was not talking about how unjustly his country had treated him and his family, nor how angry he was about it, but instead trying to explain to me how very hard it must have been for the Anglo-Saxon community to understand the love the Japanese-Americans felt for their country. They had in a very real and concrete way proven their love and loyalty. They did it by the only means which is effective. They went inside of themselves and brought forth their best feelings. They put their love at the feet of those who had incarcerated them.

I felt very proud to belong to the Human race. I know you may say, "but . . . what does that have to do with you?" What they did, I did. I take joy, strength, each time I see people expressing who they are. **Anyone.** He was telling me in different words what I have believed and lived all my life: Don't retaliate, go inside and bring out more love.

I often thought of Mr. Onoda telling us this story when I felt sad, when the pain of wanting Allan was becoming too great. I took refuge in the knowledge of belonging to this body, Humanity, which even in the midst of inhumanity, which war is, can in fact be Human.

There was a hilarious associated event. During the entire seven days it took to drive from New York, I had savored an imaginary **Japanese** meal. Eleanor's mother gave us a fantastic **Chinese** meal!

As soon as I arrived at Stanford University, I wanted to know who was doing what. I was a very curious person, I loved to know.

I quickly learned that even though the students had access to some of the best brains in the world, they did not go outside their departments. Neither did they feel that they could just introduce themselves to Nobel Laureate Linus Pauling or any of the other well known scholars. I wanted to know what Nobel Laureate Professor W.B. Schockley of Electrical Engineering had to say and why he said it, and the same about Professor John McCarthy of Computer Science, and Professor William Tiller of Materials Science.

I knew I could be of service by providing the students a chance to meet and talk to these interesting professors. When I found I wasn't the only one interested in hearing them, I organized luncheon seminars. Over several years, authors, Gina Germinara and James Fadiman and Professors Tiller, McCarthy, Luigi Cavalli-Sforza and Schockley, among others, came to talk.

Professor Tiller had just returned from Russia and brought a film showing psychokinesis. For me the thrill of being in a place where something new was happening, is indescribable. He was excited about it too. He knew he had to fund his own research since it was too new to go through regular channels.

There was the talk given by Professor John McCarthy. It was like being in the year 2000. Remember, it was only 1969-70. Here was someone anticipating things way ahead of times, like cars driving themselves on the freeways by computers and people getting all the news they wanted or needed through a home terminal, without editing, as if one had a wire service at home. How exciting I found all these new ideas! . . . the feeling of a brand new world!

I wanted to know if a robot could be built to clean house.

He told me, "No, not yet. It would be almost impossible to program it to clean, since each house is different. Even if you did it for one house, you could not move anything around after that."

Professor W.B. Schockley was kind enough to come several times. He said we should be concerned about the quality of life, not the quantity and that genes play the determining role in us, not environment. He had a well-documented presentation and his logic was impeccable. I saw he truly believed what he was saying and that he felt he was a humanitarian. He felt we were asking certain people to produce more than their capability allowed, and that was inhumane, it created misery.

Being who I am, I wanted to hear the other side of the argument. I went to see Nobel Laureate Professor Joshua Lederberg in Genetics. He was too busy with a satellite. He recommended an Italian, Professor Luigi Cavalli-Sforza.

From Professor Cavalli-Sforza's seminar I learned that with optimal nutrition, the IQ of a human being could be raised. He said that if we spent our resources on food, instead of arms, we could create the most intelligent nation on Earth. He said Food is a greater weapon than Arms. Unfortunately, I did not feel that he had refuted Professor Schockley. I wanted to hear both sides, but I had only heard one.

So many things were happening on campus! Professor W.C. Dement was beginning his dream research.

Professor Philip Zimbardo presented the ideas of a reported study which brought interesting and disturbing results. Two dozen students from all over the country, in the Bay Area for the summer of 1971, were divided into two groups. One side became the jailers, the other the inmates. After a short time they behaved as in a real jail. They became inmates, feeling and acting as such, and jailers, feeling the power and acting inhumanely toward their own classmates. In this we could all see that I wasn't the only one who had this animal I was taming; it is under the skin of **all** of us.

My husband was studying in the Communications Department. Professor Wilbur Schramm had been instrumental in getting T.V. into India. Apparently there was a lack of protein in some area in India. The people were eating the protein, but not properly cooking it. So although the food was eaten, it could not be assimilated by the body. The trick was to teach the people how to cook what they ate, in an India with 36 major languages.

To see and feel the concern to help the world was good! It felt good to be at Stanford. I gathered interesting data.

But the most important learning was to see how each Department trained the minds of its students. After the training I observed how a person thought as a Lawyer, a Doctor, or a Mathematician. I used to laugh and call Stanford "the sausage factory."

For this to occur, there had to be certain premises which were accepted by and for all in the specific department.

For example, as a universal example:

1 is called One.

2 is called Two.

No one says: In this case 1 is One, but in this other case 1 is called Two. No. There is a premise which is universally agreed upon. 1 is One and 2 is Two.

What I REALIZED is that they don't have a universally accepted premise for interpreting Human behavior, in other words, a **way** to universally read Human Beings. And I realized I had it. The formula is very simple:

Any action which is loving, kind, joyful, is Human, healthy.

Any action which is not loving, kind, joyful, is an expression of Human pain.

With this simple formula we can feel compassion for anyone

117

who "tries" to hurt us, because in the moment that someone says: "I don't believe you have good intentions;" "I don't believe you have worth because you are a housewife;" "I don't believe you are intelligent;" "You make no money, you're just a mother, therefore you have no value;" "I don't believe you can do what you say you will;" you can see how the person who is talking to you views himself. You can see his pain. Isn't it sad he feels like this? Don't you feel compassion and a desire to help him?

By the time we left Stanford, I was **sure** the answers I wanted were not in any great university. I realized I was smarter than even I had thought, but it was not useful to be only smart.

I found myself analyzing every word, every action, mine and everyone else's, to see how the pieces of the puzzle called "life" fit! I realized the mind had a better use than just questioning, analyzing, concluding, and publishing. Publish to get a promotion, publish to keep a job!

All those years at universities confirmed for me that I was not my mind — which I had known since childhood — and that my teen-age decision not to go to the university — because I wouldn't find the answers I was seeking there — was absolutely correct. I also confirmed that all those geniuses were not their minds either, nor their work. I did not love them for their intelligence, but for their human sensitivities.

When the proverbial question came, over and over, "What do **you** do?" I would always answer, "I am a Human Being, it is a full time job." They would all laugh. It was not a laughing matter to me. They were applying their minds to the acquisition of data. I was applying mine to the full development of myself as a Human Being, by expressing who I was.

One is a Human Being when one expresses Universal Love, and I was doing so. I was very happy one day in March of 1978 to hear Andrea say, "Beatriz, I have finally found one person whom you don't like!" By saying this, she was informing me of her awareness of my love for almost everyone. Also I saw I had to go one step further to love everyone. I had to try a bit harder. I did. There are final exams at the universities. There are final exams in life also!

My offerings to God as Mind were many. One of them was hunger. I went hungry many times because Allan (my husband) and Freddy (my little brother) were studying. I felt they needed fruits, vegetables, and chicken, nutritious food for their minds. I knew I could buy rice, potatoes and bread, and stretch the budget for all of us to get through the month. But that possibility was not acceptable to me.

Palo Alto, California
November 17, 1969

My love:

Life is certainly difficult for both of us now.

The sacrifices we need to make to the great God Education seem to really hurt us and drive us into ourselves and our dream worlds. Somehow we must not let this happen. We must not quit when defeat threatens; we must choose freely, not with guns at our heads. I must learn to work and carry through jobs that I don't like or that require me to do my best, not just my better or my good. If the choice is to come between completing the Ph.D. and the foreign service, I want to be able to say honestly that I don't want the Ph.D. because I don't need it, not that I don't want the Ph.D. because it's making me sweat a bit. It's sort of similar to the hope that we will have the chance of turning down the foreign service, not vice versa.

Somehow we have to make a stand and win! Not just slip through as has been the case so far, but win. We can help each other I know because we have strength for each other.

We can do it! I know!

We must learn to face the music, not turn aside, as I am doing now, and write letters or watch TV or take a bath or sleep.

Somehow we, especially I, must learn self-discipline so that our love can grow and bloom into a beautiful flower of creation that will please us both.

If we can make this happen, then I will become a good writer. Right now, I suffer from fuzzy thinking that shows itself when I tackle a problem. Some of my first drafts look more like notes rather than orderly thought.

I love you, my dearest heart, more and more every day,

Happily and Hopefully,
Allan

Another sacrifice was time. Allan was studying day and night so I had no time with him. I felt through this sacrifice I was contributing to the world, being part of a bigger picture. Allan was the writer. He would write the book that would endure for millions of years. I, by being there and helping him to become emotionally free, and being out of the way so he could study, was being instrumental in helping this great man to become.

I was building his confidence (which leads to personal freedom) by paying attention only to those manifestations which came out of love, talking about them, praising, and thinking about them. I paid no attention to any which came out of fear.

Allan was desperate. He felt I did not see him. People thought, "How can she be so blind? Can't she see he is not what she says? Can't she see he hides in the bathroom because he does not even know what to do? How can she say he is great and will contribute to the world?"

If I want a fire to die, I do not put wood on it. By thinking one second about his negative behavior, I would have been adding fuel. I could only help by giving my thoughts, my entire energy to the positive manifestations which were not yet visible. What **was** visible had enough energy.

Once the unmanifested side also had enough energy of its own, it would surface and manifest automatically. My pain was, "Why isn't it manifesting sooner? Why can't I have more energy, be stronger, be able to give more?"

Here is an example of my approach:

Allan took Robert for a week-end, brought him back 10 hours late and did not phone me. When he came I confronted him with his actions. Since I was not sure he really understood what I meant, I wrote him a letter:

> *Palo Alto, California*
> *January 6, 1983*
>
> Dear Allan:
>
> *. . . I was mad, yes. But I was mad because I truly love you. I know you to be kind, . . . generous, . . . joyful, . . . and thoughtful. When you negate that which you are, on this occasion your thoughtfulness, I feel pain, . . . Not because you are doing anything to me! No, you can't do anything to hurt me. I feel pain because you are harming yourself! . . . negating your true self. I get mad at you because you are not being you! . . . because you have to say "I am sorry." Oh! I know you are better and I know you will be even better. But my love is big for you and the world . . .*
>
> *Love and Peace,*
> *Beatriz*

I knew Allan could procrastinate. He came late day after day. Yet, each day I only **expected him** to be on time. Allan would say, "Don't you ever learn?"

No! **That** type of learning I don't need, thank you. A learning or reasoning which concludes with the manifestations of something negative, is not a learning I want. My childhood decision was to live to prove: "There is no Evil. There is only Good." How could I learn to expect the worst. No. The Law is: "Live in the Here and Now." Don't bring garbage from the past. What happened yesterday, happened yesterday. Today is a new day.

Therefore, the one thing my husband was asking of me, I

knew I must not change! He wanted me to think for a minute about him as he saw himself, with his "imperfections." Because I truly loved him, I could only look at the side which was unmanifested. Only by this process could I help him. It was cruel! Yet it was the kindest thing I could do.

This is like when someone decides to be a dancer. There is pain in the muscles, and sweat. But only if the teacher is cruel enough to ignore those pains, those sweats, and concentrate on the Perfect Movement inside the person, will the dancer who can Be, unfold, bit by bit! You ignore the present stage in the continuum of development, and keep your eye on Perfection, Eternity.

There is no conflict between "Living in the Here and Now" and "keeping the eye of The Eternal Perfection" towards which the moment's activities are progressing. The present moment should be experienced as fully as we are capable of doing so. In it is embodied all that there is. However a **part** of that present moment's experience is the content of our minds. By keeping in the mind a clear **visualization** of the Eternal Perfection toward's which we are working, our moment's **activities** are productive toward the goal. Any thought for visualization or notice of less than perfection, beclouds the goal view and must lead to a less-than-perfect result.

Various friends, and Freddy also, accused me of wanting them to be "Perfect." I always said they are **already** perfect. They saw themselves as "imperfect." I saw their pain, their fear, but that is not what they meant by the "imperfection" they wanted me to SEE.

There is no such thing as "imperfect." When looked at totally: inner (unmanifest) and outer (manifest), there IS only perfection. They wanted me to see only the external half, the present manifestation. The external cannot exist without the internal. Sometimes one shows, sometimes the other. Together they make the whole which is "perfect."

I used my mind as a tool for the benefit of others, giving the "gift" of understanding about themselves to everyone I met. Thus my mind was sacred, I made its use a sacrament.

But not everyone wanted to look into the perfection mirror I provided. One day a friend screamed at me, "I wish you would keep your perfection to yourself!"

Why give our power to what we do **not** want to see? If anything exists it is because we think of it.

For example: A chair is quite concrete. Yet, it is only a consequence of an intangible, thought. Someone had to think:

First Cause:	a chair	- Thought
Second step:	I want to have one	- Desire
Third step:	I will create one	- Action

The three steps do not all need to be done by the same person. One person may have the thought of it and draw the picture. Hundreds of years later, another person may have the Desire to take Action on the drawing made by the first person. Leonardo da Vinci thought of a great many things. The Desire and Action to bring about the physical manifestations of his thoughts took centuries. Nevertheless, the process has been the same.

The world around us is **only** a manifestation of first causes, thoughts. That is why we **have to** control our thoughts, edit at the thought level, not in our actions. The world tells me one can think what one wants, and just not act on those thoughts. No! If you think, you will bring about what you have thought.

To believe that you can throw garbage or flowers in the river, in the **privacy** of the night, and that because it was done in **privacy** it will not affect the river, is crazy!

To believe that you can think good or bad thoughts in the **privacy** of your head, and that because it was done in **privacy** it will not affect the river of life, consciousness (all of us), is also crazy!

What you throw in the physical river, affects all waters!

What you think in the invisible river, consciousness, affects all Beings, since thought is the connecting force.

That is why we must become **Masters of our minds.** We must make them our tools, and not allow them to be our Masters.

Minds can be trained, as anyone who has gone to a university knows. You can allow others to brainwash you — as advertising attempts to do — or to train your mind — as formal education is supposed to do — or you can **consciously** train your **own** mind to express fully who **you** are! Love!

Another mental process I used was to disassociate my feelings from my mind and change my feelings through reason. The process began when my mother showed me the other little girls did not necessarily want to accuse or blame me of anything. Through using my mind, I changed my feelings. I became so good at it that for a long time I thought I was fooling people. But I was **actually** experiencing (feeling) those emotions. At the time I did not realize the training this provided. I saw only the external results: I could make people believe what I wanted them to believe. Very much as an actor does on stage. I became ashamed of using emotions to get what I wanted, not realizing my motives were pure. That realization came much later in life.

I would put myself 100% into a conversation, knowing deep down it did not matter at all. I was constantly aware of the different levels in which my mind moved. I am sure Artur Rubinstein poured himself into each concert completely, trying hard to do his best and fearing this time he might not be able to pull it off. Yet, he and all of us know the worst that could have happened. Was it a life and death matter?

Even if it were death, do we really die? No. I know I am eternal, my energy will never die. Nature told me that. I saw transformation, leaves falling to the earth, becoming food for the snail, for the plants. I did not see disappearance. I'll become something else physically. Yet, the other level, the spirit, I know will continue. I wrote about this when my mother died.

Hamilton, Canada
May 30, 1967

Dear Ana Maria:

My dearest, how can you imagine that I felt nothing? Don't you realize that at least one of us had to be strong? Is it that all of a sudden you believe I don't love mother?

I always said that the day something happens, I will continue as if nothing had occurred . . . Maybe the love I have is illogical, maybe I am fooling myself, thinking that she is with me, as she has been during these last three years that we've been apart. But . . . I will not allow one thought in my mind that all is finished, because it is not so. We Do have Spirit, and that is the only thing that has value. I know I will feel her and listen to her when I need her, since she will look after me from Heaven . . .

Your sister who adores you,
Beatriz

The belief that "We Do have Spirit, and that (it) is the only thing that has value . . ." kept me steadfast to conclude a job. I was ready to hold my feelings aside for years and years, a life-time if need be, to control my feelings with my mind until I could see Allan strong within himself. My mind was always turned on, making sure I remembered, "I am **not** my feelings." ("I'm not this horrible pain.")

Since Allan was not giving me of himself, my heart was in great pain. My mind kept saying, "Beatriz, he is not denying you because of you. You are love. You are perfect. He is denying you because **he** is afraid. He blames you because **he** is trapped inside of himself! He hurts you because **he** fears. Love him enough so that your Love will melt his Fear."

Later he himself recognized his blaming had been misplaced.

Palo Alto, California
April 1, 1980
11:55 PM

Dear Beatriz:

. . . I've been living alone these last two months. What a simple revelation! I see clearly that all the crap in my life that I somehow blamed you for, or whatever, was still there and I was alone! So it's mine and I'm shovelling it out . . .

Love,
Allan

My love **did** hold firm until it **did** melt his fear. My mind had triumphed. It was the useful tool through which I had disciplined myself. **I** determined how to express myself (love, understanding) and, as Master of my Mind, used it as a tool to be Master of my Emotions and Actions.

Allan wrote,

Palo Alto, California
August 14, 1979

Dear Beatriz:

I love you. Very much. To the stars and all the worlds beyond, as well as right here on this earth . . . I am learning the facts that I could not face when you and I were going through our hard work. I can give. I am beginning to see that now. Thank you for your love, for your strength. I pray to God that you will regain your life . . .

Allan

and he wrote to himself on August 22, 1979

. . . it breaks my heart to think of the misery I have put her through just because I was too scared to live! So much fear and so much love. I want her to know that the fear that immobilized me has gone forever . . .

CHAPTER 5
GOD OF FEELINGS

To me, emotions are like a wardrobe. Through a wardrobe I get to know a person; it tells me a great deal. But I am perfectly aware as I look at the wardrobe that I am not looking at the person, only at his or her clothes.

I have a shirt.

By the process of my **living,** the shirt gets stained and dirty. I know the shirt is not the stains, or the dirt. Because I **know** what the shirt **IS,** I wash the dirt off, thereby restoring the shirt to its original state: **CLEAN, PERFECT.**

I have feelings.

By the process of my **living,** I feel anger and frustration. I know I am not the stains of anger or frustration. Because I **know** what the BEING **IS,** I change the emotions, thereby restoring myself to my original state: **CLEAN, PERFECT.**

When I see **you,** I see you perfect. Your stains are no more **YOU** than mine are ME!

I have dealt with my own wardrobe in this way. I used my emotions to get to know better and better who I was through how I dressed. I was always aware that what I felt was not me. That is why I was able to ignore what I felt and act according to who I was: **love** and **understanding.**

This process started when I was a very small child. I was born with a very serious face. I have pictures with Grandmother, Father and Mother all imitating my serious face when I was a few months old. They laughed at me for it. When I started to understand, Mother made me learn to control that face, to change it.

She would say, "If you want to look miserable, go be by yourself. If you are around people, be fit." (Meaning: "look happy"). I was love. I should **express** love at all times. When I did, I was rewarded with Mother's company. When I did not, I was sent to my room. I did not get punished for breaking things. My parents thought that is how one learns. But they did withhold their warmth if I did not express my own.

So I learned to control my face, and in the process, to self-observe. I learned to appear any emotion I wanted. I knew I could fool people and that did not feel good. But I wanted to be with Mommy, and the only way was by **looking** happy, even if I didn't feel it.

When I was three and a half years old, I had my first experience of selecting which emotion I would "wear," not just on my face.

My parents and I had gone to visit friends who invited me to sleep over. I said, "Yes." Mother warned me that if I stayed, it would have to be until morning. She would not come to get me in the middle of the night.

I waited all night and controlled how I felt. I said nothing. I behaved as if I was perfectly happy. The friends were surprised and told Mother over the phone that I was fine, she did not need to hurry. Because of this, Mother didn't come for me until noon. I was in the middle of the living room. I saw her and rushed into her arms. I cried and cried, I was so happy to see her!

I decided then I would never sleep away from home. I never did — except when out of town, at school, or with Roberto — until I left home for Canada. Even as a teenager, if a party finished late and they invited me to stay, I never did. Whatever the time — even if it was 6 o'clock in the morning — I went home.

Home was protection, a feeling of well being. Home was love, a place I loved to be. I learned I felt safe at home and I learned it without going to pieces or showing how unhappy I was.

I had acted happy and loving towards the people with whom I was staying. My emotions did not interfere with my actions.

By the time I entered school I was an expert at appearance control. I used it consciously throughout my school career. I only studied when I wanted to be called upon, not otherwise. When I knew my lesson, I appeared very insecure and frightened. Therefore, the teacher, thinking I did not know it, would call on me. Internally, I was radiant, it was precisely what I wanted. When I did not know my work, I was very vocal and acted sure of myself, screaming at her to call on me. She, seeing my eagerness, called upon those who appeared as if they had not studied.

Since then, I have done this many times: not just looking at my feelings to learn about myself, but then putting aside my emotions, because I knew that what I felt was not Me. As I practiced, I was able to accomplish bigger tasks, to override my emotions for a greater period of time, no matter how much pain or other distracting emotions I felt.

I am **not** talking about repressing my feelings, nor am I a cold fish. I am a very emotional Human Being. No one can be with me five minutes and not see me go from tears to laughter. I am talking about looking at my emotions and deciding which I would "wear" (experience, express) and which I would leave behind. This meant my life would not be driven by what I felt. I was in the driver's seat, my emotions were not!

I did not know then the future usefulness of this training to keep distance between what I felt and how I looked. I did not recognize that I was/am an actor in this play called Life, reading the lines in front of me, making **you** experience the feelings the script requires. The actor is aware at all times that it is just a play;

he is not the part. At the time, I felt this separation-ability was a fault, as if using my emotions was "wrong." With inner development, I realized the vital role this separation played in bringing me to the center of myself! Only a couple of years ago I completed the circle by returning to a natural, unposed face, without losing the hard-won awareness of self or the continuing ability to express what is needed for the purpose at hand.

Because of the great amount of love I received, I was convinced I was perfect and lovable. I also felt beautiful, intelligent and powerful. It did not occur to me there was anything I could not do. If I could think of something, it could be done. And I did it! I never experienced not being able to do something I wanted to do. I had no conception of limitation.

As long as I can remember, I have had just one relationship with the entire world: Mother/Child. I was a mother. When Mother fought with Father I would advise her on what to do or say to Dad. She was really my child, not I hers. The same with Father. They taught me; yet emotionally I supported them. I was only four years old when Father would come home tired, needing to talk, and unburden himself to me from all the worries of his work.

I was not always at home. I spent years at a boarding school. But Sundays, winter holidays and three-month summer holidays were spent at home.

Home was something else! Father and Mother fought like dogs and cats: Incredible fights full of violence! Sometimes I felt very frightened! I saw two choices: I could hate them or love them. How do I love these people who hit each other and say cruel things to each other? I realized that what they feel is not who they are. They may feel these terrible emotions sometimes; they may even act on those feelings; but they really were Love. Any action which was not loving was not really them. I decided to only judge them for their real intrinsic value.

It is as if you have a very valuable diamond covered with mud. Do you throw it away because it is covered with mud? Do you appraise it at no value because you see the mud? No one would do that with a diamond! Yet, we judge each other on that basis. We do not look past the mud!

I could never do that! So I am **accused** of being blind, not seeing the "reality," the Mud! I treat people according to the real, intrinsic value. With or without the mud, they **are** perfect! With the mud, the diamond appears opaque, but can shine just as well. The diamond **itself** decided if and when to reveal itself and let the light shine. I love the light. So, I give my energy, my every thought, knowing that with my thought process I can help the shine I love to come through.

I did not like fights. I felt one should live in Peace as much as possible. Mother used to tell me I would make a boring wife because I did not like to fight. It seemed to her fights were the spice of life. Not for me!

They seemed to fight over nothing. When Father came home from work Mother would be listening to the radio. He wanted her to change to classical music.

Mother would say, "If you came at a specific time I could arrange to listen to my program when you are not here, but since you come any time, you will have to put up with listening to my program until it is finished."

He would not! He would pick up the radio and smash it into a hundred pieces. He always demanded and she always replied in the same way.

To me, changing the radio station would have been easy; I would have done it. Mother would say I was a "lamb." To me there was no difference between one station and another, but loud voices and fights mattered a lot. Peace at all costs, for me!

In the middle of their fights they would call Ana Maria and me and ask us, "Who do you want to go with?"

Ana Maria immediately would say, "With Mother!" I would take no sides: I did not want to be part of fights. I kept saying to Ana Maria, "Don't choose. They will make up in a minute. It will all blow over. Feelings are temporary things."

Father had a gun. Mother would put down the gun next to Father and say she could not live like that any more. "Kill me, kill me," she would beg. At this point Father, in the midst of his anger, would crack up and chuckle, "You would like that! You would want me to kill you so I would end up in jail. No. I am not going to ruin **my** life. If you want to die you will have to do it yourself!" What melodrama!

Within two minutes they would be in each other's arms: crying, kissing, asking forgiveness of each other. They never went to bed angry in all the years I lived at home. Mother felt one can die at any minute during sleep, so one should be at peace with everyone before bed.

Father would hurt Mother by saying she was a bastard, as if Mother could be guilty of what **her** mother had done!

Mother would reply, "Your mother does not love you!" That hurt him! (Both accusations were true.)

I could not stand Father hurting Mother with something he knew she couldn't do anything about. I was mad at Father for that. I would go to Mother and say, "Don't speak with him anymore."

Mother would respond, "Never do that! He was angry, that's why he said those things. He did not mean them."
"Then he should control himself," I'd say. "One should not say something one does not mean." I meant those words. In 16 years of marriage I never said anything for which I was sorry afterwards. I never opened my mouth unless I knew what I was saying.
Mother, however, would look at me and say, "Remember, he is a kind, loving person. We all are. Sometimes, in anger, people say or do things that are not from who they are, that don't represent the truth about themselves. On those occasions we have only one choice: to forget those words and actions, because they were not really meant."
Thus I had the example from which to learn to see only the real actions of love, and to ignore anything that was not kind. This training was hard. I felt the pain which came from the violence. She taught me the **violent** actions were **reactions** to hurts, **not** from the **real** person.

I experienced violence also on a national level. I was told how lucky and proud I should feel to be a citizen of Argentina, which had not been in wars, while the rest of the world was at war. War was an abstraction. I never experienced it. (Besides, I was brought up so differently I did not feel part of **any** country!) But I **did** experience enormous manifestations of public violence.
Mother would take me to demonstrations about Peron. Millions of people came together screaming, "Peron, Peron!" I felt them pressing against me and I saw the horses charging the masses, hitting them with sticks and cutting at them with sabres. Even though they were saying this was a country of peace, my experience was violence. I felt violence from the people, who seemed to have a single mass mind. There was an out-of-control feeling. And I felt violence from the police, above ground on their horses, trying to control the mob. I got the feeling they were scared! So many people and so few of them! I was out of it, just observing. I did not know fear.
People would ask Mother, "Why do you take Beatriz to such danger? Stay home!"
She would respond, "Nothing will happen to Beatriz. She has to see and feel it."
She was right about both. We would arrive in time to hear Eva Peron, after Juan Peron spoke. The violence occurred at the end of the assemblies, when the Police were trying to send the people home.
I saw the woman. I saw how she could make the masses move, get to their hearts with her words. For what purpose, I did not know. I did **experience** that power. I knew it not as a foreign

129

concept, nor as something I read about.

These experiences taught me that women are very powerful Beings. I had a mother who was strong and fearless. I had a grandmother who had worked to create the first Labor Union in Argentina. I saw that Eva Peron, a leader of my country, was a woman who could move millions. Nothing in my up-bringing told me that women were helpless.

Father took me to other types of assemblies. As a Protestant in a Catholic country, he took me to see Billy Graham. Thousands of people were there, charged with a different energy. There was a translator.

Father turned to me as if he knew something I didn't, "You see Beatriz, you don't need to know the language. You only need a good translator. Now, remember that. With a good translator you can go throughout the world and speak."

I looked at him, thinking, "What is this man talking about? Why should I remember this?"

I put it down to, "Father is a bit 'kooky!'" What else could I say? The same with Mother. She kept insisting that I needed to be in the middle of that turmoil, to feel it. It was as if they were training me for something they knew, but of which I knew nothing. I decided they were just eccentric, and left it at that.

I was a good student at an English school when I was around six. There was a boy there who was the "Black Sheep." He never did his homework. When we did not do it, we were whacked on our finger tips with a ruler. I got it once. It hurt. Never again! He was continually being punished!

One day we were on the patio waiting for the bell to ring before entering the class-room. I said I was frightened because I was going to get it, since I had not done my homework. The "Black Sheep" looked at me, took his homework (the first he had done!) and gave it to me, saying, "Give it to the teacher. Say it's yours."

I objected, "You'll get punished!"

He replied, "One spot more is nothing to the leopard."

I presented "my" homework. He got punished. The "Black Sheep" was big enough to take a punishment he did not deserve, to pull himself up to a higher level of Being through conscious choice.

I, on the other hand, had the chance, as he was being punished, to stand up and confess. Yet, I was concerned with my reputation for being the "good one." I failed in that instance, to act from strength; I acted from Fear. I could also have pulled myself up, if I had talked then instead of now. I wonder sometimes where that extraordinary person is . . .

I looked "good." I was not. What is "good"? Neither was he good nor I bad. He just was able to use the opportunity which my failure provided, to raise himself to a higher level, against all appearances, by giving through a conscious sacrifice. I learned not to judge a book by its cover! Appearances are all too deceiving.

While growing up, I took great pride in my mother for tenaciously daring to BE and in my father because he was bringing me up differently. I was proud that Father continually tried to convert everyone he knew to his Protestant religion. I was not Protestant; what mattered to me was that he was doing what he felt he had to do.

Also, he loved his work. He often said, "If I were born again I would be a builder again." He had found how to serve his fellow man and express who he was through that medium. He did it well. He gave "life warranties" on his buildings, and never bribed anyone to get a contract. He lived by principles. Yes, I was proud.

Grandma Belly was quite a lady! "Discipline, self-discipline!" was her motto. She taught it well. One example was her reading every afternoon from two to four. When 4 o'clock arrived she would close the book until the next day. She would tell me the story after each day's reading.

One day she left it at a cliff-hanger: a few pages to go and the mystery would be solved. The book could have been finished by 4:10 pm; but she quit reading at four.

I was horrified, "Why didn't you finish? How can you just sit there? Don't you want to know how it ends?"

She looked at me very seriously, "Haven't you learned anything from me yet? Yes, I am eager to know how it ends. But what I want, how I feel, is irrelevant. I must do what I have decided.

"I am a Human Being, Beatriz, not an animal. My actions are not based on what I feel, or wish, at the moment. I am in charge, not my emotions."

The message came clearly to me: I am **not** my emotions.

What did I do with it? I determined what I was going to do. I always felt I was in control, life did not do things **to me**. I put **myself** through life. This brought me great pain and frustration. But I eventually learned the rewards were far beyond what I could have dreamed.

Another lesson that had an impact on me, was the importance of doing what I felt I **had** to do, even if everyone talked negatively. My parents talked at length about this.

There was a couple, living at the corner of our block, who went shopping and everywhere else together. The neighbors said, "How terrible she must be, that her husband doesn't let her out of his sight."

My mother loved dancing, movies and going to theaters, and she went with her friends (male and female). My father stayed home and listened to opera. The neighbors said, "Your mother is a prostitute." I would come home and repeat what the neighbors had said. The world out there was inflicting pain. How could they say that about Mother?

Father and Mother said, "There is no way to please other people. You see the couple on the corner? People talk because they go together. They talk about us because we don't. Beatriz, forget what people say, look within; decide if what you want to do is going to help anyone. If the answer is 'yes,' go ahead and do it. If it will do harm, then stop. People may not agree with what you do; but that is not harm. As long as you don't harm, keep on going."

I felt I had known everything since childhood. To me life was like an old movie I had seen a thousand times. While I was yet a young person I could feel what old people felt and talk with them about their problems and feelings. They felt they could speak freely with me when they could not with anyone else. I also had friends my own age and younger.

DAR	GIVE
Dar amor al que te da	To give love to those who give it to you
Que merito tiene?	What's the merit in that?
Dale al que te odia	Give to those who hate you,
Por que no lo tiene.	Because they haven't love to give.
Dar al que tiene	To give to someone who has love,
No da satisfaccion	Brings no satisfaction.
Dale al que no tiene	Give to someone who has none
Un consejo salvador	a saving advice and
Y alegraras su corazon.	joy to his heart.
Dios te da todo	God gave you everything.
Y tu no das nada!	And you give nothing!
Porque? digo porque?	Why? I ask Why?
Dad como te da El	Give as you have been given,
Y agradecido sed.	and always be thankful.
Dad una sonrisa al triste	Give a smile to a sad one
Una mano al caido	a hand to the fallen,
Un camino al perdido	Give a way to the lost
Dad como recibiste.	Give as you have received.
De lo mucho que Dios te da	Give the much which God gave you
Dad aunque sea un poquito	Give even if just a bit.
Sed maestro del ninito	Be teacher to a child
Da tu brazo al Cieguito.	Give your arm to a blind one.

Apoyo al cieguito	Support the blind one
Apoyo al ancianito	Support the old one
A todos los que necesitan da	Give all that they need
Por mas que des, deras poquito.	For as much as you give, it's only a little.
Todo lo que tengo lo doy	I give all I have:
Mis bienes, mi trabajo, mi yo	My possessions, my work, my very Self
Asi mayordomo de Dios soy	Thus I am caretaker for God
Bien satisfacho estoy	I am well satisfied
Y muy feliz porque doy.	And very happy because I give
Hago feliz a otros si asi doy	I make others happy if thus I give
Gozo tendre, si asi todo lo doy.	I will have joy, if thus I always give it.

by Federico Caprotta (in Spanish)
"Dedicated to my Grandchild, Robertito"
September 15, 1974

(From "Porque Quiero al Mundo . . ."
© Beatriz G. Prentice, 1981
Ore Press, Inc.
Sunnyvale, CA 94088)

Father would say, "If one wants to teach people to read, one teaches illiterates, not at the University. It's the same Beatriz. We are here to be an example of Love. To give to those who are loving is easy, and seems a waste of time. We must give love to those who are not able to give, who **need** our love. These are the people who are mean and rude to us, who blame and hurt us. Train yourself to love those who do not know how to love. Only by example can you teach."

I did not have any problem liking people. I liked almost everyone. If I did not like someone at first, I knew it was because I was failing to see who he or she was; I had not yet found the way to know him. I kept at it until I saw God within that person. Bingo! It always worked!

I tried to become friends with people who thought mine were the thoughts of ignorant people, who felt I had no value because I was a full time mother instead of earning money, or who doubted my motives. The more they withdrew the more I reached out. The more they kicked, the more I gave. I felt that if they didn't like me it was because they didn't know me. This sounds pretentious, but since I never felt superior, people from all walks of life, levels and ages, liked me and were my friends.

I took it as a challenge when someone did not like me. I knew myself to be light, to be love. If they did not see that, it was because I was not showing it clearly enough, and I felt frustrated **at myself.** Why couldn't I love more? Why couldn't I express myself better, so that whomever I touched, whatever I looked at, would beam? Why couldn't I light their lives, just being a moment with them? I called and called those who did not call me.

When I entered the second Catholic school, at about six, I found a big girl 18 years old who was nearing graduation. I deposited all my love in her. She paid no attention to me whatsoever. Day after day for the two years until she left, I tried to do nice things for her, with the hope she would notice and give me a smile. I never got it. That didn't stop me from trying harder each time.

At the same time, Elvirita was sleeping next to me. I spent nights up with her asthma attacks, giving her my pillow. We loved each other. Now I can see how she served me, instead of the other way around. She was beside me when I needed to give, practicing to Be Human.

My sister was there also. Oh, that soul! I had the love and understanding of my entire family; she had only me! I would do anything for her! She knew it. She would only obey me. I had to be the protector, the big sister, no, really the mother. I made her feel that whatever she needed I would provide for her. That is how our relationship has continued over the years.

Father used to tell me I had to follow Jesus. I would get mad. "Who is Jesus anyhow? A man! I am not to follow or imitate anyone!" I felt Daddy wanted me to enter a race I could not win. No! "If Jesus came and did what he did, someone else has to come and do more! Yes, we know that can be accomplished, so it's time for bigger things!"

I'd say these things and Father would get very upset. The people around would ask Father to make me shut up! He'd look at them and laugh, "**You** make Beatriz shut up! Just try!"

I am 40 years old and I am still saying the same things. We are here to do more, much more: **not** to Love our Enemies, but to realize **There Are No Enemies!**

I only knew I had to look inside of myself and do what I felt was right for me. If the entire world did not understand, it did not matter. The one thing was to make sure I did not lie to myself. I needed to know **why** I was doing whatever I was doing. I had to act as the CONSCIOUS being I am.

I surrounded myself with people who did not think like I did. Most of them thought I was just plain crazy. That continues today.

When I was 13 years old, Mother tried to push my emotional buttons. She had taken me to Luna Park to see a sports event at the boxing gymnasium. Peron was there. Thirty thousand people stood up and yelled, "Peron! Peron!" The energy and emotion were very high! My mother was next to me, standing screaming with all those other people.

I was sitting down, looking, wondering, "How can she scream 'Peron! Peron!'? This is the woman who yelled, 'Kill her! I'd rather see my child dead than living in a country without freedom!' How can this woman who has always felt so strongly **against** this man, be swept away in this mass hysteria?"

She looked at me, furious, and pinched my upper arm until it was blue. "Don't you have blood in your veins? Is it water? Can't you feel?"

Yes! I could feel! But no one would sweep me up from that seat, no matter how much emotion was in the room. I would not move because of any outside force! No! I'd move only when I decided to do so. I'd move only from within.

I loved my mother very deeply and we were very good friends. She always behaved differently with me than with anyone else. But one more time she tried to push my emotional buttons.

Since childhood, Mother had had a game: "If you love me, you will do this for me. If you don't, I will kill myself." As a child, when she got a "No," she would climb to the top of a telephone or light pole. The police would come, promise whatever she wanted, and she would come down.

That game continued when she grew up and married Father. If she wanted something and Father said, "No," she would shut herself in the bathroom and threaten to drown herself. Father would break down the door, promise what she wanted, and everything would continue as before.

All through my childhood I looked in amazement at this game, unable to understand why Father did not put a stop to such insane behavior. Mother never did it to me . . . until I was 17 or 18 years old.

I can't remember what she wanted, but I said "No." She said she would swallow some pills and die, if I did not do what she wanted.

I am not what I feel. I WILL NOT be manipulated nor played with through my emotions. Therefore, I looked at her with an incredible calmness. "Are you sure this is what you want, Mother? I love you. Because I love you I would help you do whatever you want to do. Are you **sure** this is what you want?"

"Yes," she replied.

I got a glass of water and the pills and gave them to her. She looked at me, daring me, and swallowed them. I looked at her, kissed her "Good Night," and went to bed.

Ana Maria was on the phone like a mad woman, getting the ambulance. They rushed Mother to the hospital and pumped out her stomach just in time.

I slept through the night, got up, and went to work. The next night when I came home, I saw true pain in her eyes for the first time. She looked at me and said, "I love you like I don't love anyone else. How could you do this to me?"

I returned her look and said, "I love you Mama, like you were never loved! Just **because** I love you, I can't allow you to control me through that feeling." She never played that again — on anyone! It seemed so cold, yet, it is just a clear behavior separation between who I was and what I felt. It seemed cruel at the time, and for some people, even now. Yet I could not act any differently, then or now. My emotions had nothing to do with what I knew I had to do: stop that sick game. It seemed to me the kindest action I could do.

I knew well the old adage:

"I pray for the serenity to accept the things I cannot change,
The courage to change the things I can,
And the wisdom to know the difference . . ."

But I also knew what it means:

Things we cannot change: Others.
Things we can change: Ourselves.

I am **not** responsible for a Being coming to me and choosing to die, or be negative. He has his own job to do, and is doing it. I **am** responsible for being such an example that those around me will decide to change because they see it pays off to do so.

No one could or can push a button and make me jump. No one. I was and am in control of Me.

At age 15 I read *Knulp* by Hermann Hesse. Until then, books had been only confirmation for me. First I would think. Then if I had a question I would go to a book store, pass my hand over the books and, when I felt an electric discharge coming from a book, pick it up and open it. Behold, there would be the answer. I never learned to use libraries.

This was the first time I had read a book that did not confirm something I already knew. But I felt, "Hesse is right." To read it and **feel** it was right was not enough for me. I had to **know** it was right. There is only one way: to live it, experience it. Only in this way can anything become a part of me, and only then do I "know" it.

I read the book from 5 a.m. until noon. Then I went downtown and bought a backpack and borrowed a sleeping bag. I already had blue jeans and a red leather jacket. I put up an ad on a bulletin board, giving my phone number and name, and saying I was seeking someone with whom to go hitch-hiking, leaving at 4 a.m. the next day from my house.

That evening I told Father and Mother I had read this incredible book about a man who wandered around Europe all his life. He went from place to place feeling he was light and knowing he would find only good. Wherever he went he found friends and love. When old he had a talk with God about his feeling that he had not accomplished anything with his life. He had no wife, no children, no home. He had done nothing.

136

God told him, "... the kindness and tenderness you gave ... Can't you see that you had to be a gadabout and vagabond to bring people a bit of child's folly and child's laughter wherever you went? To make all sorts of people love you a little and tease you a little and be a little grateful to you?

"You were a wanderer in my name and wherever you went you brought the settled folk a little homesickness for freedom."
He had left behind spiritual works. I knew I had found "my life" in this book. I said to myself, "I will live freely, I will be an example of freedom."

I am not talking about the Freedom my mother yelled about — as if by screaming, "I want to be free in this country," one can become free! No. I wanted to be an example of Real Freedom, the Freedom of the Self. You can put me in jail; I can live in a totalitarian country; you can say I have to change my life because I just had a child; or, I can't paint my house because your estimate is more money than I have ... You can do or say whatever you want, but you can't make **me** stop loving you. You can't make me a slave **if** I don't allow it. If I stopped loving you, I would become a slave.

Therefore, I told Mother and Father I would go hitch-hiking to the south of Argentina. I needed to confirm by my own experience that one meets what one Is. I knew myself to be light, nothing could happen to me. They listened and I saw they did not believe a word I said.

The next morning at 4 a.m. I got up, dressed, and the phone rang; someone had seen my notice. We made arrangements to meet at Once (a train station). I went to the bedroom to kiss Father and Mother goodbye.

Father was half asleep. "Where are you going?"
"I told you last night."
"You were serious about it?"
"Of course!"
He was getting up to stop me. I knew it, and left very quickly. I would not let him stop me!

This was 1956; the hippy movement had not yet happened throughout the world. Teen-age girls did **not** go hitch-hiking by themselves in South America. I did! I had to know if the theory was correct! I needed to prove I was light! Later, when the hippy movement began, I felt, "Go my children. I know what you are doing. I did it too!" But I looked very square, so the hippies could not quite identify with me. When I opened my mouth, the squares could not quite believe me!

I had only enough money for the train to go outside Buenos Aires Province. (Later trips I made this a practice.) I put the sleeping bag on the platform outside the last wagon of the train, and slept.

When I awoke and opened my eyes I found eight people looking at me! They had never before seen a sleeping bag. They were frightened! They didn't know what it was . . . and sometimes it moved! My head was inside so they could not see me.

When I came out we all laughed. I could not convince them I was not cold. My interpretation was, "We love you Beatriz, we don't want you to be cold." I talked with them, we laughed, we sang, we parted.

I was invited to sleep indoors in the mail car. The mailman and I became friends. When we arrived at the end of the line he took me to his house. I met his wife, spent a beautiful day with them, and decided to continue my travels that evening. They were worried about me, so he introduced me to a truck driver he knew and told him to take good care of me. In this way I was passed from person to person like a precious crystal.

My travels became sacred to me. They were extraordinary, but the important part to me was my purpose for taking the trips: to meet that which I was. I knew that even if I met someone who usually kills, to me that person would be kind. I just knew it. But one must test oneself too! First one develops the theory, then it must be tested — the mind, the body, the emotions, in other words: spirit!

One cannot become a surgeon on paper, a pianist by reading music, or a gymnast by looking at the movements in a picture. To Become, one must practice, one must **Do**. Through Doing, one Is, one Becomes. So I took action: First I thought, then I talked, and last I did!

At one point a truck driver said to me, "You know we rape women, no kidding."

I looked at him, believing every word he said, and smiled. "I believe you, yet, you will not do that to me!"

He looked back and said, "You're right. I don't know why, but I couldn't. Not only that, but I'm terribly worried people will think badly of you at the next town because you're wearing those blue jeans. Don't you have a skirt?"

"No." Wearing blue jeans in the interior of Argentina in 1956 was **not** done. One who did, must be "bad." What else, alone and wearing pants? But, he was kind. I was only receiving love.

There it was I knew it!

I traveled twice a year, summer and winter, until I left Argentina. I went to be with nature and with people, to mingle in worlds which were different from the one where I usually lived, but above all, to experience how truly we are one. They were life-giving trips! My travels gave me a place to test my theory. As a consequence, I met people whom I love and who love me to this very day, though we met for a few hours and continue our relationship through the years only by mail. We met in a place and space where distance does not dim the caring, where time does not seem to matter.

Here is a story of people with whom I still correspond:

On this trip I went to Iguacu Falls, on the border of Brazil, with a group of people. When I arrived at the Falls everyone was happy and wanted to sing along as they walked the trails.

I was horrified! I wanted the silence of the forest — as if the forest were silent! I wanted to hear the birds, to delight in the noise of my feet against the ground. I wanted to contemplate the incredible diamond produced by the dew on a spider's web with the rising sun shining through it. I wanted to be part of it all but did not have the concentration necessary to ignore the singing, since I was not Master of myself.

I broke away from the group, deciding to do part of the trip alone, and hitch-hiked back to Misiones.

In El Dorado I met the Alegre family. They owned a furniture store and a hotel. She was a school teacher and they had one child. First I met him and told him of my adventures. He invited me to meet his wife and child. This in itself was a miracle. Men did not meet women and then take them to meet their wives! Yet, it always happened to me. They gave me supper. We talked and laughed. I helped their child with his school work and retired to sleep. They gave me a room in their hotel.

Next morning I got up, had breakfast and washed the dishes. We kissed, hugged and said goodbye, and I went on my way.

We have written each other for years. I was almost 17 when we met. After my 23rd birthday they wrote me in Canada.

El Dorado, Misiones
June 1964

Dear Beatriz:

. . . we never imagined we could visit Canada, but now that a member of our family is there, that is a real possibility . . .

I returned from the first trip after one month. Mother and Father were settled down by then and I told them my adventures. I was sick from eating mutton for a month in the South. My stomach was not accustomed to it.

I had discovered a few things. One was how the land affects people. In Misiones the earth is red, full of life and strength, as are the people. In Patagonia the earth is arid, the vegetation grows slower than in Misiones, and the pace of the people reflects that of the earth.

Another was that if something is beyond one's experience, one tends to deny it. A man in Patagonia had a question he had asked many people before. He said every one of them had lied to him, but he knew I would not lie. The question was: "Is it true that in Buenos Aires, people get on a bus full of people who do not know each other?" (Buenos Aires was already a city of eight million people.)

I answered, "Of course!"

He looked at me heart stricken — I had failed him — and said, "I trusted you. I believed you would be the one person who would tell me the truth." I realized there was nothing I could say to convince him I had not lied to him. How could he believe this story? In Patagonia everyone knew everyone else for miles and miles. There was nothing in his experience which even suggested the possibility of so many strangers. Since he could not fit it into his categories without having to destroy his understanding, he chose to believe we all lied to him. That way he was sad, but intact.

In the dating game, I found it very difficult to put my emotions aside. I felt enormous pain through each person who came near me. Each time I thought this one would allow me to love and make a home for him, and in a minute I had lots of dreams in my head. Then, a few hours or days later, I would discover I had been used, that the person had only wanted to go to bed with me.

Oh, yes, I could have changed! I could have not trusted the next person and said I would not give myself completely until the wedding. I felt that was wrong. I saw it as a form of blackmail (If **you** give me this, **THEN I WILL** give you myself!), of legalized prostitution. I did not want someone to give me something because I was withholding his need. No! I wanted to satisfy the other person completely and **then** receive from his fullness and overflow of love. The game of making one's body scarce so the man would marry, seemed sick to me! I would not play! I would not change. I would not stop trusting, no matter what! Naive? Yes, I would rather be naive all my life than learn not to trust!

Time went by; the pain increased. As more men went through my life, I wondered, "Will I ever find the Human Being who will understand that I can set **no** limits in my life? I express who I am only by giving 100%. Will someone see **Me** someday, buried under all this pain? Can anyone see the diamond inside, that goes against all conventions?" I did not know. I just kept Being. (**I WILL** continue **EVEN IF** it hurts, and **EVEN IF** I do not know.)

Morality was not my concern. I was not eating of the Tree of Good and Evil. I ate from the Tree of Life. Everything that came to me was from God. I could see God in everyone. How could I say, "No"? Each time I learned to know myself better. That was the job: to get to know myself; to go wherever the road went.

When the pain was too much I locked myself in the bathroom and, standing in front of the mirror, talked to the U.N. about Peace in the world. I cried because they would not listen. I talked for hours. Then I would look at myself and remember how Castro had spoken for hours at the U.N. "Who do you think you are, Beatriz, Castro?" I would laugh at myself and feel better. Then I would come out.

That has been my retreat: the bathroom and my talks in it about Peace. Now I am out of my "closet" (bathroom) and talking about Peace publicly. I did not see the connection then between my pain and Peace. Now, I do. Pain was the road to my Peace, the inner Peace we will all have.

I started work selling patterns door to door, and was good at it! After a few months I decided to sell something intangible. I felt that was my line. So I sold insurance, among other intangibles, and realized I could sell anything invisible. I could actually trap people with my words! But, as my father pointed out after I became aware that I could do it well, I did not feel good about how I was using my ability! I was profiting by exploiting their fear, using the formula: "If you . . . THEN . . ." Since the formula was wrong, I stopped.

Then I worked for Compania Continental S.A., in the Department of Exchange, and there learned the great part intuition plays in the process of doing business. The spiritual purpose of business is to help the person develop more fully as a Human Being and get closer to God — the One Source, the Force, the Self . . . whatever you want to call it — through the development and use of Intuition.

The more one trusts his "hunches," the more he can do what no one else has done, and the more successful he becomes. Intuition takes one to the "Central Library," the source of all new ideas. The more a person goes there the more sure he is of himself. With practice he learns that his "hunches" do not lie to him. He becomes a better businessman.

I practiced getting "hunches" every day by reading the paper and trying to read between the lines to know what the banks were going to do. Will they start selling today? Are they going to buy? I kept a record of my own findings. I stopped when I became aware I could completely trust my Intuition. I had refined my skill.

A "hunch" is Intuition speaking to us. Intuition speaks in many languages. Dreams are another way Intuition communicates with us, telling us what we need to know. I don't dream, but when people tell me their dreams, I find they always have to do with something I need to know myself, as if the Universe is talking to me through others. Weird? But true.

Freddy was born when I was 18 years old and I never believed he was my brother. My son was born! I took every taxi in town and told them Freddy was mine. I never believed he was not. I knew he did not come through me, but he was mine!

When Mother had announced to us she was pregnant, I'd exploded, "How could you do this to me! I will have to take care of him. You know that." That came from way down deep. I don't know why I said it. She died and I did raise Freddy. I continued saying he was my child.

People kept telling me, "Don't say that. One day you will have a child, and then you will know you are talking nonsense."

I do have a child of my body now. I am no longer 18 years old. I still say Freddy is mine.

When Freddy was a baby, Mother changed his diapers every four hours. Each time she said, "Oh Freddy, how beautiful! You are extraordinary. Your bowel movement is perfect! What a nice color! What a great smell! I did not know you could do so many things so well, being so small, . . ." She would go on and on.

I could not believe my ears! "What are you saying? What do you mean, what a great smell? He stinks!"

She looked at me as she had never looked at me before, with a very stern look, as if trying to impress me with something of great importance. "Beatriz, how do you think **you** got to be so strong, so sure of yourself? By **me** telling **you** from birth that the one and **only** thing you could **do**, to shit, was horrible, smelly, and how **dare** you give **me** work?

"No! To build confidence you tell the person how wonderful he is **even if** he stinks! He will change. Remember, no human condition is **ever** permanent."

I burned these words into my mind. It was the formula:
"**I will** compliment them, **even if** they . . .
"**If** I do it **then they will** have confidence (because nothing is permanent)."

A complete circle:
From: **I will** . . . **even if** they . . .
To: **If I** . . . **then they will** . . .

I will tell the person how generous he/she is **even if** he sees himself as tight.

I will tell them how powerful they are **even if** they see themselves as weak.

I will tell the person "you are a leader" **even if** he/she sees himself as part of a group.

If **I** tell him, he/she will experience his own generosity, and **then he will** want to continue Being.

If I tell him, he/she will experience his own power, and **then he will** want to continue Being.

If I tell him, he/she will experience his own leadership, and **then he will** want to continue Being.

One day Allan will feel confident. He'll find his inner strength! Nothing is permanent.

My father had an accident one year after Freddy was born. The economy of our household was terrible. While Father was in the hospital, the cash flow stopped. I felt the problem. It never occurred to me Mother could or would solve it. Anyhow, she had Freddy to keep her busy. Ana Maria was studying — a brilliant student — no need to distract her.

As the economic situation deteriorated I thought I should leave the country and take my family somewhere outside, where life could be easier, social class would not dictate our economic needs, and Mother would feel she could work. Needless to say, no one believed I would leave.

At that time, I had a good job and very good salary working from 12 to 3:30 p.m. or a Casa de Cambios. I had friends. Leaving was **not** what I wanted for myself. It was what I thought I needed to do for the family. This was a task that had nothing to do with what emotions I felt. The training for doing what one must, and loving it, was continuing.

A month before I left, my sister went to see a lady who told her fortune using astrology. I did not know much about astrology then. The lady told Ana Maria she was going to have a great life and lots of money, etc. Since I was feeling a bit depressed, I wanted to visit someone who would tell me wonderful things too. My attitude was definitely **not** one of a believer. I went, hoping she would lie to me as well.

Well, I was in for a surprise! She neither lied nor told me wonderful things! She told me I was going to leave the country, which was true. I would meet a tall man with black hair who had something to do with engineering but who was not an engineer. She could not see **what** he would be, she said, "Because it depends on what you do." Then she said, "You will return to Argentina before the second year after you leave, and you will always have food, but . . . that is all."

How would you feel? That was the last thing I wanted to hear! I was about to leave Argentina. Who wanted to know, "You will always have food, . . . that is all"?

As you can imagine, I forgot all about it. This was not something I wanted to remember. I did not believe in all that anyway! But when I met Allan a year later — a tall man with black hair, who had studied engineering — I had to give it a second thought. I wrote Ana Maria from Canada to say I would definitely not go back to Buenos Aires as the astrologer had said. But then I **did** return for a visit one and a half years after I left!

143

That was the first time I tried to use astrology to soothe my emotions. It back-fired. But life proved to me that what she said was true. Later I learned to use astrology as a guide, a recipe. The astrology charts give me the ingredients of a meal; they tell me with what I am working. It is up to me to use those ingredients in any way I choose. The same ingredients in a recipe can produce different cuisines. I can burn the dish, but then I should **not blame** the recipe for **my** inability to carry it out.

While I was on the way to Canada I received more proof that we meet what **we** Are. The plane stopped at Lima, Peru. While waiting at the airport, I was looking at some gold rings when a man asked which one I liked. He bought it for me. Out of the blue he bought me a beautiful gold ring! The first Gold Ring (shades of Tolkien)! I would have it until the end of an era. That ring got lost on the beaches of the Mediterranean the day I sent the telegram asking Allan for the divorce.

Later, on the plane, the same man, Dr. Enrique P. Durrieu, D.V.M., offered me a job as his representative, selling horses in Canada. I said I would do it after I could speak English well enough and had gotten organized. He got off in New York. We kept in touch for a year, until I decided I could not be his representative. I truly admire people who can put 100% of their energy into a career and then go home and put 100% of their energy there too. I simply can't and I knew it. My choice was marriage.

From Lima to New York I also met an Egyptian gentleman. He gave me the name of a person whom he hoped would give me a job. I had not arrived in Toronto and I had a recommendation plus a job offer.

The Egyptian and I kept in touch for a few years. Through his letters I learned about his family and how much he missed them while on his travels, now that he was working for the World Bank in Washington, D.C. He felt he had to make sacrifices because he was doing important work for the world. He spoke a language I understood.

It gave me great pleasure to know that there were people in the world working to improve conditions, while I was still trying to find out how I would help. But that is not why I kept in touch and still remember him. He was not only helpful by giving me a connection — which I didn't use — but he also gave me confidence by lifting me with his words at a crucial moment. When I confronted obstacles in the first few years in Canada, his words kept coming to my mind. "When you are forty years old, the world will know about you." These **words** helped me to keep going.

We think guns are the only powerful weapons? Words Have

More Power! We can use them to kill or to uplift. Guns destroy fewer people than the Power of the Word. The killers are the "put downs," the judgments coming from every corner telling us, "You are No Good!... You are not good enough!... What you have done is rotten ... What you have written is unpublishable!" Words are more powerful than any atomic bomb. They have kept us in pain, acting in fear. Words **can lift** so much that we feel, "I am, I can and I will." We are afraid of guns, but we **can** fight them with the invisible Word. The invisible **always** wins!

TO YOU	A TI
To you, who confronted the world to your own conscience.	A tí, que enfrentaste al mundo a tu propia conciencia.
To you, who forgot customs, luxury and convenience.	A tí, que olvidaste costumbres comodidad, conveniencia.
To you, who love freely without criticizing others.	A tí, que amas libremente sin criticar lo ajeno.
To you, who entered my soul and have seen what I have not.	A tí, que entras en mi alma y ves lo que no veo.
To you, who gave me light of I Am, I Want, I Can.	A tí, que me diste la luz del soy, quiero y puedo.
To you, who soon I will lose because that is my presentiment.	A ti, que pronto perdere porque asi lo presiento.
You, yes, you have my truth and for that, I love you.	Tú si, tu tienes mi verdad. y por eso, te quiero.

By Maria Auxiliadora Lopez Fortes

Winter, 1980

Dedicated to Beatriz

Nerja, Spain

(From "Porque Quiero al Mundo . . ."
© Beatriz G. Prentice, 1981
Ore Press, Inc.
Sunnyvale, CA 94088)

I arrived in Toronto knowing I did not have the $500 cash required by immigration. But I knew I had examined my motives, and if I had not lied to myself, I was going to get through. The officer looked at me: well dressed, standing erect, sure of myself like a queen — as I always felt. My knees were trembling. I did not know if I could walk out of there in one piece. When I threw my purse at him, looked straight in his eyes, and said, "Look for yourself," he was surprised and a bit flustered. He did not even notice I had not answered his question. "It's OK," he said, without looking into my purse. I was counting on my knowledge of feelings. I was 22, and I got through.

No one was waiting for me in Canada when I arrived on February 29th, 1964. I was alone in a country I did not know. Within 48 hours I met Estherelka and Robert Kaplan, who became my dearest friends. She was Matron of Honor at my wedding. Today he is the Attorney General of Canada. It is right for loving people to be in high places. It is through love and compassion that we will all get the Planet moving in the direction in which it **must** go. They made me feel whole, cared for and loved.

I started to work immediately, taking care of their child, Jennifer. I threw myself at her. I had a child again! When later I had to separate myself from her, I felt such pain I could not go see her for a long time — I was so wrapped up in my own pain, I was not even aware of the pain she must have felt. She was mine! Who says our children are only those who come through our bodies? That was certainly not my experience.

I was so happy! Canada was home immediately: the green, the snow, the squirrels — which I had seen before only in cartoons — the people. It was an enormous change of pace for me coming from Buenos Aires. In Canada, things were slow and easy. People did not push and rush to get into buses. Bus drivers were polite and helped old people. I was in Heaven. My love for Canada was recognized in Argentina.

Ramos Mejia, Argentina
August 7, 1964

Dear Betty:

I hope and wish with all my heart that you are well. You don't know how long the days are without your presence. I say that you are absent because the postman goes by and does not leave me a letter . . . Well Betty dear, we are already in August; it seems incredible: already six months since you left! Many times you left, but never was your absence so long and never did I have the feeling I would not see you again. But what are we going to do? It will be what God wants. I ask Him that He let me embrace you . . . once more. We all love you and wish you success in that country which you already love so much and we have learned to love too through your words.

We received your cheque but not a line. I hope you are all right. Please write. Kisses from everyone.

Mama

Note: I couldn't take time to write "a line" because I was so busy "Here and Now." I was already beginning the Latin American Association and organizing dances for us.

The love I felt for Canada, and which my family had recognized gave me the clarity to see **Who** Canadians were, **What** they had done, and **Why**. This clarity prompted me — at this time when Canadians were searching for an identity — to write to the Governor General and his wife, pleading they make Canadians realize they DO have an identity.

Hamilton, Canada
April, 1967

Dear Mr. and Mrs. Roland Michener:

I read about you both, I guess like everybody else. But I got the feeling that I must write . . . to let you know my feelings about you.

Through "the great medium" the "press," I read that Mrs. Michener was concerned with having a quiet room in the new residence; this was her main concern.

Somehow there is human warmth through your statements, and that makes me feel more than happy . . .

I am a new Canadian, as you can see by my English (slightly corrected for this book). I came three years ago and married a Canadian young man who, like your daughter, chose journalism as his profession. Right now he is preparing for his Masters in Journalism. As you saw when I said "the Press," I was being prejudiced! I guess we all have our little ones.

I think you both will have a great deal to do with uniting Canada. Make Canadians realize what they are! Make them see that they do have an identity. The role that Canada played, plays and will play in international politics shows very well what Canada is. Canada was able to go to the Crown and convince the Parliament that she was able to look after herself. This was not done at that time. No other Colony was able to become a Country without a fight first. Canada did it. THIS IS CANADIAN IDENTITY. It seems to me that nobody sees it. Through the little I read about you I can see you will do something for this Country, because you are not afraid of doing something which was not done before . . . These are excuses.

I can see Mrs. Michener is very thoughtful: the fact that she writes guides . . . (for government wives) shows it. She realizes how much a wife has to learn when a husband is in a new position, and how many times his career depends on the kind of wife or hostess he has. And she likes to ease the road for those who come after her, by doing these guides. Good for you! . . . I always knew that there are people who are in the right positions and doing what they feel is right.

"There is nothing wrong with Power, it is what we do with it." How much I would like to have a talk with you both! . . .

For a while, my husband will keep on studying, and I keep on working, and in this way we may achieve our goals. I wish you the best of luck and I would like you to know that you can count on our spiritual support in this highly difficult task of uniting Canada.

By the way, I am by birth Argentinian. I guess that is all. I do not want to take more of your time.

Peace and Love are my sincere wishes for you both,

Mrs. Allan Prentice

I saw Canada as a Peacemaker, Moderator. Only by using this skill could she have so peacefully won her independence.

After seven months of sending money home, I had received letters from Mother releasing me: ". . . please Beatriz, if you find a good man and you love him, please accept him and don't think of us. You have to build your life and I do not want you to refuse anyone because of us . . ." and ". . . Don't worry about sending money, God willing; we will manage . . . with the new rentals." So in December I announced I would be married in March and have the reception at the Granite Club — the best club in Toronto.

Oh! People were delighted and asked me who was the lucky guy.

I would say, "I don't know, I haven't met him yet!" (Actually we had already come in contact, but had not truly met.)

Everyone laughed! This is crazy Beatriz again! But the 26th of the next March I married Allan Prentice, and the reception was held at the Granite Club.

This was to be the biggest job I had undertaken. Life for me is a spiritual job. So marriage was just that, a job! I was looking for two things. First, I **needed** someone who would need me and see what I could do for him. Second, I **wanted** someone who would want all my love and also understand who I was. I did not want ever to be expected to say, "I'm sorry, this is what I did. I'll not do it again!" No! I was who I was because of what I thought, felt, and did. Not only did my prospective husband have to love me as I was, he also had to love every minute of my life previous to our meeting; including loving Roberto. Total acceptance. Those were the ingredients.

Upon my arrival in Canada, I had contacted Subud, the World Organization I had joined just before leaving Argentina. Through it I had met a wonderful family. The lady was kind and frequently invited me for lunch or dinner.

She would send her son, Allan, to pick me up. Our conversations were always the same: incredibly boring. Although English was new to me, I could understand everyone except Allan. I thought the problem was his. He made language jokes, puns. I did not catch them. Seeing that they had gone over me, he would laugh. When I saw him laughing, I laughed, thinking he must have said something funny . . . Can you imagine those conversations?

I told his mother, "Such a nice family, what a pity Allan is retarded!" She said he was not. So I told her about the speech problem her son seemed to have. She looked at me but said nothing. Later she turned on the radio and informed me that the news we heard was read by Allan. So the guy was a radio announcer! And I thought he had a speech problem!

After that you would think I'd put two and two together and realize the man did **not** have a problem; I had the problem. Not a chance! That's Beatriz . . .

One day when Allan came to pick me up, he looked up the stairs at me and I felt as if I had been undressed. It was **not just** a physical thing: I felt as if someone had looked right **through** me. I asked, "Why did you look at me like that?"

But he only responded, "I did not look at you."

I knew there had been a moment of spiritual union, even if he denied it. So later the same evening, I asked what he thought about God — my long-time stock question. His four-hour answer showed me he was the person for me to marry.

He asked me for a date. He was to pick me up at 10 o'clock in the morning. He did not come. I **knew** he was interested in me. I **felt** it! I sat on a rocking chair and waited all day to see when he would show up.

At the time I was living with another woman. She asked, "Why are you waiting? Why bother with him?"

"I have a feeling I want to check out," I answered. I felt he needed me.

By 8 PM it was time to go to Subud. I knew he would be there. If I went, that would make it easier for him. If he needed me as much as I felt, he would have to come to me. (I am female energy, I attract **to** me.) So I continued to wait.

Allan called after Subud, at 9 PM, and said he would come. He arrived at 10 PM. During that last hour, I had a long talk with my roommate. Through it I clarified and decided what I was going to do.

She questioned me, "Why did you say 'yes' about him coming now? Why go out with someone who is 12 hours late on the first date? **Obviously** he does not care. Can't you see that?"

No, I did not see that. What I saw was someone who was so frightened that he would do anything to sabotage whatever he started. Since I knew I could love anyone, my problem was to find someone who wanted **me.** Right then I decided, "If he wants me, I will love him so the fire of my love will dissolve his paralyzing fear. He will be free. I will do it!"

Again I decided what emotions I would have and how I would work through or with them. All my life I have only one enduring feeling: Love. It grew from love of one person to two, three, larger groups, to countries. But always those I loved were known to me. More recently, I have learned to love those who are not known to me.

Those 12 hours were the beginning of the longest training I have put myself through. Oh, I know I could have walked away. But only through hard training can one achieve progress, not just in spirit, but in anything.

The work began. "He is not late because he doesn't like you. It is because he is afraid. I will be here day after day for as long as it takes to show him my love, to show him there is nothing to fear." From that day on I ignored what I felt, and only kept my eyes on him, reminding myself constantly that when he did not give of himself, come, take me out, it was because he was afraid. "Just be there, just call him, day after day, and he'll realize that **he is important.** Not just one day, one month, but consistently through the years. You will succeed, Beatriz."

On one of our first few dates, we visited the home of a friend of mine. I happened to reach out and put my hand on Allan's. He tensed slightly. Suddenly, he began to imitate Donald Duck extremely well. I was so delighted (this was the first time I heard that voice) — he sounded so funny — I jumped next to him on the couch and kissed him in front of my friend, a perfect stranger to Allan!

Allan froze! I continued Being myself.

Later, Allan told me I had "crowded" him. It would take 15 years before he would be strong enough to deal with his own responses to other people.

Meanwhile, I had to keep reminding myself that his "crowding" problem had nothing to do with me.

I also soon came to realize that although he was a capable journalist, he would only speak his **own** mind through that self-effacing Donald Duck voice, because he was deathly afraid of what anyone might think of Allan Prentice.

I realized that I had to **decide** whether or not to marry Allan. That decision **could not, must not,** be based on my **feelings.** Feelings are here today, gone tomorrow. My commitment had to be based on things that are firm, stable, solid, eternal.

I needed to know how he felt about children: how were we going to raise them? Was he a healthy person? Was there any serious illness in his family? What was the possibility of having a retarded child? Would I have to decide not to have children? If so, did I want that?

We sat down and I asked Allan and his mother every conceivable question about the mental and physical health of his family. I needed data.

Meanwhile, he thought if he showed any disagreement I would walk away. He didn't want that, so he didn't disagree; he just said nothing. I thought if one presents a point of view and no one speaks up, there must be agreement. I was very **wrong** in this case!

He was right, I would have walked away. Marriage is serious business. I loved him, but I knew I could love any Human Being. I would not marry just because I fell in love. I could ignore such feelings. I needed to know for what purpose I would be undertaking that spiritual job. What was my love to contribute, accomplish? With Allan I saw an appropriate purpose.

I imagine football players must feel something like this. They have a purpose: to play. But they also want to stay up late, eat junk food, etc. They ignore their desires which might interfere with obtaining the results they want. **Self-discipline** is what life is all about. This is **not** denial from outside, but from oneself. It reveals the real Freedom: to be able to do anything and yet be able to firmly choose what one really wants to accomplish, no matter how difficult. The same self-discipline is learned from fasting, not because one does not have money for food, but because one chooses to control oneself.

This is the training of oneself: conquer the emotions, so that they are what one wants them to be, master the body, to obey and move exactly as one wants it to move, and school the mind to thoughts which lead to feelings of Peace and Freedom (from which ecstasy is a result). This training is accomplished by choosing "conscious pain." A smart person chooses the hardest university when he could go to an easy one. That is a choice of hardship, yet the world sees it as a good, clever choice. If you choose to develop your body, the world understands, "No pains, no gains." However, if one chooses a life situation clearly providing emotional pain, therefore exercising one's emotions, the world thinks one is mad, or a masochist. Why?

Only through absolute Control of every muscle can one freely express movement . . .

Only through absolute Control of Mind, Body, **and** Feelings can one express spirit.

Once all my questions were satisfied, I was able to make a conscious decision. I said "Yes" to Allan. We both were happy. But I warned him, "If you marry me, don't expect me to clean or cook. I'll share your **life**." He did not believe me. He should have!

I knew he was emotionally stuck. I also knew I could unstick him, make him realize he could give. Only through being emotionally free could that extraordinary mind bear fruit. I saw my marriage to him as that job of helping him to Become free. I knew I could not go where he would go then. But I wanted to be part of the preparation. Through this Human Being the cosmos was going to have something from me.

I told him, "In seven years you will be all right. We will have to part then." I do not think he believed it. I took the job knowing what I was getting into, what I wanted to accomplish, and that I would not be there to collect the fruits. I was telling him, "Love is a creative principle which I will channel to accomplish a specific purpose." I intended to use love to burn out his lack of confidence — Fear — so that he could become aware of his own true self — Love.

What I did not know was what it could cost me, nor what I would get out of it. Getting something out of it did not occur to me. I had no concept of myself benefitting from my helping others. I only learned that in March, 1981.

It did not take me long to realize I was not to have emotional contact with Allan until he was really emotionally free. This began to unfold a few hours after the ceremony. He did not want to leave the party! He showed no interest in being alone with me. Beatriz — "if you give her lemons she makes lemonade" — looked at the situation, laughed and said, "How many times are we going to get married? Of course we want to enjoy the party to the last minute."

But then there was the second day, and the third . . . We visited and dined with his immediate family, went to see friends of mine, and then to see members of his family whom I had not yet met. We laughed about our unorthodox honeymoon, but I knew then I had to wait. My only personal wish, from that first day, was to have two hours of Emotional contact with Allan, with him entirely focused on me . . . like lying on the floor **together** listening to a record . . .

When we see a light flickering on and off we know there is an open circuit somewhere. When we see a sick person we don't seem to realize there is a problem circuit in his/her mind.

If we observe the type of illness, we can tell what type of thoughts the person has. Allan was all in knots emotionally; he could not let go. Was it strange then that he experienced constipation? No, of course not.

As a child, I went to Mother twice with physical complaints. "Mommy, my throat hurts."

Mother looked at me and said, "Why are you telling me that, I am not thinking your thoughts!" Her cold eyes added: "Why come to **me, you** are responsible for that."

After the second time, I realized I better keep healthy, control my thoughts. I could not put dirty gasoline in my car, and expect a smooth ride!

The one overwhelming feeling I had had since I met Allan was, "I am a virgin." I told Allan. Oh, how I felt it! I wrote to my mother of this incredible feeling. "I am a virgin!" I wanted to scream it to the world. In fact, everyone thought that I **was** a virgin in the traditional way!

Since I look at every thing from the spiritual point of view, I looked within for the basis of my virginity. Bingo! There it was: It did not matter with how many men I had been. I was a virgin just as a spring of water remains pure, no matter how many travellers stop and drink its unadulterated, virginal water. That was the meaning of virginity. I knew it was true. My mother wrote: "You are mad . . ." But when I explained, she understood.

Allan wanted to know every thought I had. I could barely speak English! I wanted him to read the book which could say so much about me: *Knulp* by Hermann Hesse. But that book was not translated into English until 1974! Never mind that book, few people in Toronto in 1964 had ever heard of Hermann Hesse (1946 Nobel Laureate in Literature). They spoke of authors I did not recognize. I felt culturally deprived.

I wanted him to understand my pilgrimage on Earth and why I talked so much about death. Death was my friend. Because I remembered it every minute I was full of life. I never passed up an opportunity to tell someone, "I love you." I did not want death to take me, or them, before I had said it.

Hamilton, Canada
March 20, 1967

Dear Anita:

We wish to thank you for your companionship this last week-end. As Esther said: "She is as beautiful as a flower." Your soul daily peeks through your face more radiantly.

With all carinos
B & A

But people don't speak of death at 22 in this society. They don't plan when they are going to die, or how, as I was doing. He was frightened. So were my friends.

I did not fear death. Because of it I was free to try anything. The thought of death propelled me to be more open, to appreciate everything much more. I am very aware of how temporary everything is. I could not procrastinate for I knew I was going soon. "There is so much to do! . . . and so little time in which to do it!" Its presence made it possible for me to continue. How could I give up?

But I did not live in a rush. I never run. I just was always 100% with whomever. People call it intensity. I say it is the focusing of all my energy on one point at a time, treating everything as if it were a matter of life and death — and at another level concurrently knowing it really does not matter.

When Mother died I looked back and knew that each moment I had done my very best, precisely because I had treated each moment as if it were the most important moment in my life. I loved her and had shown her my love. We were friends.

Buenos Aires, Argentina
April 17, 1967

My dearest Betty:

. . . I speak to you as my best friend because that is what you are for me, and I know you will understand . . .

Chau, besos
Mama

She was right about my friendship. Since childhood she had always confided in me. I understood. I often asked myself, what could I not understand?

If I had it to do all over again I could not do it better. With what I knew, with what I had, with what I felt, I had done the best I could at the time. My conscience was clear. That is why I showed no remorse. What I could have done, I had done while she was alive!

Soon after the wedding I realized Allan would not take me anywhere except to bed. He was frightened.

Since Father and Mother had been such an example of independence within marriage, I decided to go to movies by myself. I also went out to dinner with my friend Brian. Nothing else I did meant as much to me. It was like minor jobs, keeping myself in as much balance as I could until Allan needed me, and at the same time being available when and if he wanted to open his door and come out.

The owner of the South America boutique wanted to go to Mexico to buy new merchandise for her shop. This was the same lady who had helped me begin the Latin American Association.

To go to buy — to generate more money — she had to leave the shop. Since I was not working at the time, I offered to look after it for the month she would be away — gratis.

One day while I was working at the boutique, I was robbed of $2.50. I told her husband and offered to reimburse him.

He said, "Forget it."

When she returned she did not get in touch with me. I heard from other people she was saying I was a thief.

My first reaction was of outrage.

Esther was furious. She wanted me to sue for slander. She felt I could not just sit on it. This person was hurting my reputation.

At that point, I felt very good to see Esther loving so much. (She loved justice and she loved me.) This gave me the clarity I needed to think it through:

"Could I sue from a loving place? No.

"Did I steal? No."

"Then . . . my conscience is clear. I don't know why that woman is telling this lie, but since I am not guilty I can just let it go." The system my mother had taught me as a child, when the girls blamed me for something I hadn't done, was useful. This was not the first or only time I applied the system she taught; it works! I can't change what the woman feels about me. I can't change others. But I **can** change my feelings. I am Master of them. If I change what I feel, I have changed the situation.

I wanted Allan to be Emotionally free, and then I would leave. Whatever else I wanted for me at other levels, was irrelevant. When asked what I wanted, I would respond, "It's not what I want; the question is: 'What does Allan want.'" I would say to myself, "Beatriz, you will have to wait until you find out what Allan wants. Then and only then will there be something for you to do."

Whenever Allan said or hinted that he wanted something, I tried to bring it about. I wanted to show him that there are no "pipe dreams." Dreams are the seeds of reality. If we can think of something, we can certainly bring it about. The only thing that can't be brought about is what we have not yet thought. By this process I was hoping he would see and feel what he did and did not like, really wanted, or wanted to throw away.

Columbia University was a real "pipe dream" for him. I exerted myself to show him he could do it.

We spent a year at Columbia. The department was a close-knit unit. The energy was high; the hours of work long: I slept no more than four hours in twenty-four. I worked during the day and kept Allan company until late at night. I read and criticized everything he wrote. I kept myself abreast of everything. I would not be one of those wives who are left behind!

The greatest of my discoveries that year occurred when we visited West Point. This was at the height of the Vietnam war. I went, determined to confront those military people. I wanted them to understand **Love,** Not War!

I sat at their table, ate their food, listened to their talk . . . and felt so very small! It was not hate that propelled them to fight, it was Love! They, far more than any of us on campus, felt the horror of the war. Their friends came home lame, or dead. Yet, they kept on marching. I realized then that the motivation to be nonviolent and the motivation to be violent were one and the same. Only the expressions were different. But I knew that the ones who decided for nonviolence would have a greater victory; and the ones who chose to fight would experience greater pain. Somehow, when I realized that, I could not confront them. I just laughed with them, felt compassion and really wanted to hug them, heal them, and tell them it would be all right.

Later, I realized that the ones who chose to fight would experience greater pain because they were operating from a smaller frame of reference: Love for only their own country. The others would have a greater victory and suffer less, because they were operating from a larger frame of reference: Love for their own country and for the other country as well.

Stanford was a shock. Maybe because New York City has the reputation of being the big cold city, everyone at Columbia had extended themselves. The Department of Journalism allocated money for a get-together every week. The campus is such that whatever happens, everyone knows. Because of people gathering together, one is bound to run into familiar faces everywhere, and therefore strike up friendships easily.

At Stanford, the school is geographically so spread out that when the Cambodia riots occurred, I heard about them on the radio and had to drive the car to the other end of Campus to see them. Because of the bigness and decentralization of the campus, one really has to make an effort to see and meet people.

When I arrived at Stanford I immediately looked for a job. I wanted the same type of job I had had in New York, with the same pay. I was told I could not get it here; the training was not good enough for California, where pay depended upon papers from schools. For the first time in my life, the outside world told me: "You can't do." . . . and I bought it! This began a nine year period of accepting more and more "social limits."

I dealt with this first "You can't," by volunteering my services. When Stanford saw what I could do, they offered me a job, which I left when Freddy came.

I discovered the Bechtel International Center. When I arrived the place was full of Arab students. This was my first close contact with that world. I had never thought about it before. But at a critical moment, when I could have felt lonely and disconnected, they were there. All those students were talking about home, telling me their stories, sharing their warmth and humanity, allowing me to cook for them and therefore making me feel useful. So much warmth! There were many stimulating discussions.

Bridges, bridges of love, of sharing, of becoming aware how very much alike we all are! Without all of you I could never have made it through. Oh . . .! We argued! We laughed! The newlyweds from Egypt: She was so terribly intelligent and so incredibly feminine! What a rare combination!

Fred Nassime, from Iran, lived with us for a while. He was the one who bought a bottle of champagne to celebrate my pregnancy. "A New Human Being is going to arrive. We have to celebrate!"

Once there was to be a T.V. program, "90 Minutes with Ben Gurion." Since they knew me well and loved me, I asked them to sit with me and watch the program. They did! While we were watching it together I knew it was a miracle of love. It happened because they loved me. Somehow on a small scale I was able to achieve, for a few minutes, a human bridge above old ideas. I knew again I was on the right track.

The argument I used to invite them was: if they thought Ben Gurion was an enemy, they should know what the enemy thought, to be able to fight back more effectively! I was trying my abilities to get others together. But I was doing it by presenting sides in terms of enemies. I myself could not yet see the way to explain that **There Are No Enemies.**

In December of 1970 or 1971 a few scholars from Russia came to Stanford. They brought their brains, their knowledge and their humanity. They cooked a sit-down Russian dinner for 120. They sang for us, played the piano, recited their poetry. The sweetness and feeling of their language was such that I got goose pimples.

One of them was Professor Tolstoy, the father of eight children, a big, warm man. He loved to talk about his family, his children, his music. He played piano superbly. I felt his pride, his love, his warmth.

I am sure his contributions in his field are many and great. But to me the human bridge was the most important one. The knowledge he may have will be washed away sooner or later. It will be outgrown. But the love left, the bridges made, will never die. My love for his land not only lives in me, but — through my talking — in the minds and hearts of many,many people, my son included. Those ties are not outgrown; they multiply. Through him I was able to feel close to a nation about which I otherwise

157

did not know much. Oh, yes, I could read about it. But as I wrote Ana Maria in 1967, "It's very difficult to . . . feel something for someone whom one does not know . . ." The level of human interaction is where we can feel each other, discover each other, experience the diversity and oneness of us all. Thanks to you, Mr. Tolstoy, I arrived at my center. Because you gave of yourself, you helped me to expand my world.

Since I knew very well that I do not own anyone and no one owns me, I was free to be of service to anyone. I never had a thought, "I have to clean, cook, wash, or whatever people think their obligations are, . . . or I can't be with so and so because I must do such and such." Never. I was there for however long it took, and only when finished would I go home. My only obligation was to be with people until they felt better, then move on to the next and the next.

The stronger I became through this giving, the more people noticed and remarked, "You are strong." The more they said that, the stronger I wanted to be.

But when they started to say, "You are wonderful," "You are such a spiritual person!" Oh boy! It was all lost! I felt my ego expanding. Since I could not allow my actions to be motivated by outside approval, I had to pull away from the approval and withdraw into myself. I would not allow myself to feel that important!

Everyone around me was giving workshops. They asked why I didn't. I even wrote some outlines and a proposal to the Whole Life Center. They approved it. But I did not feel right about it, so I withdrew. I had wanted to do it for validation from the outside. I knew my validation had to come from within Me.

During Woman's Week at Stanford I participated as always, and women from different groups, the city (San Francisco), and political women's organizations, wanted me to speak. They felt I was powerful and had a lot to say. They were right. They had the best of intentions, but they were saying nice things about me. As I heard them my pride ran higher and higher. I did not go; I did not speak. It would have been giving fuel to my pride, my ego. That, I would not do.

So in Palo Alto in the 70's I retreated and sat looking at an oak tree for several hours every day, for almost four years. I didn't tell anyone. I felt like such an idiot! I could not explain why I was doing it. I simply felt I had to, so I did.

For three years nothing happened. During the last six months an incredible experience occurred! I lost the sense of the limits of my body. I could see my arms but not feel where they finished. It was as if my skin opened and connected with the air and with the tree, so that each became a part of the other. There was a feeling that we were all one, with no divisions.

I realized how much like an oak I was: very strong, but not flexible. If a strong wind came, pieces of the tree or of me broke away, leaving a sense of loss.

Behind the oak I observed a poplar. This tree was tall, sometimes green, sometimes bare, but always flexible. It bent so that when the wind had gone by, the poplar would regain its posture without losing anything of itself.

I realized then that the poplar was stronger than the oak. I felt Allan was the poplar and I had great admiration for it!

So my retreats were to teach me I am not better! Yet, I am unique, as we all are! We are different only in our expressions, not in the essence. That became clearer and clearer as years went by.

I was born into a Latin culture. In that culture, when the youngsters become teenagers, their parents — because they love their children — want to keep them close by, at home. "Stay here, we love you."

I observed in the Anglo-Saxon culture, when the youngsters become teenagers, the parents — because they love their children — send them away, as the birds do. "Go out, try your wings."

Each of us **feels** the same; we **express** it differently.

Allan was the product of his culture, as I was of mine. When he was sad he expected me to leave him alone. On the other hand, if I saw anyone sad I would never leave until I could make them laugh and be happy. Well, it was a while until we were both able to understand that neither of us was trying to hurt the other, rather that each was trying to be loving in familiar ways. Our lack of understanding brought pain to both of us, until we understood. It is impossible to feel pain when one understands.

I was happy whenever I saw someone accomplishing what he had set out to do. People thought I was riding other people's trips. No. I just have no sense of where I end and the next person starts. There is no such place! I am one with each person, the plants, the animals, the world, the cosmos. What others have done, I have done. I could not distinguish between my happiness and their happiness.

It is like using a library. I can make use of the knowledge of someone else; it does not all have to come from me. If someone discovers the light bulb, we all can use it. It is in the body of public knowledge, where no one person possesses it. Happiness is the same.

Everyone had happy times and I shared them. If they were sad, I was there to support them at whatever hour for whatever length of time they needed.

I knew Allan thought about different people he loved: his mother, father, brothers, friends, professors. I knew his desire to communicate his feelings to them. He had tried to express himself even in his fear, through newsletters, radio, etc., behind various roles. But he did not take action on his desire to express himself face to face. He was breaking the Law: Thought, Desire, **No** Action. As a result, he was very unhappy. Only while he learned **to do**, to take action, would he begin to find his inner source. I knew I could teach him, but only by example. I had to follow the Law. (Thought, Desire, **Action**) It drove him crazy!

If I thought someone had a nice blouse — a perfect stranger — I would tell the person, "What a nice blouse you have." His embarrassment was tremendous! He'd ask me not to speak with people I didn't know. I could not do that! I would be breaking the law. I would be saying, "**You** + **Me** are **not US.**"

A stranger is a friend I have not yet met.

He wanted to hide. He thought I was the source of his embarrassment. His fear was that source. He constantly **blamed me** for **his** feelings. I constantly felt his lack of approval . . . yet I had to do it. Years later he realized and wrote:

Palo Alto, California
April, 1980
11:55 p.m.

Dear Beatriz:

. . . I've been living alone, these last two months. What a simple revelation! I see clearly that all the crap in my life that I somehow blamed you for, or whatever, was still there and I was alone! So it's mine and I'm shovelling it out . . .

Love
Allan

The first step Allan took to reach out face to face to show his feelings and share his actions, was when we began the sexual workshops in 1976.

Allan and I decided to tell our parents and friends about the sex experiences we were exploring. We could have done what we wanted and not told anyone. But . . . would these people love us for ourselves, or for the idea they had of us?

So I knew we had to talk. We agreed: No Secrets. I'll write my father in Argentina and phone Allan's parents in Toronto. Allan will talk to Andrea and Sean.

I was nervous; I did not know how they would react. Allan came from a strict family. He was still a virgin when he married, at age 26, and his two brothers are celibate in their thirties! You don't get three celibate boys out of a permissive household. The risk was enormous: they could disown us! We love them. We wanted them to love us, but US, not a lie! They accepted US.! We were scared about Sean and Andrea. They could turn and live without us as friends. We care for these people. We knew they were judgmental. These were not people who sit in the middle. They view the world as, "This is Good; that is Bad." And now, we wondered where they would place us. We hoped, in their hearts! They did.

My father answered with this letter:

Buenos Aires, Argentina
November 22, 1976

Dear Daughter:

. . . I am advised of all you have communicated to me. Congratulations! I hope you will find satisfaction in this new manner of living. I have never interfered in the lives of my children or of anyone else. Let people live their lives as they please, as I have lived mine . . .

Kisses,
tu papi

This is STRENGTH. What I do is an Open Book! No privacy.

WEAKNESS is to do what we want to do and keep it quiet in **fear** that others will take an action we may not like.

At the national level also, STRENGTH means NO SECRETS.

WEAKNESS generates: "TOP SECRET," "NATIONAL SECURITY!" This translates to, "**If you** know, **then I will** lose," at both personal and national levels. Thus "Privacy" is born.

We were strong. But is it a wonder that one can be strong, when one has received incredible unconditional love from birth? Is it possible **not** to respond with love? This little computer named Beatriz only responded to what programming was put into it. It recognized and filtered out any entering information which was not loving, as wrong information which did not belong in the computer!

It has taken me many years to recognize that other people were not told over and over how good they were. They did not receive Love from everywhere. I was a "privileged Being" because I knew what laws to use.

This was obvious to family and strangers alike.

Dear Betty:

. . . *you can see what life is, therefore we must expect anything and*
we must not tremble. To be strong as an Oak and continue ahead
without fear, without looking behind. This I do not need to tell You,
because you are one of those privileged beings who inhabit this planet
and who are full of virtues and of a strong spirit . . .

Good bye or so long
Maria Rosa
(lady who prepared
my wardrobe just be-
fore my departure from
Argentina)

Now, I just want you, all of you, to receive more Love than I
have received — if that is possible — by following these Laws.

When I went to sexual workshops I uncovered that when I was
four years old I had decided, "I'll show the world There Is No Evil,
There Is Only Good," because the girls at school had told me,
"You are Evil." My life had been based on that decision to live to
be a "Christ."

But at 36 years of age I realized I was not 4 anymore. No one
was saying, "You are Evil." I did not need to continue to live as I
had. But how **would** I live?

I began to operate as I saw the world operating ("keeping
accounts"): **If you** call me, **then I will** call you. **If you** will play
with me, **then I will** clarify your ideas. **If you** buy me a card for
Mother's Day, **then I will** buy you a card for Father's Day. **If you**
go camping with me, **then I will** be happy. **If you** do what I want,
then I will do what you want.

The feeling I experienced while operating in this manner, told
me clearly I did not want to live like that. It diminished me; I felt
insignificant. My actions were dependent on others; I was giving
my power away. I had never before acted this way.

Once I had learned the ways of the world, I was free to choose.
I chose my **old** formula. **I will** call you, **even if** you never call me. **I**
will buy a gift for you, **even if** you never reciprocate. **I will** care
for you, **even if** you think little of me.

Not to be a saint also meant it was OK to say, "No, I can speak
with you tomorrow, but not now," or, "I am having dinner now,
I'll call you later," instead of listening at the moment the person
called, as I always had. When Freddy would come to me,
expecting to find support right at that moment, I would say, "I

am busy now. I had planned to read (or whatever), but let's arrange for another time that is convenient for both of us."

It all seemed very reasonable, but I was changing one fundamental rule in my life. I had always been immediately available 100% to anyone who needed me. There never had been any conflict of time; things had always flowed one after the other. And now I was not available to anyone exactly when needed — for the first time in my life.

I felt terrible inside, trapped: the flow stopped. I had less time for myself than when I hadn't even planned time for myself. It was not only time, I had less **of myself for myself** (like stealing from your own bank account). So I returned to my old way.

The thought of society is that, "It is OK to think about something but one does not need to act on it." My philosophy was that the control must not only be in the action, but also in my Mind. So I continued looking into myself through what the world was saying.

Anger was the theme through some of the workshops and with some friends. "Everyone carries anger," they said.

I had never felt it. I decided maybe it was just buried; I must find out. I decided to take a course in "Intensive Journal."

The teacher asked why we were there. This was my answer.

Intensive Journal Class

I am Beatriz, a person who has been trying to answer the questions: "Who am I?" and "Where am I going?" since birth.

I am here because I'm trying to get in touch with my anger. I am not aware of it. Yet, since I have discovered what I decided as a child and therefore lived my life according to that decision, it makes sense that it was resentment. The decision was logical and justifiable at that time. Now, . . . it does not seem appropriate, so I am trying to change it. While doing this, I want to see or feel the anger that I must have felt, and get rid of it.

Exercise in Class

Twilight Imagery log.
A beach, a jungle — great peace within.

Stepping stone period (teenage)

Dancing, singing . . . pain . . . the pain . . .
The feeling of not being accepted . . . of not fitting.
That feeling through my entire life. Dreams . . . hours dreaming of a home, children, a husband, of peace in the world, of talking to the U.N., of feeling that everyone felt I was bad. The lack of approval.

163

Inner stepping stones

Got married against having career.
Pursuing relationship instead of putting energy into buying
houses, . . .

After this search I discovered I had no anger to get rid of. I understood! How can anger survive the light of understanding? Pain I felt, sadness too, compassion a lot; but anger, no.

Since I have friends of all different backgrounds, socio-economic levels — whatever that means — education, political persuasions, etc., when they get together in my house, things do not mix well at all. I can relate to all of them; but somehow the pacifist can't bring himself to peacefully toast champagne with the arms collector!

One day a Jewish friend was visiting me. Another friend dropped in and in two seconds it was obvious the second was a very prejudiced person. My earlier visitor just got up and locked herself in the bedroom.

When my prejudiced friend left, the Jewess was furious. "How can you have such a friend! How can you stand a person as prejudiced as that! How can you associate with her! Don't her comments make your blood boil?"

"No. I understand."

When I enter a room and see a baby six months old, I don't become angry because it does not walk. I know it can't yet; with time it will. We are all aware of our physical development because we can see it within the duration of our physical lives.

We are not immediately aware of our development in terms of evolution. In order to understand that, we must look and understand beyond the time frame and limitations of single physical life spans.

We fail to realize that just as there are stages of physical development and of evolution, there are stages for inner development. The time span for inner development is longer than for physical development, as is that of evolution. Therefore, for us to understand it, we **must** look from a longer time frame. It may take a Human Being a whole life-time being prejudiced, to learn not to be. The development of each Being is on a different time scale.

Just as I would not walk away from the baby because it does not yet walk — I would stay near so that by observation the baby might learn sooner — neither does it occur to me to walk away from any other Human Being. Any person may walk away from me. I don't abandon anyone for lack of **understanding** on my part.

164

For 16 years I badly wanted to emotionally share two hours with my husband. He never gave me that. I knew he was doing as much as he could. He was fearful. I felt pain for him because it is hard to be a prisoner of oneself, and for me, because I was not strong enough to melt his fear fast enough. What was there to be **angry** about?

Once I was feeling so badly I could not move. I was perfectly healthy, yet my legs would not obey me, my arms would not move. It was as if my will-to-live had left my body. I knew what I needed. I called Allan — he was in the bathroom — and implored him, "Please Allan, sit 5 minutes with me, hold my hand, just 5 minutes."

He looked, realized I was in bad shape, and said, "Beatriz, you better call Silver or you may not survive the night." I did call her, at one in the morning.

My angel came the following morning and touched me by applying Tiger Balm. I heard, "I love you Beatriz. I can stop my life for you."

The day after that I was new again.

Allan had walked away to his computer the first evening. Although he understood the situation — with his head — he had felt he did not have what I needed. Of course it was not true that "he did not have," but **he** thought so. To feel he did not have anything to give, anything to contribute, **has** to be the most painful of all experiences! So, although other people may have felt anger, I could not. That is why I **never** withdrew my love, my support, my caring. I understood.

I realized I had a great pain deep within me always, yet I was always happy, feeling well. In fact, I actually felt pain when it was relieved! Only when I got water did I realize I had been thirsty at all, and how very much. It really was weird!

I talked. Oh, did I talk! Why? Well, if I decided to be on my knees, after a while my knees would hurt. If I kept quiet, the pain would be so great I would have to stop and rest from that painful position, from doing what I had set out to do. That I would not do! So I talked, and while I talked about different subjects — or my pain — I didn't feel it so much because I was diverting my attention. Thus I could remain in the same position. In summary, talking was a way to keep my mind occupied away from the pain of the job, so I could continue doing the job.

The one trip I could not seem to ride was Religion. Each person seemed to identify with one specific religion. I felt I was a Jew, Protestant, Muslim, Catholic, Buddhist; you name it, I felt it.

I grew up as a Catholic. My father was a Protestant, my close friend was the daughter of a Rabbi. At age 22 I was "opened" in Subud.

What is a Religion for me? I compare Religion with the great cuisines of the world. The French are accustomed to eating French cooking. They are really satisfied with their cuisine. They could not be satisfied eating Chinese cuisine every day. They claim there is none better than theirs!

The Chinese are accustomed to eating Chinese cooking. They are really satisfied with their cuisine. They could not be satisfied eating French cuisine every day! They claim there is none better than theirs!

It is good they all feel satisfied with their own cuisines. But it is not the cuisine that keeps the outer man alive! It is the biochemical components in the food, the proper balance of proteins, minerals and vitamins. The same components ("essence") are in all the cuisines.

The ritual, or how it is cooked and presented, provides the satisfaction for the inner man. The colors of the meal, where and how it is served, the aromas, all the outer signs contribute to the satisfaction of the inner man. The whole, the inner and outer together, produces an extraordinary satisfaction . . . as it should.

But most of the time we forget that it is not the cuisine, but what is in it, the "essence" of it, that keeps us physically alive!

So it is with Religions. It is not the Religion itself but the "essence" or "spirit" that works through it, that is satisfying. Through all the religions of the world there is but one spirit, one Energy: Love. And that energy also exists outside of Religions. No Human Being can say, "I do not know what love is!" No one! And that is the **One** energy which unites us all.

So to me, to kneel and pray in Spanish, to light the candles in a menorah or kneel on a prayer rug in a mosque, are the rituals, the outer symbols. I can do any one; it is irrelevant to me. But the **feeling** of it is sacred to me in any way I do it, in the forms of any religion, or none.

Again, what is praying? To me, it is Being. When I can sit with you and be 100% there, I feel I am praying. When I learned to be able to clean my house, putting 100% of myself into it as an action through which I could express who I was (Love, Spirit), without feeling I was wasting time, I felt I had reached my highest goal! That has been the most difficult lesson for me to learn. That is praying! That is meditating! That is loving! I owe the "I am of house cleaning" to Pilar.

Robert and I went to Denmark and then Spain in July 1979. When we arrived in Spain we landed at Malaga Airport. Robert then asked, "Where are we going Mommy?" I took my Fodor's Book, opened it at random as always when seeking information, and there was a description of Nerja: "A small village on the sea, away from the maddening crowds!" I thought, "The Universe has decided for me!"

"Here," I said. "It looks like this is it, Robert!" We took a bus and spent the first night in Nerja at a hotel.

I wanted my child to learn the culture. So the following morning we walked the streets, saw a group of ladies all dressed in black, and asked if they knew of a family who would board a mother and child for two months.

One of them led me to a house. No one was there, so she took me to another.

As we entered, the lady in black asked the lady of the house if she would take me in. Immediately, I started to talk with her. Before she realized (according to her own words), she said, "Yes."

We installed ourselves there, with Pilar and Manolo and their children.

While in Nerja I observed several things, among them that they clean and go shopping every day. Coming from the States, I thought, "What a waste of time!" I can be really blind sometimes, and not see past my nose!

I thought I should teach her how not to "waste" time! Oh boy, I wanted to teach her! She is the one who taught me!

One day I wanted to put some trash in the trash bag and couldn't find one.

Pilar saw me and said, "Throw it on the floor!"

I realized she really wanted me to put it on the clean floor! She is the one who cleans. I took a closer look.

Through cleaning she was expressing who she was. When she finished she wanted everyone to enjoy it, love it, yes, dirty it — so she could start all over again. Crazy? No! How dare I say she is wasting her time! How dare I judge her offering as a waste!

When I hear Rubenstein in a concert, he is giving me the best of himself. When he finishes, he starts to practice all over again. Do I feel he is wasting his time by practicing? How dare I believe his practicing, his expression, is superior to that of Pilar? How dare I judge one medium of expression as better or worse than another! Both are ways of expressing Being, through discipline. Both are ways of learning to Become, through service to others.

This was the most difficult trial I passed in my life. I had refused to clean my house because I had believed I was not born for such things! How dare I! So I came to realize "The I AM of the Housewife." I learned and became free!

Another observation I made in Nerja was that when I would arrive at the house, Pilar would already know where I had been and what I had done. There is no newspaper in Nerja. They don't need one! Their system works!

At the beginning I was annoyed. "Why can't they leave me alone? Why are they so busily occupied with who does what where?" But again, I knew better! I should not be judgmental. So I looked again, closer. Why is this occurring? Things **never** are what they appear to be. (I learned that in kindergarten, from my friend the "black sheep!") So . . . What is really happening here? I realized that someone had told Pilar, "I saw Beatriz having a cup of coffee." Pilar listened. She registered the time, discounted how long it must have taken the person with the news to walk from the coffee place to the house, and made a mental note of the time. Later, someone else said, "I saw Beatriz having a cup of coffee." Pilar registered the time again. Then she deduced that from such a time to such a time Beatriz must have been in that coffee place. I arrived. She checked it out! Bingo! She is happy because she realizes her deduction was correct! So what appears to be gossip, is the need of each person to exercise his/her logical mind! Who, what, when, where, why? How is that different from someone writing a bunch of questions, putting them in the computer and arriving at a conclusion? . . . or me answering who, what and why of myself? Why is either one more valid? Is it not the same? So I became more than willing to tell them where I had been.

All our minds need information. I would not be surprised if we all had the same number of pieces of information in our heads. The information is different. The process, or "what's" and "why's" are the same. I can't help but look at the Law within the Law: In Every Instance See The Whole (Including the Commonest). Connect the Particular with the General.

My child, who had been born at Stanford and surrounded by literates, was growing up to believe reading and writing were what a Human Being Is! I was not aware of this.

Every day I bought a newspaper and a magazine. Since I felt it a crime to throw them out, I brought them to the house and left them on the table for the family to read.

After a few days the magazines and papers were in the same position. I realized then that these people did not know how to read!

That is when I became aware that just as I hurt them by assuming they were literate, the people at Stanford hurt me by assuming I was college educated. The hurt comes from the assumption that everyone around is in the same fishbowl . . . Neither I nor the people at Stanford were intending to hurt.

When my son discovered they were illiterate, he decided they were subhuman. His world crumbled. His conception was false! In any case he was hurting! He began to spit, to kick, to behave with a lack of respect I had never before seen.

I was so embarrassed I wanted the floor to open up and swallow me! I told Pilar, the lady of the house, that if she wanted me to leave, I would.

She said, "Mrs. Prentice, I am not an educated person. I work the land. I do not know much. But when I take my mule to work and she kicks, I know it is because she is hurting. So I usually caress her until she calms down. Please, don't leave."

I looked at her with tears in my eyes.

She began to be nicer with Robert. Robert got worse and worse. After four months, in the middle of one of his tantrums, he looked at her and screamed, "How can you be so nice to me when I am being so mean?"

She looked at him and very calmly replied, "Because I don't have a problem, **you** do."

All of a sudden something fell into place inside Robert and he changed. He started to compare what he knew in California: the swimming pools, good libraries, etc., with what he saw here: no degrees, no education, no psychology of this or that, just Being Human.

From that day Robert loved them. His world view reconciled that though it is important for him to read, there are other things just as important.

Who **has** more? Who **gave** more to my child? The person who bought him a ticket to the theater but did not go with him, or Pilar?

These other things can only be passed on by living, no University can teach them, no money can buy them. Let's not miss the boat . . . Let's not allow our Humanity to go out the window.

Let's wake up and recognize values! Then we will be able to deal internationally from strength, as the **equals** that we are. Yes, we do have technology and it is, important. We also have tangible economic power. But Pilar, and millions like her, have an intangible which is just as important, or more so. We can always create another car in the factory. But if our Human values are not passed down, if they are lost, we won't be able to go to the libraries or factories for them. And without our hearts, all the knowledge in the world is meaningless.

Can we imagine if we could act like Pilar among Nations? When one nation acts aggressively, the others can refuse to react violently and instead make the aggressor feel the real problem, as Pilar did. Can you imagine what a difference that would make in the world? Who are the literates? Who doesn't understand?

Manolo, Pilar's husband, observed me reading the newspaper and magazines for two hours each day. The third day he asked me what I had learned. I was very excited to be able to tell him all that was happening in New York, Buenos Aires: in the world. After all, I am a well-informed person!

He looked at me, amused, was quiet for a minute, and then

169

asked, "How long has it taken you to read all this?"

"Two hours," I replied.

"That means you spent six hours in the last three days.

"Beatriz, I don't mean to be rude, but . . . is there anything you can do with all that information from the newspaper? Couldn't you have spent those six hours doing something useful in this town?"

I felt very embarrassed and didn't buy another newspaper for the rest of the year. I was not the less wise, and began to utilize my time in the town. He was so right! Are we **sure** that the literate people are the ones who think more clearly?

Manolo and I talked with each other, our hearts open. I felt I wanted to help them; I felt sorry for them!

He told me his thoughts. "I figure that Spain can be without the King. I figure Spain can be without lawyers, without accountants.

"But I figure Spain can't be without food. I am a farmer. I grow food. I am doing the most important work in this country. I know no one else sees it; I know people look down on me. But since I know what I am doing, and the importance of it, I am happy doing it."

He was right! He knew Who he was, What he was, and Why he was! Therefore, He was happy.

I looked at him and heard him. I could not help but feel he could be a Great Leader in the world. Yet, here he was . . . and my heart ached.

> Nerja, Spain
> July 25, 1979

> Dear Allan:

> . . . *talking about my pain. I always see greatness, intelligence. Why? And people always get scared! Why?*

> Love,
> Beatriz

I stayed in Nerja for one year. I saw how hard Manolo worked to plant the potatoes and that after the harvest no one wanted to pay the price. He had to practically give them away or they would have rotted on the ground. I was furious! I would organize them, I felt.

I did not know then: everything works together for the good of all! I was reacting!

I asked him, "Did you think of not planting for just one season, so that Spain would feel the lack of food when this part of Malaga, Andalusia, did not produce?"

"Yes, I thought of it. I know it would make a difference. I

would have more food in my 'fridge, more money for my family. But I can't do it. The land needs me! I can't do that to the land!" False or true, it was clear as water, the Law at work: Living Your Life for a Purpose Higher Than Yourself. His "reasons" were incorrect, but he was "Sacrificing the few" — his family — for the **benefit** of **the whole.**"

I had wanted to solve a problem at the level of consequence: changing the outside. I felt very small with such an answer. I shut up! Solutions must come at the invisible level first!

I left there very much richer as a Human Being!

There was one more thing I realized while in Spain: I am not **just** a Human Being, as I had always claimed, but also an inhabitant of Planet Earth!

While I lived in Argentina I had learned to have strong feelings for that country. Even though I felt I was not one of her people, I did feel I was an ambassador: wherever I went I must be an example; people will judge Argentina by me.

While in Canada my feeling was so strong I became a Canadian!

When I came to the United States I was even happier. My life has been a continuous growth of loving and enlarging my world. I felt American. The frankness, directness, of America suited me. So I became American too!

In Spain, my fourth country, I realized I was a Spaniard. I started to feel the pride of a nation which not even Napoleon could conquer!

At that moment it came to me that I really was an inhabitant of the whole Planet Earth! There was no country with which I could not identify; no country I could not love. I have had three passports! I would like to have just one, as an "Inhabitant of Planet Earth!"

I felt Spain's blood. If anyone in the world understands the Arab world, a Spaniard can! If any country could play a leading role to bridge the two worlds, Spain can!

By the time I left Spain, I realized I was to be an example, yes, but the example had nothing to do with one country or another. I was an ambassador of Love for the Whole World.

The era with Allan ended with that first trip to Spain.

While in Spain I examined the histories of Allan's pain and my own. Allan had written in his first letter to me that he was dealing with his "facade problem" and counting on me "to puncture . . . (his) balloon." I did. I helped him back from drinking when he was so frightened he chose booze as a way to hide. I brought him back from madness when he saw that as the way to avoid confronting life. Dr. Allan Cott's diagnosis was schizophrenia. I attended the Schizophrenics Anonymous meetings. I felt he should go, but knew the healing was at a different level.

If a water pipe is broken, a bucket should be put under it, as a **temporary** measure while the **cause** of the leak is solved. Allan had to go to the doctor for first aid for the **visible result**; I was concerned with the **invisible cause** of his problem.

The cause was in his Spirit. His fear would drive him anywhere, rather than to face life, to face himself. I was there to turn him away from any lie he chose and show him that each time he was running away from himself. Oh! It was painful for him. Who wants to live with someone who constantly puts a mirror in front of you and says, "Look, this is You!" when the picture is beautiful but you feel ugly?

Little by little he gained confidence in himself. Little by little my love melted his fear. I knew he knew. I knew he could feel my love.

That gradual melting and growth is documented in the love letters we exchanged over a decade and a half. The first letter was written a couple of weeks after our real (spiritual) meeting.

Hamilton, Canada
January 13, 1965

My dear Beatriz:

I'm still pinching myself — Can't believe it's real. Am I really in love? Do you really love me?

You've been on my mind ever since you got out of the car Monday morning — before that too — but you were there for that part.

When I got home Monday, Mother asked me if I'd been up all night. I said yes. Very wisely she asked no more questions — except to inquire whether I was capable of driving to Hamilton.

Maybe I'd better explain one thing — you remember I compared your face with another girl that I had met in Hamilton? I neglected to say she is 17. Come to think of it — when you are happy and relaxed and I look at you, you do look younger, without the cares of the world that your elderly, knowledgeable spirit normally mark on your face. So it's a special compliment — not that the other girl is important, but the changes love has brought you, are important.

You may be wondering why I write small — It's my only piece of paper!!!

There are a lot of things I wanted to say in this letter — As I drove or walked along they flocked through my mind — beautiful — ineffable (look it up) thoughts — that fled as soon as I filled my pen.

172

But I can only think "I" for some reason. I want to tell you everything I'm thinking and I want to know everything you are thinking and I want your opinion — which, because I love you, and in spite of loving you, I value most highly — You're so smart you frighten me!

Second side of paper

I am trying to overcome my "facade problem." I just hope I'm not exchanging one false front for another and I depend on you to puncture my balloon regularly.

I am considering the question of returning to University very seriously. You're partly right when you say I need it as a crutch. But there is the feeling in me — right or wrong — that what I will be called upon to do next will require all the learning and studying power I can muster. And God knows I need all the help I can get, especially where somewhat uninteresting subjects are concerned . . .

Oh, by the way on the subject of nothing to do in Toronto. Get a Globe and Mail for Wednesday, turn to page six and read Richard Needham's column. I retitled it "Get off the Pot."

That's enough for now — Remember —

> *(I loze (crossed out))*
> *I love you (can't spell it)*
> *Allan*

The first side of the page told me how very accurately Allan judged me. He saw clearly my deepest concern: The World! "Without the cares of the world that your elderly, knowledgeable spirit normally mark on your face." He saw my soul! I had had my breasts removed because men did not see Me, my soul; and now **he** saw Me! He realized I carry within me an empathy for the suffering of the entire world. Therefore I knew he would understand my working for that world. He would let me serve, let me Be! He did not understand at an emotional level, but at a much deeper one: a soul level.

He would never ask, "Why didn't you cook, instead of being with so and so?" He clearly understood, "One does not Why's the Musts!" as he himself had said to his aunt when a small child.

Also, he saw my intelligence. That was important to me. The world could look at me and think I was silly, crazy, stupid and ignorant, but I wanted the person next to me to recognize I was brilliant.

On the second side of the single sheet of his letter, Allan asked me to bring him back from lies to Truth! "I depend on you to puncture my balloon regularly."

I knew I could do that! I had already started work on his "facade problem."

173

When I met Allan he had an extraordinary ability to imitate different cartoon character's voices. It was cute and I had loved it.

But soon I became aware that any idea he held — of any weight or importance — he said **only** through those voices. He was hiding behind them. I had begun to make him aware of it.

He also asked me to help him study: "God knows I need all the help I can get, especially where somewhat uninteresting subjects are concerned."

I knew I could do that.

Later, people thought, "Beatriz is the one who wants Allan to study." Nothing could be farther from the truth! I knew it was a "crutch." But once he replied that that was what **he** wanted, I worked for it with all my might, **as if** it was something I wanted. What I thought, what I felt, became irrelevant. If I allowed myself to dwell for one second on what **I** thought, I could not put all of me into what **he** wanted.

Also, he had scratched out the misspelled word, "love" on his sign-off, rewrote it and then said, "can't spell it." This told me he needed me — another confirmation of my feeling.

I considered that letter my Marriage Contract. I knew the marriage would be over once it was accomplished.

(Hamilton, Canada)
January 28, 1965

What a beautiful day! I look out the window and everybody seems happy — because I am happy. I got a beautiful surprise when I got to work yesterday — I DON'T have to work Monday!!!!!!!! I work Saturday night and Sunday afternoon. So I'll go right from Hamilton to Subud and then rush right over to see you — If you're not at S.

Also I feel much better today than I did yesterday. When I woke up yesterday I felt like I'd been clubbed — tired, sick — just like before. I don't know why — maybe leaving you — maybe just the bad air in Hamilton. Anyway I feel brighter today — partly I think because I've written to Ruth about a 13 year old son of a friend of hers who ran away last fall and was never heard from again. She wrote asking me to pray for him and I don't think I really took the letter too seriously. I just let it go. Last night as I cleared off my desk of all the junk that had accumulated, I re-read the letter and felt a strong urge to pray. I did. Then I wrote Ruth, asking her how young Anthony was — if there had been any word, if the hunt was continuing, and asking after the father — I think for the first time I realized what he must be going through — to come home at night and not have his boy there.

Oh, by the way, I asked her what she thinks about you. Like a specialist doctor, I'd like to have an unbiased, outside opinion before going ahead anyway.

> *All my love*
> *Allan*

This letter provided the first evidence of the effect my love had on him. He had cleared his desk, prayed and taken action on something he had previously neglected. This was to me a clear indication that with time my love could free him.

It had begun. Eventually, if I was patient, he would feel emotionally **free to act,** continually giving **care** and **support** to others.

> *(Hamilton, Canada)*
> *February 6, 1965*

My dearest darling delightful Beatriz:

I was just reading a book where on Christmas morning the man "romanced his wife," and I fell to thinking how we would make love Christmas morning and one of our dozen children would run in and say, "What are you doing mummy and daddy?" and we'd say,"We're making love," and he's say, "What's that?" and we'd tell him as much as he needed to know.

And one day our daughter, all of 13 years, would come home to tell how her boy friend had kissed her, and we'd rejoice with her that she'd found something new.

And our son would come to us to say he's made love to a girl, and what should he do now, and we'd tell him what we thought and leave him to make his own decision as a man.

And a little girl would see me in the shower and say, "What's that, Daddy?" and I'd turn red and roar, "Get her out of here!" and you'd explain to her and would calm me down.

And how did I start thinking about all this? Because I read a book and thought of you, so if you don't like, it's your own fault, and if you do like it, it's your fault too.

And God bless you my beautiful, bountiful little chickadee!!!

> *Your own,*
> *Allan*

This letter told me of his dreams to have a family and of his expectations about who took care of what. But I knew he was too frightened for the giving required of a parent. I wanted a family right then. But I knew I would have to wait for Allan.

We were married on March 26th and after that we both wrote. On my birthday he gave me this note:

Hamilton, Canada
June 24, 1965

My dearest, darling Beatriz:

As you sit behind me now — talking of nudism, cross because I am laughing, and thinking about the freedom of Canada — I love you. You throw me a kiss — I love you. There may be nothing to go with this because there is no money — but I love you, I love you, I love you.

Allan

I replied:

Hamilton, Canada
June 24, 1965

Darling, my love:

There is nothing more important than your thoughts . . . I do not need gifts, you know that . . . I need you!! Your love . . . !! I could not be happier today!!

I am sorry I make you mad sometimes, I will try to be better. But you know that I have no pride, no wishes, no nothing; with you I just have love. And maybe because of that I am blind. I love to be blind because of you . . . !

You are a nice sickness! I can not be more proud of you! No one can compete with you; it is true that you are smart but that is not so important. But you are thoughtful, kind, loving, honest, with a heart of gold . . . for all that and much more, I love you darling!

Thanks a lot for the wonderful card.

Your Pussy-Cat
Beatriz

My description of Allan as ". . . thoughtful, kind . . . with a heart of Gold . . ." caused people at various times over the years to think I was blind. This is what I do see:

The Sun is: Brightness, Warmth, Dryness. Sometimes I experience: Darkness, Coldness, Wetness. That does not mean the Sun has changed. I am experiencing the clouds that cover the Sun. Even if the Sun never comes out, it is NOT Darkness, Coldness, Wetness. This simply is not true.

It is the same with Allan, or with any Human Being. He is considerate, kind, loving, with a heart of gold. That is the unchanging Truth. I was experiencing not him, but the clouds that covered him. Clouds are here today and gone tomorrow. I always knew that. If he could see the Truth about himself, that he was all I was saying, then he would burn away the clouds and be free. Only the Truth could set him Free. Because I knew this and acted upon it, I appeared to be blind.

My dear Husband:

*Here I am, in the office thinking about you . . . warm feelings
arouse me and you were in my mind . . . I do not know why . . . but
certainly I remembered a fireplace — full of cards, you . . . and me
looking at them . . . but neither of us interested in them . . . I could
feel your presence behind me, your and my feelings, a world of words,
none spoken. Then, your warm hands on my shoulders . . . your
body near me, your hands working on my feet. Bad Boy! and you did
not like it! The radio on, music is soft and I invited you to dance.
Don't ask me why I am remembering all that, but it just came to me.*

*Did I tell you how much you mean to me? Did I ever say you are
the most important thing in my life? No . . .!? What a bad girl . . .
but believe it or not,*

I love you,
Beatriz

Soon after I got married I had special stationary made. I bought
white paper and had a golden cross printed on one upper corner
and my new name on the other. I thought I was making a clear
statement of what I had embarked upon: I was gladly putting
myself on the cross! To me it was clear as water.

I was surprised to find people kept asking me if I had married a
minister. That was when I began to see how very differently
people interpreted things than I did. If I had received that letter I
would have thought the person was trying to say, "I have picked
up my Cross," minister or not.

This reading symbolically was like my interpretation of Allan's
first letter. It was divided onto two sides of the paper. One side
spoke of me, the other side of him. This very format, the
division, told me the unconscious message. He may not have
consciously planned it that way, but I always read the
unconscious, the invisible, very clearly. Apparently many people
do not.

Toronto
April 2, 1966

My love:

*I look — and look — and look for a card but — no words, no
card could express what I feel for you.*

*So I felt the white of this paper may give you an idea of my pure
love and cross of my sacred feeling toward you — I love you but
not only that — I respect you, admire you and only pray that I can
be your Valentine for ever and ever.*

Yours,
Beatriz

Toronto, Canada
February 22, 1966

Sweetheart:

    I sit here at my desk, amid the pile of papers and reels of film and I think of you . . . loving, sweet, soft lovable you, You!!! I love you. Yup, and I don't like the idea of sharing you, even on paper, with some other fellow. So I write. Wondering where you were tonight when I was wanting supper. Had pancakes. What is love? A soppy feeling when one wants sex? I don't think so. Rather a soft feeling in the heart and soul — a desire to be near and live fully with someone, of which sex is a part! A feeling of protection toward the loved one. A blessing of two people where mere physical characteristics mean little (although are meaningful) and the mental communication is very close. They can consider argumentative ideas and reach friendly conclusions or even compromise.

    My sweet, I love you, with all my heart.

Yours,
Allan

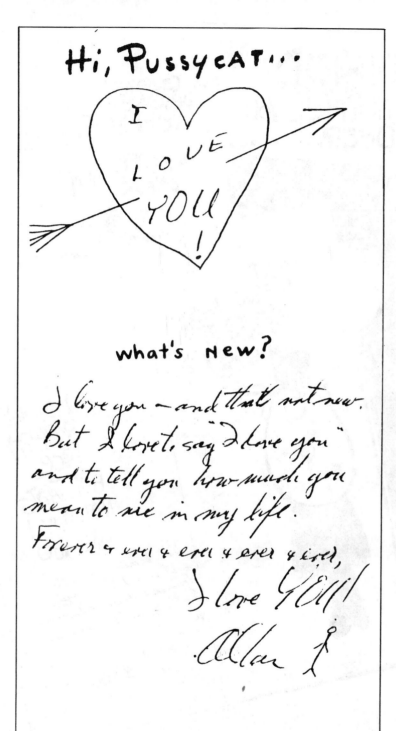

Hi, PUSSYCAT...

I LOVE YOU!

what's NEW?

I love you — and that not new. But I love to say "I love you" and to tell you how much you mean to me in my life.

Forever & ever & ever & ever & ever,

I love YOU!

Allan

I'M GLAD I MARRIED YOU DEAR........

....'CAUSE YOU DESERVE THE VERY BEST.

✩ HAPPY ANNIVERSARY

I DON'T LIKE YOU JUST BECAUSE OF A PRETTY FACE!

I DO HAVE A PRETTY FACE, BUT THAT'S NOT WHY I LIKE YOU.

It's because you are the most interesting, intelligent, lovingest, beautiful woman I know — and besides I like sex!

Love,
A.

LOOKING FOR SOMEONE WHO'S
SWEET, AFFECTIONATE, WARM,
UNDERSTANDING & BEAUTIFUL TOO?

.....NOW THAT YOU'VE FOUND
ME WHAT ARE YOUR PLANS?

— o —

Sweetheart:

I love you. I sit here freshly bathed, wanting to write you a note to tell you how much I adore you, love you, admire you and appreciate you. You have become my whole life — my joy and my sorrow, happiness and despair. When you are happy, I am overjoyed; when you are sad, I am stricken.

Please say you'll love me — if not forever, then at least until tomorrow and tomorrow and tomorrow ,,,,,,,,,,,,,,,,,,,

I know it is tough to keep going under the pace of both our jobs, but remember that I love you and I wish it could be different; we will win through together.

To my one and only love,
besos, cariños, abrazos
Allan.

I had said to Allan before I married him, "Don't expect me to cook for you, to clean for you . . . etc." I had followed through. In this letter Allan is **wondering** where I was. Of course, I was helping someone I felt needed me. He was wondering, **not** complaining. I will be forever grateful to him for letting me Be. I would have done it anyhow, but to be able to do what I felt without having him complain, was so extraordinary!

(New York, N.Y.)
December, 1968

Dear Santa Claus:

I would love to receive copies of the letters that my husband wrote to the people he was supposed to write. This would lighten my heart no end. Nothing else could make me happier . . . I know you will give them to me because although I was not a good girl all year round, I tried most of the time. So . . . Give me an "A" for trying . . .

I wonder what my husband would like for Christmas, I hope he will write you too, so I will know. He has been very good this year. It is a pity the bank account is so low. But . . . Our love for each other runs sky high . . .

Beatriz

I knew Allan would read my letter to Santa — as I was hoping to read his.

I was asking Allan to Be by expressing his love to others (his parents, brothers, old friends, professors)! He had not written those letters. This reminder was part of the task of puncturing his facade, as he had requested in the "Contract." No greater Gift could he have given me! I knew he thought and felt. But he did not **DO.** I wanted him to Act; thus the trilogy is lived! (Thought, Desire, **Action**).

I was not the only one who was asking him to express his love. I felt very deeply the pain his mother was experiencing because he could not express his feelings of love for her.

After Allan took his Masters from Columbia University in New York City, he received this invitation to Canada.

Toronto, Canada
July, 1969

Dear Allan:

I was just talking to . . . (your mother) and she tells me you are not quite up to par these days. I've been looking forward to seeing both you and Beatriz a bit before you go on to California and now I thought I would encourage you to come ahead and spend about a month or more here.

If you are not working, then why not do so here. Better still, what I want you to do is this. Come in a week's time and you will be able to go up to the chalet and spend a whole week there.

. . . (friends) will be up there from August 1st or 2nd to the 10th and I have an idea it would be good for you to spend a bit of time with those three fine persons . . . The value of being in that air, and with those three guys, can not be underestimated.

You should see my cousin R! Already he has a bit of color back in his cheeks since he came here. Not that this air is any good, it's just not so bad as Con Edison's (New York City).

Think over my advice seriously and I hope you will come next week. Love to Beatriz and tell her I am really looking forward to a good discussion.

Brian

Allan accepted and spent the rest of the summer in Canada. I remained in New York, working, until he came back and we got ready to move to Stanford, California. While he was away, I wrote:

New York, New York
August 11, 1969

My dearest Love:

You have no idea how much I love you, and how I was taking your love for granted.

You know . . . I'm afraid to be alone now. I close the door with a chain . . . I just realized my strong feeling of security, it flew to Canada . . .

I just had to tell you this.

I think, you think . . . but neither of us is telling the other what we think: it is dangerous . . . Let's go back where we left (off) and communicate again, shall we?

Enjoy yourself. I like to be alone for a while too, so do not hurry home, stay until you want. Love to every one, but especially to my husband, if you find him . . . Will you try?

> *Love, Love, Love*
> *your Sweetheart*
> *Beatriz*

Note: From my wedding day, I was still waiting for my husband. There was much correspondence from Canada as a result of Allan's trip.

An old friend of Allan's family wrote me:

> *Toronto, Canada*
> *August 5, 1969*

Beatriz dear:

Just came in last night from spending a week-end at the chalet and I have regards from Allan. It would do your heart good to see Allan. He was so busy and so absorbed with the electricity that I always had to remind him to eat and his sense of humor was terrific . . . We are sorry you won't be dropping in Toronto on your way to San Francisco or wherever you are going — But good health and good luck . . .

. . . P.S. You are the best thing that (has) happened to Allan. There aren't any other duplicates like you — so . . . (brothers) will be bachelors and . . . (father) will have to live on and on. Allan was so sentimental when he saw us that he hugged and kissed me.

> *"L"*

She knew very well that earlier Allan could not have expressed his affection.

> *Toronto, Canada*
> *August 15, 1969*

My love:

This has been two wild weeks.

First at the chalet — no rest cure — just hard electrical work . . .

Well there is a lot more — I should be home by Saturday 23 August maybe sooner.

> *I love you and miss you,*
> *Kiss*
> *Allan*

Dear Beatriz:

. . . I decided to write you a letter and tell you how pleased we all were to have Allan with us this last week.

Firstly, the work and the location had just the effect I had anticipated. He is well and happy and told me he did really enjoy himself while working with us. In fact I don't ever remember having as much fun with Allan as in these last two weeks.

But not only was it good for Allan, it was **great** for us. We have had many different fellows work on the electrical aspect of the chalet and believe me, it is a complicated job electrically. For a smaller building; it literally bristles with electrical outlets . . . a good deal of the work had been done by the other four guys ahead of Allan; there were dozens of unfinished things . . . what Allan did was to bring it all on line for us. He never stopped — in his Scorpian indefatigable way — until every lamp holder had a lamp in it with a switch that worked when you turned it on.

Then he used all his e.s.p. to discover hidden power sources, sealed up behind the drywall, and other such oddities, and began to install the fluorescent lamps over the fireplace. Saturday he worked until 1:30 A.M. to finish the lighting beams over the front entrance hall, and (thus) brightened an area that had been gloomy too long.

But most satisfying of all for me was how he got all the soffet lights working. The roof overhang (soffet) . . . has ten . . . lamps . . at night, with these on, the building is truly beautiful. All the men are putting forth such an effort . . . rather than having a place that looks like a bunch of amateurs had done it, on the contrary, the standard of workmanship is miles ahead of what we ever expect to see in our regular inspection tours, . . . (of other buildings).

. . . I hope somehow you can see it one day when it is all completely finished, I know you would love it. I am designing the master bedroom as a room for love making. I feel this is essential to the atmosphere of any good master bedroom. It will be . . . Isn't that a delightful idea for the bedroom, Beatriz?

Don't forget to hire me when you and Allan are rich enough to have a lou.

Love
Brian

As should be obvious, Brian is more than just an architect! The chalet was designed, built and sold as a fundraiser towards the acquisition of the Toronto Subud Center.

While Allan was in Canada, Kirsten came to visit me in New York. Upon her return home, she wrote:

Dear Beatriz:

I wish I could express how happy I am I came to visit with you. There is something you transmit to me, every time I am with you. My awareness is increased and I begin to care.

Furthermore it is marvelous you could arrange for us to see what we did. I am glad we concentrated on the four plays, rather than getting me muddled.

We had a pleasant busride home, the temperature was kept more even this time and our fellow-travelers were really pleasant. I am learning from you; it is so easy to get valuable contacts; most people are just waiting for you to thaw . . .

I guess you know now, Allan will come late this week — (I) will remember to send things with him.

I hadn't any problems in Buffalo — they did not even open the suitcases and I declared only $12 worth. I am really pleased with the things I got — the candies cannot be eaten with the paper though (sic).

Thank you again, you are truly the most exceptional friend I have ever had.

> *Love*
> *Kirsten*

When I received this letter I was so glad! Kirsten was telling me that I was accomplishing what I felt my job was: to bring awareness (light, love) and caring to people who did not know how to care yet, by being with them. How did I transmit it to her? By showing **her** how exceptional **she** is! What this required of me, I clearly expressed in my letter of May 30th, 1967 to Ana Maria on the occasion of mother's death.

. . . we must continue as she wanted of us . . . day by day, a step ahead each day . . . Place your head high. It does not matter how many times we fall down; we must get up and continue, erect and happy with faith and hope, looking for new horizons and knowing that she will be proud to see that we are trying to be generous and knowing how to forgive, like she knew how to do, to know and learn to see the good side of everything and never escape, to live with the people, in the midst of apathy and uncaring and preserve that which we have, to be a duck, swimming in dirty water and coming out clean and dry . . .

> *Beatriz*

We are born WHITE, PURE, CLEAN, PERFECT

6. You didn't finish high school? You'll never amount to much!

14. You don't want to spend anything on Defense? It's not safe! It's not done!

13. You can't park your truck in **this** neighborhood! No sir!

9. You'll have to do things you don't like to do! That's life!

1. Stop talking to strangers! You embarrass me!

8. It's time you learned you **do** have limits! Grow up!

5. If he didn't have a diploma, he wouldn't even try to produce. He **needs** my love. I don't need to change.

14. This nation is so insecure! Too scared to try the untried! It **needs** my love.

12. They'd feel inferior if they lived in a blue-collar neighborhood! They need my love I don't need to change.

9. She's not aware she always has a choice. She **needs** my love. I don't need to change.

1. He doesn't know he embarrasses himself! He **needs** my love. I don't need to change.

8. He must have lived within limits for a long time! He **needs** my love. I don't need to change.

. . . And so we clean, heal and purify ourselves! No one can heal us! No one. "Physician Heal **Thyself**!"

Each and everyone of us is a healer!

The process illustrated by the duck not only heals the emotional and mental bodies, but the physical body as well, since we are one machine, thoroughly connected as the fingers of a hand.

As we do it over and over, we restate our rightful place: we are Humans when we think, feel and act humanely towards Ourselves first, and Others as a consequence: "Love your neighbor **as** you love Yourself." Having two eyes, two legs, one nose, and 195 IQ **does not** make us humans!

We can make this planet a humane place to live, when we learn to be humane with ourselves.

Getting Dirty	**Getting Clean**
1. Stop talking to strangers! You embarrass me!	1. He doesn't know he embarrasses himself! He **needs** my love. I don't need to change.
2. Do you need to move your hands to speak? It's not done	2. He feels my gestures show others he is "different." It's his lack of confidence! he **needs** my love. I don't need to change.
3. Is it necessary to set a formal dinner. We're informal!	3. He can't relax in a formal setting. He feels ill at ease. He **needs** my love. I don't need to change.
4. You're a secretary? I certainly wouldn't want to be one!	4. If she were a secretary, she would not feel worthwhile. She **needs** my love. I don't need to change.
5. You didn't finish High School? You'll never amount to much.	5. If he didn't have a diploma, he wouldn't even try to produce. He **needs** my love. I don't need to change.
6. You want to make a mark in the world? You're dreaming!	6. She feels impotent. She has given up! She **needs** my love. I don't need to change.
7. I don't believe you're pure. You're lying.	7. She doesn't see she's pure. She **needs** my love. I don't need to change.
8. It's time you learned you **do** have limits! Grow up!	8. He must have lived within limits for a long time! He **needs** my love. I don't need to change.
9. You'll have to do things you don't like to do! That's life.	9. She's not aware she always has a choice. She **needs** my love. I don't need to change.
10. He is sick, he's poor. You can do better than that!	10. She doesn't know the pleasure of loving for its own sake. She **needs** my love. I don't need to change.
11. You can't marry him. He's beneath you.	11. He'd judge himself by who's next to him. He doesn't have a strong opinion of himself. He **needs** my love. I don't need to change.
12. You can't park your truck in **this** neighborhood! No sir!	12. They'd feel inferior if they lived in a blue-collar neighborhood! **They need** my love I don't need to change.
13. You don't want to spend anything on Defense? It's not safe! **It's not done!**	13. This nation is so insecure! Too scared to try the untried! It **needs** my Love! I don't need to change.

Palo Alto
17 Nov 1969.

My love, — Life is certainly difficult for both of us now. The sacrifices we need to make to the great god Education seem to really hurt us and drive us into ourselves and our dream worlds. Somehow we must not let this happen. We must not quit when defeat threatens; we must choose freely, not with guns at our heads. I must learn to work and carry through jobs that I don't like or that require me to do my best not just my better or my good....

Somehow we have to make a stand and win! Not just slip through as has been the case so far, but win. We can help each other I know because we have strength for each other. But it must

be happy, uncomplaining, cheerful help that
encourages us to really make a good of it.

We can do it! I know!

We must learn to face the music, not turn
aside, as I am doing now, and write letters or
atch TV or take a bath or sleep.

Somehow we, especially me, must learn
self-discipline so that our love can grow and
bloom in a beautiful flower of creation that
will please us both.

If we can make this happen, then I will
become a good writer. Right now, I suffer from
fuzzy thinking that shows itself when I tackle
a problem. Some of my first drafts look more
like notes rather than orderly thought.

I love you, my dearest heart, more and
more every day.
Happily & hopefully,
Allan

194

Valentine's Day the following year I sent this to Allan:

Palo Alto
February 14, 1970

There are no words to express what and how I feel about you . . .
warmth? Passion . . . ? I do not know; all of them are words . . .
meaningless . . . How I really feel only God can transmit to you.
And little by little it seems he is doing it. When you are inside me
. . . when I feel you right in me sometimes I know nothing will ever
separate our souls, our minds are like chains . . . Allan . . . Oh!
my sweet Allan! You are such a surprise for me, yet!!! I can't quite
realize I married you!!!

I see you so big, and wonder how such a little me could get you. How
could you put your eyes on me? I see ahead and can see you right at
the top. I wonder, would I be able to get that far with him? Would I
have to stay behind? There is so much in my mind, so much
uncertainty except in one thing . . . YOU! You'll get there! You
are all the things I thought you were . . . You are this gentle man,
living childhood . . . full of love and understanding . . . full of
emotions screaming to get out, and soon they will come out . . . What
a Valentine's Card? I'm crazy, I'm only supposed to tell you I love
you, and I almost forgot it!

Yours and only yours,
Beatriz

I had been daily helping an Argentine couple to adjust to life in the U.S. almost since they first arrived here at Stanford. When I was pregnant with Robert, she had come to the house and seen me in bed, vomiting all over the bed, with crust on my body, and Allan ignoring all of it. Only Freddy (at age 13) was feeding me, coming home from school even at lunch time to do so. Not wanting to interfere, she said nothing, but continued to visit me almost daily.

One day her husband arrived unannounced, scooped me up in his arms, and took me home to their house. She was waiting for me with a hot bath already drawn. I stayed there the remaining couple of weeks until the morning sickness was over. Freddy and Allan ate dinner there daily and she cleaned up my house while I was away.

They could not understand how I could love this man, who seemed to them a monster. I knew he was ignoring me because he felt he could not give. I knew his pain had to be worse than mine. Therefore, I kept loving.

Even if I wanted to, I do not know how to stop loving anyone. I know how to grow in love; that, I can teach.

After I returned home, Allan cooked dinner for all three of us every evening.

Allan became ill and went to Canada for a prompt and effective cure. While he was gone I wrote.

Palo Alto, California
March 8, 1972

Oh . . . ! Allan . . . !!! We missed you . . . !!! The house is empty without you . . . No one said "I have a headache," "Be quiet, I feel bad, I didn't sleep." How funny . . . !!! Hope you have a good time and remember us as much as we remember you.

The baby wonders why no one is asking how "it" is. I told "it" soon Daddy will come back like new.

Give our love to . . . (the family).

Your wife went to Dr. on the 9th. He said baby due June 15th . . . Well, love, keep writing in your mind at least. I might get something. Did you get the indirect?!!

Chau papi,
your mami,
Beatriz and Freddy

Note: He **did** write from Canada that two-week trip, but saved up his letters and mailed several together.

Sunday a.m.
Toronto, Canada
March 5, 1972

Dear Beatriz and Freddy:

We have just had three rounds of the battle of the basement wall. I think I'm getting my way, but OH, the lobbying, the backroom arguments! You remember the wall at the foot of the basement stairs, Beatriz? The one I have sought to take down for maybe 10 years? Well, I mounted my horse again this trip. Talking to mother: the wall stays . . . Later father comes down. I outline the proposal to him . . . The plan is approved, as they say in Parliament, "in principle," but father (and I too) does not want to go ahead if mother is opposed. Fair enough. He goes off. Some time later he returns to say mother has given in, sort of, . . .

I got down to Subud Friday night. Subud House is Here!! Ta! Ta! They have purchased a two story commercial bldg. . . . Yes, Brian is hard at it, continuing peculiar installations for peculiar people . . . As an interloper, of course, I have much to say about the whole

*thing. I walked in, saw some lighting and said something like,
"Brian, are you responsible for this mess?" Wiring as usual is a little
peculiar. They had the same fellow (a professional) working as (they)
did on the chalet. But it is going to be beautiful! All wood strip along
the staircase and so on; indirect lighting . . .*

Dr. Browett says I have . . . I am *feeling better and I hope the
trip will be very successful all around.*

Love
Allan

Toronto, Canada
March 8, 1972

Dear Beatriz and Freddy:

*Greetings from the frozen north! As I write, . . . (brother) is
outside chopping holes in 4" thick ice covering the driveway, which
arrived over the weekend as a welcome for me no doubt.*

The flight was fair . . .

*Then after walking through the maze, and waiting for my bag —
20 min. — I popped out to find no one waiting for me.*

*I called home several times. No answer. Was I abandoned? Finally I
went upstairs and sat down. A few minutes later, . . . (brother) appeared
. . . At the airport, he waited but I never seemed to appear. I guess he
wandered off for a while just as I came out.*

Anyway. Mom and Dad are in Ottawa or Montreal or both.

*The house looks much the same: full of stuff. The basement is
crammed even more. They still skimp on storm windows and it's still
cold inside.*

*When we arrived, H and his girl friend were there. We all traded
friendly insults and laughed a lot. I haven't had so much happy talk
over nothing for a long time — it's very refreshing . . . (brother)
came home from work about 1 a.m. — he is still at . . . still
unhappy a bit with his job, but prospering as usual . . .*

March 11, 1972
Saturday a.m.

*Well Sweetheart, as you can see I was trying to give you a complete
history of the trip but it appears it doesn't get down on paper very
well.*

*I have been to Dr. S. . . . She checked my neck for an adjustment
but says it's OK, it's just nerves, not physical tension . . .*

Tonight I go up to Dr. Browett to see what the guru has to say.

*One thing though, remember my project to clean up the basement?
Finally we will begin it next week — removing the ceiling at least.*

Everyone says I look very healthy. Even . . . (Dr. S.) is surprised . . . Everyone asks for you — Brian and all the rest at Subud, most whose faces I remember but I can't quite place the name. They all send their love and their best wishes for the baby. Please remember me with love as I do you with mine (you too Freddy!) . . .

I will try to write more frequently; maybe just a daily account.

> *Love and kisses and Peace*
> *Allan*

> *March 11, 1972*

Dear Allan:

. . . I am so glad I'm married to you. Hope you get better physically and keep a schedule well. Discipline!! Discipline!! I wish I could help! But I do . . . !! Because my love is with you, and Freddy's and the baby's!!!

We all three love you a lot. Doesn't it give you strength and give you purpose? No . . . ? too bad . . .

Enjoy yourself and eat, send smell by mail if possible!!! Well, love, a big kiss to you and all from tu media naranja y media.

> *Beatriz and Freddy*

My decision to quit my job and stay home, where I felt my energy was needed, had for a year created a scarcity of money. I had solved it by not eating. My hunger pains at this point were really poignant . . . therefore: "send smell by mail . . ."

After Robert was born, Allan gave Freddy this card. Clearly, he had known and appreciated what was happening in my early pregnancy.

> *Stanford, California*
> *July 9, 1972*

Printed:

"To Thank You. 'Little things mean so much.' Thank you so much for your thoughtfulness. You have a gift for making others happy."

To which he added:

I thank you for all the care that you took of my mummy when she was feeling badly.

> *Love and carinos from*
> *your new sobrino,*
> *Robert Allan*
> *(Robert's complete name)*

Note: Although much improved, Allan still found it necessary to express **his** thanks in the name of his new son.

November 11, 1972 I entered the hospital because I had attempted to commit suicide. The pain . . . the pain . . .

My father was staying with us at that time and Robert was four months old. I felt Father would take charge, I could let go. He stayed with us until Robert was 11 months old. We talked a great deal. Father told me I was not asking Allan for anything. I was not pushing him to go and get a job or to finish his degree. He asked me if I had not learned anything from Mother? "Don't you remember how she kept spending more and more? Haven't you learned?"

"Yes! I learned I would never, ever, ask my husband for more than what he was providing. I will stretch my budget even if I have to starve, but I will never demand more money, thus making him feel inadequate, . . . and I will never fight."

He looked incredulous . . . "Your mother was the best thing that ever happened to me! Because she demanded, I went out and pushed myself more and more. Because I loved her, I wanted to bring the world to her. Without her push I would probably have been nothing!"

My mouth dropped. "You mean all those fights, all those arguments . . . you think were the best thing for you?"

"Yes."

Once Father left in June of 1973, I told Allan he had until October to resume serious work towards his Ph.D. at Stanford, or drop out. If he did not decide and take action by then, I was moving out. I could not live in that limbo anymore.

The one thing I had learned from my suicide attempt was: Yes, I have a job to do, but it takes **two** to accomplish that job. I had done as much as I could. Now it was Allan's turn to make the next move. If he really wanted the job finished, he would make a decision. He had to begin to **Act**, to **Do**, to **Move**, to **Give** (to stop hiding).

Through all this pain I grew. Each time, I delved deeper inside myself to bring out more strength with which to know myself better. We may be two tree tops mingling, but we have different roots. It was important to keep them apart, to retain my own roots, especially after seven years of marriage. We separated for six months.

My friends were telling me Allan was no good, because they saw my pain. I was telling them Allan is very good, and if they knew him they would like him a great deal. Of course later, when allan finally opened up and expressed himself, they liked him so much that when they saw **his** pain as I pulled away from him, I became the "no good." Finally, we all knew that we are both OK.

After four months of separation Allan had decided, quit Stanford University and taken a professional technical writing job. He sent me a card for Valentine's Day, 1974, printed: "I'm not very experienced, but I'm willing to learn." To this he added:

— what the card says is true — I'm not very experienced but I'm willing to learn how to love.

I love you so much, my heart hurts when I think you might be gone forever.

I want you to care for me.

I want you to hold me and teach me.

I want you to love me.

I want to love you and be the husband, lover, friend that Freddy and Robertito need so very much. And I'm going to strive to show you that I am sincere . . .

I know it's easy to write cards, but I really want to change, to be what I ought to be. You may say I'm just trying to hang on — It's more than that — I need you — you are my life, my heart, my hope for the present and the future. I pray that you have not ceased to care, but I will strive to make you care again. I believe it is important to both of us.

> *Love from*
> *Allan*

There was no way I could refuse to go back to him, once he wrote "I need you." There was no question in my mind that I was here on earth to teach how to love. I was feeling pain, I wanted out, but as long as he needed me, I could not quit. I had to finish the job. I knew the day would come when he would **not** need me anymore.

So I said, "Yes, let's get back together. But **no books** to hide with, **no television!**" If he wanted to learn to love, he had to get rid of anything in which he could bury himself, escaping from life. No "drugs!" I was willing to continue only if he agreed to my conditions.

He did. From this point it would take the seven years I had originally predicted. I knew we had **begun** the final road.

I also knew he didn't love me. He had said it himself, "I want to love you." But he needed me, and I would remain as long as there was a need.

From the next year we began to execute what I had begun to discuss in June 1965. Allan had described the scene that night, "as you sit behind me now — talking of nudism, cross because I am laughing . . ."

It was true: I was cross. He had asked me to help him overcome the fear which had produced his "facade." I was trying to do exactly that, in broaching the subject of nudism. He did not realize that only through nudity (complete vulnerability) among

200

strangers, could he begin work on the unblocking which would set him free.

After ten long years, he was ready. We began to go with Sean and Andrea to hot springs where people bathed nude. He felt very safe with them. I was delighted.

By 1979 he knew how to organize his time and was no longer afraid to show love to other people or to shop at a store for himself and for gifts for women.

In June 1979, he bought me a gift **late** in the afternoon of my birthday. Knowing I was hurt by this apparent omission, he wrote:

Palo Alto, California
June 24, 1979

No matter what else I do or I don't do, I do love you and want to be with you.

I hate myself when I hurt you in these thoughtless ways. Please forgive me. God bless you on your Birthday and bring you many more happy ones.

Love,
Allan

The next month I finally made the long-delayed trip to Europe.

Copenhagen, (Denmark)
July 6, 1979

Dear Allan:

. . . The world is one. It's hard for me to see what is different from one place to another, so somehow it seems futile to travel now. Denmark is very picturesque! I'm OK. I really am. I'm sorry I sound strange, I feel so . . .

Dear Allan:

. . . How are you? How is Bb? How are you finding life as a bachelor? Is it better? Are you happy? Please let me know. My heart is aching, and I don't know how to make it stop. I love you. I'm glad I am a lamp for you, that brings clarity and understanding as you (have) said. Call Sean, Andrea and S. and say "Hello" for me. Tell them I am thinking what good friends they all are . . .

Love
Beatriz

Allan was going with Bb. — a friend of his was a friend of mine. She wrote me:

California
July, 1979

Dear Beatriz:

I was really sorry you were on your way to Europe when I got back from the workshop last weekend, because I had a lot of thoughts I wanted to share with you. I'll try to do the best I can on paper, since I don't want to wait until you get back.

The workshop was unbelievably fantastic and I fell in love with about 50 people. Of course you probably know the feeling since you've experienced the workshops too. The most important thing that happened was I fell in love with me; *something I don't ever remember feeling before.*

I've talked to Allan about our relationship the way it was before the workshop, and I know I was trying to possess him or the love that I felt was coming from him. I was so desperate for that kind of love and he was the only place I could find it.

I guess what I really want you to know is I've found that within myself and all the other people I met, and my relationship with Allan has changed quite a bit.

I still don't understand a whole lot about open marriage and specifically your agreements with each other. But I know Allan could never love any woman as much as he does you. I only hope that you know and trust that love. I think we've both experienced some jealousy of each other in fear that he (Allan) couldn't love both of us, and one would eventually lose out. Since the workshop, that jealousy has totally disappeared from me and suddenly I have the same feelings for you that I did when we first met at F's. I really liked you and felt you were a beautiful and warm woman and later covered that up because I felt I had to compete for Allan's feelings. God, it feels so good to be rid of all that shit. I hope we can pick up on that and continue a new friendship.

I still treasure my relationship with Allan as a very close friend and lover, but the desperate possessiveness is gone. I just want you to know that I never could or would want to take anything away from his relationship with you. And if he ever made the decision not to see me again I would truly miss that friendship, but it would be all right.

I don't think I've said everything I've wanted to, but I hope we can spend some time together when you get back. I hope you and Robert are having a wonderful trip. Take care and stay happy.

My love
Bb

The jealousy she had felt, she had projected upon me, assumed I also felt. I had not felt any.

Palo Alto, California
July 17, 1979
11:30 p.m.

Dear Beatriz:

. . . Bb has really come to terms with her version of "crowding" and is beginning to see that there are a lot of bees that like her honey. I am finding it easier to deal with the "crowding" as well, being able to bring it up for discussion and express my opinion and feelings. I am growing. She and I are becoming friends.

. . . so much has happened since you left two weeks ago. Time has been vanishing rapidly and yet it seems so long ago! I miss you both — the love, the warmth, the affection — and yet I am content to be by myself, inspecting myself with no one else to answer to: I am happy, and yet I am not happy.

. . . workshop . . . I had a good time . . . we . . . went roller skating . . . dinner . . . breakfast . . . open house . . .

. . . studio apartment . . . painted the whole room and bath . . . took me . . . Saturday and . . . Sunday to finish it, but it looks good, and I am proud!! . . .

Love
Allan

P.S. There are a million more things to write and I will write them.

He knew he was happy and unhappy, but he did not know why. I knew. I felt **he** felt that he owed me, that he **had** to give. So if I did not make the move, he would never harvest what I felt I had accomplished. If/when I did let go, he would have his freedom and be completely happy.

Nerja, Spain
August 4, 1979

Dear Allan:

I need more time by myself. For Robert as well as for me. Robert needs more time with me; he is improving a lot in behavior. He needs more time for the language too. But above all I want time. I need it. I did not realize how much out of balance I was . . . In the last two days I have begun to relax; I just started. Can you let the house go and send us $600 a month for us to live on? Please answer in a telegram since the letters take 15 days and we have no time.

I forgot, being in the States for so long and in Canada, and especially being with you, that life is not to work, but rather one works to be able to live.

I received a letter from Bb saying she had a good workshop. I am glad for her.

Your letter seems to say you are spending time with people you like, enjoying new activities and doing work like painting and feeling good about. I am truly glad. I am sorry you miss the warmth, love and affection you are accustomed to, but you must be receiving a different kind, I am sure.

Sorry to have to say, I discovered I do not miss anything. I do not have anything to miss except the great pain and longing for you that I always have when you are there and yet not there. Now, since you are not here, the pain is gone and that seems to be what my love affair seems to be: the love with my pain, always trying to have you. To want to be with you. Why? I do not know but it seems so futile now, to spend all my life wanting someone who does not want to spend time with me. I am very incidental in your life, and as time goes on, it is more and more. Well, please answer.

Robert misses you terribly, he cries he wants his Daddy; He says you need him, you need someone crazy around you; and he feels that is his role. That feeling of his makes it very difficult for me, because I am contemplating the idea of staying in Europe. For $25,000 we could buy a house or apartment. Europeans of all nations, spend three or four months of each year in Spain just living, and the rest working. Three or four months! If in years we could squeeze a few days, it is a lot. There is never time. There seems to be always that new project: the B.A. the Masters, the Ph.D. and now the new projects at work — always something else. I knew I had to be deeply dissatisfied to fall like this for John, but I did not know how much.

Please answer, I really feel we can let go of the new house. Talk with R and see if we can salvage some money out of it. I don't know; I am not there. So pay no attention to what I say. You do what you feel is right.

I just want time for me now. I am starting to discover how many deaths I had, and going through all the skeletons, and trying to find out who lives inside of me. Who is this new person, who is definitely not the dynamic 20 year old, but yet, the old 20 year old, who still wants a home, where people eat together, sit together, talk together — where what is natural to me, does not need to be worked on and changed, but shared and enjoyed?

Well, Allan, I am truly happy you are growing and you and Bb are getting along better. When two people can be friends and play together, they definitely have a great deal going and can certainly share their lives together. As you know, life does not need to be work . . . Yet that is all we ever did of it.

*It may be too difficult for Robert to remain here for so long
without seeing you. Maybe you could come in October or November
for two weeks. Think about it.*

    Please answer.

Love
Beatriz

Meanwhile, he was writing this letter, which passed mine in the
mail.

Palo Alto, California
August 5, 1979

Dear Beatriz:

    *I was so happy to receive your third letter (from Nerja) —
especially to read that your unhappiness has dropped away.*

    *Life here has been hectic for the last three or four weeks. House-
sitting . . . turned out to be a little more energy-dissipating than I
had bargained for — not her fault or the house's, just added
responsibilities and especially a division of my energy when it seemed
to have a lot of calls on it.*

    *Our house has not been sold yet, . . . but I am confident that it
will go alright, . . . E recommended some exterior and interior
painting to make it more attractive and I agreed . . . I repaired . . .
and totally repainted it . . . A beautiful job if I do say so myself!
However it was a lot of work and just about killed me for the next
week.*

    *That was the weekend of N's party and I chose not to go. A good
decision, I think.*

    *A painter recommended by E said he would paint the entire
exterior walls . . . plus . . . plus . . . for $ . . . I agreed. He did a
perfect job in four days. The house really looks sharp now and I'm
sure the energy put into it will attract the right buyer.*

    *There are so many things to tell you. I miss you and wish you
were here to tell in person. My life has been full, and hectic and I am
learning to be by myself, to be my own person, and to trust myself.*

    *Last Wednesday I visited S (finally!) and I told her all your news.
We talked about our problems with crowding. She and I seem to be in
the same boat versus other people. She has been seeing R quite a lot
lately and because of his high energy, etc. she feels somewhat pushed
to see more of him than she feels comfortable doing . . . But she also
feels he is so aware of her feelings that it is possible to deal with the
"crowding" reasonably well. I told her how I viewed our (your and
my) relationship in these terms and how it was repeating itself
somewhat with Bb. It was good to talk with her . . .*

. . . I drove . . . up to the Super Advanced Sex Workshop — all alone.

The workshop was super. The energy was so different, even from the Advanced. We were all gathered in the center of the floor, very close to each other, but not really touching. And it felt right to me, We were close, sometimes reaching out to touch each other, as if to say hello, I like you, yet we were in our own "spaces," not needing to touch. Looking back, I see that the touching at the end of the Beginner's was more needing than it seemed at the time.

The energy was very even and calm, a lot of peacefulness even in the turmoil of self-understanding that was taking place. For me, the revelation came (doesn't it always?) on Saturday Night and Sunday Morning. I had expressed the conflict of feeling that I did not have enough to bring to a relationship, even a friendship, and yet also feeling that people wanted more from me than I wanted to give — a doublebind if ever there was one! On Saturday Night at dinner, I did not have a date and when I went to sit in one or two empty seats at full tables, I was told they were taken.

Suddenly I felt I had not planned for the evening, had not taken care of myself. I sat at a table all alone. Even Stan noticed me and felt my bad vibes. He sat elsewhere. Then Sh came alone and rescued me. I knew it was a rescue and yet I was glad because I needed it and I realized the dumb stuff I was putting myself through. She and I and others who came to join us chatted and I got out my anger at myself and learned something.

On Sunday, I found myself looking around the group very dispassionately and realized that, although I would be happy to be with anyone there for a time, there was no one I really wanted to be with. A good feeling, a feeling of self-satisfaction. And I realized too that I don't need to be anything more than I am to be a suitable friend or lover Thank God. Finally one of the men . . . came up to me and . . . D . . . and told us how much he especially felt we two gave him a feeling of caring and support. It was so good to hear that, I can't tell you.

I learned that I can say what I want even when it conflicts with other's desires, and not have the roof fall in. A little more experience like that and I'll be perfect.

Bb and I . . . have been learning a lot about our relationship. She is aware that she wants a lot from me, and I am learning how to say no in a positive way. Last week, we took an hour to really go over the problems we were creating for ourselves — . . . my difficulty in expressing my feelings, wants, desires, etc. If she is to learn to be happy with herself, I have to learn to be clear about what I want (and to be happy with myself). We do love each other, but I finally made it clear that, even if I wasn't married and didn't have a

primary relationship, I was not ready to have a primary relationship
with her or anyone else . . . I expressed my realization that I do not
plan very well at all and that I feel I need to learn to do that.

A few of us went to a Moroccan restaurant . . . a beautiful dinner
— and behaved outrageously . . . and having a great time. I felt like
I ought to be embarrassed, but I wasn't . . . A very happy-go-lucky
occasion . . .

. . . called today . . . we are getting together . . .

. . . I'm having dinner in the city . . .

I don't know if that's everything, but it's a lot! I'm still working to
put myself on an even keel and slowly but observably I'm getting
there. I hope you and Robert are enjoying your farm life and the
beach and that the money is holding out. It sounds like you are
having a peaceful, reflective, relaxing time and I hope you are happy.

Love
Allan

This letter signaled the end of the era which had begun with
his letter of January 28, 1965, the "CONTRACT." At that time I
had determined that if I was patient my love would make him feel
confident in himself and thus emotionally **free** to **act**.

The time had come. He knew how to give care and support and
was **doing** it (others were recognizing this, as he mentioned in
his letter); he was expressing what he felt. Also, he was
beginning to believe what people were telling him about himself,
that he was a caring Human Being. I had told him a million times,
but now it was coming from unbiased sources. He was free. The
trilogy was finally being lived. He Thought, he Felt, he Did. My
job was done! It was time to let go.

TELEGRAM   August 16, 1979

Will stay in Spain until end of September. Send money and numerology
books. M address urgent please. Initiate Fast Nevada divorce procedures. I
want to be free by October 1st. Beatriz.

As I put down my hands to draft this telegram, I noticed my
ring was gone. The First Ring. It was the end of an era.

TELEGRAM Back   August 17, 1979

Nevada Impossible I want you. We need to talk. Send phone (number) and
time. Love. Allan.

PHONE CALL   August 22, 1979

Beatriz said: "My pain is good, purifying. I am not rejecting
You and I am not saying I don't love you. I want us to remain
friends. What YOU want is not in me. (looks, speech, etc.)"

I also told him about Jose, our meeting, and that the divorce had nothing to do with him.

Allan informed me he was coming to Spain. I told him I would be busy until Jose left, and that I would use the time of Allan's visit with Robert to go to Brussels to check out schools.

Allan said that he loved me, he did not want the divorce.

Reaction to my telegram, from a friend:

California
October 24, 1979

". . . I think the telegram you sent Allan was rotten — after 14 years he deserved more than a demand for a quick divorce with no explanation . . .

Somehow the "injured party" did not seem to need explanation. Why do we jump to conclusions so fast, to point the finger at someone? Why can't we wait until we have enough data to arrive at a positive conclusion?

Meanwhile, in answer to my August 4th letter, Allan had written:

Palo Alto, California
August 14, 1979

Dear Beatriz:

I love you. Very much. To the stars and all the worlds beyond, as well as right here on this earth. I feel the pain that you suffered because you were with me and loved me and stood by me when I truly needed you. And I feel the love that led you to do it. Even in my blackest most fearful moments, when I did not like you, or felt you wanted out, I knew you loved me. In my heart of hearts I knew. My sorrow is that I did not show my love for you. It was always qualified, reduced, rarely full and free. I believe that as I see myself better, through different people's eyes (not just Bb's) I am learning the facts that I could not face when you and I were going through our hard work. I can give. I'm beginning to see that now. Thank you for your love, for your strength. I pray to God that you will regain your life.

Allan

I had asked for a divorce **because** I love him and because I had **succeeded** in the tasks agreed upon. Only success permits us to move on. For me there is no such thing as falling **out** of love. Love can only grow. Because I wanted the best for **him,** I had to say, "let me go," so that **he** would be free!

Allan wrote "Notes to Himself" after receiving my divorce telegram. August 17, 1979 1:43 a.m.

I feel so empty — my heart has broken — suddenly I realize how much Beatriz and Robert mean to me. They are the lights in my dark life — good things that have happened to me. The divorce is impossible. I can't do it. I must stop it. I know the peace of my soul depends on it.

August 22, 1979

The phone call with Beatriz made me happy. She cried; she laughed, her voice touched my heart. I want to see her, to touch her, to show her how I am today; to feel her strength, her softness, her love, her caring.

And yet I feel I am still depending on her for approval and strength.

I was frightened at the thought of caring for Robert alone for a week (while Beatriz went to Brussels). But as I walked, I realized the fear and knew it would be all right. We would be happy together, reading, swimming, playing, being children together, and my "child" is truly joyous now!

To go dancing with Beatriz, who spent six hard months pushing me into others arms, all the while longing for me. It breaks my heart to think of the misery I have put her through just because I was too scared to live! So much fear and so much love. I want her to know that the fear that immobilized me has gone forever, burned out of me by the loss I felt when she sent me the final bomb — I knew I could and would do everything necessary to show her the new me — to keep her beside me, but only if she wanted it. I want her to want me and I want me to want her — that seems a little weird. I do love her and want her with me, but I would rather have her happy if it is not possible for it to be with me.

How much I see now that I have been escaping all my life — there is work, always work, the safe place to be, day and night — and even there I escape. "We have nothing to fear but fear itself." So simple, yet so profound. Now I know, feel, understand what that means. It is my inner strength that leads me forward. Now I do, rather than procrastinate . . . I feel Great!!! Everything I do makes me feel better, stronger, powerful. I thank God that I have found this inner well.

Note: "I want me to want her" . . . but he did not, and I knew it. "Want" is different from "love." This is a "divorce of love": "I would rather have her happy, if it is not possible for it to be with me."

Sept. 2, 1979   5:00 a.m.

Beatriz came into my life when I needed her desperately. That need has gone. I would repay it, but how? By letting her go about her business of helping those who need her? Jose needs her strength and breadth of view. Stephan also needs her to open his eyes and heart and strength.

Perhaps Robertito does not need her now. When I was not strong in myself, he had only her to turn to. Now her strength and need to help may overwhelm him, rather than settle him, make him more "hyper."

It is time for the tide of Beatriz to flow out and the tide of Robert to flow in?

These decisions cannot, must not be made on emotion.

Note: Just what I had said about the marriage decision! This is a **Being** acting Consciously.

He was well aware of what had been accomplished. His desire to "repay" was **acted** upon (Thought, Desire, Action) in his divorce settlement, designed to provide support for Robert and me for a few years so that I would not immediately become occupied with making a living.

There was much work to be done to undo the purchase of my "dream house," begun just before I left for Europe.

A friend wrote to me:

> Berkeley, CA
> October 27, 1979

". . . You created the situation of the house but you left it to other people to sort out the mess. You instruct Allan to do all those things for you, which anyone with backbone would resent . . ."

Allan **had** backbone. But he knew I had followed instructions from him for years and years — when he had been too scared to even face a salesperson.

I had bought **everything** for Allan.

> July 28, 12 mid day

My love:

They are too small, darn it!
Better get 36-32: 36" waist
32" leg

Pls: note: one pair is 33" leg the other is 29". Anyway, the 34" waist is too small. Also, if possible, could the legs be a little looser in all 3 pairs, because these are much too tight.

> *Thank you my sweet,*
> *Yr ever-loving*
> *husband, Allan*

It was not easy, to go back and forth — especially when I did not even know the materials of North America. I was accustomed to cotton and silk and found myself in the midst of polyesters, rayons, etc. I was accustomed to being served and here had to go and look for the clothes myself. I knew centimeters and had to buy in inches. I was so confused! It felt as though I were in another world. But I did it. I learned because Allan needed a go-between until he could grow strong within. Finally, after all these years, he was strong.

So the facts are: neither was Allan without backbone, nor was I abusing my relationship with him. And Allan knew it!

Allan himself talked about his scaredness later to his brother:

Palo Alto, California
April 10, 1980

"... for me reaching out to other people has been the hardest thing, having grown up totally scared of what people think of me. It's gotten a lot better ..."

It was much better by the time I went to Spain.

Berkeley, California
August 8, 1979

Dear Beatriz:

... we had dinner with R and An two nights ago ... An said to Allan: "But you can talk! It's so nice. I never knew before that you could talk!"

Love
Sean

It was so much better that he wrote to his Mother about his participation in a sex education movie. He continues:

April 9, 1980

Dear Mom,

... I love you, and you are very strong, despite all your illnesses. And now I believe I am becoming strong too, Thank God, and thank all the friends and teachers who have come my way — a real blessing.

I told my friend Sam about ... (it) and he said he envied my guts and adventuresomeness. That's odd, he is so outgoing and talkative and charming — I envy that in him. But we will learn from each other, and that's one of the true meanings of life ...

I have discovered that I still do all the things I dislike in myself, even when I am alone. Now I don't have anyone to blame but me! So I have to get my act together! I love you, and Dad, and ... (brothers).

Bless you all
Love Allan

Allan had developed to this from a person who could not shop for his own clothes, nor assert himself with a waiter if service was not given!

Precisely **because** Allan had backbone, he did not resent it. He had all the facts and therefore came out with positive conclusions.

When are we going to learn to withhold judgment until we can arrive at a positive?

When Allan came uninvited to Nerja in September and met Jose in person, I had soon followed Jose back to Brussels. I returned to Nerja after Allan had gone back to California, and found this note on the table of Jose's apartment, where Allan had stayed. We had talked of all coming to California for Christmas.

September, 1979

Dear Beatriz,

. . . I look forward to seeing you all in December, including Jose. Any friend of yours is a friend of mine, if he wants to be. I am glad he makes you happy; you deserve it.

Please write and so will I. And remember that I love you very much and I care what happens to you, and I care for you.

Love and Kisses,
Allan

P.S. I wanted to buy a teddy bear as a parting gift for the child. HE wanted a rifle! (It's always hard to give people what they want, instead of what one wants).

Please keep The Powers That Be *and the lighter and scissors,*

Love, blessings and peace.
Allan

Again Allan mentions caring and loving me. Yet his love is for my happiness, and so he offers Jose his friendship and is glad Jose makes me happy.

The first P.S. referred to Robert, "the child." This story told me Allan was finally free. He was now following the Law: Not my Will, but Yours. He had converted a simple action into a sacrament.

Dictionary definition of "sacrament": "An outward and visible sign of inward spiritual grace."

Dictionary definition of "grace": "favor, goodwill, kindness, **disposition to oblige another;** short prayer."

He had produced an outward sign, which was based on giving up (sacrificing) **his own** desire and acting on what another person wanted. By that action, he prayed. He bowed to Love for his son.

This is **not** the bowing because "I am afraid of you;" "You are my boss and I value my job," or, "I can't contradict you because you may leave." No. That is the bowing of weakness, which leads to death. He had bowed to Love, which comes from Strength. This bowing takes one to freedom.

But first of course, he must know what he really **wants.** And that is his next journey. To discover what he likes, and enjoy it to the fullest!

The last sentence, "Please keep **The Powers That Be** and the lighter and scissors." He had left a lighter and a pair of scissors. But I always read the unconscious. To me the Universe was saying . . . Reading from right to left, as all sacred writings: "Use your scissors, (your mind) to cut your confusion with the lighter, (your inner light) and you will arrive at **The Powers That Be.**" That was precisely where I had always wanted to go. **The Powers That Be,** would give me the answers I had been looking for so steadily all my life. Who am I? What am I? Why am I? Where am I going? That is why I had decided to stay in Spain: to clarify. Allan gave me the recipe. We constantly give pearls to each other! I thanked him so deeply in my heart for that last note!

He wrote to himself while still in Nerja:

Nerja, Spain
Sept. 2, 1979 5 a.m.

— *I love Beatriz.*
— *Beatriz loves me.*
— *We love Robertito.*
— *Beatriz has recognized a lot of pain from our past 14 years.*
— *She has not yet gone through that pain and must, before we can ever (if ever) come together again.*
— *Jose is a return to the strength, attentiveness and energy of her father; he is an attempt to regain what she sees as the good part of her life.*
— *What Beatriz sees as her "Mommy role" with me is that of a wife helping her husband to become strong in himself. Now when that strength surfaces, she has trouble dealing with what she has accomplished.*
— *At this point I know I do not need Beatriz to make me strong.*
— *At this point Beatriz needs to realize she can be dependent on someone (or everyone or anyone) without giving up her own sovereignty and that in fact, she must allow herself that freedom and intimacy and vulnerability before she can be truly free.*
— *I believe her realization must come before we can truly ever be husband and wife again.*
— *And yet I have thought this evening that I should offer her one last (?) chance to end this process by coming home with me on September 10. She will refuse. But I will have taken my best shot.*

— Beatriz still cares what other people think, although she disguises it as protection of Jose. I believe she believes what she says.
— In spite of all this, I believe that Robert is better off with her than with me for the short term at least. (I mostly believe this, but something in my heart says it is not true.) Perhaps this decision can be left over until Christmas, when she, Robert and Jose will come to California. I feel much emotion and fear about this, so perhaps the belief is invalid. This will take more reflection and thought.
— I know I do not feel "saddled" with Robert if he comes to live with me. Perhaps the peace I feel . . .

COMMENTS —

Allan was assessing the situation quite accurately:

— Yes, I loved him and he loved me. Yes, we both loved Robert.
— Yes, I was experiencing a horrible pain which I did not know how to stop.
— Yes, Jose was a return to the good part of my life. Someone was next to me who was proud of me, who wanted to be with me, who thought how I dressed, spoke, moved my hands when I spoke, ate, interacted with the world, and my size were all perfect! Oh! Yes, I felt good, after all those years of feeling Allan's embarrassment about me! His lack of confidence made him feel "others" would not approve that I looked so formal, moved my hands while I spoke, spoke with strangers, like to eat in a very formal manner, had to lose weight, (always more, never enough) and was never perfect. Yes, it was good to hear Jose say, "Don't lose one pound, I think you are beautiful, you are perfect."
— Yes, he could clearly see he did not need me to give him strength anymore, I could see that too! My time had come, I had to go. I had followed "need," I was not needed anymore.
— Yes, he could see I needed to become dependent upon someone, anyone, or everyone, to be truly free. It was true. I had never ever depended on anyone. I had never ever allowed myself an intimacy and vulnerability with anyone. Now, I have opened myself totally, and as he said, to Everyone. I am all or nothing.
— Yes, he saw that his strength was the result of something I had accomplished. The one and only point which I disagree strongly is the negation of my own feelings. He denies I feel like a Mommy. I felt like his Mommy, not his wife. And now I feel like the Mommy of the world. Never, except with Jose for a little while, had I felt anything other than: "I am your Mommy." The lack of acceptance of this feeling from my friends in California had been a great source of pain for me.

Now what does "I am your Mommy," mean to me? A Mother **knows** the whole process of life. She knows the child is born; she will help the child go through the learning of talking, walking, adjusting to others, writing, dating; she knows her child will walk away from her to form his own life, to have his own children. She will love all of it; she will support all of it; she will see his future, his old age. She wishes the best for him. She desires to die before her child. She would give up her life to extend the life of her child. And I did feel all of that for him . . . and now for the world.

I always know whenever I see a person, how that person got to be where he/she is, and what he can do to get where he wants to go. Even if I personally may not want to go there, I will support each one to get where **he** wants to go — if that will not lead to hurting himself or others.

I will **not** support you to drink. So I will not drink with you, even if I do enjoy a glass of wine. I **will** support you to study, if it's what you want, even if I think it's a "crutch."

A mother is a person who **knows** she can read an Agatha Christy novel, and enjoy it, but **chooses** to spend the time playing blocks helping her child, laugh, play, live!

By her example she can teach her children to **know,** and to **choose!**

Nerja, Spain
October 5, 1979

Dear Allan:

I hope you had a good trip and are well. My trip to Brussels was good. I was able to see the city, and the prices at the schools. I think Robert will have to go to the normal French school and soon will learn French. The price is . . . quite a lot for a private school.

I learned too that Jose has his money because he won the lottery, but does not have any idea of how to make it grow, so here we go again.

. . . Robert is OK now, he is going to school and learning more and more Spanish and is getting to be more calm. Jose came Sept. 29 to Oct. 2 to be with us, and Robert reacted very well, and very loving. I was truly surprised! Well, the weather here — after your storm — is back to warm and sunny, so when I came back it was good again.

I would like to know what happened with the divorce. I don't want to move in with Jose without being married and I don't want to spend my life in Nerja. Did you see a lawyer? Did you find out how to go about it? It is possible to do it in Nevada or in the Islands for a quicky? I know if it is with the consent of both parties it is possible and fast in Puerto Rico or something like it. Please answer me.

215

. . . About Christmas, Jose said whatever I want, he wants, . . .
Without addresses I feel lost. I want to arrange the trip . . . please
send addresses . . . I will leave Robert with you most of the time since
I will be driving Jose around, and I think in this way Robert will be
near . . . (friends). See if in December Robert can be enrolled at . . .
sometimes I can take him, sometimes if you have to work, he has a
place that he likes and knows to be.

I am writing on the beach so I can't write that well. Please write
or send telegram. (A friend) . . . sent a post card from Madrid and it
took 6 weeks to reach Nerja . . . !!

Allan, I was thinking that we really are good friends, but
somehow I don't miss anything . . . what's wrong with me? I have no
feelings? Freddy . . . yes . . . I miss him!!! I feel as if I am blank
now, nothing behind, and not knowing what lies ahead.

I got involved with the City Hall of Nerja and next Tuesday,
Wednesday, Thursday and Friday from 11 to 2 o'clock all the
children of Nerja will paint a Mural in the Balcony of Europe, free
subject. I am involved in that. Glad that I have done something while
here. Robert started painting classes on Friday. School seems to be
going well, in fact I think he behaves and looks softer in his way. He
says that now that he has the gun you bought he is able to get rid of
his hate. Maybe he is right.

Tuesday 9th of October: The activities of The Feria, of painting
the Mural, (which) were (expected) . . . to last 4 days; started today
and tomorrow will be finished! It looks OK!

Allan, please start sending Robert's books to Brussels so that when
he arrives he can start feeling at home there. The cards that you
bought are fantastic; please keep that going. Could you keep sending
books and cards? not those activities envelopes but the cards of animals
and such. Make him a member and give them the address of
Belgium. Please keep sending books, new books; they are very
expensive here and bad ones — they break.

Well, I hope you can have a few minutes to write and tell me
what's going on. I do not know how you are feeling but I never felt
like this before. Today is the 9th of Oct. I hope your cheque gets here
by the 15th. It would be nice to have arranged something that could
arrive on the 15th or 1st of each month.

How is your work going? How are you organizing your life!?

Is there any news about the house? or income tax? Please send
information. When I had just come (here) I was waiting, for news.
After my telegram of divorce I was bombarded with letters, telegrams,
flowers; now I feel left dry again. Please keep me informed. Send
telegram if you can't write. Send my love to everyone, tell them I'll
see them when I get there.

Freddy, I hope you have received my letter to you. The mail here is so bad I never know if what I write gets there or not. Well, love to all. Keep well and please move for the divorce. The division of money can wait until next year.

Until soon,
Love Beatriz

Nerja, Spain
November 2, 1979

Dear Allan:

. . . Do I love him? (Jose) I do not know, I want to repay that extraordinary feeling that I get from him, I guess. I guess I wish that what he gives me you could give me; then I would have it all. I know I love you. I know I did and would do almost anything for you, and I do know I would not for this man. Yet, he has given me and Robert far more than you ever did. How unfair life is! Why can't I give him as much? Why can't you give me as much? I guess we never give to those who give to us, and we pay by giving to others?!!

Beatriz

I was saying that Jose was giving to me because he was overflowing himself — from his Love Center — **not** because he felt any obligation or need.

Allan's love had always come to me from his Fear Center, because of a sense of need, and later a sense of "had to" or "should."

I loved Allan because I was overflowing myself — from **my** Love Center.

I loved Jose not only because I was overflowing my Love Center, but because I wanted to **repay** him — from my Fear Center, a sense of "should," also.

Nerja, Spain
November 24, 1979

Dear Allan:

October 17th I received a telegram from you in which you said you sent money to Banco Atlantico. Today . . . I received $400. First I thought you would send $600 a month. You left on Sept. 15th. I had enough for 15 days. You knew it. OK, you sent it on October 16th, but . . . it did not arrive until now. The only sure way to send money according to the Bank, (is) . . .

Well, enough of money. But I had so little I could not send a telegram or anything. I was left at one point with 21 pesetas. Pilar gave me $ . . . and the grocery gave me credit to eat. I did not want to ask Jose . . .

Anyhow, I want to tell you that we'll not be going to California this December as planned, because if we were going to live in Europe, yes, but we (have) decided we'll go to California to live. I personally would like to stay and so does he, but just because we want to be happy, we can't allow Robert not to have a father.

Robert, 15 days after you left, was waiting for a letter from you. He decided in his head you would write to him every 3 days, then he decided you would do it once a week, then he decided every 15 days, because that is when Daddy gets his checks and not only will he write but he'll send me something. Then it was 21 days, 30 days, 35 days, 40 days, 45 days, 50 days, 55 days, 60 days. At that point he said to me that if he could cry all the tears that he feels inside, when we open the door of the apartment a river would flow down stairs.

I know you love him; yet you can't change that much. You can't start thinking about another person when you have never done it. To learn . . . will take time, and to keep a relationship going one needs . . . to put in the time writing, or to be there. Of course that is easier.

So Jose decided it would be better for Robert to be near you. Robertito loves Jose, he says he is his father in Europe but, when we go to California, he'll be his Tio Jose. Jose does not want to usurp your place, but can see Robert's pain, so he writes to him from Belgium and gives him cars and plays chess, and teaches him little games. Well, what I am saying is that we will go basically because Robert needs a father and we do not want him to lose you. YOU ARE IMPORTANT, you know? So, we'll be going between May and June 1980, after school finishes.

Now, do not worry about the divorce. We'll take care of it when we are there. I need to talk with you, maybe through the phone once.

Robert is really doing very well here at school. His marks are excellent in every subject; his Math is good; he is learning to multiply, etc. He is sitting down and doing his work. He is learning that he is not the center of the world, and allowing others to be. He is being far more human, more loving, more considerate. I wish we could stay. Family life here is so strong and is doing a world of good to him.

I felt very frightened for a while because I did not have any money and felt terribly dependent. I think it was good for me. But I really want to organize my life so that I can feel secure. For that I will ask you this: You know I always wanted to buy houses and if we had done so we could have had more. Anyhow, you do have your education, and when we bought the Emerson house we said we would put that house in my name alone. Well, what I want is that house just for me . . . (even if) it . . . cost one million, to me that is irrelevant. I want the house because I can live there alone with Robert and know he can go to school and no one will increase my rent. I can rent the apartment and one room and cover the mortgage, and with the $600 you will give me we could live. You can keep the cash and profit of the other house and buy a new one . . .

I guess what I want is security. I hope that (it) will work out with Jose. But I want to arrange my life in (such) a way that if it does not, I can be OK. So I want to . . . live . . . in that house. Do you understand?

Maybe later I could work, but now I don't want to. I know I am right, for me and Robert. Freddy passed lots of tests with drugs, etc. He was strong because he received love. He did not feel a void that others feel; and Robert will need even a stronger feeling, being who he is. I don't want him to be a drug addict or stealing or whatever. So I need to be there for him. Now more than ever I can see that and I can see the results. It's marvelous to see!

Maybe you think I am asking for a lot of money but I think that we did not put in a lot and I want to be able to live. So I will not take money out, I just want to be secure, to know I have a roof in a good area.

You and I know I'm smart, but I have gone around trying for jobs. Never again — in a place where to be a waitress, "Perfect Recipe," one needs two years (of) college. I feel I do not want to go back and study. Yet, I know I can't get a decent job; maybe typing envelopes, no thank you.

I feel in this way you can buy . . . a 2 bedroom house in Palo Alto or a 3 in Mountain View, to be near us. With you will always remain your education. I ask the house in exchange for all the years of school. Your earning power has gone up; mine — especially in this area — has gone down. Well . . . think about it and let me know.

Jose has some money but he won the lottery, so he really does not know how to make it. He is a (skilled) laborer. So in a few years, unlike you, he will not be able to depend on his muscles. With years, you'll be far more creative; he'll be going down like all laborers do. So I can't depend on him. I need to organize my life independently of anyone who will share my life.

The other thing: he'll have to learn English. It'll be hard for him. And he is doing all of this not for himself, but because of Robert and you, seeing what is best for all around. So don't change the house too much.

How are you? How is Freddy? . . .

. . . Somehow I feel you will agree to that even though from the *outside it does not look even. But our relationship never was, why should the parting be?*

Allan, you are a good friend, I always say that to Jose. I can see myself talking to you about him. Jose has come once a month to see us for three days and on December 18th I'll be going to Brussels to spend the Holidays there.

If you could send two or three books a month to Robert, he would be so happy. He feels abandoned by you. Allan, he loves you and by telepathy is hard for a 7 year old. It will be only until May. Write to him; send him something; make him feel you love him. I was not going to say or ask you, but it's hard on the little guy.

He is a little guy. For you two months is nothing; for him, a life time! And he is so aware of time! Just like you are not! Well, say Hello to everyone and I'll be seeing everyone soon for always.

Allan keep well.

> *Love*
> *Beatriz*

In this letter I express my understanding that life is a process and developments take time: "I know you love him (Robert), yet you can't change that much. You can't start thinking about another person when you have never done it. To learn will take time . . ."

I display my use of a symptom to diagnose and cure; "I felt very frightened for a while because I did not have any money." As **Symptom**, "It was good for me." From the symptom I was able to **diagnose** and determine the **cure**: "I need to organize my life independently of anyone who will share it."

Any symptom is there for a purpose: to indicate **how** to align oneself to what must be. If one has physical symptoms, they make us aware of how we can align ourselves back to Health! So whatever happens, I view as good. In this case, the symptom clearly pointed to the solution. Now, I could **do** something about it. Otherwise, I would have been dependent on another, and not aware of my dependency.

In the letter I also reveal how I was trying to find economic security based on predictable income, for the period when I would be performing the Primary function of the society: raising a Human Being. Without the successful completion of **that** job, there would be none to appreciate the Secondary products my employment in the labor market could have produced. Even if I could produce the greatest Masterpiece, it would be a Secondary product, and would need someone to appreciate, to see it, to use it. Any Masterpiece, without a Human Being on the other end, is useless. So to me, putting our energy into raising our children as complete Human Beings, is the **number one priority.**

The results of my efforts to fill Robert's needs were already apparent when he was five. At that age he visited his grandparents in Canada. Here is how he seemed to our old friend Brian.

Toronto, Canada
August 23, 1977

Dear Beatriz,

Well, it was love at first sight with Robert and me. He came marching through the barriers at Toronto airport and I gave him the official "welcome to Toronto" handshake and he accepted it as if he were a visiting international dignitary. What a kid! You've done a marvelous job on him. He manages to preserve all the vitality and drive he was born with, but has a highly controlled way about him. His manners are impeccable. If he's charging and comes to an obstacle of two people talking, he'll excuse himself before he goes through. I don't know how you did it.

He's also a great bluffer. He sets himself forward as one who can and will be participating in any conversation. Nothing and no words are too great for him, regardless of the fact that he hasn't the faintest idea of what they mean. I asked him, as I never talk down to kids (our mother never did with us) as soon as we got back to . . . , if the plane ride had been a hectic and harrowing experience. Within a minute he told me he had had a "hectic and harrowing" day . . .

Love
Brian

CHRISTMAS 1979

Snowflake Card

Dear Beatriz:

You are one of a kind. A beautiful, flowing snowflake who has brought joy to my life. I'm glad you are happy.

Love
Allan

This card was received in Brussels while I was with Jose. Allan has the soul of a child, pure, no jealousy, no possessiveness, with gladness for others. Again, he was showing me his greatness . . . (All the more reason for me to let go!) My mother had seen this and written many years before:

Buenos Aires, Argentina
May 16, 1966

Dear Beatriz:

. . . I am so happy to receive your letter, but especially the few lines from Allan, who returns all the love I have for him.

221

People here think I am crazy to love him as much as I do. They say I don't know him well. But I saw him and I loved him. You know that. And you know I never make mistakes when I love a person.

Allan has a great soul. It is the soul of a child, which is the purest a being can have in this world. I am so happy you tell me you are very happy! And no, it does not bore me to know you are happy . . .

Mama

The lines of communication between us while we were separating were always open. I kept my respect and admiration for him, and he continued to always see the greatness in everyone. His work was a case in point:

Palo Alto, California
October 18, 1979

Dear Beatriz:

. . . Well Peter (my boss) is leaving the company to go into business with two other former employees at the end of October. His going leaves a huge hole in the company, impossible to fill because of his breadth of interest and abilities. So what happens to me? I will be working for Sam.

Love
Allan

Nerja, Spain
November 2, 1979

Dear Allan:

. . . I hope you enjoy working with Sam! It seems so strange . . . ! He knows your superiority. It must give him a great satisfaction and create self-esteem for him to have someone of your caliber working for him . . . Usually it is the other way around . . .

Love
Beatriz

Palo Alto, California
February 18, 1980

Dear Beatriz:

. . . It may be that Sam feels superior with me working for him — I don't think so. I see him as much more attuned to the business world and therefore more managerial, while I am more artistically inclined. We are working well together.

Abrazos,
Allan

His response, as always, was a teaching for me. I always compared him to the rest of the world and showed him the areas in which he was better than anyone else, in an effort to give him confidence in who he was. It was much harder to communicate to him an idea of caliber — that he did **very well** everything with which he became involved. He always patiently showed me he was no better — nor worse — just different, and side-stepped the caliber issue. What a privilege to have lived with this Human Being! Here, I was the student.

Nerja, Spain
Jan. 15, 1980

Dear Allan:

Robert and I are back in Nerja after seeing Kirsten and April in Denmark. How big (grown up) and beautiful April is . . . !!! 15 degrees Centigrade below zero!! I had forgotten how beautiful the snow was. Jose went there for three days and met them. I was warm since Jose gave me a beautiful fur coat (Astrakhan) for Christmas.

I am still confused. I guess you were for a long time and it was possible for you to be with me. But I seem to need time for myself, and recapture my culture, my values, my self. I hope you are working on demonstrating what you feel.

Maybe still there is hope for us. I love you, I know that; yet, I never had time and Allan I need you to know that I exist. I need you to demonstrate what you feel for me and give me time with you. I want a home for Robert, a real and normal home where he counts . . . I don't want all that sex, for me. Maybe you need it, or needed it, but I don't.

I hope to be here until Robert finishes his school in May or maybe earlier. I'll let you know.

Do I make sense? My wounds seem to be healed by Jose, but I'm not sure Jose is for me. I feel connected with him for always, and all this, as part of it.

I received your checks. It was a nice surprise to hear from you and Freddy on Christmas . . .

How are you? Do you still feel you want to wait for me? or are you organizing your life with me out of it?

So much has happened to me inside!! Sometimes I think I was frightened of enjoying you. Or that now that you did not need me, I should not be there. But above all I felt for a long time the wound of you not wanting me, of the wait . . . that was OK as long as no one else had you. But then I saw you giving and starting to give to me only as a guilty feeling, as "If I want to give to so and so, (then) I must give to Beatriz." It was not, "I want to give to Beatriz," but I must if I want this or that."

I feel really well and enjoyed Denmark a great deal this time. It was great that I went again.

I feel calm in Spain: to be able to speak Spanish again, to be around people who feel that what I do, Mothering, is an important job, that every one around feels like this, is so good. It's so hard to hear Andrea speak about me as having no value, and to be there, where only a job for money counts. I tried and tried to prevent it from affecting me, but I am Human and we all need to feel valuable.

I was very happy to see the cards that you sent to everyone. What does that mean? That you are starting to demonstrate, or that it's easier without me? Answer me, Please.

Say Hello to everyone.

I will not live in Belgium. Spain, I would not mind; but I would rather that Robert have you. You are very special to him, and to me, too. I hope you know that. Let him know about you; talk to him as to a child. He is interested in games and such, and not so much in what you are going through. Put yourself in his shoes and feel it.

Well, I'll let you go now. Hope you and Sam are well at work. And I hope to see you soon. We need to talk, and wait, and talk and wait.

Your Christmas card really touched me; thank you, thank you very much.

Yes, you are right (per phone conversation while I was in Brussels), appearances are important to me: dress and environment. I don't like empty packages, but I like to feel beautiful and be next to someone well dressed. Well Allan, keep well and keep in touch.

> Love
> Beatriz

Subsequently in a phone conversation, I raved about how sweet Spanish sounded to my ears.

Allan, who has an extraordinary love for his language, interpreted these statements as an attack on English. He wrote:

> Palo Alto, California
> May, 1980

Dear Beatriz:

This is not the letter you were expecting after our chat, but I felt angry this morning about what you said about English. It may be true that for you and a million others, English is not as sweet as Spanish, etc., etc., but English was the language of the country and the people who took you in and helped you make a new life. You repaid this by complaining about the language and making very little effort to do it and say it right. You saw you were put down by me and others. *True. But I think it was due to your lack of care, your cavalier, "it doesn't matter" attitude, your "my language is better than yours." How would you like an attack on something you cared for?*

You would (and do) respond with claws and cold fury. Beatriz, your attitude toward English is a poison, like bigotry. (mine is better because it is mine) It is bigotry. I am sorry. These words had to be written. I hope you will accept them in the true love in which I send them. Please remember that I do love you, and love sometimes involves the pain of truth.

Always,
Allan

He did not understand my love of my native language and culture. I believe the distinguished Spanish thinker Jose Ortega y Gasset explained my way of thinking to the hilt, when he said in Buenos Aires (El Hombre a La Defensiva, 1929): ". . . the Argentine likes himself. If one understands these words exactly one sees there is no essential vanity. What we like, does **not** have to be the best in the world. It is not a question of value, better or worse. It is enough that we feel that it has Something and with that, that we **like** it . . ."

Precisely **because** I had made English my own, and immersed myself in its thought patterns I had forgotten how Spanish felt! In fact, I relearned it when I came to California. I may feel one language is more comfortable for me than another because I can express myself in it more fluently (because I know it better); this does not mean I think it is better. I feel more comfortable in old shoes: I can walk and walk in old shoes; new ones can give me blisters! New ones don't know me, or me them, so well! If I hurt you Allan — and I know I did — I hope this book, written in the language of Shakespeare — not of Cervantes — will stand as proof that my feeling is **Not** "better or worse," **Not** "mine or yours," but rather "Yours is Mine," **even if** I don't know it well and may never know it as well!

But before the language discussion erupted, and yet while it was already brewing, our love continued to be expressed.

Palo Alto, California
February 14, 1980

Beatriz, my love:

Just like a buttterfly, our love and friendship continues to unfold and spread its gossamer wings. I love you very much — as a lover, as a wife, as a friend, as mother, as teacher, as student. We are together in this joyful odyssey toward truth and beauty. Will you be my Valentine?

Love
Allan

Dear Beatriz:

I love you and you love me — why can't we live together? It's a hard question. Since I talked to you at Christmas, and especially since I got your letter of January 15, I've really concentrated on this question. It appears that for that to succeed, both of us have to make changes in how we relate to each other. This is the hard part.

I've come to some conclusions about my current needs — to live alone and to reach out to the people I want near me. So much of my life so far has been shaped by coincidence or someone else's idea or trip, you know: Let's go to a movie, let's have a party, let's make love, etc. When too much of that happens at once, I pull away because I can feel the pressures and I "don't know what I want" and I feel pushed around, even though it may be what I want too.

Also, I need to deal with doing what I have to do in a timely fashion — either doing it or disposing of it positively — not procrastinating.

I understand your need for having "Mothering" seen as OK. I am waiting for you. I am organizing my life with me in it. (Damn hard job for a 41 year old) How is Robert?

Beatriz, my exploration of my life in the last year or so (we met Stan 16 months before) has been hard for you. Learning new things, I found it was easier to practice on strangers than on you. But I felt you wanted so much that I had to give to you in order to be free to experiment and learn. I felt cornered by my feelings — probably guilt and your regular reminder that I gave to others what I did not give to you.

By the way, I have stopped talking about the divorce — my family is simply spending some time in Spain. I feel there is time enough to figure out the next steps when you and Robert return. And time enough to tell people when something really happens. (It's such a conversation drag to say to our acquaintances "I'm getting a divorce," especially at parties — the story is a drag and people expect me to be sad or depressed when I'm not — as you know.) I feel the separation is important for both of us to sort out our lives and our own relationships. You know, in many ways, what I want and what you want are pretty close: I want to give you more, I really do, and you want more from me. I haven't found anyone I like better than you. I doubt if I ever will.

. . . Everyone has been very supportive to me — and to you — and I appreciate that love. I love you. I love Robert. My feelings of what I want are still not fully clear — but they will be. I hope you are also becoming clear on what you want, and that we can decide what to do when you return.

Allan

Nerja, Spain
March 20, 1980

Dear Allan:

. . . When I said I am confused I did not mean that I do not know what I want. I know exactly what I want. I always knew it. What I do not know is if I should remain in this relationship, or if I should go alone, or with Jose . . .

Love, Beatriz

I had never, ever, opened myself up to anyone. What I wanted had been kept inside of myself always: To have the answers to my three questions: Who am I? What am I? Why am I? I knew that was what I had always wanted, but what road to take to **get** those answers . . . ?

I had opened the same letter with the following:

. . . One whole month has passed since Valentine's, and I have not written . . . Well, I want to say "Thank you," the flowers were beautiful . . .

Beatriz

Palo Alto, California
April 1, 1980

Dear Beatriz:

. . . What I do know is that I love you very much, and I want you home. I've had a lot of time to think and to try all the new waters that have been opened to me by my new-found openness. But for all that's gone before, you are still the only one. I know it's been hard for you — all this waiting and hoping while I spread my butterfly wings for the first time — but it had to be — I needed to go out and take chances I never took before.

When I got your letter, I was ready to sell all and move to Spain — For Robert and for you, because you seem so happy there. But I think I have a little more to deal with here. I can't yet let go of my solitary life when I am just finding myself. (A paradox, considering the words above.) But I am moving quickly through this period and I should be done with it when you return.

As far as I'm concerned, you can have the house or anything else I have, if you want it, or need it. (That feels good but scary to write.) Please remember that, whatever happens, I am who I am, and I love you, respect you, and want to do what I can to help you be happy.

Love
Allan

These words told me how naive my little boy really was.

First, he thought that because he had tried his "new found" freedom, he knew what it meant to be free. He was still married to me. A piece of paper does tie. If I was right, once he was really free — divorced — the feeling would be gone. If I was wrong, the feeling which he said he had for me would remain with him.

Second, he was just beginning to find himself, to know what he liked, what he disliked, what he wanted, what he didn't want — after long years of hard work by both of us; and now he could imagine this path could be dealt with in a few months?! I knew better.

Because the Marriage "Contract," was a finished success, he did not need me anymore; I had to let go. Just as one moves from school to a job, success is what prompts one to move on.

Dear Allan:

Nerja, Spain
April 9, 1980

. . . I am happy that this year has been of great benefit for you. I do know you needed it. If it would not have been so, I would not have given you the support you needed.

I continue the same as I was when we got married. My needs are the same and I continue with the same dreams. But now there is a difference: before, I could wait, now I have a child who needs a father and a home. He can't wait.

To form a home, two elements are necessary: First there must be a "couple." Second, the couple must have as a principal objective: to give, give, give . . . to share with their children and the world. In this way the couple grows, by learning to live for other human beings . . . They are an example of generosity, kindness, giving, giving, and patience . . . The child SEES and learns human values, the ones which can't be learned at school . . . The child feels emotionally satisfied and does not need drugs of any type . . .

. . . you tell me "I love you"; you always said it; I always believed you. But there is only one proof of love: TIME! One thing is to speak, the other is to love! I said "I love you," but my life was at your disposition: my time, if you would have wanted it, was yours; my thoughts followed you everywhere, at home and outside. How is it possible that you can see this as "Crowding"? I do not know . . .

Beatriz

Dear Allan:

. . . You said you understand how hard it must have been for me to
see you free. How wrong you are! That made me happy, that brought
satisfaction to me. What was hard was something else.

I thought I was an example, for 14 years, of what Love is. To be
there for you. To allow you to enter my Being whenever you wanted.
To never hide from you, not even a thought. To ask for what I
wanted. I was hoping you would some day do the same.

What I asked were not big things . . . things of everyday: to go to
bed together, . . . to get up together, . . . to have the hope or the
illusion everyday, that at a certain hour you would come, and this
thought could give me the strength during the day, (which) I needed
to keep going among people who are uncaring and apathetic. But that
hour never arrived; that was the pain, Allan. The pain appeared here
in Nerja, the pain drowned for many, many years. But God seems to
give to one exactly what one needs . . .

Beatriz

Robert and I returned from Spain to Palo Alto in early June 1980.

For my Birthday:

Palo Alto, California
June 24, 1980

Beatriz:

Thanks for the memories — and now something to keep them with!
(a Kodak electronic flash camera)

Dear Miss:

Ah? You are not Miss? Don't tell me! Well,

Dear Mrs:

Take my big Congratulation on your birthday, and if you permit
me, Yo te quiero mucho . . . mucho . . . mucho (I love you very
much . . . much . . . much . . . Spanish song)

I am, sincerely, your lovingly husband,

Allan

Meanwhile, in August 1979 I had met Jose the very evening of
the day I had sent the divorce telegram to Allan. Our relationship
built quickly and warmly.

Here are some of his letters, translated from the French:

> Bruxelles
> September 12, 1979

My dear:

> The time seems so long without you by my side, and the days are
> unending. Day after day I tell myself that life without you at my side
> is impossible . . .

> One, hundred, thousand
> kisses for you,
> Jose

I noted to myself in my diary:

> Yesterday I received one letter, my first love letter in my life . . . A
> letter that came not out of guilt, of not doing what one should or
> should not do, but a letter saying how long the days are for him
> without me, how life seems impossible without me . . . "without me!!!
> Me!!! Me!!!"
> I cried from happiness. He does not understand why I cried, but I
> feel things so deeply. It was happiness that I felt; it was gratitude to
> God for giving me love through Jose.

> Bruxelles
> December 8, 1979

> Dear:

> I love you more than yesterday and less than tomorrow and I will
> be waiting ardently for you at 5 o'clock at the airport. Did you
> receive the transference?

> Lots of kisses
> Jose

As if I needed to signal my second era, Jose bought me a
beautiful gold ring. It is in two colors of gold, like the one I lost on
the beach at the end of the first era. Many Inca Gods were
depicted on the first ring; the second looks like a serpent.

Jose is a very intuitive person and he began to feel it would be a
mistake for us to live together.

> Bruxelles
> February 26, 1980

> Dear Beatriz:

> . . . I need to work out my life and prove myself to myself and
> without somebody to rely on to do it. I know that I will hurt you but
> I cannot actually think of living together, I feel it inside of myself and
> I know that it would be a failure. I know my feelings for you are
> always the same . . . I need to have confidence in myself again, and
> then be able to say that I am your companion for life. I am solely a

man who is seeking himself and does not know who he is, what he can do . . . I wish you to understand that the time to make a commitment has not come yet, it will be a mistake and everybody will be unhappy, if we push the destiny.

Un abrazo,
Jose

I confronted him with these responses to his recent letter:

— It is nothing new to me that you are looking for yourself. Examples: You asked me to come to Belgium — Fear
Only things of the best quality — Insecurity
On the beach asking, "Can you accept me as I am?" — Feeling that you have no value.
Competitiveness — Need to feel above others because you feel below.
Spending money in quantities — Feeling that for yourself alone, without money, without paying for others in the bar, no one loves you. You are alone. ("I need people around me, and I don't know how to attract them to me without money.")
— Every instance serves to help one know oneself.
— There are no real errors. The only error is not learning from what happens.
— My awareness that you have no internal control. When one does things for social expectations, one is out of control.
Example: To have to keep a date for dinner — obligation. This shows lack of control in your own life. (I did not fight because I felt you loved me in spite of what you were doing.)
— Masculine energy and clarification with feminine energy. That is the function of the woman in that search. It's very difficult to find anything in the darkness. The light is only provided by female energy: the woman in us. When both are conscious of that fact, the result is two individuals growing as equals and complementaries (bees and flowering plants).
We continued to see each other.

He came to the U.S. on the 9th of July (Robert's birthday) and at that time again asked me to marry him. He left and ended up in the hospital in Luxembourg.

August 11, 1980, Allan and I filed for divorce.

October, 1980, Allan left the house on Emerson Street.

December 4, 1980 I turned to Allan and said: "You kept insisting you did not want the divorce; you kept saying you loved me. Now that you are free I can repeat to you what I said in the first telephone call from Spain. I asked for the divorce because YOU did not want me, **not** because I did not want you. You said

231

then, it was not true. NOW, time has passed. Do you want me?"
"No."
I knew it. The job was finished. I had let the bird go free and it did not come back. I never had it in the first place.

Once he was emotionally free and had tried the world, once he was in a position to know, I wanted in the deepest part of my heart for him to choose me. One can't say, "I don't like peas," until one has tried them. But I knew once he did not need me, was strong enough to know what he **did** want and free enough to go out and get it, he would not choose me. He did not. I had been hoping, but I knew all along he would not.

In front of Andrea, I asked Allan, "In 15 years of marriage, was there any moment when you needed me when I was not there?"
"No. You were always there."
I asked, "Were you ever there for me?"
"No. I was not there for you."
When we were alone I asked him, "Then why?"
He said, "Did it ever occur to you that I do not want a person who is always there?"
No, it had never occurred to me.

So, in December 1980, I let go of Allan because the job was done and he no longer needed nor wanted me. I had no bad feelings. I had done what I had set out to do (help him study and overcome his facade problem). From now on he would face himself with no more lies. He knew the truth about himself: He is a giving Human Being. He was free to enjoy life! He had kept his part of the bargain; he always recognized my intelligence and let me Be. We both had fulfilled the "Contract."

Meanwhile, Jose and I had continued to correspond.

My dear:
                                           Luxembourg
                                           October 12, 1980

. . . the hospital has 2,000 patients for 6 doctors, so you can imagine all the work they have to do . . . I stopped drinking 15 days before I entered the hospital . . . (so) I didn't need to go through the "detoxification of alcohol" program. Dr. Newberg told me if I tried to drink again, my arms and legs might possibly be paralyzed, so now it's finished, the alcohol . . .

I will go to the U.S. in December. Whatever happens I want you to know I love you and adore you in the deepest part of my heart. I want you to know that my thoughts are always with you . . .

Madame Heinen sends you regards, and congratulates you for the moral help that I have been given by your letters.

                                           Your petite love,
                                           Jose

Luxembourg
November 3, 1980

My dear love:

. . . I will be in San Francisco by December 18 . . .

I love you,
Jose

He phoned on December 2nd to tell me he was not coming. I said I'd go and bring him to the U.S. to be treated.

Eleanor was staying at home while I flew to Luxembourg. Later she wrote to me:

Miami, Florida
July 26, 1982

Dear Beatriz:

. . . before you went to Europe to see him, you asked me in a soft little voice, "What shall I do if he doesn't come?" Beatriz, it was, as you yourself said, the first time you needed help, the first time you were showing your vulnerable self . . .

Eleanor

Yes, she was correct. I felt vulnerable. For the first time in my life I didn't have a job; I didn't have a well-defined goal where I could pour out all my energy. "If he doesn't come, Dear God, what is my next job? Where do I place my love, my energy?"

I flew to Luxembourg December 3rd, 1980 to offer myself for the same job with Jose that I had just completed with Allan. Jose said he was not coming. He wanted to find himself by himself. Through me he already knew he could build instead of always destroying.

I begged him to let me give him the love and support that is necessary for anyone who embarks on that road. I knew I could. He was in such bad shape!

He confirmed my long-held belief that the only way I can defend myself is through thought, by Being. I knew only good could come to me because I think kindly. It always has. If someone was bad, with me he would be different even if it was the only time in his life. Jose told me that he behaved differently with me, but he did not think he could keep doing that consistently. So, he would try to build by himself.

I told him, "You are terribly frightened."

He responded, "Of course not, I've never been afraid in my life." (A year and a half later, he admitted it.)

While in Luxembourg I spoke with Dr. Heinen, Jose's kinesiologist. She told me she thought I was giving Jose too much. Now that she had met me she thought I had too much to

233

give to any **one** person. She said, "Go and ask. Those who seek shall find." I could not understand how one can give too much! What does she mean, I am giving too much? How can giving ever be too much?

A few days after we parted lovingly, Jose wrote to say goodbye.

Ettelbruk, Luxembourg
December, 1980

Dear Beatriz:

. . . How are you sweetheart? I have thought a lot about you since you left and I miss you. I know that you are thinking about me too, but life is that way. In any case, if you believe in your fate, sooner or later we will be reunited for more bliss. I talked about it with Mrs. Heinen. She found you extraordinary . . .

All my tenderness
Jose

My heart was in pain. But obviously God did not want to give me the big job I wanted to do.

January 20th I went to bed feeling alone. Like always since that night in February the year before, I put myself in the fetus position and remembered that night with him when I felt one, complete, whole. I slept like a baby. January 21st I did it again. On January 22nd I was about to do it when it came to me, "This is wrong! I am using **his** energy. He has asked me to release him. I can't do that anymore."

I realized he had touched something in me that made me feel well and full. If I could feel it with him in my mind, I had it in me, all by itself. I tried and it worked. I had let go of Jose — January 22, 1981.

I had finished every project and was ready. I asked God, "What is my next big job to be?" It soon came to me.

After I knew what I must do, Jose wrote to me again.

Bruxelles
June 26, 1982

Dear Beatriz:

I'm very late to write to you. I thought that I would be able to pull through by myself, but it is not possible . . . In spite of a separation I always kept love in my heart and no days pass by without thinking of you . . .

I am asking you for a loan of . . . I am sorry to be that direct but I am at the end of my rope.

I miss you because you are the only one who understood and loved me. I hope you are still free because I need you. I do not know how to say it but in my heart you are my wife. After all this time and silence I have learned what life is and a true love, but I was too proud to write you. I must admit I was a big child . . .

If you still want me I will come to you as soon as possible to live our beautiful love deep and nice. All my hopes are in you. You have all my tenderness. I love you and never stopped loving you. Write to me often if you want to help me.

Thousands of kisses,
Jose

Bruxelles
July 13, 1982

Dear Beatriz:

I have received your letters. They were a great comfort for me and I thank you from the bottom of my heart. I think I have understood your life, your feelings and your way of life . . .

Regarding sex, I want you to know that for me it has been over for more than a year. What I want is to live with somebody who really knows me well; and who knows me better than you? My qualities as well as my blemishes . . .

I have helped a lot of people and now, I have nobody around. When you wrote to me that "I had Fear" it was the truth: I do not know how to live in this actual world. Little by little I realize that I have wasted my life and lost the feeling of people for me — except you, only you did not change! I am still looking for my way but I have never found the appropriate approach.

I will be in the hospital again. Maybe I will find peace for myself and I will start to live at last a normal life. I feel a revolt against the world because I thought that everybody was like me, and as a matter of fact I realize that all of them are profiteers who used me. Now I feel more lonely than ever.

Kisses,
Jose

It is true I did not change, but what he did not see was that when one understands why people do what they do, one doesn't change. Once he can see that he was right in believing people are good, and that the profiteers used him because they were more afraid than he was, then he too will keep thinking everyone is good, and the revolt against the world will be over, Peace will be found. Once he can see it, he will be able to heal himself. No one can do it for him, we can only bring support, care, understanding, clarity; but the work must be done by the person!

235

Bruxelles
July 27, 1982

My dear Beatriz:

    I have received your letter. It helped me a lot. I relapsed and am still depressed. I must go to the hospital.

    I have analyzed your last letter and a lot of things appeared very positive to me. But I asked myself the following questions: What can I do not to be materialistic any longer? What could be the purpose of my life if I start all over again in this jungle . . . ? I am 46 and am like a child unable to protect myself. Is it lack of education or bad luck? You found your way. From reading your letter I am convinced that everything will go well for you. I must reach the point of being at peace with myself . . . Thank God, your letters make me feel good and I thank you . . . I will try to follow your advice and maybe little by little, I will achieve the same result that you did. Help me morally everyday, I need it to keep living.

Jose

He must see that his protection is the one which he used all his life: his Love, his belief that everyone is good. Once he sees this the jungle will become a sea of Human Beings in pain. He will want to help them all, to heal them all, as he has been doing all along unconsciously.

Bruxelles
August 6, 1982

My darling:

    . . . I feel useless. But in the hospital, when I will be taking care of myself, I will also be able to help people who are in worse shape than I am . . .

    You are an extraordinary girl who thinks about everything, not forgetting anything. I miss you, I love you, love me too!

Kiss to Robertito
Jose

Once more we see how extraordinary he is. He is desperate, and yet he wants to go to the hospital because he knows he can help others there. He is a healer and does not know it . . . Why do people never see who they are? Why?

236

Bruxelles
September 4, 1982

My dear Beatriz:

*. . . I was wrong to trust, I have nothing left . . . I cannot feel
peaceful inside of me. I always thought that people are good, it was
the mistake of my life (and now I pay the price). Sometimes I would
like to disappear . . . my life seems absurd and without purpose . . .
You know that my mind is with you every day . . . Please let me kiss
you,*

Jose

Bruxelles
September 13, 1982

My dear Beatriz:

*. . . I feel lost and you are the only one to whom I can confide. You
know me so well! I see that more and more when I read your letters
over again and realize what I lost when I left you. I have made many
mistakes but the biggest was not to be concerned about hurting you at
that time. I must admit that I think I am now repaying all the
wrong that I have done to others . . .*

*I wish to know if really nothing is possible between the two of us,
if we will never be together again? . . . You always finish your
letters with Love and Peace, for my part I will finish my letter with
Love without Peace. I love you and will be with you all my life.*

Jose

I did feel pain when he left, yes, he was right, but I took the
lesson that the pain had for me and ran with it, and grew through
it. It is my responsibility to transform the pain I feel into joy. He
did what he had to do: he healed me when I was bleeding, and
then he left to continue his healing road . . . We all are healers, if
we could only realize it! Some of our actions give light to others,
some of our actions give shade to others. It is up to us to increase
the light which others give us and to convert shade into light!
These were only opportunities, and I took them all!

I refused to close my outpouring of love towards him or
towards anyone else, just because I felt pain. I refused to believe
that the pain I was feeling was his fault! I understand why people
do what they do! I will never change! I will love; it does not
matter what others do! That has been my motto. I have had only
gain from it.

I had answered Jose's letter asking me for money, saying I
could not send him any because I did not have it. Then Robert's
grandfather died and left $ . . . for Robert. We spent half of it on
the ticket for Robert to go to the funeral in Canada and the other

half Robert decided to send to Jose.

After he had done so, Robert said to Allan, "Daddy, I sent my money to Jose! I am learning how not to be greedy!"

What can I say? Could a report card full of A's (which he has) make me happier? That is the type of learning we must do! That is the consciousness we must teach our children . . . My heart was happy. Robert does not have toys. Robert does not have an Atari. Robert is not learning how to program a computer, nor taking courses in drawing or tennis . . . But he has enrolled himself in the course called Life. He is putting himself through it. The lessons must be learned. The sacrifices must be conscious, just as we consciously register ourselves in Law, or Medicine or Carpentry.

It seemed fair to Robert to give to Jose. Jose gave Robert a great deal of money and made Robert feel big. Robert wrote to Jose, "Because you gave me money I was able to buy gifts for people and buy meals for you and Mommy. You made me experience how good it feels to be generous. Because of it, I am sending you this money." Robert could see both sides: he was being grateful to the person who had taught him how to be generous, and he himself was overcoming being greedy. What more could one expect from a ten year old?

True, he does not clean after himself. True, he does not put the lids back on jars. True, he does his homework a day late sometimes . . . but . . . is all that important? Is it even worth harping about? I never taught those things to Freddy either; he learned them eventually. But, to be generous, to see the need of others and do something about it, to share what he has — **even if** he does not have much — that is what I feel raising my children is all about . . . except my children are not only Robert and Freddy!

Jose responded to Robertito's gift and note:

Bruxelles
October 2, 1982

Dear Robertito and Beatriz:

. . . I thank you two very much from all my heart, especially the few words from Robertito. I was really touched. I hope that a son like him will keep his heart clean and upright, as I could foresee when I met him. I wish I had a son like him. All the time we spent together I esteemed him mine. Tell him that not one day passes without my thinking about him and all the good times we had together . . .

Dear Beatriz, your letters full of comfort make me feel a lot better, and I am anxious to get them. I thank you for the international money order that helped me for the bad time. I know that one day we will see each other again. Time is nothing if feelings are deep and true.

Love without peace
Jose

When I read this letter I knew he would be fine. Why? Because he was using the formula. "My worries will be over, . . . **I will** be able to see you . . . **even if** it takes time . . ."
We will see him again. He will recover. My love is with him; but I could not say "yes" to marriage now. The world needs me now. The world needs him too; and he will find the peace he is looking for and will work for Peace as well. To say "No" to Jose — when I could not see how I could publish the book, how I could even get it edited, who would come along to help me — took knowledge. "**I will** continue **even if** I don't see the way clear yet." Because I did not break the law, help came, the book is about to be published.

With other people my goal had been to be with them for a few hours and have them change their outlook on life and themselves as a result. This continued to bring me great satisfaction.

Boston
January 14, 1981

Hi,

   I was just looking at my picture of Ap and thought I should say hello to you. The trip home was a very long one. Everything was fine until we got to Newark . . . We had to . . . In Boston we had to . . . I didn't get home until 9:30, but I didn't go to bed until 1:30 a.m. because I was still on California time. I spent three days looking for a job, but the market is still terrible. I have spent a good deal of my time at home with my parents. I am so terribly frustrated by everything that's going on, that I needed to be with somebody. I went to see my friend who I hadn't seen since last July (You told me to see him.) and it wasn't so bad. I just hope he keeps in touch, since I told him I felt bad that we had lost contact with each other.

   Tomorrow I am leaving for Florida to see if I can't find someone to go into business with me. I will be going down not knowing anyone and the thought scares me. I have a very good feeling that something good is going to happen — at least I have a positive attitude. I want you to know that I am very happy that I had the opportunity to meet you and your family. Talking with you has given me a much healthier outlook on life. Please send my love to everybody and tell Ap to have a safe and enjoyable trip. Bye for now.

Love . . .
J.

"Talking with you have given me a much healthier outlook on life." This outlook change is even reflected in the letter itself: from dismal complaints to brave positive expectation.

Palo Alto, California
January, 1981

Beatriz!

I've thought all day about tennis.

*Beatriz I think I've decided not to continue at . . . (school). I'll miss
so much that I'll . . . "flunk" the class — we're going to be in
Washington, D.C. and we'll ski in Utah . . . I feel that I very much
need a couple more Intermediate . . . before . . . Advanced. That
word "advanced" scares me!*

In any case . . . any rate, I feel blessed *to have "bumped into"
you, and should you ever be desperate enough to want to "just bat
some balls," please give me a buzz.*

Fondly, . . .
Mo

. . . "I feel blessed to have bumped into you" . . .

Over the years I had chosen to be the "legs" with everyone.
"You be the head, I'll do the leg work, making what you want
part of me, creating a unit. We are one." As Allan wrote, ". . . if **we**
can do it, **I will** be a good writer."

"You wish. I do. You are the brains, I am your legs." It was a
purposeful way to practice the Law: "Not My Will, But Your Will
be Done." Later, an additional step emerged:

From: If **we** can do it then **I will** be a good writer.

To: If **I will** be a writer then **we** can achieve World Peace.

I had gone to a lodge to receive New Year 1981, and there met
Mrs. Kenneth Patchen, the wife of the poet. She was powerful,
loving, all woman. She had her man eating out of the palm of her
hand! I talked with her about Jose, and how I had gone to Europe
to see him and called him every other day from California. She
had said the same words as Dr. Heinen, "You are giving too
much."

At home in Palo Alto in January 1981 I had lots of company, so
I put all my feelings about Jose on the shelf. I wanted to take time
to look at them and analyze what had been said to me. As always
(except the few years I was "setting limits"), things in my life
have a free flow. I never have to plan time for myself; when I
need it people seem to go away. So by the 20th of January 1981,
everyone who was at the house left. Then I let go of Jose. (Jan.
22) My only remaining attachment was to my son: I felt I could
not live without him, that he needed me!

On January 29th Allan and I went to divorce court. The judge
looked at the agreement and wanted to know if it had been

signed in front of a lawyer. He wanted to know if Allan understood what he had signed, and questioned him. It was a divorce of love. What a strange thing! Allan had agreed to give me total control over Robert and three-quarters of his take-home pay!

We left the court and had breakfast together. Allan was feeling that he was a good man, which he is! I was feeling that he had done what was right. I thought our marriage had been a one way street: I thought I gave and he took. Now he was giving me what he could: economic support.

I had said to Allan, before we got married, that we were going to be together **only** up to a certain point. When we met, I saw a person with no confidence in himself, a person who waited for crumbs from others to come his way. I, on the other hand, was a leader. I was going to lead him to confidence, to strength, to self-assurance — with my only weapon, Love.

How could he choose the "crumb" — the one he got when he had no choice — once he found the strength to which I was going to lead him? I knew he would not. I was right! That is what Love is! **I will** love you **even if** you don't choose me! When we married he wasn't in a position to choose. I was and I did. After the divorce, he was and he did.

When we parted I went to a Christian bookstore which I had never entered before and bought a card for him. It said, "Thank you for being who you are." What a thing to send your **ex**husband! But that is truly what I felt.

I felt pain, uncertainty. Where would I go from here? I can't be without a job! To me a "job" meant a spiritual task for which I knew the "invisible" reason. For the first time in my life I felt insecure. One job was finished and the other I thought I had found, had said, "I don't want your help!"

I called Esther. She came immediately, my angel, and gave me a shoulder on which to cry. Someone loved me. She had cleared her busy schedule to be with me. She gave me all her Time. To me it meant: Unconditional Love. That love healed me so that I regained my balance and could see clearly again. Love does not have to come from the opposite sex.

Our decision for me to pursue Real Estate and make money made me feel more secure. That I could do. But . . . for what purpose did I want that money? I wanted it to make me feel less afraid! That would be an action based on Fear, the wrong reason. My actions were always based on Love. I would not break the Law! I could not do it. Because of Esther giving her love, I was able to see that the security I sought could not come from money.

I had left money before. When grandmother died, Ana Maria kept what my grandmother owned. My father was upset. He wanted me to fight. Some people said, "You should fight for Freddy's part, if not for your own."

I spoke with Freddy, saying, "I know what the world says, but there is nothing in this world that is worth fighting for. I will fight for the perfection of myself; but that is my inner fight. I will fight to climb the highest expression of love to everyone; that is my inner fight. The enemy is not out there! The enemy is **in** me!"

Freddy agreed.

Having freely decided money-making was not the road for me, I knew I needed to clarify my feelings. When I am trying to clarify an emotional entanglement, I read myself a children's story and try to see what the story is **really** saying.

I knew man created numbers as symbols to interpret the material world. They are used to explain, so that we can understand it better. I knew stories and myths are the symbols man created to help us interpret the psychological world, our inner world, the world of the invisible. These stories are like maps and I use them as such.

This is the story I selected at random (by my old method of responding to an electrical discharge) and read and reread to myself on this occasion:

> *There was a couple who wanted a child very badly. So, with all their hearts, they asked for one.*
>
> *As they were asking they heard a noise in the kitchen. They went into the kitchen and found a seed of a baby! Oh, they were happy, so happy! The child was born, grew a few years, and one day a witch took it away.*
>
> *The mother and father wanted their child back. They went into the forest to look for it. After a long time they found the child.*
>
> *By then the witch was fond of the child, so she wanted to give the mother a few gifts to take home with the child.*
>
> *The mother was furious. She did not want to take them. She wanted to run away.*
>
> *But the child said, "I want the gifts." So the mother agreed to take them.*
>
> *The End.*

Looking at the story I saw:

1st: Father = Adult in me
Mother = Parent in me
Child = Child in me
Witch = Pain in me
Gift = Gift for me!

242

2nd: "a couple wanted a child. They asked with all their hearts. They got it."

If I ask with all my heart I will get what I ask for. I knew that. (I had asked for someone like Allan and gotten him. I had asked for someone like Jose and had gotten him.)

3rd: "they were very happy!"

After my wish was granted I would be very happy. I knew that. (When my wishes for Allan and Jose were granted I was very happy.)

4th: "One day a witch took the child away."

After the happiness something would happen that would take the happiness away. I knew that. (Allan and Jose were both taken away from me by their own fears.)

5th: "the witch wanted to give the mother a few gifts to take home for the child."

If I listen to the child (my inner child) and pay no attention to the mother (my parent, judgemental self), then the witch (my pain) has a gift for me!

That was it! I had to look at my pain. I did not get my two emotional hours with Allan, but the pain of not getting them had something else for me. What **did** I gain from the pain? I recalled the letter I had written:

Nerja, Spain

Dear Allan:

. . . I am trying to get in touch with that part of me that is tender, and let it feed me . . .

Love
Beatriz

Ah! I am searching for my inner well, from where I can draw what I need for myself! The pain forced me into myself to find the core of the spring within me, from which to draw again and again: pleasure, laughter and joy!

Allan needing so much had provided the opportunity for me to give, which I needed to do. Without him I could never have grown in Love. Each time I felt I could not stand it any more, I had gone deeper into myself and brought up a bit more. "Oh! Thank you Allan for **Not** giving me those two hours! The pain I felt pushed me into myself, so that I got to know myself better. Oh, thank you Allan for the pain!" "Oh, thank you witch (pain) for the gift I could not have earned without you!"

At that moment I knew my business with Allan was finished. "Now, I **am** completely divorced," I said to myself.

California was good for me. It was the period in my life when I experienced the so called "human life." This means I learned to set limits for myself. I always felt I walk in the opposite direction from everyone else, and I did. While everyone else, during the 70's, was trying to break **out** of boxes, I, who had never experienced one, was learning how to live **in** a box. The experience lasted from 1969 to 1978. It went like this:

If I had degrees, **then** I could do so very much. Intellectual Slavery!

If Allan does not come to take care of the baby, **then** I will be stuck with Robert. Physical Slavery!

If Allan does not make love to me, **then** I will be frustrated. Sexual Slavery!

If I buy the house I want and am alone, **then** I might not be able to keep it. Economic Slavery!

I felt all these emotions in Horror! I sat and meditated hours and hours looking at my Oak Tree to counteract these feelings. Finally I said to myself. Do you, Beatriz, want to live like this?

No!!

Always, I had waited for Allan, for hours, for days — but that was my Choice. I could have left. I was free to stay or to go. I chose to wait for him. Once Robert was born I felt stuck, **if** Allan does not come I **can't** leave!

He did not come, once, twice!

Oh . . . no . . . not even **you** do that to me; I am free! I'm not a slave! I'll not be stuck.

Who says I can't leave Robert alone? Who cares **if** no one else does it? I will!!

No one has the power over me to deny **me** a choice about **anything!** I acted much like Chienne . . . our dear dog: I'll escape no matter what, if confined. But see, if Free, when I had a choice, I voluntarily waited for Allan for days . . . and days . . . for years . . . and years . . . But don't put me in a box!

One day Allan and I agreed he would come at 7 p.m. He did not come on time. I waited 15 minutes. Silver and I left for the movies leaving Robert alone. This was hard for me to do.

Allan was furious! Robert was alone!

I said to myself, "My responsibility is until 7 o'clock. It ends when the responsibility of the other person begins. I am not responsible for Robert after 7 p.m." I explained this to Allan later.

He began to come on time when Robert was concerned. Once we set a time and Allan clearly understood it was **his** responsibility to take care of the child for the period agreed, Physical slavery was solved.

I began to masturbate. Sexual slavery was solved.

I chose my "dream house" **even if** I did not have all the money

— by getting someone else to put up the rest. I knew I could rent the house for weddings and to important professors from out of town, if I were alone. Thus I knew I could keep it all by myself, **even if** the investor at some point wanted his money back. Economic slavery was solved.

I will contribute to the world. I am writing this book **even if** I don't have a degree. Intellectual slavery was solved.

I could not choose to act freely until I had learned to set limits. To learn, I had to live among people who lived very restricted lives. They were my teachers. I owe them my freedom, my very life.

Sean once said to me, "Thank you for teaching me."

I am saying it to him now, "Thank you, Sean." Your life had an impact on me. Because of you I learned to be a better person.

The same goes for Silver. Without her it would have been impossible for me to learn. She sees clearly where something begins and ends. I could apply that in the case of responsibility for Robert. That is something she may never do, but one takes from others what one needs and applies it as one sees fit! If I have not said it before, "Thank you Silver," you were a great teacher.

I loved Allan; but no human being would make me a slave. I was free and I acted freely. Responsible, yes, but freely undertaken. If free, I would choose to enslave myself.

Thus I returned to my original state of strength, as when Allan had met me.

1

Only By choice ◄ does not crawl ► has No choice

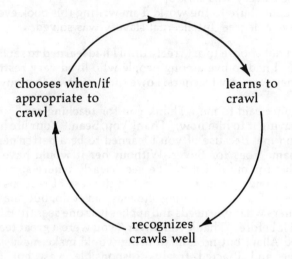

chooses when/if
appropriate to
crawl

learns to
crawl

recognizes
crawls well

2

Only by choice ◄ does not talk ► has No choice

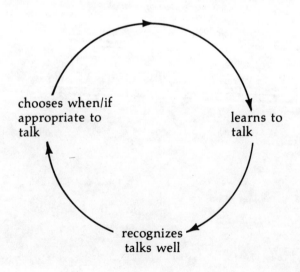

chooses when/if
appropriate to
talk

learns to
talk

recognizes
talks well

3

Only by choice ◄ does not express ►has no choice

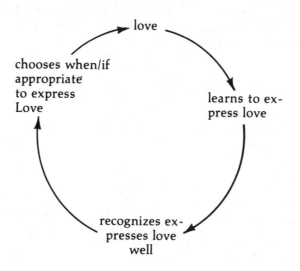

love

chooses when/if
appropriate
to express
Love

learns to ex-
press love

recognizes ex-
presses love
well

4

Only by choice ◄ does not kill ►has no choice

Humans

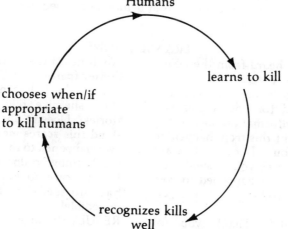

chooses when/if
appropriate
to kill humans

learns to kill

recognizes kills
well

What makes each person arrive at the point of choice? — SUCCESS.
a skill is learned and then one can choose if/when/never to use it.

I did not change or blame anyone to get out of my box. I just changed myself, my ideas. The world was trying to tell me it was good that I was "growing up," learning to set limits. I feel it is a pity people learn such "growing up," going only half way around the circle! If there is a "growing up" to be done, it is to **complete** the circle by learning to feel, think and act, making free choices as when we were children, but consciously.

I will play, **even if** there are no toys anywhere.

I will go poo, **even if** I go in my pants.

I will like you, **even if** you are white, black, yellow, purple.

I will fight injustice, **even if** I am alone.

I will prove there is no Evil, **even if** no one shares this belief.

I will free India, **even if** the British are materially stronger.

I will freely express my love for you, **even if** you don't freely express yours.

I will because Facts don't count. I have moral strength. No visible is stronger than any invisible, and Love, an invisible, is stronger than Fear, another invisible!

I feel I can teach how to unlearn that which has been learned, which causes pain. We all used to know! We have just learned to cover it up. Now we have to reawaken it.

In order to keep open and loving, I learned to hear from the Center of Love, my heart.

Example A: **A friend tells me a story**

"You know what happened at Stanford? There was a rape! The girl was leaving the church at 10 p.m. There were no lights and a man attacked her from behind and raped her . . . (more details)"

TRANSLATIONS

When heard from the Love Center **(heart):**
She is telling me, "I'm concerned for you. I give you this information so you can prevent this from happening to you. I care. I want to protect you. I would feel badly if it happened to you. I love you."

RESULT: Thank you for loving me. I love you too.
You + Me = "US"
Together

When heard from the Fear Center **(pain):**
Why is she telling me this? Does she like telling gory stories? Doesn't she understand this scares me? Whatever happened to that person has nothing to do with me! I don't care to know! She has no sensitivity! It's incredible!

RESULT: If you love me you would not be telling me this!
"Me" & "Them" are Separate and Opposed

I have **two ears** physically. Which Ear am I going to use? The Ear which hears from my **heart**, or the Ear which hears from my **pain**? The choice is mine. I choose to hear from my heart. If we reverse how we listen, we'll find ourselves in the New Era of Peace. We do need to translate what people tell us, **but** the translation **Must** create an "US," not separate "Me" and "Them." Everything in the physical world tells me of the invisible world.

Everything in the invisible world tells me of the physical world.

Example B: **Jose.**

"I want to marry you. I don't want to marry you. I want to marry you. I'm a family man. I'm a drunk, a gambler, a womanizer. I want to marry you. Release me from my promise to marry you. I still love you."

TRANSLATION

When heard from the Love Center **(heart):**
He is in such pain, he goes from woman to woman, booze to gambling, desperately trying to find Love, to find himself. He is not doing this to me. I will remain constant until he finds his own strength. I **can** cope with anything: poverty, sickness, booze, gambling, vacillations! I can love; therefore I am powerful.
RESULT: Thank you for accepting my gift, my Love. I feel grateful, I have a job now.
You + Me = "US"
(together)

When heard from the Fear Center **(pain):**
Who does he think he is? First one thing, then another! He can't do this to me. I don't like to be treated like this. I **can't** cope with poverty, sickness, booze, gambling, vacillations! I can't keep loving him. He is a creep! Therefore, I am powerless in our relationship.

RESULT: I can't give you my love. You are a creep. "You" & "Me" are separate and opposed.

Love Center (Heart) decisions at crucial times in **my** life:

My Wedding reception
To cry from the realization Allan did not want to spend time alone with me — or — To celebrate, laugh and enjoy the party to the last minute.

249

Love Center Choice	I laughed and enjoyed the party even though my heart ached.
Mother's death	To cry for her — or — To celebrate Allan's graduation the same day.
Love Center Choice	I celebrated even though my heart ached.
Father's death	To cry for him — or — To celebrate Allan's opening night singing in the Gilbert & Sullivan operetta, "Pinafore."
Love Center Choice	I celebrated Allan's triumph even though my heart ached.

It is impossible to live in other than past, present and future time when one hears with the heart. On these occasions present time was appropriate. (The Here and Now.)

My heart may be aching; I can still love, laugh, sing, enjoy. The pain is a feeling. But I am not the feeling. I am love. I can still love, regardless of the pain; I can still laugh regardless of the pain. I do not need to give power to my feelings. They are **not Me**; I am their Master. I can direct them. They are tools I can use by directing my mind only to Positive conclusions.

Any conclusion which will lead me to view an Individual or a Nation as "creep" "egoist" "tight" "worthless" — and therefore lead me to walk away — is a conclusion I do not want. I can direct my mind to see the situation in such a manner that the conclusion can only be compassion and understanding. Therefore I **never** walked away from anyone because of lack of understanding. Would you stop multiplying if you did not understand multiplication? No. You keep at it until you do understand.

Silver knew very well I could — if she needed me — stop everything and just be with her and sit in her house, for whatever period she wanted me.

She felt badly because she felt she could not do that. She felt she was not giving to me, or that I might perceive her as not giving. It never occurred to me! A tree gives shade according to its size. I take what the tree can give, or wait until the tree has grown and is therefore capable of giving more. When the tree is **capable** of giving and is **choosing** not to give, **then** I leave.

Andrea loved to go shopping. I went shopping with her. As we shopped I heard, "I love you Beatriz, that is why I am sharing my shopping with you."

250

Sean took pictures like no one I know. He brought out the souls of people and nature in his pictures. Each time he made a copy and gave it to me I heard, "I love you Beatriz, that is why I took the time and money to make a copy for you."

Mark had so many problems . . . each time he came and tried to clarify his emotions I heard, "I love you Beatriz, that is why I come to you when I feel I need to talk."

Each single day I came home from being with anyone and Allan did **not** ask me why the house was not clean, why the food was not cooked, I heard, "I love you Beatriz, that is why I let you Be, that is why I understand your need to give."

Mo wrote in January 1981 ". . . In any case . . . I feel blessed to have bumped into you . . ." When I read that I knew she had felt **me**. Yes, I blessed her. I bless everyone I ever met. Webster defines blessing as, "To express a wish for the good fortune or happiness of" . . . and that I do.

Not a day in my life has passed that I have felt unloved. What I did feel was that I did not fit . . . so very different . . . such a strange duck I am! But love . . . Oh . . . I felt loved! Come with me . . . I will teach you how to think so that it does not matter **what** the outside world does, you **will** experience Love. I will teach you to Love in such a manner that you will end up loving the whole wide world! The world needs us all. I can't live with all this love and no place to express it . . . Come with me, experience Happiness, Ecstasy, Fulfillment . . . It is for all of us!

For my birthday my father once wrote me:

Buenos Aires, Argentina
June 14, 1964

How fast the time passes, Betty! It seems yesterday when, three days before you arrived in this world, your mother and I, who couldn't help ourselves, wanted to go out and have fun. We arrived at our love nest (home) at midnight and she began to feel the labor pains. We had three days waiting for Betty with anguish and worries. You did not want to come to this world of pain and happiness. It looked as though you felt well where you were — so much so that the doctor had to take you by force. What do you think about that? The funny thing was that you were born all red and wrinkled and your mother thought you were a monster . . . But, thanks to God, we had a beautiful daughter.

How many things have happened since then: a lot of beautiful moments and of the other kind — but those don't count, because when we focus our minds, all your experiences fill them with your eagerness to live and how you demonstrated y ur presence. You always wanted to be noticed. You wanted to say, "I am here. I have come."

I do not know why there are people like you on this earth. But the truth is that the few months in Luis Viale, where you were born, you were very popular. You have continued being so up to today, with the result that you have forged a strong character — tenacious, resolute, firm, fearless — which has been useful for overcoming all obstacles which life has presented in front of you. And you have succeeded without hurting anyone — which is what counts in this life — so that one can have a clear conscience. Otherwise one can not live in peace and happiness. You have succeeded and I want to congratulate you. Your modest life on this immense planet be a torch which will illuminate not only your way, but the way of all those around you . . . In this manner you will make others happy and be happy yourself. You will have more and more strength to continue on the road you have decided.

On the 24th we will not be physically together. But we will be spiritually remembering different times of your life and our lives to be able to feel you even more present. Remember that I love you and that I have great trust in you. Don't betray my trust. Happiness on your day.

Kisses
papi

. . . "on this immense planet, be a torch which will illuminate not only your way, but the way of all those around you . . ."

Oh . . . ! I had done that, but I had always wanted much much more. I had wanted to know **how** I could illuminate the **whole world**! And I had not found **how** — yet . . .

BOOK TWO
BETWEEN TWO WORLDS
FROM 'I' TO 'WE'

CHAPTER 6
THE EXPERIENCE

At this point, I began a fast and locked myself in the house for three weeks. Every day, after Robert had left for school, I sat and thought. I wanted to know where I should put my energy next. What did God want me to do?

I felt that I was finished. I had done every single job I had set out to do.

The job with Allan was finished. I had succeeded.

The job with Andrea and Sean was done. I knew that they could separate without a complete break. Both of them had assured me they would not separate. I knew better. But they had said that if they did, they would never again see each other. That was their pattern. I felt that pattern had to stop. They had to learn to integrate, to part in peace. And they had learned. My energy had helped them do that.

I had known Silver for nine years. Every day I had followed her with my mind to send her energy. For years I had hoped she would recognize that she had to work for herself alone, that she was a leader. And now, I felt that this job was done.

I had helped Mark, Freddy's friend, see that he could graduate from film school. If he could see that, I knew he would do the rest on his own. Now I felt that job was done. Even Mark's father had realized what I had done. He had told me, "We had a war going on: light against darkness. I am glad light won. But darkness is necessary too." He was right! I had known that as long as I did not let go, light would win.

Every job I had ever started was now finished. I had a clean blackboard. I could write what I wanted.

Over the years, people had always come to me with their problems. I had strong friendships all over the world. I might not see someone for ten years, but when we came together, we would immediately pick up where we had left off. People called me from Canada or New York. If they needed help, they thought of me. Nothing gave me greater pleasure.

I decided that I had accumulated a great deal of wisdom. I could speak on any subject because I could see any subject from the spiritual point of view. With me, it was not a matter of subject, but of how to look at that subject. I decided I would open myself up to the public. I would lecture.

But it was not wisdom I had gained. I had simply gone through a love growth, or hollowing, process; the process of bringing love to each situation. I had created a hole inside of myself where the energy called love came through. The greater the hole, the greater the amount of energy that passes through, and the greater the number of people who can be touched.

I had recognized one more law, "the Law of Harmlessness." Because I win, you win too! I had done each job, and as a result, the other person had won too!

I decided that if I wanted to go on the lecture circuit, I would need a degree. The only subject I wanted to study was metaphysics, so I wrote to the Metaphysical University in Los Angeles and filled out their application as soon as it arrived. I was happy with my decision. This was the beginning of a new path. I gathered all the application papers together on the dining room table and then, very ceremoniously, placed them inside the envelope and said, "I, Beatriz Prentice, a Human Being, an inhabitant of Planet Earth, one of the many spiritual leaders of the Aquarian Age . . ."

But before I could say, ". . . is taking her first step toward the lecture circuit . . ." Suddenly, the voice of my father filled the room. "And with what authority do you call yourself that?" the voice demanded.

I turned toward the voice and quite calmly replied, "Because I know Who I am, What I am, and Why I am."

Then a voice surfaced within me, communicating to me: "I am that I am. I am the law and have come to fulfill it. The law is to bring Heaven to Earth."

At that moment, my entire life became ordered. I felt peace. The degree that I had wanted became meaningless.

This event began a week of revelations which I have described in the final chapter of this book. Abruptly, my life underwent a complete change. It was as though an eagle had lifted me up and I could look down on the world from afar. I could see the pattern because I was no longer immersed in it. My entire life now made perfect sense. Until that moment, my life had seemed like a box of loose puzzle pieces. Some pieces fitted, made sense, some did not. But now, everything fitted, I saw, I felt, I understood.

I also saw the lives of Sophia Loren, Richard Nixon and Prince Charles.

I saw the pattern of Sophia Loren's life. She had learned from the poverty of her youth. This poverty had given her the desire she needed to acquire wealth. At the same time, I saw a steadiness, a loyalty of feeling, a wisdom deep within her. Once she had found wealth, she had realized that money could not bring her happiness. I felt the frustration which she has experienced because people do not "see" her. She wants to spread her inner beauty and wisdom, her inner "perfume," but has not yet found the necessary outlet. I saw how our two puzzle pieces could fit together, how we could work together for peace.

I saw that Richard Nixon had been given spiritual values when a boy. I saw that he had wanted to be of service to the world, but had attached himself to power, to money, because of his fear, his insecurity. And, as a result, he had paid a terrible price.

In his actions as President, his inner imbalance had been manifested outwardly. He had kept his eyes on the international world and had ignored the national world. He had forgotten that the way is as important as the final product.

I saw that he had a great desire now to be of service. He experienced pain by not being able to find a place for himself. I also saw that if he reconnected with his spiritual values, he could satisfy this inner desire, he could be of service in the endeavor to turn the world around towards peace.

I saw that Prince Charles had felt like a very normal boy growing up. But then, when a young man, he had realized he was "stuck," that his life was set out for him and he had to follow these directives, and he had become very insecure. He had had to struggle with himself to find out who he was and express himself within the limited, rigid, confines of his role. I realized that he could see cause as well as consequence. At the international level, he could see beyond the surface to the depths; he could become a Peacemaker.

My ordinary routine was disrupted by what was happening to me. I could not sleep. Energies were shooting through me. A powerful energy would soar up from my lower body and exit through the top of my head. Another energy would go down from my heart until it reached my toes, where it seemed to collect and build up. It was as if my heart was a glass being filled with water, and the water was love, and the love was now overflowing down the sides of the glass. Twice, without warning, I shook uncontrollably. Once I was at the supermarket, trying to decide which brand of toilet paper to buy, when suddenly it hit; I began to shake like a blender. It lasted for a minute or so. I didn't know if people were watching me, but I wanted the floor to open up and swallow me, I felt so embarrassed!

One day in April, I took Robert to the swim club. Once we got in the pool, Robert began to make "war" with another boy — as usual — and I was trying to intervene to bring "peace." As I was talking to Robert and the other child, suddenly Robert turned to me, and, in an authoritative manner, said, "When are you going to learn? When? How long, how long?"

I was stunned. It was not Robert speaking, but that being, who, from time to time in Robert's life, has pushed its way through. This was not a boy, but a man with a deep voice and a stern, strong manner.

I said nothing. I left the pool and went home alone. I sat on the couch and became quiet within. My mind was asking, "What do I have to learn? This child is here for a purpose; he is telling me something, trying desperately to teach me. But what?" Then, like lightning, it came: "War." He was trying to tell me that negative energy is necessary. "But how?" I asked myself. I had denied negative energy my entire life because I could never find a place for it. If something was not good, it did not exist for me. And now my child was telling me, "Look! Look at it and learn its highest use."

Soon I found my answer. We need to use negative energy, the energy that kills, inwardly to kill the false-self and, in that way, merge into a larger unit. When negative energy is used outwardly — as Robert used it — instead of inwardly, it shows the imbalance of the whole. I realized then that as long as I denied negative energy, I too was unbalanced. I had to use both positive and negative.

Thank you, Robertito, thank you.

Robert always loved school. Whenever I wanted him to mind, I would say, "Tomorrow, I will not take you to school!" Immediately, he would obey. So the next morning, when he looked at me and said, again in the manner of that older being, "Mommy, today you are not going to take me to school. Today, you and I are going to Santa Cruz and we will talk," I listened and obeyed.

We drove to Santa Cruz in silence. Neither of us spoke until we lay down on the beach. Then he looked at me and said, with the voice of that other being, "Mommy, I want you to know something. It has been very hard, very hard. You are very strong. I needed to be stronger. You had to learn.

"You know we went to the doctor last December and he said I had the beginnings of multiple sclerosis? Well, don't worry, I will not get it. Keeping my energy was hard. When the energy begins to accumulate, the body begins to misfunction. I could not let it flow. You had to learn. But now, I can begin my life. You have learned."

He said we should go to Spain. I could not believe my ears — this child had been incapable of planning anything. We always called him the "now" kid.

I couldn't speak. Poor child, he was serving me — me, the one who was always trying to teach him to be positive! I was the one who had to learn! Tears rolled down my cheeks as he continued to talk and plan. Love poured from my heart. Every being is constantly serving. Every being was doing what was best for me, and for everyone, but I had been blind.

Before, I had always thought that I gave to people, but now I realized that I only took — I took the best of someone, the positive. I realized that I was no more, no less, than what each person who had passed through my life had given me.

Yes, I would follow my child. We would go to Spain.

I had to tell everyone I knew about this incredible episode. I went to San Francisco to tell my friend Silver. As we were walking down the street, I smelled chicken cooking. My desire rose sharply. I thought to myself, "I have arrived; it doesn't matter; I can finally let go of my energy for once." So I gave in. We bought a half chicken. Immediately, I began to eat it with my fingers. I gave in to my animal desire to devour. It was so good!

That evening I was in the bathroom, squeezing out toothpaste onto my toothbrush, when I glanced at the mirror. What I saw there shocked me: my cheeks began to sag; the flesh under my chin drooped down. My face, usually firm and young looking, gradually deteriorated into the face of a tired, old woman.

"Okay," I said, "I get the message. If we control our energy, we can stay young forever. But if we allow the senses to dominate, we age. Okay, I won't do it again."

The next morning, I jumped out of bed, hurried to the bathroom and looked in the mirror. My face was young, firm, and fresh again.

I had arranged to visit my friend Sean in Berkeley. As I was preparing to leave, my cat, Miaws, came to me, attracted my attention, then led me to my car. She looked up at me, then went under the car for a moment, then came out and looked up at me again. She went under the car two more times.

After the third time, I said, "I got it. I got it. I guess I need to fix something in the car. Well, it has to wait because I'm going to Berkeley."

Sean and I had a great deal to talk about. We went to dinner. We danced. I wanted him to be happy. I wanted the whole world to be happy.

That night I stayed over and left in the morning. Sean lives on top of a hill. Driving down, as I approached the first stop sign, I pressed on the brake. But the car did not slow. I felt calm; I started to laugh. "Ah . . . you were right!" I thought, remembering my "conversation" with my cat. I decided to let the car take me to safety and let go of the steering wheel. The speedometer rose to 70 mph. It passed through four intersections without meeting any other cars. When the road leveled out at the bottom of the hill, I was able to park the car. Then I hitched a ride to the rapid transit station.

While waiting for the train, I began to talk with a middle-aged man who said he worked as a fisherman. I told him I was going to gather people, that we must work for peace. If I called him would he leave everything and come work with me? He said, "Yes," then gave me his name and phone number. I felt as though I was becoming a fisherman of men.

Later that week, my neighbor asked me why my driveway never had the trails that snails usually leave on cement. I told her that when we had moved into our house six years before, the gardener had asked me to buy snail poison. I had refused. Instead, I had gone around the yard and talked to the snails hidden among the greenery. I had told them that I didn't want to harm them. I wanted them to eat, but could they please not ruin my garden. And they had obeyed.

When I told her this, my neighbor said, "You must be psychic." I did not think of myself as a psychic. I felt that I was a prophet. I wanted to reach the people, all people.

In April, I went to speak with a Catholic priest. He asked me to talk at his church on May 3rd. I did not prepare for the service, knowing that when I got up, I would be able to speak. As I stood before those people, a voice came from within me and gave the speech. It came through me, not from me. The following is a transcription from the tape recording of that talk.

. . . I am here because of my need to reach each and every one of you. I am here out of the knowledge of Who I am, What I am, and Why I am! I am here because my push button is need. It has always been (need). And now the world needs us, all of us. We look around and see all sorts of things we don't like. I always said I was "the expert of the spirit world." That's what Beatriz was! and I laughed. I knew how to bring peace wherever I went. And I laughed. But now it's no joke anymore.

As I look around, I realize that the problems that we have are not hunger, but greed; not lack of things, but frustration, hate. (These) are the problems of the spirit. And I thought, "This is my line, I know about that!"

So when we have a problem, what do we do? We try to solve it with the raw materials that we have. What are the raw materials of the spirit world? What are the energies that we have?

I feel that we have the energy of Moses — who gave us the foundations on which we all can build the road on which Mankind can walk behind us — and lead us inside with the energy of the

Buddah, with the determination and free will of the Krishna, to serve mankind like Jesus — with love, tolerance and patience.

But we are in the Twentieth Century and we need something else. This is the New Age. A new element of the spirit has to come (forth)! "What is that new element?" I thought, "It has to be there." And it is . . . It's violence! It's war.

Everything that exists has a highest use. Everything! and I was to learn, that war too has a highest use. We are to take that energy and kill self. We are to take that energy, each one of us, and kill the frustrations that we have, the anger that we feel, the hate. Kill self . . . and as we kill self, and as we use that energy within, we get to the "I am." We achieve peace within, and we know who we are.

And when we know who we are, we can have courage to do and serve. Some of us are for the few. Some of us are for the many. Some of us are for the all. But each (one) of us has a place and we have to take it.

We can change the energy of the world around. We do not need to live in fear that somebody will push a button. We can change it, if we are big enough to face ourselves. The solutions are not out there, in Washington, in China, or in any place else, but in us!

We have the power to be who we are. We have the power to use that energy which is (now) undirected and use it for its highest purpose for which it was intended; to help us; to make us Be who we are. I am a healer of men. Who (ever) I touch, I love and heal. I do want so much to give that which I have, for which I worked so hard. Take it. Ask the question, "Who am I?" and know that there is an answer . . . I know because I have it. And it is for you to have too. It is for all of us. The promised land is here, it is within, and we are all to get it. We can change the world.

We saw in the sixties, the hippie movement. We saw the hippies roaming through (out) the world. I did that too, when I was 15, in the 50's. I had a purpose when I did it. I wanted to prove that I would meet what I was. I knew (myself) to be light, when I was fifteen. I knew that I would find nothing that could hurt me. And nobody ever did. The doors opened one after the other.

Now I am forty years old and I know I am here to lead man(kind), because I worked for 20 years with thoughts of peace and love. Now is the time to mature. Now is the time to take up the challenge that we screamed in the sixties. We grew, we thought, we went on, we meditated. We began the growth movement. Now is the time (for action). There are answers. They are within. It is possible.

At the service I also played and sang along with the recording of a song expressing the idea that the only important thing is to

Love and that "all the sages of the world came just to tell us that." Another line of the song says, "Let's throw our conditioning aside, and reunite . . ."

After the service, each member of the congregation came up to me and said exactly the same thing: "We know what you said to be true."

Later I went to the director of the International Center at Stanford University and asked for a room where I could gather people. But I did not speak to this person in my usual voice. Although I knew what I wanted to say and said it, when the words came out, they were in a different voice: a strong, commanding voice which sounded preachy. I could not control it. My entire facial expression changed. At one moment, I was pleasant and friendly, then suddenly, my expression would become stern and authoritative. This happened several times. It got results. People listened. I was given the use of a large room at the International Center for my meeting.

It was a small meeting. I informed people about it mostly by word of mouth. Silver, Andrea, April (Kirsten's daughter), Robert, and Allan were there. Allan told Robert, "Mommy has become a teacher." He came humbly — he, Allan, the one who will remain in the All, who is much more evolved than I.

Often I would sing alone and I would cry. I cried because the joy I experienced brought tears to my eyes. I was in rapture.

But at the same time, I began to feel the fear of the world. The news of the Atlanta murders filled the papers every day that summer. As I watched this episode unfold, I cried because I felt the pain of the man who had done this killing. I realized how much pain he must have felt to strike out at the world in such a brutal manner. I felt that instead of judging him, we should love him. I wanted to heal him, to tell him I didn't judge him bad or evil, but that I understood. I felt the tremendous pain that he felt.

One time I was with Andrea watching a television program called "The Christians," about how the Jews, Christians, and Moslems have influenced each other. I felt the pain of each group, the pain of its history, the tremendous fear. I felt the pain physically and in my very soul.

I had felt a similar pain when I visited The Alhambra in Granada, Spain, in 1979. I was not able to take the tour and enjoy the magnificent buildings and gardens because I could see the turmoil and feel the pain of the place.

When the TV show ended I began to cry. I no longer had problems of my own. The only pain I could feel, the only problems I had, were the problems and pain of the world. Before, if someone had said to me, "You can love the world," I would

262

have laughed. Before, "the world" had always been abstract for me. I loved only those around me, the people I could touch, hear, see. But now, "the world" had become alive for me — its countries, its people. I saw the pattern and spiritual purpose of each country.

I felt that I had to go to the world and tell the people all that I had discovered. My past now made sense. I realized why my mother had taken me out to experience the masses. She was showing me that I too could lead the world. If Evita could lead her country — for whatever purpose — then I could lead the world to peace.

I can because I Am. And I Am because I Know, Feel, Think and Act. And I Know, Feel, Think and Act, because I Am.

My father had said, "You can talk to the world, but remember, you'll need a good interpreter." He had showed me how to eat weeds and said, "Now you know you can eat and survive!"

I realized now why I needed all this information. All the pieces fell into place. I had been **trained**. I had prepared myself my entire life to be the next Christ — but not in this life. Perhaps the next, or the one after that, but not this one. I knew someone must come and do even more than the last spiritual man. And now I knew it was to be me!

I told the principal of Robert's school, "We only need one, just one Human Being: one Buddha, one Moses, one Jesus, one Mohammed — just one. I need all of you. We'll make it. We'll make it."

Needless to say, many people I talked to thought I had gone off my rocker. People would say, "Be careful," or, "Think about your child, think about yourself."

I realized that people might not like what I would say. Some might take my child to shut me up. But I realized that I couldn't let that thought stop me. No one could kill me. No one could kill Robert. It just wasn't possible. What **Is**, does not die. I was eternal. Immortality was no longer just an idea — it was real.

I felt secure with this realization. This security allowed me to sell my house. I believed that I needed to organize a large meeting. I called to find out how much it would cost to rent the Flint Center in Cupertino. I called Bill Graham, the concert promoter, to find out how much such a meeting would cost. I realized that to get the money for this meeting, I would have to sell my house. I planned to travel all over the world with my child. If I had to, I would eat weeds in order to survive.

I thought I needed the money to reach all people. It was only later, when I began to meet people who seemed to communicate with me telepathically, that I began to realize that the meeting was with the Cosmos. The "all" I was to meet was not all people, but The **All**.

That summer, April arrived from Brazil to stay with me a while before going to Denmark. She brought her fiancee, Patrick with her. I had wired money to her for the trip. Her mother, Kirsten, was supposed to wire the money from Denmark to reimburse me.

At the time, I needed this money very badly. I called her bank in Denmark several times. Each time they confirmed that they had sent a wire to my bank. But my bank had not received the wire. Kirsten said she had paid an extra fee so that the money would arrive within twenty-four hours.

April left for Denmark and Patrick remained with me. He was frightened because he thought she would never send him the plane ticket so that he could join her. Because he was so scared, it was a real stress having him around. I was only able to be kind and loving with him because I could let off steam with Andrea. Again she did not even know what service she was providing.

April wanted me to use the money her mother was wiring, for Patrick's trip. But if I did, Kirsten would be furious. I felt trapped in the middle. But since the money hadn't arrived, the matter was out of my hands. Finally, Andrea decided to charge his ticket on her American Express card. As soon as he left, the wire arrived. When my bank checked into the matter, the bank in Denmark said they had sent the money the same day Kirsten had placed the wire. There was no explanation for the holdup.

For years I had wanted to expand my relationship with Silver. This year, for the first time, she had invited Robert and me to Sacramento as a present for my fortieth birthday.

Once there, I found myself in strong conversations with her. She would try to present a viewpoint opposite to mine. This was usual for us. But at that particular time, I was trying to make a big decision: Do I take the job? The voice had told me to give everything up and the job was mine, that I could bring Heaven to Earth.

But now my mind was saying, "**Should** I give everything up?" I had always been a black or white person, all or nothing, no compromise. But now, after I had seen how Silver lives her life, I knew that one could do things in stages. Thanks to her, I had a choice.

One statement she made that weekend stuck in my mind: "You want recognition." When the weekend ended, I went home and prayed. I prayed like I had never prayed before. "Oh, God, sweet God, you know I don't want recognition." I had worked all my life to kill ego. But what if Silver was right? What should I do?

I decided to give only $20,000 of the house sale money away, instead of all of it. Giving it all away meant taking the job. I decided that I would work, but not as a Christ. I felt that this would show God, the Force, the Cosmos, that I wanted to comply with the command. But in case Silver was right, that I did really want recognition, I would not take the job. I would not try to gather all people. I would go to Spain with my child and become a writer.

And so I followed the word of Man instead of the word of God.

The money I would give away would be seed money to the Cosmos, and would return to me multiplied. Anyone who lives in the United States is here, among other reasons, to learn to deal with money. I could only deal with money in the way that I dealt with everything else — from the spiritual point of view. So I would give the money to the Peace movement.

I sold the house at a time when interest rates were extremely high. Everyone told me I might have to wait a year to sell.

I just told them, "The first of August, I am leaving."

Soon after I put the house up for sale, I had two offers.

The real estate agent told me, "I hope you realize this is unusual. This is not a seller's market."

I only looked at her and laughed.

If Beatriz is selling, it makes no difference that for everyone else it is a buyer's market, for me it is a seller's market.

Before the buyers came, the real estate agent wanted me to make sure the garden was well watered. So I watered more than usual. But there had always been one corner that the sprinklers did not reach. Every summer the plant in that corner had turned brown from lack of water. Now that seemed to make no difference. The plant seemed to be in tune with me. If I felt elated, its leaves would be up. If I felt a bit down, its leaves would wilt and droop slightly.

Throughout that summer, I continued to feel an extraordinary sense of joy. I would sing at the top of my lungs, anywhere, anytime. At a Fourth of July street barbecue the band let me have the microphone. I sang, "Last Night I Had the Strangest Dream I Ever Had Before."

In two weeks I had a booklet printed, of Spanish poetry which my family and friends had written. In the prologue I wrote, "Thank you for helping me find peace within, the peace I wish to give you all."

When people first met me, they would think I was crazy. As I talked to them, I slowly won them over. I reached out to each person at his own level of understanding. To physicists, I talked energy. To cooks, I explained my ideas in terms of cooking.

I began to feel as if certain people that I met could read my mind. Often they seemed to know what I had done several years ago.

In early June, I went to hear Dr. Helen Caldicott give a lecture at Stanford on nuclear holocaust. I talked to Dr. Caldicott before the lecture and told her that I had something to say to everyone there. She agreed to call on me when her talk was over.

As soon as I sat down in the auditorium, a young man came and sat down next to me. Without introducing himself, he began to urge me to talk. During the question and answer period, he kept saying, "You have something important to say! Put your hand up. Talk!"

No one had ever needed to push to get me to talk before. But I thought that Dr. Caldicott would call on me. She, on the other hand, expected me to put my hand up. By the end of the lecture, the man was furious, his face red with rage. He got up and talked to her. I was embarrassed by his rudeness towards her. Yet I was also amazed at his concern for me.

After he left the auditorium, I went outside and found him.

Immediately, he asked me, "What happened to you two years ago while you were in Spain?"

I was stunned. How could he have possibly know about that trip?

"Who are you?" I asked him.

He refused to answer.

He told me to come to a meeting that he had organized. "You must be there," he said, and showed me a paper which concerned this meeting. The paper referred to the meeting as the "August 6-9 Coalition Meeting."

I went to that meeting and also several others which he organized. The purpose of these meetings was to organize Greenpeace and other groups for the peace movement.

I discovered that his name was Cristopher. He did not seem very articulate. I could see that people thought he was off his rocker. Yet I knew he was not!

For one meeting, he rented a large room in St. Mary's Cathedral and paid for it himself. The other people thought it was foolish, but I knew it was not. Although I did not realize it at the time, he was working at cause level. He was creating in spirit, working with The Force. I would become aware of this later. At the time I just knew we were on the same wavelength. We felt the same way towards the world.

I decided that I should give him the money I felt I had to give the Cosmos. I gave him $20,000 from the sale of the house. The last time I saw Cristopher, I asked him, "When or how will I know about the meeting?"

He replied, "One day you will see a film with lots of candles. And after that will be another film. This film will tell you." Though this all sounded very mysterious, I was joyous. My head was burning. The sensation was so strong that I could not reason as I normally did. I felt perfection itself.

Shortly after this, Allan took Robert to a spiritual retreat which offered readings of past lives. He had asked me to go with them, but I had declined.

That Sunday I decided I needed to know more about world history. I saw an ad in the paper for a movie on the subject and thought it would be fun to go.

After I had bought my ticket, with an hour to kill, I went to a cafe and ordered some coffee. I sat at my table, smiling, full of joy, looking at the air, feeling strength, power, peace.

A man at a table nearby looked at me and told me that I seemed very happy.

I said the world was an extraordinary place.

He invited me to drink my coffee with him. He was a historian who had taught at Stanford. He told me that Russia had all the raw materials they needed in their country, but that the United States would need to go to South Africa to find the proper raw materials. When we did, Russia had only to wait for us with their boats in the middle of the ocean.

This reminded me of what I had said when I was twelve years old: "Russia will win and at that point the world will turn and the planet will become a spiritual place."

He talked about Carl Sagan's book, Cosmos. He said that Cleopatra was a brunette, and kept looking at me with knowing eyes. "Do you know about Dante?" he asked "Do you know what Beatriz means?" He took a page from a novel he was working on and made me read it. Then he told me to criticize it. "You know," he said, "you know how to."

I felt he was testing me. How deep did I go? How much did I know?

He said, "What if we bring the donkey to the water and there is no water?" He wanted to know if I could provide the water for the masses.

I told him that greed is a consequence of fear, and fear a consequence of pain.

That seemed to satisfy him — I went deep enough. He said I should read Shakespeare and told me to start writing immediately.

For the first time in my life, people were pushing me, people stronger than I was. I did not like it.

Later, I went to a bookstore and found the book Cosmos. The

first page I opened showed the numbers of a crystal. I saw that there was a remarkable similarity with my own numbers. (See Table, page 307.)

I remembered what the man had said: "Cleopatra was a brunette, you know." I recalled that I had given Allan a Valentine's Day card, years before, which had pictures of several famous couples on it: Napoleon and Josephine, Romeo and Juliet, Marc Antony and Cleopatra. I rushed home and quickly went through my files. Where was that card? I found the card I had given Allan in 1970, eleven years before. Yes, I had underlined "Cleopatra and Marc Antony!" So that was one of my past lives! That certainly was good preparation for me to lead the world to peace. Cleopatra had been a ruler, so I had already learned those skills.

Though I hadn't gone to the spiritual retreat, the Universe had brought my reading to me nevertheless.

While I was still wondering whether I should give all my money, I went to a cafe one morning for breakfast. A man at a table near mine, looked at me and said, "Why so pensive? Have you ever lost? Why so hesitant? Tell me, tell me, did you ever lose at any time in your life?"

I looked at him. "No," I said, "never. You are right. My entire life has been one of growth."

"So? . . . now you have your answer."

He said no more. I was stunned. I left. How did he know? Or did he? Was I going crazy?

I got up the next morning, looked at myself in the bathroom mirror, then closed my eyes and called the man with my mind. "Be there. I'll be there at seven."

I went to the cafe at 7 a.m. He was already sitting at a table. I walked over to him and, acting very surprised, said, "Oh! You are here!"

He looked at me with a serious expression and said, "Of course, didn't you summon me?"

My mouth dropped open. What was happening?

We started to talk and he asked me what I had done to my husband. "What happened in Spain?"

How did he know about these things? Whenever I answered a question, he would say, "I don't understand that."

Soon I realized I was speaking with the spirit of Jose. I just knew it — I could feel it in his presence.

He began to ask me about literature. Who wrote this book? Who wrote that one? He told me to take the job. "Don't write," he said, "What can you write that hasn't already been written? You see," he said, "you thought I did not have any brains."

I almost fell off my chair. It was true! I had always thought that Allan was mind; Jose, feelings. I had decided before that Jose and I could not relate intellectually. Now his spirit was showing me that he actually knew everything, but he had chosen to close himself to certain kinds of knowledge so that he could do what was necessary for his journey.

I felt ashamed.

He said I would marry and that I would serve. He was telling me to go for spirit instead of mind. He was trying to serve me.

I was humbled — here he was, out of work but all smiles, maintaining a positive attitude. He had the same ability as I did, and I had dared to complain about the grand task God had given me.

But I was still not quite sure I wanted the job. I still planned to write. In August (1981) I would visit Argentina for the first time in seventeen years. Then in September, Robert and I would go to live in Spain.

Before going to Argentina, I stopped in Los Angeles to attend a spiritual congress at the University of California, Los Angeles (U.C.L.A.) I hoped to meet with Bapak, leader of Subud. I had heard a taped lecture in which he had said, "Why do you think I am traveling at my age? — I am looking for a leader to come forth!" I knew he felt he had a divine mission. I felt I had one too. He was old and would die soon and I would be here to pick up the "job." The show must go on; the actors must take their places.

Freddy, Robert, and I went to register at a dormitory on the U.C.L.A. campus. The lady at the reception desk kept telling me how extraordinary Freddy was. I said that Robert was too. She said, "Follow Freddy," then turned to her husband and told him, with extra significance in her eyes, "This is going to be a good one for her to figure out."

Then she told me she needed an iron. Did I have one?

I ignored this remark.

She told me to sleep at another dorm nearby. Though the congress was being held here, I accepted her advice. I felt she meant I did not belong at the congress.

Perhaps she was right. I did not get to talk to Bapak, but only an assistant of his.

Later, I found her again, and again she mentioned the iron, looking at me with knowing eyes.

Suddenly, the picture of my realtor lady came to me. The last day that I was at my house, she had stopped by and said, "I want to take something from your house. Do you have anything?"

The house was totally empty except for an iron.

"Ah! I'll take the iron," she had said.

The interaction was very strange.

And now this other woman was looking at me as if I was supposed to make some kind of connection. I decided it was a spirit coming to me through two different people, identifying itself with the word "iron."

At U.C.L.A. I met David, who teaches "The Course in Miracles" in New York. We went to breakfast and talked and I told him I felt he was a peacemaker.

He said, "This meeting is not me, but through me."

For the first time in my life, I felt as though I had a complete interaction with another person, spiritual, intellectual, emotional. Yet I also felt it was not a person, but a being, a spirit. I had fallen in love with a being. I knew that I would meet that being again in the near future.

During our four days in Los Angeles, Freddy, Robert and I decided to visit Universal Studios. While we were waiting in line to enter the grounds, a lady began to talk to me. She said she could tell me lots of things, but first, I must follow Freddy and not Robert. I should stay in Argentina. I should not go to Spain. She said I was surrounded by envy, by forces that wanted to pull me down.

I looked at her and said, "No one has ever harmed me. No one ever will."

"Please, follow your older son," she said. "Your older son. Everything is ready for you there." There was compassion in her eyes; there was a plea; there was love.

I wanted her to explain what she meant, but suddenly Robert pulled me away with such force that I lost her in the crowd.

"I never paid attention to the outside world before! Why should I obey now?" I asked myself. "Why listen to people whom I don't even know? I will not! I refuse to! It's crazy!"

The next morning, while sitting in the dormitory lobby, I overheard two cleaning people talking in Spanish. The younger man had a Bible in his hand. The older man was saying, "If you want to come to my house, come, but don't speak religion in my house." The younger man believed you should read and talk about the Bible. The older man thought one should simply live as it says to live, and be filled with good feelings.

Suddenly I felt that I was listening to Father and Mother. They were in these two bodies. The younger man with the Bible was my father; the older one, my mother.

A lady carrying a broom joined them. She looked at me with an incredible love in her eyes. I recognized that love at once — it was Belly, my grandmother. Belly with a broom!? Belly cleaning? I had never seen her wash a dish in my life, much less carry a broom. Yet, I knew it was her.

The next morning, August 4th as Freddy, Robert and I were getting into the car to drive to the airport, the cleaning lady, my grandmother, leaned from a fifth story window and yelled down to me, "I was so glad to see you again!"

Though I knew it was Belly, I said, in my mind, "Beatriz, are you going mad?" I waved goodbye to her with tears in my eyes. Freddy looked at me strangely, unable to understand why I should have tears saying goodbye to a maid I'd just met.

I could not talk; I could only cry and smile at him. He looked at me and said, "I don't understand any of this, but I am here for you."

He was living up to his poem he wrote and sent me in 1979:

> ". . . Friends are Forever
> I've come to find out
> But for one special one
> it goes on longer than that
>
> Whether help with a car
> or a beautiful smile
> it's always been there
> without having to call
>
> I guess, I've sometimes forgotten
> to show my love
> to a truly good friend
> That I've always had
> So if you ever need anything
> anything at all
> Don't hesitate,
> give me call . . .

Since I had been away from Argentina for seventeen years, I was prepared not to fit in. I would be coming back to a nation completely different from the one I'd left.

But as usual, my scenario did not fit. Everything was exactly as before. I found all the love that I had left, and even more. Now, the neighbors understood my odd behavior, my "pre-hippie days," of twenty-five years before. They apologized for giving me such a hard time.

I found my sister, Ana Maria, weighing well over 300 pounds. She showed me the house. It looked old and abandoned, like a "manger."

She looked at me with great satisfaction and said, "Don't you think it looks depressing? Don't you think it is really dreary?"

But I, who was seeing the perfection of everything, even

271

garbage on the sidewalk, said, "No, not at all."

She got angry. "What do you mean — it's not depressing? What do you mean, it's not bad?"

All of a sudden, I realized that Ana Maria had been serving me like no other. She had been the negative energy that had enabled me to be the positive one. She had worked hard to create this manger. As soon as I realized this, I told her how truly depressing the place was, how terrible it looked.

She smiled, a great smile of satisfaction. She had succeeded! If I was to be a Christ, she had prepared a manger for me. If I was to be positive, she had to be negative.

Later I bought some flowers and opened the drapes, the windows and the shutters. Ana had said over and over that the house was dark — but she had kept the drapes, windows and shutters closed! Soon the house looked much better. Even Ana Maria said so.

I could now see clearly what Ana Maria had given me. For me to have the opportunity to be who I was, she had to be **that** sister. Since her birth she had been the negative energy, giving me the opportunity to love her, or to side with Mother, Father or Belly, all of whom continually put her down. My heart broke. Anita knew I loved her. She had listened to me as a child. She had come to me for anything, all through her life. I had had to disconnect from her when I was in California because I was learning to set limits, learning how to say, "No." But that had had nothing to do with her.

How could I express my love — besides feeling it and thinking it? Saying it was not enough. I had to manifest my love in a way that she, as a negative energy, could understand. I had to do it for me too! Because I am, therefore I Know, Feel, Think and **Act**. I would use the money that remained from the sale of my house. What did she want? What were her dreams? I would buy her anything.

While I was thinking all this through, I went to my room. A few minutes later Ana Maria came running from the kitchen, asking me who had lit incense in the house, and where was it?

No one had. I knew it was me. While I had been concentrating, seeking inner guidance, my inner aroma had spread throughout the house. I had gone back several lifetimes, to when I cleaned incense. The letter Ana had written to me in February of 1964 had become a reality. Yes, I brought fragrances back to her without wind.

Dear Beatriz:

God placed on the earth flowers, messages of love and peace. Today one goes to a much colder and harder country. I tell you, don't stop illuminating, don't allow men to step-over you. Send your message. To the man who would love you, don't show false thorns, but resistance. Don't forget that your smile, your message of love, peace and unity, must reach your children and grandchildren. That will be fertile ground for all your seeds, robust from faith. Your parents and your siblings will wait here for a favorable wind which will bring your fragrance.

Do you know that cactuses do have a heart and cry during the night?

Do you know that your sister is a solitary cactus in the humid pampas?

Ana Maria

I felt, "Yes, I have come back to you; after learning to say no, after years spent learning how to close when everyone else was learning how to open; after learning to see you as negative, to see you as the cactus. But now I can see how the cactus fits in the all. Oh, my dear Ana Maria, how could I have existed without you! You were here, preparing my manger, and I have chosen another road! I have chosen not to be the Christ, but to be the writer. Please, please, take my money and begin your life! Thank you for serving me so well."

Ana Maria and I went to the "Casa de Cambios" (currency exchange) to cash the check, the money from the sale of my house. The man said he could not cash it immediately, but could I please come back the following day. He wanted to sell me an apartment. We went to see one. He was insistent that I buy an apartment. I felt that outside guidance was trying to force me to stay. I decided I would rather let go of the money than be coerced into doing something I didn't want to do. So, in my mind, I let go of it. I endorsed the check and left it with him. Ana Maria was furious. She felt I would never get the money back. But I knew that if one trusts, if one really trusts, one is always rewarded. Now I realize that this was the first step that I took out of fear.

The next day, before going to the Casa de Cambios, Ana Maria and I had lunch at a Brazilian restaurant. When we went to the exchange, I mentioned this to the man and then told him, "I knew someone from Brazil who stayed with me in California." As I said this, I heard him communicate to me, "I am the one who held up your transference. I did that so the money would not be used for the Brazilian, because of his different energy." I felt that a spirit was acting through him, and that this spirit had held up the money from Denmark with which I had planned to pay for Patrick's trip.

Again that day, the man would not cash the check. Again, I left it with him.

The following day, when I went to the exchange, he gave me the check back, refusing to cash it, and took me out for coffee.

Later, I went to another exchange, which cashed it immediately. This was to remain a pattern with me throughout the month: I would receive guidance, but refuse it, then receive the same guidance again and refuse it again. But on the third time, I would be allowed to do as I wished without any interference.

First, I had met the spirit of Jose, then the "iron" spirit and the spirits of Father, Mother, and Belly. And now, I had met the one responsible for withholding the money in June. Needless to say, I was acting a bit shaken at times. I couldn't explain all this. My head kept burning. Before, I had believed in guidance; I had believed that someone — or "something" — had taken my hand and led me from place to place throughout my life. But now I was being visited by the spirits of the past, the present and the future! It was like something from Dickens.

To understand and to believe is one thing, but to make something your own is quite different.

After cashing the check, Ana Maria and I visited a lawyer I had known since my youth. In the old days, he and I had often talked about Lanza del Vasto, a disciple of Gandhi, the first man to bring Gandhi's idea of non-violence to the West. Just before I had left Argentina, seventeen years before, he had told me, "When you come back, I will want to know if you have realized why you didn't go with Lanza del Vasto."

Now I told him that I knew. I had made the right decision. The path away from the mainstream of life was not for me. I had to immerse myself in life; I had to swim the muddiest waters to reach the opposite bank and emerge dry, clean, and pure.

My friend began to talk about the trip he and his wife had taken. They had gone to California and he told what they had done. I could not speak; I was petrified. He was describing the trip I had taken with Jose the year before. Every **detail** was in place: the cities, the restaurants, what we ate at each restaurant, the motels, were all the same!

Then he said, "Bring me a picture of you and him. He was no good. We have to do something."

I knew he meant Jose.

Then he said love was important to me, but "you do not want

274

this man", and made a face that was a perfect impersonation of a man I had just met in Buenos Aires and who had shown a strong interest in me.

"Come in two days," my friend told me, "we will talk about the one that is for you."

We left his office and Ana Maria said, "I do not understand that conversation. How did he know about Jose? How did he know any of it? What did he mean?"

I was too stunned to answer her. I would not bring him the picture of Jose. I did not want harm to come to anyone. I began to fear and therefore, I began to use my judgment outwardly.

Before, I had had the distinct feeling that the Jose I had experienced in California was a different man than the Jose I had met in Europe. But at the time, I just thought, "He's different because it's a new situation." Never in my life had I imagined that a spirit could enter and act through a person the same way that a car can have many different drivers. I had always said, "If someone is unkind an entire lifetime, with me that person will be kind." I thought that I was lucky enough to get that one "good" action; never had I imagined that a different spirit would come through just for me.

We took a taxi home and for the entire twenty-minute trip, the driver kept saying he could go the faster road, the super-highway, but it looked as though we would have to go the long road instead. He was taking the only possible route to our home! He kept on and on about the fast road and the long road.

I knew he was talking to me. He was telling me that I was not listening to the Universe, that I would take the long way around instead of the super-highway guided by spirits. My head kept burning. I was trying to make sense of all this.

Ana Maria thought the driver was crazy. "What was he talking about?" she wanted to know. "There is only one way home. Anyone knows that!"

I cried; I smiled at her. I knew that I could not explain; she could not understand.

I began to observe that I was hearing different messages in what anyone was saying, from what the other listeners, and even the speaker, perceived. It was like reading an ordinary letter and immediately seeing a secret code in it — a code that the writer had not intended to produce. I had a hearing within a hearing.

Still trying to decide exactly what to do, I was asking the Cosmos to guide me. I wanted to give away everything if that was what God wanted — but was it? In addition to the things I bought Ana Maria, I paid the legal fees for the probate of Father's estate and signed away my part of the family estate to her. The instant I signed the form, hail came down hard outside. It lasted just a few minutes. Stunned, we went to look outside. There was only a light covering of clouds and no wind. I thought the Cosmos was telling me I had made the wrong decision.

It seemed that every time I let go of more of my money, I received more energy. This energy seemed to attract people. Robert noticed that if we entered a place that was empty, within two minutes, it would be filled. This happened in grocery stores, restaurants, everywhere. It became a big joke with us.

One day the sky was very gray; it looked as if a heavy rain would come any moment. August in Buenos Aires is usually the rainy season. Ana Maria said, "It's too bad you had to come this time of year."

I have never worried about the weather. The sun has always followed me. When I went to Belgium in 1979, the rain stopped. The day I left, the rain began again. During the winter I spent in Spain, it only rained when I went to Belgium and Denmark. Before, it had been a joke with me, but now I decided to test my powers.

"Look, see," I told Ana Maria, "The sun will come out."

Then I stood in the middle of Florida Street and looked at the sky and thought and felt. Within five minutes, the sun came out. I told Ana Maria it would not rain until the day I left. It did not.

Ana Maria kept telling people, "Beatriz is crazy. She believes she can control the sun."

Ana told me she could never get anything made well. She always got inferior quality.

I wanted to prove her wrong. She needed a corset, so I took her to a very expensive shop in the best part of town. I saw the quality of the work done there and was certain that this time, Ana would be satisfied. The woman took the necessary measurements, then told Ana Maria when she could return to try it on.

But when we came back, I was shocked. Not only was the color wrong, but the corset was very poorly made. Since I had paid in advance, she had to take it.

Looking back, I realize I was being shown how one attracts energies identical to one's own.

Before leaving Argentina, I spent a few days with a cousin whom I love dearly. She told me that she could look at someone and know immediately where that person had lived in a past life — Atlantis, Egypt, Syria, etc.

Like so many others, she felt the effects of Argentina's poor economy. I felt that I was in possession of great intuition. I could help her. I would buy her a lottery number with which she would be sure to win. I concentrated until I came up with a number I felt was right, then we drove all over until we found a store which could sell us that number.

But the number did not come up. I was truly surprised. How could I have been so wrong?

My stay in Argentina lasted through the month of August. My mind kept burning. I had trouble talking; I did not make much sense; my logical mind and reasoning were going. But the power, peace, happiness and joy I experienced were enormous. People would say, "There is something about you, one can feel it," or, "Beatriz, you give me energy."

When I left Argentina, I had less than $500. A month before, I had had $60,000. But I trusted God. I knew the Universe would take care of me.

When I had to leave Ana Maria, I cried and told her I loved her. I think she finally realized that I did love her. I told her that if at any time I didn't talk to her, it would not be because I didn't love her; I had to work for peace. I had work to do for her, her child, the whole world! She understood.

Freddy would stay in Argentina. I would fly with Robert to Miami, visit a friend there and then go to Spain.

At the airport, a lady stopped me and told me she had lost her son. I looked at her and felt that she was trying to tell me something which I needed. She left, but a minute later I decided to look for her.

I was about to step onto the escalator, when she appeared as if from nowhere, and said, "My son is the taller and has black hair." Then she disappeared again. Her statement made no sense. What was she trying to tell me?

I was looking at every action as the spiritual manifestation that it is. I lived in the "now," loose and free, having broken the barrier of time. Yes, time is an illusion. Everything in the "now" told me what was to come. I had eyes to see.

But my mind had started to melt. I, who constantly thought, who always had to understand and reason things out, who regarded the "mind" as a precious object, could not think. My mind was burning. I could hardly talk.

Yet the peace, joy, security, freedom I felt were beyond anything I had ever experienced in my life. I was home. All my wishes were satisfied; all my desires, fulfilled. I was whole. Ecstasy! It was like a cosmic orgasm. Not like an orgasm which lasts just a few minutes, but like one that had begun in March with "I am that I am" and was still continuing.

I had arranged to meet my dear friend, Eleanor, in Miami on September 3rd. I wanted to talk with her about my experience. In March, I had received her name, but nothing more. I felt that she and I were in this together.

Since leaving Los Angeles, I had looked for the spiritual being I had met through David. In Buenos Aires, I had read a book about the life of Julio Iglesias and decided that he was that being. Julio Iglesias knew what discipline was. He had overcome paralysis and was now a singer and songwriter who had opened himself up to millions. He loved and was loved by the so-called "little people" — the poor, the illiterate, those whom I loved too.

He believed in throwing himself into life sexually, just as I did. He was red wine. He had to make love with many women. Through his sexuality, he passed his being on to others. Just as a drop of red wine changes the color of white wine, so his soul, his "color," touched and changed those of others. I knew I did not want to make love anymore, but I knew what he was doing.

I made a numerological chart using his name and date of birth and found that he had master number 22, the number of those who can open new roads for the masses. He knew how to have friends on all sides — Arabs and Jews, capitalists and communists, the rich and the poor. I felt we could work together to bring peace, by bringing love to the world — not human love, but Divine love. Yes, he was a peacemaker!

Before, I had always seen the inner reality through the outer reality. Now I perceived the opposite: it seemed as though the outer reality occurred because of my inner being. My inner reality was projected on the outer reality.

Eleanor and I were in the hotel room, talking, and Robert was watching "Captain Kangaroo." I became aware that the television was "talking" to me. A man on the show said, "Pay attention. We are going to play a game. Everything is going to be backwards. Left will be right; right will be left. You are me. I am you."

Suddenly, what the woman at the airport had said made sense: "My son is the taller and has black hair." Freddy is taller than Robert. He has black hair; Robert has brown hair. I'd always known that Freddy was mine. Now I had been told.

Freddy himself had written of this in the second half of his poem to me in 1979:

". . . 'cause after all
If we don't take care
of each other now
who'll take care of us
when we grow old

You say you're my mother,
I say you're not, . . .
it don't make no difference
we both know what's what.
so
just enjoy my loving
and leave it at that
because whether mother or sister;
it don't change one dot,
The feeling I get
when we share our thoughts.

Freddy, my sweet Freddy, had helped me through so many crucial moments in this experience! Just by "coincidence," he had come all the way from Alaska to California to stay with me for one night, that night in March when I had felt the weight of the world, and cried and asked God, "Why me? Why me?"

Freddy had been there to comfort me, to assure me that whatever I would need for the job, God would provide.

On the other hand, Robert, the one who had come through me — through me but not **from** me — had pulled me away when someone was trying to protect me. I knew that our children are not our own, but this was more than I had imagined.

So . . . the television was instructing me. I kept asking myself, "Am I going crazy?" At the same time, there was another part of me that knew, that said, "NO, you are not crazy, you are in a new territory, a territory that you have never known before."

Often while Eleanor and I were talking, the television would present our thoughts to us. First I noticed it. Then Eleanor saw it too and began to understand. The moment she did, someone on the TV said, "An intruder is getting into the wave length."

One day, while we were relaxing on the beach, a lady selling mother-of-pearl pendants approached us. The pendants were displayed on a board which she carried in her cart. She did not offer me the whole choice, but took two from the board, a dove and an owl, and asked me which one I preferred. I chose the dove. She **gave** it to me and said, in a very insistent manner, "I'll be back on Tuesday."

Both Eleanor and I had the distinct feeling that I should obey.

But what? I was supposed to leave for Spain on Sunday — why should I cancel my plans because someone I did not even know was telling me to stay? I felt the woman was saying, "Tuesday your dove will be here." Did that mean I would meet the being I was looking for?

I took the dove pendant to a jewelry store to have some gold added to it. The man at the counter said it wouldn't be ready until Tuesday.

I decided to follow these different messages and stay until Tuesday. I wanted to look beautiful if I was to meet my "dove," so I went to a salon to have my nails done. The salon was closed; it would not be open until Tuesday. To my surprise, the name of the place was "The Cleopatra."

The book about Julio Iglesias had said that his parents had wanted to call him "Julio Caesar." "Ah! It all makes sense!" I thought to myself, "I was Cleopatra. He was Caesar. He and I are to meet again. We will go all over the world to reach the people, to burn out the fear they experience. Through his songs and my words, we will conquer. Peace will come, not only through Popes, politicians, and special interest groups, but through all of us. He and I have a lot to do. We will be a couple who love and understand all people, of all cultures, from beggars to tycoons, slaves to kings. We will open all hearts. They'll believe us! We'll go from country to country telling each how the other countries want peace too! They'll believe us, because we do have a key. Our key opens all hearts!"

I noticed a small display in the hotel lobby the next morning. The display contained reproductions of Cleopatra's rings. I realized that one of them symbolized my very Being. A short rod projected from the base of the ring, and around this rod, three smaller rings revolved, moving freely. It resembled a gyroscope. To me, each ring represented an energy: mental, physical, emotional: Spirit!

So Cleopatra bought the ring (the third Ring, three in One). She had to meet Caesar.

The man at the counter studied me with a significant expression and then looked past me. Eleanor saw a man sitting outside the store on a couch in the hotel lobby. He nodded to the jeweler and the jeweler told me, "I have a gift for you." He went to the back of the store and returning, handed me a small box. At the time, I had not wished to acquire any object, no matter what, so I said to Eleanor, "This is my gift for you."

At that the man at the counter became very hard, very strong. "No, it is for you," he said. "This is for you. You must know this." Then he softened a bit and said, "Well, if you want to give it away, that's okay. But at least read what it says. Read it. Please. You'll need it."

To please him, I opened the box. Inside was a sand dollar with a paper rolled up in its hole. The inscription on the paper read, "When this sand dollar breaks, a new being will emerge."

I wanted to have a nice, peaceful, dinner with Eleanor before she had to leave Miami. So many strange things had happened, I wanted us to relax. But when we walked into the hotel restaurant, we found a long line of people waiting to be seated. As we approached the maitre d', a man came up to him and said something in his ear. Then the maitre d' looked at us and, without a word, seated us immediately.

During dinner that evening, I had the distinct impression that we were sitting among spirits. The people at the tables around us "felt" like spirits. Eleanor perceived it too. There was a strange feeling in the air.

Eleanor described her impression of all these experiences in a letter to Allan, and of the restaurant in a letter to me.

June 14, 1982

Dear Allan:

. . . Regarding the "experiences" in Miami . . . One thing I can recall that both Beatriz and I felt took place in a restaurant. It was our last night in Miami, so we decided to go to a nice place in the adjoining motel. The maitre d' told us we would have to wait, and it appeared there were people waiting (sitting on chairs in the small lobby inside the restaurant entrance); then a man came and whispered something in the maitre d's ear. In a moment, he told us to follow him and showed us a table. While we were looking over the menu, I looked about because I was getting an uneasy feeling, as if the place and the people in it weren't real. At that point, I mentioned this to Beatriz. She responded, "You feel it too?" We looked around and both felt it was as if we were looking at something staged. Don't ask me to explain, I just had a queer feeling which was independent of Beatriz'.

When we left, Beatriz stopped at a gift shop in the same motel lobby. She purchased a ring. Before the purchase transaction was completed, I stepped out of the shop, into the main lobby. I was leaning on one of the sofas, when I noticed a man looking into the shop. He seemed to be trying to catch the eye of the proprietor who was facing him. When he had, he gave an imperceptible nod. Then the owner went to the back of the store and as I reentered the shop, he brought out a gift box containing a large sanddollar on which was painted a pelican. Enclosed in its gift box was the "legend of the sanddollar." He said she must have it and gave it to her, free. Of course, the proprietor may have been feeling generous, but it was unusual to hand out something that wasn't junk.

Re: the hotel scenes. Perhaps there is a logical explanation of the above, but I can't explain the uncomfortable feeling I had; a feeling independent of Beatriz's cues.

Another thing which I can't explain, and which may also be subject to interpretation, is the TV business. While in Miami, it was true that when Beatriz went on about a subject, that evening there was something on TV that was related. Of course, this can be interpreted as coincidence, but?

I cannot pretend to understand what Beatriz is going through. However, I cannot disbelieve what she says. You know better than I, that everything cannot be explained on an intellectual level. I try to understand, but as I told her, I am not where she is. I love her . . .

Love
Eleanor

(From letter to Beatriz 6/14/82)

. . . As I looked around the restaurant, the walls were a vivid embossed red; the waiters in black, and the customers with their painted faces, stood out against this red. Their seemingly affected manner . . .

At this point, my experience became very strong. The period I am about to describe lasted from Sunday, September (9th month) 6th (9/6/81) to Saturday of that same week. I had given $20,000 to a man in California organizing a group called "The August 9-6 Coalition." Coincidence?

I was in my hotel room Sunday morning, when I heard someone on a children's television show instruct the viewer to thank God. I would not have noticed it, but the words were repeated three times in a row. Suddenly, I felt that I must go to church. I went to the church at the hotel, but discovered they did not allow visitors to participate in communion. I felt that was not right; God belongs to all, so I left before the service was over. I did not have much time to catch my plane. I would leave my clothes in the room — God would take care of Robert and me. I just assumed that I would meet someone, fall in love in two seconds, and we would be taken care of. That was normal for me.

On our way to the airport, while waiting at a stoplight, I gave a canvasser for Muscular Dystrophy some money and the person handed me a paper decorated with Walt Disney cartoon characters. One picture in particular gained my attention: a cat trying to get at a fish in a bowl. The colors of this cartoon seemed to come off the paper toward me. I felt it had a message, but I could not decipher it.

Before we reached the airport, it suddenly began to rain. It rained so hard that I could not drive. "Okay, I get the message," I said in my mind, "I'll turn around. I'll not go to Spain." As soon as I turned the car, the rain stopped. I decided to turn back towards the airport. The rain began again. So I turned around once more and headed back. By the time I reached the hotel, the church service had ended. I apologized to the priest for having left early. "Why am I judging?" I asked myself, "Why? Why now, for the first time in my life, am I going back and forth and judging? Why can't I just accept?"

I still felt that I should catch the plane. I still had fear. And this time, on my third attempt, I was able to do as I wanted; there was no rain.

When we finally arrived at the airport, I stopped to ask a security officer where I should go to return the rental car. He looked at me and said, "I know about you Argentinians." Then he made Robert get out and step inside a glass booth. "You behave or we'll deal with you!" the officer warned him, then let him go. A sharp chill went through my back. I returned the car and as I walked toward the airport bus, an inner voice told me to let go of my fur coat. So I did — I couldn't have cared less about furs, gold, money; I just wanted to do what God wanted me to. Robert was surprised. "Why are you leaving the fur coat, Mommy?" he asked. I told him that I had to. I was told to do so.

Inside the airport, a voice instructed me to go first class, so I had my ticket changed.

While waiting in line with my luggage, I realized that I had to check something out in another part of the airport. I did not want to drag my suitcase along. I had the distinct feeling that the two persons in line in front of me were there to protect me. If I left my luggage, they would take care of it. When I returned fifteen minutes later, the suitcase was still there. As soon as I stepped back into line, the two people looked at me inquiringly, as if to say, "All done now?" and then left.

Before I entered the plane, I heard a voice say, "Leave your purse." So I set it on the floor. Then I stepped inside first class, sure that I would meet the spirit who had talked through David. A stewardess called my name. Someone had found my purse. After handing the purse to me, I heard the stewardess say to another, "If I were to meet him, I would lose my purse too."

But I was not nervous. I knew he was shy, insecure. I knew of his feeling of being one apart. He could be with the masses, loving them, yet feel apart from them. I wanted to give him confidence and security so that he could realize his full spiritual potential.

Once we were in the air, I had the distinct feeling of being watched and judged. I turned and saw two women across the aisle, both very refined, very astute. "Yes, they will be able to do OK," one said to the other. "The boy has manners. He can sit and eat with royalty. So does she."

I had once told Silver, "I must marry someone whose station in life will allow my child to be Prime Minister, if he wishes to be. He must learn to be with royalty, as well as with peasants." And now, I felt I was being watched and judged to see if I could play the part.

We had a layover in New York and as I stood in line to register my luggage, I felt that a man standing nearby was trying to communicate something to me. He looked at me, then moved his arm and jiggled the hand bag he held, then glanced at me again. His bag was identical to mine! I thought he was communicating that I should carry the bag on the plane with me. Again, someone was trying to tell me what to do. I decided to ignore him.

As Robert and I were about to enter the plane, the doors closed in front of us for a second. I became scared. I thought this was a sign — like the rain. We should not go to Spain. A man from the airline took me aside and asked me whether or not I was getting on the plane.

"But remember, you already have your luggage on the plane," he said.

I decided to get on the plane. The stewardesses examined our tickets and told us to wait before boarding. My head was burning; I could not think. Was the Universe telling me not to go?

I saw a lady holding a single rose. The rose was small and pinkish and had turned brown at the petal tips. It looked exactly like the rose I had given Jose in Spain two years before.

The stewardesses let us board. When the doors closed, I panicked; I wanted to jump out. I went to the stewardess, but she told me the doors couldn't be reopened. I knew they thought I was crazy. I felt I was living in the world of Orwell's *1984*. We were all being watched. I could not make a move without "it" knowing.

The movie shown in first class concerned a couple who were able to break the central computer program on Earth, at a future time when the entire planet is run by computer. I felt this was my assignment: a Cosmic program existed in the world on an invisible level, and I was to decode it. There existed a super-human control for which I was working, the Cosmos.

I felt complete, in union; I had a sense of freedom, serene understanding and joy unlike anything I had ever experienced before. "Heaven is here!" I thought to myself, "here for all of us." My head kept burning; the sensation was gradually increasing in intensity as if more and more of my brain cells were actively functioning. My "Cosmic Orgasm" was becoming even greater.

We arrived in Spain on September 6 (9-6) and immediately took a taxi to Nerja, where my friend Pilar lives. In the taxi, I opened my hand luggage and found that the contents were not mine. Inside were an expensive Pierre Cardin towel, white thongs, and sun lotion, plus some ragged clothes of children's size.

"You see," I said to Robert, "with great pleasure I gave away everything I owned and got Pierre Cardin stuff back. You did not and you got old stuff back."

He looked at me and said, "You are right, Mommy."

I knew that whatever happens, happens for a reason, a lesson is to be learned.

I planned to stay with Pilar and her family at first. I had only ten dollars left, but I did not care; I knew the Universe would provide.

When I got to Pilar's house, the entire family greeted me and then we sat around and talked. Pilar insisted that I go to the bedroom with her and see the gift she had received only a week before. When she showed me the corset she had been given, my mouth dropped open and my eyes began to tear. She looked at me, puzzled by my reaction. The corset she held up was exactly the same quality as the one I had **ordered** for Ana Maria in Buenos Aires. I realized that Ana had received the corset which matched her energy and Pilar had gotten the one which matched hers. I had given to one person, but the person who had received from me was not the person to whom I had given. I was not the doer! I did not control the way the energies worked!

I could not speak; I could not say, "How nice, Pilar, it's beautiful!" I was trembling. As she looked at me, Pilar realized this was not the same Beatriz she had known a year before.

This was a simple event, but the events kept mounting; my beliefs were being confirmed. I was getting weaker. With Freddy next to me, things had seemed easier.

I recalled a strong conversation I had had with Kirsten seventeen years before. "Beatriz," she had said, "you must understand that all these wedding gifts you are receiving are because of the Prentices. People are not giving because of you. You seem to think they are giving because of you."

"You are wrong," I had told her. "Each person receives what he/she deserves. Down south in Argentina, my mother gave to everyone all her life. And now, her daughter up north in Canada is receiving what she has planted."

At the time, I knew she thought I was crazy, but I was used to that — no one ever thought quite as I did. But now I could see that what I had thought was right.

Later that day, I went to look the neighborhood over. All the people I had known a year ago came out on the street to greet me and talk. The point of reference in all their conversations was the date I had left the year before.

They had to tell me the latest: some poor man had won the lottery last week. When they mentioned the winning number, I began to shake. I was stunned. It was the same number I had bought for my cousin in Buenos Aires. I realized that I was misusing my power, deciding who to help, judging. I was playing God.

Everyone stopped talking and stared at me. I was supposed to be happy at this news, but instead I was crying, "Oh, God!" and thinking, "We have no idea how the universe works. We know nothing." After a few moments, they all said goodbye and left.

I found out that "La Feria," the open market, had been moved from the downtown district to "El Barrio," near Pilar's neighborhood. It had happened one month after I had left the previous year. I had said "La Feria" should move to El Barrio because that would bring business to the poor section of town.

I also discovered that someone had opened a health food store. I was very pleased; the year before, I had told everyone in California that a health food store was needed there. I went inside and asked the owner what had made her decide to open this business. At that moment, a man burst in through the front door behind me and exclaimed, "Your seed has sprouted! Look, see, and enjoy!" He held a jar with alfalfa sprouts in it. Was this my answer? Yes, I knew it was.

Later, I passed a kindergarten I had seen many times the previous year. It had been a dreary place — no toys, no bright lively colors on the walls, no decorations. I had wanted it to have all these things. Now I found it had been transformed completely: the walls were painted with fresh, striking colors, mobiles hung from the ceiling, the children had toys. Life was there!

The year before, Robert had had only one wish for the town — a pizza place. And, as I continued to walk, I found one in the next block. It had just opened.

My scenarios, I realized, never fit. I had expected to see Argentina completely changed and it had been exactly the same. I had expected to find Nerja the same, but it had changed totally. Everything that I had wanted for the town — including yoga lessons — had come about.

I realized the power that we all have. What we Think, Becomes. Control is in the mind. That is how we build! I decided to use my power.

I ran to the fair and began to touch all that was displayed out in the open — fruits, vegetables, fishes, everything — hoping that my power could somehow help these people to have more. Each time I touched something, my eyes would catch sight of a number. First, I saw the numeral "1"; next, the number "10." I thought that as I exercised my power outwardly, these numbers indicated how much my power increased inwardly. The numbers continued to grow in multiples of ten. I could feel the power mount up inside me. I realized then that math was a product of the spirit; an outer manifestation of an inner reality. By the time I had finished, I knew I really was a Christ. I could do anything! I could multiply fishes.

I kept thinking of the fish that the cartoon cat was trying to catch, so I decided to go to live with the fishermen. Robert refused to come; he did not want to live in the worst section of town, where the so-called "undesirables" lived. But I knew they were the kindest people, always willing to share what little they had.

That night I slept at the home of a man and wife whom I had met the year before. Early the next morning I got up and went to the beach to work with the fishermen. I helped them pull in their nets from the sea. It was hard work, but I was determined to do it. I thought, "If you can, so can I."

I believed that my power would help them bring in extraordinary catches. But they got the same amount of fish as always. I was crushed. They gave me an octopus and I returned to Pilar's.

She was worried about me and offended that I had not stayed at her home. I apologized. I had no intention of hurting, only of loving.

That day my perception began to alter, to open up. I started to see people projecting energies. I have great difficulty describing what I perceived at this time. Imagine trying to describe red to one who sees only black and white. Yet the experience was very real.

I saw a woman in a grocery store become very angry. Suddenly, an energy shot out from her forehead in a single beam of force — not light or "visible" in the usual sense. I could see it, feel it, and see its effects. This force struck down a small boy walking beside his mother outside the store. The mother yanked the child up and exclaimed, to no one in particular, "This child is always getting into accidents." As soon as she said that, an energy came soaring out from her, projected from her forehead.

This energy travelled quickly until it struck someone riding a bicycle a block away. The bike teetered, swerved, then came crashing down.

Later that day, I became able to see, not just one energy, but three different energies coming through people. One was a positive energy; one was the negative already mentioned; and the other was neutral. I could sit in a room full of people and see how each one projected different energies in conversation. It was very disturbing. It was like sitting in a room full of radios with each one tuned to a different station. Yet, at one point, through all that noise, I did hear someone say, "After Saturday everything will be all right."

Monday afternoon, I took Robert and Manolo, Pilar's son, to the beach at Nerja. I was wearing black and white. These seemed to be the only colors I could wear. I was to wear only black and I was to meet my being, Julio Iglesias, who would be all in white. These would be the uniforms for our work. We would lose ourselves touching the very souls of the world.

I had only 1,000 pesetas left (around ten dollars), but decided to spend five hundred pesetas to rent a "pedalo," a boat propelled with the feet, for the children. The young man renting the boats gave me 1,000 pesetas back. "Not for you," he said.

After the children had taken the boat to the water, the young man suggested to his male friend sitting beside him that he run on the beach. But his friend was relaxing and obviously did not plan to run. I knew the suggestion was meant for me, and so began to run up and down the beach.

As I ran, something quite extraordinary happened. A curtain raised — I could see! Not only did I have a hearing within a hearing, but also a sight within a sight. I could see several windsurf boards (surf boards with sails) gliding over the waters of the Mediterranean. I noticed that as long as I kept my thoughts on God, the boats, the sails, remained upright and stable. But if I let my thoughts slip away from God, the boats would begin to tip until they formed forty-five degree angles with the plane of the water.

I started to tire after a short time; I was not used to running. The boats began to tilt. In my mind I began to sing a song to the Virgin Mary, a song I had not even thought of since I was ten years old. As I sang in my head, I started to feel less tired; it became a pleasure to run. The windsurf boards stood up straight on the sea. The boats were serving me, reminding me of my proper thoughts. I felt very grateful; full of joy; complete. I thought, "Thank you for helping me! What Ecstasy!"

After a while, I sat down near the young man who rented the

pedalos. Almost immediately, he said to his friend, "It is not we who are helping you, but you who are helping us." Then he took out a pair of binoculars and said, again to his friend, "You are looking at it backwards," glancing at me from the corner of his eye.

I thought to myself, "I am tired."

"Don't play martyr," he said.

That made me get up and run again.

Now I became able to see the connections among human beings. It was like seeing the connective tissue of cells under a microscope. I saw how the connections among us form one huge web. I also noticed that my thoughts could control the movements of the people on the beach. As I ran along the shoreline, if I happened to think of how tired I was, certain people, in front and behind and to the side of me — in the distance — began to move toward me. If I had a mental reaction, if I thought, "Am I going crazy? What's going on? Why are these people moving?" They would stop, and another group of people would begin to move. It was as if I had a set of three buttons, blue, red, and yellow, and each button controlled the movements of a different set of people.

When I sat down again, the young man's friend said, "Well, for her first day, she didn't do too badly."

That night I realized that the television also had different energies. One was loving, another war-like, and the third, neutral. I saw that what people watched, matched their energy. The conflicts over which program to watch seemed to be about which energy would dominate.

On one of the programs that night, a male performer sang, "Look how she walks . . . She thinks she's a queen . . . She thinks she can do anything, wait and you'll see . . ."

Then, on another program, a woman dressed as a black cat was travelling through space in a crystal and singing, "Go, go on, you'll make it."

From this program, I picked up the message that I **should** run only on the right side of the beach. But in my mind, I decided, "No, I am not a cat or a dog. There are no cats or dogs, no divisions. We are one." Though I did not want to judge, I **was** judging: I was arguing in my mind with the information the Cosmos was giving me.

On Tuesday I went to the beach again with Robert. I ran, but on **both** sides of the beach — left and right. The beach was divided into two sections. The people on my right were solely in family groups. The section on the left had a few families, but also some nudists and homosexuals who sunned themselves at the far end, away from the family groups. When I ran along the left side, "immorality" seemed to occur. What I mean is: the nudists and homosexuals soon stood up and, glaring at me with defiant expressions, walked over to the right side, to "invade" the territory of the families.

On television that night, I watched another performer sing, "Look at her, she thinks she can change the world."

Then, on another channel, a woman dressed on one side as a dog and on the other as a cat, was dancing from one side of a stage to the other, singing something about "uniting us all."

Wednesday I decided to try an experiment. I went to the beach and performed some loosening-up exercises. But I did not run or try to control my thoughts. The young man said to his friend, "She is paying attention to the noise instead of concentrating on working with the force."

Then he began talking directly to me, demanding that I run. I could not answer him, I could not make myself speak. I wrote on a slip of paper, "I'd rather die standing than live on my knees," and gave it to him. When a photographer wanted to take a picture of Robert holding a lion cub, the young man came up and offered to pay.

I refused. Did he think he could buy me? Did he think he could control me, get me to obey him, by giving me money? I felt angry, but I was also afraid. I was judging, rejecting, closing myself off, resenting. I was feeling completely opposite to how I had felt all my life. Normally I would have thought, "Of course you can buy it for me. Of course I deserve it."

That afternoon, while watching television at Pilar's house, I saw a woman perform a dance which included all the movements that I had done on the beach, exactly as I had done them and in the same order. I was stunned. I was immersed in the world I had always believed in — the world of telepathy, guidance, invisible connections; the Cosmos. But it is one thing to think and feel and quite another to experience, to make it truly your own. For the first time in my life, I was petrified.

I decided not to go back to the beach. I felt I was being controlled. My inner peace began to melt. I wanted to do what God wanted me to, and yet, I was rejecting what the Universe was giving me.

As I began to feel fear, the colors of all the objects I saw became intensified. Different colors would come forth according to my mood. If I was able to control my fear and have a loving thought, I would see blues and greens. But when I felt fearful, the red on different objects would become accentuated, glowing brilliantly.

I had received the message that I had until Saturday to learn how to use the force. As the end of the week approached, my fear became stronger and stronger. I could not sleep. I would walk all day and all night. I wanted to unite the Sun and the Moon which were within me. As I walked, I sang to the moon.

I began to think that "they" were after me — those forces from another place. There was nothing I could do which was not known. Of course, I had always believed this before; I believed in the akashic records. I had always tried to control my mind because I knew thought was the communicating force.

I remembered how, as a child, I had played "Mata Hari" whenever the neighborhood boys divided into armies for "war." I would go from one camp to the other, gathering information. I realized that now was the time to sprout the seed I had planted as a child. I would discover how each force works. I had to decode the cosmic computer — no matter how terrifying the job. That was my assignment.

I began to receive answers from everything around me — even trash on the floor. I had eyes to see. If you know the language of a totem pole, then you can "read" it. In the same way, I could read every object I saw. I began to take my guidance from objects. I followed the clues which each force — each energy — gave me. I received messages everywhere — in the way that merchandise was displayed in store windows, for example. I saw that people bought things which matched their energies. I could tell what someone was going to pick up and buy before they did so. I saw how the clothing a person wore matched his energy. Every object was a totem pole of information.

It was time to register Robert for school. I decided to let the forces guide me to the correct school for him. By following certain clues, I ended up in the attic of one school, and there found a blue baby carriage. Even today, I am certain this was the same carriage I had discarded in California years before, the same one in which I had put Robert as a baby.

I decided to hide in the attic — I didn't want to be led anywhere else. But then I thought, "No, no one can harm me. I do not need to hide. I must remember I am working. I am decoding the Cosmic program."

Yet, I still felt fear.

I went to the principal of the school and told him what I had found in the attic. "Big Brother is watching," I said to him.

He was very kind. He listened to me and tried to calm me down.

That night on television, the woman dressed as both a dog and a cat sang, "She is falling, she is hiding . . . and while hiding, found a crib."

Later, on another program, a woman sang, "A lady was singing like a clown, entering a cemetery with a red-and-white checkered handkerchief, she put it on a pole as a sign."

The next day, I went to the town cemetery. In one corner of the grounds, on a pole, was a piece of red-and-white checkered cloth. I felt enormous fear and went to hide in a small room behind the cemetery chapel. But again, the other part of me said, "No, I am just decoding the Cosmic program. I do not need to hide."

After I left the cemetery, I could not maintain my inner balance; the Fear Center continued to win. Instead of using my fear inwardly, as I had always done before, I was using it outwardly. My inner imbalance was affecting my outer reality. Because I had fear, I created an "us" and "them" situation.

By Friday, I was horrified. Where could I go? — there was no escape! Taking Robert with me, I went out, found a taxi and told the driver to take us to the airport. My eyes were going everywhere, seeing forces, signs, clues. The driver kept glancing at the rear view mirror to check on me. He thought I was mad. Near the airport, he stopped at a doctor's office and instructed me to go in. I obeyed. I overheard the taxi driver talking with the doctor. The doctor said I might need to be hospitalized. I knew that if they took me to a Spanish mental institution, I would be stuck — perhaps kept there for life.

I grabbed Robert by the hand and ran from the office. I stood in the middle of the highway with my hands up and forced a car to stop. The driver agreed to take us. As soon as we stepped into his car, an announcer said over the radio, "The police are looking for a woman dressed in black with a child about ten years old," and then gave a description which fit us exactly. I thought "they" were after "us." Robert heard the radio report too and was scared. I told him to lie down. When the man saw my reaction to the announcement, he wanted to let us off.

I began to cry. "Please take us to a safe place," I pleaded, "Take us to a boys' Catholic school where I can leave my child." I offered to give him my expensive gold watch. Finally, after I had assured him the watch would buy a three bedroom apartment in Spain, he drove us to a school.

I felt that this day was for Robert. Today Robert had to experience God. He had to accept him, to turn to him. I felt he could not continue to exist in the lower energy in which he had been born.

We entered the main building of the school. A man suddenly appeared in front of us, as if from nowhere.

"Please take my son," I said to him, "Keep him for the length of time you think you need, for this experience. I don't have any money."

The man looked at me and said, "What you want will be done. We are ready for you."

At that moment, another man entered the room and said, "Even the Yerba Mate is ready," and he left a little package.

Yerba Mate is not usually sold in Spain. I felt that this man was trying to identify himself to me. I panicked and left immediately, with Robert.

We walked through the streets on the outskirts of Malaga. We were hot and hungry. Our feet hurt. I asked for help in my mind. Suddenly, three men walked out of an apartment building and stopped on the sidewalk in front of us. They all looked the same. Each one wore a white shirt and a blue pair of pants. They stared at me and said in unison, "We are here to serve you."

My head was burning. I said, "I need to take my son to a Jesuit school for him to experience God. I have no money. Can you help me?"

"Yes," the three said, again in unison. Then the first man told the second one to take us somewhere.

We followed the second man and got into a jeep with him.

The man whom I had spoken to at the school walked past on the sidewalk, carrying a package of Yerba Mate, his back hunched, a peculiar, mischievous expression on his face. He turned his eyes to me as if to say, "Bye . . .", then went past us and stepped into a Number 11 bus. Eleven — the number of illumination. Did this mean illumination was out the window for me? Did this one man represent the one force, the All?

Again my fear took control. "No, no thank you," I said to the jeep driver and hopped out with Robert.

As we hurried away, Robert protested, "Why are you doing this, Mommy? Why? Are you mad? Why are you doing this to me?"

Again I asked for help in my mind.

This time I saw two workers picking up stones and piling them alongside the road to build a wall. I was not frightened and decided to help them. It was hard work, but I was not bothered. My head was in God. "I will do whatever work God wants me to," I thought.

But the men did not want me to work. They said I was a lady; I should not be doing this. They told me I would ruin my nails. After awhile, they gave us some money so we could eat. As we left them, I felt happy and unafraid.

We had something to eat, then continued to walk along the road toward Nerja. Each time I glanced at the road, I saw a dropping of excrement; a larger dropping each time. I took this to mean, "You are doing it, bigger and bigger." My frustration mounted; I wanted to do what was right, but felt I was moving farther and farther away from God.

Although I was fearful, I decided to stop a car. The driver said he could take us to Nerja, but "there is only one thing: I'll take you if you don't mind if I get undressed and drive nude."

I was shocked. Although I had been naked in front of many people, from hot tubs to orgies, for some reason, this seemed very wrong. I just couldn't; I could not ride with him if he was nude. At that moment, I felt as though I could never be nude in front of anyone again.

I said "No" to him and he left. Was this last man the last energy, a physical energy, on the negative side? Was this feeling of not wanting to be around nudity because I was now out of Paradise?

Robert was exhausted. Suddenly, for the first time since March, he began to speak with the authoritative voice of that other being. "Mommy, you have been born to work, yes, but spiritual work — not picking up stones. You are confused. You need to go to Nerja and be with the ladies. They'll understand what you are going through. Don't be here in the middle of nowhere and with men. Please Mommy, let's go home. Let's go to Pilar's."

I looked at him and said, "OK, we'll take a taxi."

We managed to find a taxi, but I did not have any money. I offered to pay for the ride with my Cleopatra ring. He saw how alone and exhausted I was and took pity. He did not want to take the ring, but I insisted.

By the time I reached Pilar's house, I could no longer talk. I was beyond speech or mind, Pilar was trying to help me, asking for names and telephone numbers of friends or family. Robert told her about Kirsten in Denmark. I looked like a lion. My child was scared of me. The people of the town had decided that I had gone mad. They said to Pilar, "Aren't you afraid of her?"

"No," she replied, "I know that woman. She will never hurt anyone. Not even mad."

She washed my clothes, fed my child, put me to bed, brought me hot milk, caressed my hair and said, "There, there . . .", thinking that I had gone mad because I had no more money.

The next morning, Saturday, I decided that from now on I would accept whatever the Universe gave me. I had just been through the most terrifying day of my life. I felt that I had reached the end of the road. I went to the beach, wanting to speak with the young man, the one with the kind, loving eyes, the one who had given my money back, who had wanted to buy a picture for my son; the one who, when he had asked me to run, I had judged because of my fear; the one who I had thought was trying to control me.

I could give, but I had mistrusted someone when they had tried to give to me.

When I spotted him on the beach, I was so glad to see him, I rushed up and went down on my knees before him. I could only say, "Please," as I looked up into his eyes.

He looked at me with cold detachment and said, "Terrified, eh? Why do you see the speck that is in your brother's eyes, but do not notice the log that is in your own eye?"

Later, I discovered that this quote came from Luke 6-41.

I put my head down on the sand and cried. I realized that I had been judged. I was out, out of Heaven! I was not pure enough yet. There was still more work to be done.

I was breathing hard. My heart was pumping fast. The waters of the Mediterranean, usually so calm, so stable, never knowing a tide, began to rise, covering more and more of the beach. I could still hear the young man's words in my head. I felt tormented. The water continued to rise. Twice, the young man and his friend had to move their paddle boats further up the beach.

His friend said, "Doesn't she know the power she has? What does she want to do, wipe out the beach?"

"Does he mean I'm responsible for the rising water?" I wondered, "If I calm my feelings, will the waters go down?"

I tried to pacify myself. The waters began to recede. The young man said, "That's good."

When the sea had returned to its normal level, I ran from there as fast as I could, crying and screaming, "No, no, no, God, why, why? Have I been so bad? Have I been such a bad Human Being?"

People stopped and stared at me as I ran through the streets. I was hysterical, crying at the top of my lungs. I ran up to someone and asked him, "Please tell me — am I a bad person? Why does God want to scare me so? I only want to bring peace!"

Of course, God did not want to scare me, but Laws do work. I had used my Fear Center outwardly instead of inwardly, and so had created my own hell.

I went back to the beach one last time that day and approached the young man. He said that night I should go dancing and stay away from Pilar's house. It was a test. I had to let go of all my security. Then, and only then, would the Universe pick me back up. I had to prove that I could stand completely alone.

I decided to get some rest before going dancing and so returned to Pilar's house.

A neighbor was there and told us how she had painted all day; first the living room, then the dining room. She said she was very tired; it had been hard work. My head kept burning. As she talked, I knew she was telling me what Freddy had done in Argentina that day. Later, when I checked with him, he said he had painted the living room, then the dining room of our house. And yes, it had been hard work; and yes, he had done it during the second week of September. The information the woman had given corresponded exactly with what he had done! What does this mean? Can one be informed about all places at once? Yes, we are Gods! We are Gods!

I went to bed early and got up to go dancing after everyone else had gone to sleep. But I discovered that Pilar had locked the front door. She was afraid that I would escape and do something crazy. The windows were all barred; there was no other way out. I wanted to scream, "Let me out, let me out — this is my last chance to enter Heaven." But the voice of "sanity" kept saying, "No, Beatriz, you'll wake up these people. You've been enough bother."

As I crept back to my bedroom, I began to relive the negative energy which I had experienced from my son Robert. He was always trying to put the television on a channel of negative energy. One day he had bought some plastic "Vampire" teeth at the store. I saw a Dracula rising from his quiet, sleeping body as he lay there on the bed. A voice in my mind began to say, "And God gave his only begotten son . . ."

"Lord, are you asking me to kill my son to prove my love for you?" I questioned.

With tears overflowing from my eyes, I went to the kitchen and found a long, sharp knife. I approached my son's bed and knelt down beside it.

"Robertito," I whispered, "I love you, Robertito, you came to serve me. You forced me to see, to recognize negative energy as the necessary force that it is. I love you. But God is asking me to give you up. And so I must. I must. My allegiance must be to him."

He continued to sleep peacefully, his head towards me, tilted slightly on the pillow. I lifted the knife up slowly, carefully, then lowered it towards his neck. The blade was an inch from his throat.

At that moment, a voice in my mind said, " 'Give' does not mean 'kill.' " I froze. Then I quickly took the knife away. Now I understood — the giving up was in my consciousness. I had fought like a tiger to have sole custody. Robert was mine! Mine alone! . . . or so I had believed. I had refused to let any divorce papers deny my feeling.

Now I realized that God wanted me to place my trust, my faith, my love in him and be completely independent of anyone or anything. I had already learned that my child was not my own, that he had come through me, but not from my energy. "Yes, that's why I was so sick when I got pregnant," I thought to myself. Something which was not mine was in me, and I had not wanted that negative energy. I remembered the words of Maria Bun at the Stanford International Center: "You don't want it, that's why you are so sick." At the time, I had been very offended; I had awaited a child with so much love; no one could have been as happy as I was, when I found out I was pregnant. But now, nine years later, I understood her words.

That night, when I went to bed again, I knew it was the end of "the experience." When I woke up the next morning, the curtain had come down. I no longer had a hearing within a hearing, a sight within a sight. I felt completely drained; destroyed. I could not think; I could only lay there in bed.

When Robert woke up, he looked at me and said matter-of-factly, "Thank you, Mommy. I am free now."

I watched the television news that evening and saw the vigil Greenpeace had been in Livermore, California. The film clip showed a crowd of people holding candles. Then a movie came on, starring Liv Ullman, the Spanish title was: "She Capitulated."

I remembered asking Chris, the man to whom I had given $20,000 for the Cosmos, when I would find out about the meeting I was supposed to attend. "One day you will see a film with lots of candles," he had said, "And after that another film. This film will tell you."

During the previous week, I had entered a strange land. Trees that talked would not have been as frightening as what I had experienced. I, who had always used the two centers — the positive and the negative — in balance, could not balance them when I met my unconscious. But it was as it should have been. If I was positive on the conscious level, I had to be negative on the unconscious level. The negative is in matter; the positive is in anti-matter. And so, the two together are balanced.

I knew only too well that I, who had never judged before, had judged throughout the experience. I had feared and therefore, I had judged. Before, when people spoke to me of fear, I had no concept of what they were talking about.

I felt as though I had been with God, but that now I had been dropped like a hot potato. I had been unable to receive what the Universe had tried to give me. My chariot did not even want to obey. My body had wanted to rest when the order was to run. Now the story of Pinocchio made sense to me. Each time we behave in a way which denies our true selves, the nose gets bigger; a long nose keeps one away when one wants to go near. Each time I did not obey the guidance given me, I got further and further away from the All.

I cried and cried. To have been with God and then to have lost it is devastating. I felt incredible desperation.

Robert kept trying to comfort me, saying, "You are all right, Mommy. You are good."

All my life I had felt that I did not ever want to experience any kind of test. Now I understood why: the one test that I would care about, I would fail.

The memories I have of peace, wholeness, freedom, the realization that we are all brothers, the Divine ecstasy, the awareness that we could live together without sex because we could enjoy something far greater than any sexual experience, will remain with me for as long as I live. I am not in ecstasy now, but I am outside happiness and pain in relation to the external world. The only pain I know is the pain of separation from God. I will not feel complete until I renew that union.

Pilar eventually got in touch with Kirsten in Denmark, who called Allan. He contacted Silver and Andrea and they all called me while I was still in Spain.

I told Andrea of my overwhelming sense of being nothing: "I am nothing. I can do nothing. I have done nothing." Andrea, poor dear Andrea, thought I should go to a psychiatrist. I knew this was not from feeling inferior, but from knowing my place in the Universe.

I am writing from memory now, but here is what I wrote then:

"I realize how ignorant I have been. I thought I needed to sell my house to organize a large meeting for all. I thought "all" meant all people. I did not have any idea that "all" was the collective consciousness that I was to meet as I let go of everything and trusted myself and my child to the Universe."

My last day in Spain, while Pilar was washing and packing my clothes for me, I suddenly became aware that I was inside a pyramid. I could feel myself inside it. I saw how its different points had different symbols which related to my life. I realized that if I wanted to join Heaven again, I must peer up a narrow hole cut diagonally through the structure, to the top of the pyramid, to Heaven, to the highest, to God.

Looking back on my life, I began to realize what the various symbols meant. These are the ones I examined:

The last time I had made love with Allan, I had seen an Eagle. I had cried with happiness then, feeling that "I am home; I have done it."

The energy which began flowing up and down through my body in March. Was that the serpent?

I had tried to multiply the fishes.

I had written to Andrea at one time and told her that I perceived her as a lamb.

While Allan was in Nerja in 1979 a tremendous thunderstorm had broken. I had felt that the storm was the manifestation of his inner negative energy colliding with his inner positive energy. The positive energy had won when I had asked for a divorce, when I gave him that last blow. I had conquered thunder. Now he is searching for himself instead of hiding. He will be a Sun.

The temperature had dropped from five above to twenty below zero and it had snowed, the day Jose came to Denmark in 1980. He was snow. When I had left him, he had told me, "Because of you, I know how to build now. I will build alone. I will find out who I am by myself." He too will be a Sun.

I had conquered him. That is the power of a woman. That is what beauty is for: to attract Human Beings to peace. His search for self will lead him to peace and love.

Father brought rain with him on his visit to California in 1972. Not since 1845 had the Bay Area had such rain. He had always called himself "Rain;" rain had always followed him. When he left he had told me, "You have conquered me. But your son is stronger than you." He came to California as rain and left as a Sun.

The first winter Ana Maria experienced in Toronto, we had very strong winds. The wind seemed to be significant for her. I realized now that I had conquered her too. She could start anew. She will be a Sun!

Yes, I had conquered; I had conquered with the only power I know how to use — sun energy: love.

Is this what the pyramids mean? Are they physical manifestations of our very Beings?

While I was still in Spain, I received a letter from Andrea including the following:

*. . . For years, you have been there when other people had problems
and needed you. Now you need yourself. The part of you that is
fighting for recognition is very lucky because it has a world-famous
helper right there in Nerja — Beatriz G. Prentice — who has lots of
time to listen to it and sooth it . . .*

Andrea

Her letter brought me great happiness: for the first time in my
life, someone had said I was a world-famous helper, or praised
me in some way, **and my ego was not touched!** I **now** realized that
I was not the doer, so I no longer had any ego. But with the
knowledge that I was nothing, knew nothing, I also realized that
I could get up and do. Yes, it seems I can only talk in riddles these
days!

When the curtain came down and I could no longer see the
world as it really was, I felt crushed. I just lay about, with no
energy whatsoever.

When I realized that I could no longer take care of myself, I
reached out to the most logical person — Allan. We had parted
lovingly just over a month before at the airport. I needed him to
take care of me and Robert.

He said, "No." I needed money; he said, "No." The one I loved,
the one with whom I spent seventeen years, the one for whom I
had gone hungry, who was once weak, but now was strong, told
me, "No."

But by this time, I was not just living a belief; I was living a
knowledge. And so I asked myself, "Where did I originate this
response?" And I soon realized that I had originated it on the
beach in Spain, when the Universe had tried to provide for me
and I had pulled back. I had feared and judged.

Then I had gone back to the young man. Yes, I had to learn.
Beg, Beatriz, beg. I realized that Allan was a vehicle for me to
learn. When the learning came from him, the lesson was even
more potent. I felt sorry for having put him in such a situation,
for making him say "No" just so I could learn what I needed to
know.

This mental process took a few months. But I knew that by
using my mind correctly, I could make my feelings arrive at the
only place I wanted them to reach: Love — not only towards
those who were helping me, but also towards those who were
not extending their help.

Long before I had figured all this out, I wrote Allan:

I am glad you are getting to know who you are . . . You are the nicest being you will ever know. I know. Be of service to Ann. Love her and sacrifice for her. Give to her even if you don't get. Conscious sacrificial service will get you to Heaven . . . Heaven is Here, for all of us to have. There is not much time. The work must begin soon. I wish I could do some of the work for you . . . yet . . . you must be enjoying seeing yourself so sure and doing things. It is a good feeling, the feeling of control of oneself and the power that it gives as long as one does not hurt anyone else. I hope Ann is satisfying your thirst, your emotional hunger. Enjoy, enjoy . . .

Love
Beatriz

It seemed crazy; foolish by normal standards. I sell my house in July. I have $60,000 — **cash.** Then I go off to write a book. All nice and neat so far. Then I give all my money away, experience absolute chaos and end up yelling, "Help!"

Why shouldn't the world say, "She got herself into this, let her get out by herself! Now she will finally have to go out and work and forget all this spiritual stuff!"

But I had never reacted, I had always acted. I had addressed myself to causes not consequences. I knew that just because I now had nothing, I should not alter my original plan. I wanted to write, so I would still do so.

To do this, I had to manifest on a physical level what had already happened at the inner level — I had to physically let go of Robert. He would stay in Argentina for a while. I loved him very much, but neither more, nor less, than I loved all the children of the world whom I had never met . . .

When I returned to the United States on November 27, 1981, Andrea took me in. All the years I had known her, people had asked me why I was her friend. You can't find two people more unlike — on the surface — than she and I.

Andrea constantly gathers information. She has to tell everything that she finds. That's how she expresses herself, how she gives of herself: through mental energy. God forbid that she should have information on any subject and not give it! She would give to the first person on the street, if the person would let her. "Oh, you don't know about Loehmann's?" (a clothing discount store) she would say, "Then let me tell you . . ." and on she would go. If I had told everyone how giving I saw her, they would have said, "Beatriz, you are blind."

Obviously, I was not.

301

We are all so loving . . . if only we understood how each person expresses love.

We truly had a great stay together. I wanted to do everything her way. It was a test. "Well, Beatriz," I said to myself, "you are water. Let's see how adaptable you have become. Can you mold yourself to any shape? Can you do whatever she wants and feel perfectly happy doing it? Are you really water? If you can bend, Beatriz, then you have become truly strong. Only those who can yield completely and realize they do not lose themselves, are really strong."

I did everything her way. I had become as strong as the Oak and as yielding as the Poplar. She is very exact. Things must be done in a certain way and only that way. The toilet seat cover must be down! — so the cats can't get to the water. For each of her rules, she has a very logical reason.

She began to feel a bit guilty that I had adapted so completely to her, that she had not had to adapt to me. I never had to say, "I want," or "I need"; she looked, she felt, she gave.

During this time, my body kept saying: I have no strength. But I just told it: "You are going to keep on going as if you did. Obey! You did not obey before at the beach. Now you will, because I love you; I will conquer you through love — not through will, as I tried before through diets. I will treat you well so that you will get me to God. You are the instrument to get me to him."

As I was writing about this experience, I phoned Eleanor to ask her what the woman on the beach had offered me besides the dove. She told me it was the owl (when she said it, I remembered). As we continued to talk, I glanced out the window of my second-story apartment to notice an enormous mural on the wall of the building directly across the street. The mural consists of some wavy lines which resemble wood grain, and two huge **owls**, one in profile, the other facing the street. I glanced over to the phone table and saw the letter from my writing instructor. "Beatriz, you are an extraordinary philosopher and intellect . . ." she had written. I realized then that I had wanted the dove, but had chosen the owl. I had not been willing to wait till Tuesday, as bidden, for the dove.

My story is like the story of the "Three Little Pigs." I built an inner house in which I hid. This inner house was strong enough to survive a lot of pain, criticism, and judgment, and yet put forth love and joy. But when the second wolf — the Force of the Cosmos — came, it blew my house away. Now, while I work for peace the next sixty years, I will build my inner house strong enough to withstand any wolf. I will have a house secure enough so that, if the television speaks or the world turns itself inside out, I will not fear.

The experience of becoming aware that we are all Gods, the experience of being omnipresent and omnipotent, was too much. I am not trying to justify what I did. No, I was just not prepared well enough. Now, I know that all the knowledge we have as we go through this "forest" becomes rot, becomes absolutely nil. Some of us are for the All. Some of us for the many. I came for the many, but while working for the many, I'll carve my way to the All. Next time, maybe I can enter Heaven and not make it a Hell. At present, I am in purgatory, free of pain. That is a great improvement, but the taste of heaven will never leave me. I was in Heaven! I will be there again, and next time, I pray, I will be able to use the Center of Fear inwardly, where it belongs. **Fear is for internal use only!**

Nerja, Spain
September 29, 1981

Dearest Andrea:

As I spoke with you I could feel your love for me. I never imagined you really love me as much as you do. I want to say thank you. How does one repay love? What does one say?

After I hung up (from our phone conversation) I realized my whole experience (was for my development). I realized that until now I always said: I believe in Numerology; I believe what Einstein said about the Universal Symphony; I believe what the books said; and I understand. But now, for the first time in my life, I can say I know each to be true. I know it with my whole being. I knew light, and now I know darkness and from there I will come back to light with a strength superior to any before.

It is right for a little while longer for me to be here (in Nerja). But not for always, I know. Silence is important.

I was glad to hear (from you, it) gave me strength. Thank you.

I went to hell, but not because I lost the luggage or the money; in fact I did not even notice any of that until I had stopped the flow of things. I got scared. Yet I want to do what God wants me to do. It is so incredible! Life is so powerful; Heaven so near. And yet one can fall so fast!! I knew that sanity may be gotten through madness, but I had always thought of it as WORDS. To live, to experience, to incorporate it into one's essence, is more than I had ever hoped or thought possible.

*As you see, I am better. I will be having low moments, I know,
but your calls, your caring, your showing concern, heal me, more
than anything else could. I love you Andrea. I do. You are the lamb
that takes the Sins of the World. My lamb. Your Christ. See you
soon.*
                                                    Love
                                                    Beatriz

                                              October 5, 1981
Dearest Allan:

*. . . Allan my dear, please, please, I know how much you want the
Union with God. Please be ready, please jog, please eat well, please
make your body a perfect instrument to receive and be obedient. I
thought I had concentration, enough to control lions. The lions are
easy to control, . . . but our thoughts . . . our bodies . . . I thought I
exercised. I would not eat . . . I mean I would sit at table and not eat
on purpose. I would put myself consciously through incredible stuff.
You know. Unless it is conscious it is worthless. I thought I exercised
the body, emotions, mind, yet what is required to stay there forever,
is beyond what I have done, much more. I am grateful that God let
me experience what now I read St. Augustine and other mystics have
experienced. But I want more, I want more of that fire, . . . through
which he speaks. And yet, . . . how scared I was! The power . . . to
see what one can do . . . Oh, Allan, what one can do is beyond any
imagining! The Bible is true. It is not a tale to be interpreted; it is
true. We are all Peace Makers. I know you are. But Allan, train,
not just love, unselfishly. Don't just serve, get ready physically.*

*I was told not to follow Robert. My love for Robert won. Oh, how
sad to be tied! One can't be tied, not even to one's child. I am not
anymore, I believe. But what a price to pay to learn! What a pain to
be far from Him, I mean from God, when I was one with Him . . .*

And to express my feelings after the splendor broke and
Robert had gone to Argentina, I wrote:

                                              December 1981

*Oh God . . . ! My God, my sweet sweet God . . . ! Here I am
crying . . . crying over the paper just remembering: How it was
when You were with me and how I want to be with You again.*

*There is a part of me that says "You, Beatriz, are crazy." One cries
because a lover left, because you lost your house, your money, your
child . . . yet . . . nothing matters to me . . . I gladly gave and
gladly would give everything and everyone away for the purpose of
being with You again. Oh! my God . . . is this selfish?! Am I being
selfish? Wanting to be with You, wanting to feel that union, that
peace, that power, that love . . . Should I forget about all that and get
on with what the world calls life? I can't.*

I can't forget You talked to me, "I am that I am." "I am the Law and I have come to fulfill it." The Law is to bring Heaven to Earth. But Heaven is here, . . . for all of us. Why then do we fear? I never did before. Allan used to say, "The only thing you, Beatriz, fear is fear itself." How true! I knew there was nothing to fear, nothing but fear.

You were guiding me towards the Kingdom, and I was tired and wanted to rest. The splendor was great, miracles began and they were so big they were more than I could take. I was astonished. I began to doubt my own sanity and I began to fear . . . As I did so, the splendor broke . . . I onlyl have Your memory now. How can I explain how one feels? I look everywhere for You.

Now it is as if there are two of me: One before You revealed Yourself to me, and one after, the one before felt pure, sacrificing, selfless, good. The good after — the one that received Your grace, the harvest — feels the opposite. I feel selfish and greedy, for wanting to be with You again. It is so strange . . . to pursue that . . . Is it bad? How can it be? No human being can provide the happiness You do. No human being can make me feel Whole. No one can make me see the World so Perfect, so Harmonious. Something was lifted and I could see, my ears could hear, my nose was able to smell. I saw the bondage in which we all are. I saw how what we think, affects us and others around us.

I wasted my life looking for love in sex, food, money, mind, feelings. Oh, those delights! . . . those meals! . . . those warm evenings! . . . But alas, they were not complete; they never are!

In sex . . . from arms to arms . . . giving, feeling, listening to men talk about their pain, their frustrations, their fears — and . . . The more I gave, the better I felt. Yet, it was not complete. The union did not last past our physical union. I seemed to need to disconnect again, to retain my identity: just after we were one, I needed to be one alone again.

I looked for love in Mind. Yes, in the workings of minds, the pleasure of intellectual talks, the playing of ideas, . . . forth and back; the arguing from white to black, and from black to white. By doing that — creating a new concept each time — Oh, I was stimulated! I could truly have a physical orgasm just by this process. The God of Mind . . . What did I not do for it? I went hungry . . . knowledge was important.

Yet, I did not obtain knowledge the way that other people did. I went inside of myself and got a whole theory, brought it out . . . and behold . . . someone informed me that I knew a lot about Nietzsche, or the Summerhill program or whatever, though it had invariably come from inside me. Whenever I was stuck . . . when I needed confirmation of facts, I went to a book store, ran my fingers over the books, and picked up the one that "pricked" me. I would open it. The answer was always there. That process started when I was a child and continued until last February, when all of that left me. Even thinking seems to have gone out the window.

I used to just sit and think, analyze, bring facts together and logically come to understand about people, myself, events. Now, there is only the overpowering feeling: to restore my union with God and tell the world that those questions "Who am I?" "What am I?" "Why am I?" do have answers. They are not just questions that one asks in philosophy classes in the cloisters of great universities.

Now I read Dante's Paradise Lost (part of the Divine Comedy) and realize he must have had the same kind of experience that I had. I believe every human being whose work has succeeded over the ages has used that same energy . . .

Now I know that a lot of fiction is true. How else but as fiction can one transmit something so above and beyond the normal understanding?

Now I know that Present, Past and Future are illusions. One can break the barrier of time and see and live in other dimensions. When one is there, it is very simple to see that time does not exist in the way we think of it.

When a person writes, and 50 years later what he wrote comes about, people think what he "imagined" came true, or what a "visionary" he was. It is not vision to enter into a room, see what is there and sit down and write about what you have seen! But, how does one explain to the world precisely what one has done, when something so out of the ordinary person's experience has happened? One can't. So fiction comes into being. How could Dickens say, "I was visited by the spirits of yesterday . . . I was talking with them, they presented themselves to me . . ." Would anyone believe him? No! Would anyone believe it today? NO! Yet . . . I know better . . .

When I had all sorts of opinions, I did not write. I am writing at a moment when I feel I know nothing; I can't judge anymore, I hold no opinions. I can only speak about that which I have lived, that which I know. I write not from Understanding — which comes from the Brain — nor from Belief — which comes from Faith — but from Knowing, which comes from Being, from Experiencing.

But all these feelings, all these experiences, would mean nothing unless they were for a purpose. I know the purpose. The world must know . . . (and) decide. Yes. Out of loving individual persons, I got to loving the world, feeling its pain, its fear. The fear mounts to its frustrations. The frustrations mount to its judgment; this mounts to its hate; and hate mounts to violence. I read this . . . it sounds *impossible. The World . . . ! Such an amorphous thing . . . ! How can I love it? Yet . . . I do love this world and . . . I do feel one with the people of each country, each culture. Each is different, yet each Being knows what Love is. That is what Unites Us. There are differences, but only of expression. There is but one force; Love.*

From now on I don't want to use the word "God" anymore. This is not because I don't believe in Him, but because it is a confusing word. someone could say, "I don't believe in God." I want to talk about something that not a single Human Being on Earth can say: "I don't believe in it." I want to refer to that force which every Human Being on Earth has experienced . . . , Love. That is the energy I am talking about. Some of us Love a house, some-animals, some-plants, some-places, some-people, some-humanity, some-the world, some-the universe, some-the cosmos, some-beyond that which is known.

TABLE OF NUMEROLOGICAL RECORDS OF IMPORTANT DATES

A.   Employment at Compania Continental:

Began   2 July 1962

$2 + 7$ (July) $+ 1 + 9 + 6 + 2 = 27$ $(2 + 7)$ $= 9$

Finished	7 Oct. 1963	$= 9$
Arrival Canada	29 Feb. 1964	$= 6$
Return Argentina	25 Aug. 1965	$= 9$
Become Canadian Citizen	27 April 1967	$= 9$
Become U.S. Citizen	8 April 1977	$= 9$
Return U.S.	3 June 1980	$= 9$
Arrival Argentina	6 August 1981	$= 6$

B.   Date of Birth: 24 of June of 1941 $= 9$
     Name: B E A T R I Z
               $2 + 5 + 1 + 2 + 9 + 9 + 8$ $= 36 = (3+6)$ $= 9$

This is derived by assigning each letter a number from the following chart:

1	2	3	4	5	6	7	8	9
A	B	C	D	E	F	G	H	I
J	K	L	M	N	O	P	Q	R
S	T	U	V	W	X	Y	Z	

C. Saying of young man on the Beach: "How come you look at the little dirt in your brother's eye instead of looking at the big log in your own eye." Luke: **6-41** My birth: June=6. Year **1941**.

I looked at the whole Bible and found only this other **6-41**:

John **6-41**: "People are murmuring because he is saying: I am the bread that has come from Heaven."

This is what I am saying:

"I was in Heaven and here is the bread (book) I have brought back."

D. My signature design at age 3: Designed in Year 1944 = 9

Spiritual life leads to illumination? 7 to 11

Coming to inner power to project after illumination? = 8

I designed it by simply adding all the letters for each name. I did not know how to write, but I wanted a signature, I kept it until in Canada they did not allow me to use it. It appears in all my legal documents from Argentina.

Question: Are all these 6's and 9's coincidence? What is the probability of it? I was told to remain in Argentina, everything was ready for me. Argentina has been in the news and I know if I was there I would have spoken and changed the course of history. I panicked, I did not obey. From being a dove and a Sun, I became an owl, and therefore a Moon (Reflection).

BOOK THREE
BECAUSE I LOVE THE WORLD
(AN OPEN LETTER)

CHAPTER 7
BECAUSE I LOVE THE WORLD
(AN OPEN LETTER)

I. To Individuals

Science
"Science: the systematized knowledge derived from observation, study and experimentation carried on in order to determine the nature or principle of what is being studied."

This is exactly what I have done with myself. I observed, studied and experimented to determine the nature of the self.

My premise was: I will prove there is no evil. I am love. After 40 years, I know this to be so, and I know what principles I used to experience this. There is no doubt in my mind, that if these principles are followed, every single human being on earth can find Happiness! This is not happiness which depends on someone else, on a car or on a degree, but happiness which comes from the Self, way deep within, an unending source!

I now understand how every piece of the puzzle fits. At the same time, I now know that I did not know anything; do not know anything and do not know if I will ever know anything. But I do know how I got to Know: "I Know, I do not know anything." That is precisely our destination. Why? Because when you reach that state, you really experience universal love. There you find real humility, not a make-believe one by trying to be less than what one is. I am Light, Love and Power; I am all and I am nothing. I know all and yet I know nothing.

Through being scientific, I have arrived at the center of myself. I respect science a great deal. We just have to use it on ourselves — the Science of Self. It is very exact.

When I did things or told people what I did, they felt I had courage: "You came here without a job? You did that?! I could not do that!"

To me, they were the ones who were courageous. It requires a great deal of courage to move to a new place and base your decision on a new job there. What if the company does not like you — or you it? What if something goes wrong? To me that is courage. You are putting yourself at the mercy of others, you are making decisions when the steering wheel is out of your hands. I would be scared stiff to do that.

I feel I could go anyplace; wherever I go I have myself — no one can take that from me. What courage does one need for that: None!

My Love Affair With Death:
Because You Have Been My Friend, Now You Are My Enemy
The first recollection of death I have is when the baker man died.

311

I was around six or seven years old, and I remember how we went with all the neighbors to the funeral. We were standing by the open casket and several people were talking about how wonderful this man had been. My eyes opened wide, incredulously. Who were these people talking about? Surely not the baker we all knew. He was mean, grumpy, unkind to all of us children, and had no concept that one could, from time to time, wear a smile on one's face.

In my innocence, I looked up and asked, "Why are you all saying these things? They are lies — this man was not kind, generous or gentle. He was unhappy, bad tempered and irritable. I don't think he would like to be remembered for anything but what he was." Everyone looked at me, my mother quickly took my hand, before I could do any further damage, and led me home.

For a long time, I thought about how people had acted around the dead body. I realized they were afraid. None of them behaved as they always did. Somehow, it was as if they were presented with something that they respected a great deal, because they did not understand it.

Since all the women in my family had died by age 45, I decided when I was 12 years old, that I would die by age 40. I decided I was not afraid of death.

In fact, I decided that far from keeping death at arm's length, I would make her my friend. And since that day, she has been my daily companion. Every night since then, when I go to bed, I reflect upon my day. I think, "Tomorrow is another day. If it were the last one of your life, Beatriz, how would you live it? How would you plan it, whom would you see, what would you want to tell them?" And with death in my mind, I organize my next day.

As you can see by my life, the fruits I have had from this approach are far from morbid. Because I was constantly aware of death, I lived fully. I never missed a chance to say, "I love you" to someone if I wanted to. I never missed an opportunity to investigate, to feel, to explore. Because I feel I may die, life becomes all the more precious, more luminous.

I am now 40, so talking about death is normal, but when I thought and talked about it at age 15 or 20, people were quite uncomfortable. They felt I should not be thinking about death, that I was too young to think of such things. If I would have paid attention to them, my life would not have been so rich, so full. I owe my incredibly rich and full life to death. I want to thank you, death, because of you I have truly lived.

Because I lived, I died, to be born again. Now through love I will conquer you, death. Through my words I shall live, and others long after I am gone will receive nourishment from them.

I will survive long after you come to take this body. I shall conquer you!

And so it is with the world. Because, as a planet, we have become conscious of death — of total destruction, we will now live consciously. We will prepare to survive, we will make every action count, and by so doing we will conquer death. We will choose life and arrive at peace, at eternity — we will break the barrier of time. I am only presenting my life, to show how one cell lives: How in a microcosm, the macrocosm exists. We have only to look at it, understand it and act.

If we begin to look at each human being as though that person is a cell of a body — humanity, we will then begin to understand far more clearly who, what, and why that person is the way he/she is.

We may encounter a person who is very rigid, inflexible, and quite insensitive.

We may encounter a person who is very sensitive and reacts to the smallest thing.

We may encounter a person who is very isolated, and who relates only to people who are like he/she is.

We may encounter a person who relates to everyone.

Now, where do they fit? Who are they? Why are they like this? What purpose do these specific characteristics have?

Well, if we look at a person as though he/she is a cell, it makes perfect sense to have a cell that is very rigid, inflexible, and insensitive if that cell belongs to a bone. It would be atrocious if we had a cell that was flexible and sensitive to the outside world in our bones.

But when we encounter the very sensitive person and we view that person as a cell which belongs to the skin, it makes perfect sense that this cell has those characteristics.

When we see a person who relates only to others just like him/herself and we envision that he/she is a cell which belongs to the nail, for example, the behavior becomes quite appropriate.

And when we see that human being who relates to everyone, as though she/he is a cell which belongs to the brain, in contact with all the parts of the body, it makes perfect sense.

The view of people in such manner makes us aware not only of who they are, what their function is, but why they need to be. The desire to change them dissolves. Acceptance enters your Being. With acceptance, Peace!

In the same manner we can translate that to countries.

Each country is serving a very specific function and we must make sure that we don't change each other, but that we grow "consciously" to incorporate our parts.

If we want to "change" anyone, we are saying: "What you are is not good enough." Needless to say, the person or country will

313

react to that. If we can see and therefore accept, then we have the trust of the person or country and thus we can work together towards a common goal. It's common, it's real, it's desired by all of us! The result will be enjoyed not by the few or the many, but by **all** of us. We can have it, but we must learn to "think" anew.

We are growing. The body, Humanity, is in an evolutionary process. We'll act, we'll move, and we'll arrive. There is not just physical evolution; there is such a thing as spiritual evolution, and we are in the midst of it. The parts are forming; just like once certain parts of our physical body changed, so our consciousness is changing and, with it, the physical manifestation of our very lives, our institutions, our countries. Finally we will have a Unified Planet.

First Cause

The basic hard work is making sure we agree on the following: What are we going to do? Open a restaurant? Achieve peace?

What is it — a visible, like a restaurant? An invisible, like Peace?

Who is going to be involved? Just a few people? The whole planet?

Why are we going to do it? Profit? Charity? Survival?

Only when we have answered these questions — the what, who and why — can we begin to address ourselves to the how. How are we going to do it?

If we follow the idea of opening a restaurant, we will need agreement on the type of restaurant we want to open. Failure to agrée on this would prevent success. If we want a high class one, certainly we should not go and buy mismatched cutlery. If we want to serve people on the dock, we do not want to hire waiters who were trained to serve at the Savoy. It is all very obvious. It is understood that first must come the **Idea**: "We will open a restaurant."

Then we must agree that we are all willing to work on bringing the idea to manifestation, that we really **Desire** to open up a restaurant. Once we have an idea and a desire — an agreement on both — **Action** will follow. A **restaurant** will appear on the planet.

The restaurant is the consequence of the first cause. The cause is the idea of opening the restaurant. What we see is always a consequence of the invisible. The idea is an invisible. The physical restaurant is the consequence of the invisible.

You and I are physical beings. You and I are here on this planet because our parents felt "something." We are the manifestation of that feeling — it does not matter if it was physical passion, falling in love, or one partner feeling rage and raping the other, the other feeling mistreated and unable to get free. Whatever

314

the feeling was, there was a "feeling." Good, bad, planned or not, spontaneous or not. There was a feeling. Out of that feeling, an action followed and you and I materialized. We were born. The Cause of our own existence is an invisible: a feeling. The Consequence is visible: our bodies.

Once we understand that Cause is an invisible, we recognize that if we want to change what we see, we must change it at the Cause level, at the invisible level.

As we look around, we have the feeling there is something "Wrong" with the world.

We see hunger in the world. We go and try to alleviate it. We make donations.

We see polluted rivers. We go and try to clean them.

We see polluted air. We go and try to purify it.

We see the proliferation of nuclear arms. We want to stop it.

All that is very good. First aid is important. But this is dealing with consequence, not cause.

Why are the rivers dirty in the first place?

Why is the air polluted in the first place?

Why did we create bombs in the first place?

Why are the people starving in the first place?

People are not starving in the world because the planet cannot provide for all. It can.

But there is Greed. Greed is merely a manifestation of Fear. Fear is a manifestation of pain. Pain is an invisible. Pain is the Cause of the problem. Only by healing pain can we then solve the other problems. Once we heal the pain, the Cause, we will see the consequences diminishing.

Because we are in pain and afraid, we feel we need to accumulate. So we live by Fear. We have made all our decisions at a personal, national and international level based on Fear. Fear is an invisible, therefore it belongs to the Spiritual Domain.

How do I connect dirty waters with Fear? Let's look. Let us say I have a factory which dumps waste in the river. The reason for my having a factory is profit, which I want to accumulate. I want to accumulate because I want to feel secure. I want to feel secure because now I feel insecure — afraid. So being afraid is the reason behind wanting the profits which supposedly would provide me with a feeling of security, which supposedly would get rid of my feeling of insecurity, my fear. Because I want more profits in order to feel more secure, waste is dumped into the river. And because it is not just I who fear, but you and he and we and they, the river is polluted.

We are trying to solve an invisible problem with a visible: money; an intangible Fear with a tangible: money. We can't. When our body — which is tangible — is hungry, we can satisfy it

315

with a tangible: food. But we cannot satisfy an intangible with anything but an intangible.

Alarms = Symptoms

Let's look at some of the alarm symptoms the planet has given us and let's look at what we do, and what we **can** do instead! During the 40's a Hitler comes and does his thing. What is his action telling the world? It is saying, "Hey, world, look at us, we are out of balance."

What do we do?

We look at Hitler and judge him "bad." So in a minor way we do exactly what he does. He is judging someone else to be "bad." And we too are judging, by pointing our fingers at him.

What can we do?

We **can** look at him and realize he is showing us that each one of us is not bringing forth enough love. We must begin to understand that the whole world is starving. We **can** go inside of ourselves and bring forth greater understanding and greater love for everyone we meet. We **can** judge ourselves internally.

The outside is only a manifestation of what really goes on at the level of consciousness. As each of us looks at the Hitlers of the world and brings forth compassion for them, and understanding and love, instead of condemnation, we **can** actively work toward turning the world situation.

But as long as the alarm symptoms are there and we look at them and judge them as separate from us, we can never have peace. There can never be peace where there is "us" and "them." Peace means **all** of "us."

All of this is not only national and international. This must be done at a personal level continually. We go to work, we see someone pushing someone else. We can choose to be upset to see people act like this. That means, not only one person is angry, but now two people are angry, he has won you over to his side!

Or, we can see him pushing and think, "He must be very hurt, very frightened, to need to put another person down to make himself feel better! I would not like to be in his shoes, to feel so frightened!"

By this thought you have brought forth into consciousness a positive feeling; contrasted with the other! That person, his action, has given you the opportunity to bring from inside yourself a better self, a more understanding self. If you did not take the opportunity he gave you, there are now two of you on the side of fear! Balance means that we have two things, or feelings, of equal weight, one on each side.

When a person was rude to you and through the use of your mind you brought your first feeling of anger to one of understanding, compassion or love, you created balance within yourself.

One person being rude, negative, and one person understanding, positive, created a balanced situation at the level of two people.

In terms of energy formulae, the various combinations are as follows:

1. When a person was rude, and you got angry and remained angry, this is what you created:

1-	= one person negative unbalance
+1-	= other person negative unbalance
2-	= double negative unbalance as part of the whole

2. By creating a balance within yourself by experiencing the negative and making it move to the positive, you created positive on the outside. The outside is a manifestation of the inside. This is what was created:

1-	= one person negative unbalance
+1- + 1+	= one person neutral balance
2- + 1+	= negative unbalance as part of the whole.

3. When one person was rude, and the other went from anger to understanding, and the first from rudeness to understanding his own rudeness, and changing his own feelings, there is a balanced picture:

1- + 1+	= one person neutral balance
+1- + 1+	= one person neutral balance
2- + 2-	= neutral balance as part of the whole

4. When someone is rude and you know that no one acts like that unless operating from fear, you can respond with, "I know how she/he must feel, I have had those days." You are thinking from knowledge, which manifests itself as understanding, leading to compassion. That is what is created:

1-	= one person negative unbalance
+1+	= one person positive unbalance
1- + 1+	= one neutral balance as part of the whole

5. When someone is rude, and then that person changes his/her feelings (even if you never know about it — we are talking energies here), and you had acted from your love center with understanding arriving at compassion, this is what is created:

1- + 1+	= one person neutral balance
+ 1+	= one person positive balance
1- + 2+	= positive unbalance as part of the whole

6. When a person operating from love center brings understanding, clarity and compassion to another, who also brings understanding, compassion and clarity, this is what is created:

$$
\begin{array}{rl}
1+ & = \text{one person positive unbalance} \\
+\,1+ & = \text{one person positive unbalance} \\
\hline
2+ & = \text{double (\textbf{perfect}) positive unbalance as part of the} \\
& \text{whole}
\end{array}
$$

We create the perfect balance by manifesting the perfect positive unbalance, and having the perfect negative unbalance unmanifested. As all of us use our minds to change our feelings, the entire world will manifest the inner reality of personal balance.

When we use our minds to bring about positive balance of our feelings, our health will be optimal, since illness is the outer manifestation of an inner unbalance.

This meditation done consciously 24 hours a day, is the greatest thing anyone can do. It requires no time, just 24 hours within your 24 hours. What I have tried to show is how the energy travels by positives and negatives.

Now, here is another example, without numbers. If we hold a sock in one hand, all rolled down, and little by little we pull it out inside out, it finally unrolls to its limit. (That is precisely where we are right now. At the ultimate negative manifestation of energy.)

Now, to proceed, we begin to pull the toe of the sock inwards little by little, until the sock is completely right side out: the inside is in.

With the sock we can clearly see one item in two situations. One could not exist without the other, since they are one and the same!

This is the process we are all undergoing. While some of us are beginning to pull the sock toe inwards, there are still some who are outside doing what they must, until the whole sock is finally as it is supposed to be: all of it right side out. Peace.

The whole sock balances itself by first going out, in a negative unconscious way, and then coming back inwards in a conscious, positive manner. Once the sock remains there, we have the outer sock, which got out by the process of going in, and the inside of the sock, which finally is in by the process of having been out! Riddles . . . riddles . . . I am out, because I have been in! I am in because I have been out! I am in process as well! I looked like three, yet I am one!

This is the process, a beautiful one! Look at it. There is a task for each and every one of us. We are equal, no one person has more power than any other. If just one person does not achieve peace within by this process, the sock can't be turned completely. So we need each and every one of us, all of us, all. If I could do it, so can you!

Is it clear now? How important the alarm symptoms are? How

they had to be there? How they are part of the whole? How we can use the alarms to see how much more we have to pull the sock inwards? They are the barometer of our progress in turning the sock inwards. By looking at the symptoms we can tell how far "in" the sock has travelled. So let's say "Thank you" for the terrific job the alarms are doing, and let's get on ourselves with our inner judging, inner killing.

Peace to and for the World, I

First, I thought myself perfect. The world said, "You are crazy!" Not true . . .

You may say, "How can this person that kills be perfect?" I say that the killer is showing us the imbalance of the whole. He is in fact doing us a great service.

When we are sick, it is not the parts of our body which keep functioning normally that are the greatest help to us. It is those parts which malfunction, which show us symptoms, that are truly helping us. Because of symptoms, when we go to a doctor, we find out what ailment we have and can seek the cure. So, when we are sick, the cells which take upon themselves to hurt, or go crazy, are the ones which in fact are giving us the greatest of help. Without them, we would die without knowing we were sick.

It is not different with the body of humanity.

Second, I saw my husband perfect. The world said, "You are crazy!" But after 17 years he is healed by my Love vs. his Fear. Love always conquers.

And now, here comes Beatriz again, except this time Beatriz is saying: "Hey . . . World . . . Look! You are perfect! Yes, the world is perfect."

Now, what do I mean by, "the world is perfect"? I mean that it is working perfectly. How does it do that? By giving us the signals, the symptoms, that tell us, "Please take care of me, I am not well." The symptoms are violence, economic collapse, polluted air, all consequences of causes. The cause is: Fear, which comes from Pain. Frustrations, hate and violence are but three stages of Fear.

Let's look at this scene (the microcosm). A person is very sick. Fever, colds, sores all over, bleeding profusely.

What would anyone do in such a case? We realize there is something wrong. We rush the person to the doctor. The doctor sees the patient, sees all those symptoms and feels grateful for them. The symptoms tell what is wrong with the person. The outside tells what is wrong inside. The symptoms help the doctor realize there is an illness in the first place, and what type of illness it is. Because the body of that person is functioning 100%, or, in other words, because the body is functioning perfectly, the body is producing alarm signals so that it can be saved. The doctor knows only too well that if there were not symptoms, and the body was ill, it would die without being able to get help.

Let's look at a different scene (the microcosm).

A person is very sick. Fever, colds, sores all over, bleeding profusely.

Everyone looks at the person:

"Look!"

"Look! Isn't this terrible!"

"Look, the carpet is getting dirty with all this blood!"

"Have you ever seen anything like it?"

People gather to look at the scene.

"Such a thing should not happen!"

"Why do we have to be subjected to this type of thing!"

"Can someone do something about cleaning up all this mess?"

Some people get together and begin to clean up the rug. One spot is clean! Good!

But of course the person is getting worse, so . . . the rug is getting worse. By this time everyone is involved trying to clean the rug. No one is paying attention to the person and trying to solve the **cause** of the mess.

The second scene is analogous to much contemporary social and political policy. That is what we are doing. We are trying to clean the rivers, save the animals, clean the air, preserve the forests. But we are ignoring the cause of all this happening. We are treating symptoms, consequences, not causes. We are judging all this violence, polluted air, etc., as bad instead of seeing them for what they are: symptoms.

Not only should we look at them with grateful eyes, but we should feel an incredible compassion for those of us who are the alarms, so that the rest of us can bring the body back to health.

In the case of the world, of course, the doctor is ourselves! The healers are those who are still healthy. It is up to us to thank those people who are serving as alarms, and by so doing we integrate them as all of us as Peacemakers. When we are thankful to them, judgment turns inward, where it belongs.

"Good," "bad" — let's eat from the tree of life! There is only Good. Even atrocities, when seen as part of the whole, are not "bad."

To see that we have to be aware that each human being is but a cell of a body. Some cells are sick. They are sick because the body is working perfectly and is showing us there is an imbalance. Those cells are sick. The whole body is sick! Similarly, it is not just your uterus that is pregnant, all of you is pregnant!

Sickness is localized at the very beginning and later spreads all over. The more we let it go, the more it spreads to let us know we are out of balance! It does not help to stand in judgment of another, "Look at that man — he kills!" But rather to realize, "Oh, I did not do enough. I was not able to project myself enough. I did not put enough humus in the soil (the soil being consciousness, the humus being Love), so this plant is not getting what it needs."

The more we ignore the causes, the more serious the symptoms get. The body, of course, in its desperation to be saved, makes bigger and bigger symptoms. If we do not pay attention to causes, by trying to save itself, it could destroy itself. Most people see the world's symptoms growing.

We are all Peacemakers. It is not a matter of loving our enemies! It is a matter of realizing there are **no** enemies! The alarms are doing the greatest of service to all of us. Without them, we would die. But there is no "better" or "worse." Each piece is working together, for the benefit of all.

But alas . . . I know I could not have seen all this by myself. I was shown. I am trying to pass on to you in a linear picture what I was shown through intuition. How inadequate. I feel no one can transfer this kind of knowledge and so I want to motivate you to seek it for yourself. I am impelled to speak to you. There is Peace, Happiness, Fulfillment, Ecstasy for all of us!

We cannot bring about Peace if we think in terms of "we," "they," "ours," and "theirs." Where there is division, there can never be Peace. Peace is the result of integration, of different parts working together for a common goal. Each finger on the keyboard moves differently, but all of them working together in balance bring about a harmony: music. Each organ is different, but working together in a balanced way they create health.

We create peace in ourselves when we use our minds to turn our emotions from fear, frustrations, hate and violence to understanding, compassion and love. As one's mind hooks to the emotions to bring them to the right place, the emotions are hooked to the body. When the emotions are right, not only do we experience health, but as the three levels (mind-emotions-body) work together cooperatively, they hook to higher consciousness, where we can picture perfection, harmony, fulfillment and love for every being on earth. This is the working together of the three energies within us.

Peace to and for the World, II

Consider another example: A company has different departments. Each does a different job. Together they produce a final product. Each member of the company knows what the product is, and what part of the puzzle he/she provides. Each also knows that although as individuals each person in a department has many talents, during the 8 hours at work each will concentrate on specific tasks to bring about a specific product.

MAN

Brain	Muscles
Liver	Heart
Lungs	Bones
Blood	Kidneys

Each has **inner systems different** from the others, yet when they work together (in balance) there is an output:

A HEALTHY MAN

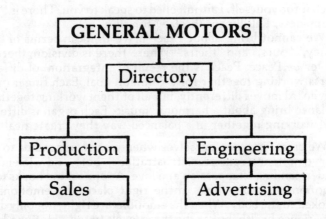

Each department has **inner systems different** from the others, yet when they work together (in balance) there is an output:

WORKING CARS

*WORLD

Afghanistan
Albania
Algeria
Andorra
Angola
Argentina
Australia
Austria
Bahamas
Bahrain
Bangladesh
Barbados
Belgium
Benin (formerly Dahomey)
Bhutan
Bolivia
Botswana
Brazil
Bulgaria
Burma
Burundi
Democratic Kampuch (Cambodia)
Cameroon
Canada
Cape Verde
Cent. African Empire
Chad
Chile
China (Republic of)
China, People's Republic of
Colombia
Western Samoa

Yemen Arab Rep.
Yemen People's Dem. Republic
Iran
Iraq
Ireland (Eire)
Israel
Italy
Ivory Coast
Jamaica
Japan
Jordan
Kenya
Kiribati
Korea, North (People's Dem. Rep. of)
Korea, South (Republic of)
Kuwait
Lao People's Rep.
Lebanon
Lesotho
Liberia
Libya
Liechtenstein
Luxembourg
Madagascar
Malawi
Malaysia
Maldive Islands
Mali
Malta
Mauritania
Mauritius
Mexico

Monaco
Yugoslavia
Comoros (Republic of the)
Congo, People's Republic of
Costa Rica
Cuba
Cyprus
Czechoslovakia
Denmark
Djibouti, Rep. of
Dominica
Dominican Rep.
Ecuador
Egypt
El Salvador
Equatorial Guinea
Ethiopia
Fiji
Finland
France
Gabon
Gambia
Germany, East
Germany, West
Ghana
Greece
Grenada
Guatemale
Guinea
Guinea-Bissau
Guyana
Haiti
Honduras
Zaire (Congo)

Zambia
Zimbabwe (Rhodesia)
South Africa
Spain
Sri Lanka (formerly Ceylon)
Sudan
Hungary
Iceland
India
Indonesia
Surinam
Swaziland
Sweden
Switzerland
Syria
Tanzania
Thailand
Togo
Tonga
Trinidad-Tobago
Tunisia
Turkey
Tuvalu
Uganda
U.S.S.R.
United Arab Emirates
United Kingdom
United States
Upper Volta
Uruguay
Vatican City
Venezuela
Vietnam

Morocco
Mozambique
Nauru
Nepal
Netherlands
New Zealand
Nicaragua
Niger
Nigeria
Norway
Oman
Pakistan
Panama
Papua-New Guinea
Paraguay
Peru
Phillippines
Poland
Portugal
Qatar
Romania
Rwanda
St. Lucia
San Marino
Sao Tome and Principe
Saudi Arabia
Senegal
Seychelles
Sierra Leone
Singapore
Solomon Islands
Somalia

Each has inner systems different from the others, yet if/when they work together there will be an output: **PEACE.** That is our STRENGTH. We are looking at it as if our different systems were our weakness. They are not!

*The question arises: On what basis did I choose the selection of the Nations. Well, I never stopped to think when I spoke of Robert and Freddy if I mentioned them in alphabetical order or not. I will **not** begin to worry now when I speak about my other children. I know they will feel my love and respond in kind, even if they are **not** in alphabetical order, or some of them get forgotten in the process. It happens in families! You will just have to put up with this Mommy, you are stuck with me! One does not choose one's Mommy! No? Oh! Well . . .

HUMAN BODY

Made of:	When Balanced:	When Unbalanced:
Cells	All cells work properly. Result: HEALTH	Some cells alter their proper behavior. They are working at the service of health by saying: "Take care of all of me. I, the body, all of us (cells) are out of balance They are showing the unbalance of the body. How do they do it? By **unconsciously** altering their proper behavior. How is balance restored? By the "person" **consciously** giving the cells what they need (protein, minerals, etc.)

Good or Bad?	Final Conclusion
Is it bad that some cells let us know that we are out of balance? Are the cells which alter their behavior working **for** or **against** health? They are working **for** balance by being unbalanced. If they did not alter their behavior and give us the "signals," the body would die without our knowing.	Thus, ALL cells are "GOOD."

Conclusion: ALL CELLS WORK TOGETHER FOR THE BENEFIT OF THE WHOLE, TO MANIFEST ITS UNBALANCE OR ITS BALANCE.

HUMANITY

Made of:	When Balanced:	When Unbalanced:
Persons	All persons work properly. Result: PEACE	Some people alter their proper behavior. Why? Because they are working at the service of peace. They are saying: "Take care of all of me!" I, humanity, all of us (each person) are out of balance. They are showing the unbalance of the body. How do they do it? By **unconsciously** indi-individuals altering their behav-vior. How is balance restored? By each **conscious** person **giving** to the other unconscious person what they need. LOVE.

Good or Bad?	Final Conclusion
Is it bad that some persons let us know we are out of balance? Are the persons who alter their behavior working **for** balance or **against** it by being unbalanced? They are working **for** balance by being unbalanced. If some people would not alter their behavior and give us the "signals," humanity would die without our knowing.	Thus, there is no Evil, since Evil is working at the service of GOOD. **THERE IS ONLY GOOD!**

Conclusion: ALL PERSONS WORK TOGETHER FOR THE BENEFIT OF THE WHOLE TO MANI-FEST ITS UNBALANCE OR ITS BALANCE.

We have taken the first step. We created the United Nations. Now let's take the second step and eliminate our "egos" from it. That will make it possible to work together. We must kill the "I" — the personal self, the national self — so that we can emerge as "us," a unit (which we already are, if we only knew it!).

By now we know we can't say: "I will throw this pollutant over here, and I will not be affected." We know we **will** be affected. If we spit up into the air, it comes back to all of us. The air does not say, "I will go pure to this country and polluted to that one."

So our solutions must be done at a global level to be effective. Now that the machinery is in motion to cure the symptoms with "first aid," let's start dealing with the cause. Why are the air and water dirty in the first place? Let's start looking, just like a doctor would, through the visible, to the problem of the invisible. If we solve the invisible problem, the visible will change.

How Cultures Differ in Showing Their Love For One Another

When I came to North America 20 years ago, I was a bit surprised. First, I had this preconceived idea that English people were cold, unemotional.

What I discovered, in fact, was that far from it, **they are** the emotional types and we Latins are the cerebral.

I began to observe how young and old people in this society get married for no other reason than "We are in love."

To me, a Latin, to follow through an emotion into action just because of the feeling has to be the most emotional behavior I have ever seen.

We, on the contrary, first decide what type of life style we want, where we want to live, what type of ideas, family background, what does the person think about raising children — all these things must be looked at prior to ever falling in love. We know that feeling will go away, and we must decide on things which are far more permanent. Even if we **do** fall in love, if all the other criteria are not met, we just walk away, with pain in our hearts, feeling "better now than later."

To see people looking into each other's eyes, and not considering how their individual value systems and private goals could merge into one, to see how they "love and go with it" was, to say the least, mind boggling to a cerebral Latin. Yet, the stereotype is quite the opposite.

What I observed is that we Latins can laugh anywhere, have fun any place, sing wherever we are and feel free to do so, even if our hearts ache, and the Anglo-Saxon people did not seem to be able to do so. But they were able to work when their hearts ached, and we weren't. That seemed to be the basis for the stereotype of our being emotional.

We are gregarious, yes. But emotional, no.

No important decision in a Latin household is made without a great deal of thought. The input leading to the decision comes from a lot of people, family and friends, not just the person involved.

The next interaction that surprised me was how parents encourage their children to leave home. That was a real contrast.

They also encourage their children, from the time that they are very young, to earn money by delivering papers, cutting lawns, etc. For us, that would be unthinkable. I remember the front page of the Argentinian newspapers when Kennedy began his political career and how people thought: "Poor little boy!" Why? Well, he had sold newspapers. Why else besides extreme poverty would someone do something like that? Only after I came here did I realize how even the international news gets completely colored by the perspective of the cultures: How we see from where we stand and are unable to comprehend that there may be a different motivation for actions than we presume, based on our cultural experiences. Needless to say, I realized they were sending their children to earn money out of love, just as we give all the money we can, out of love. Of course Mommy and Daddy buy you an apartment when you get married! Of course Mommy and Daddy work double shifts to do it! Of course we take care of our grandchildren when the parents go away, even if the kids scream and are loud!

The other difference I noticed was how we each show our humanity differently.

Every institution in this country is humane. Everyone can go to a hospital and be treated equally. Everyone who needs food can find some program (a food stamp program or local church) established by people who have found it in their hearts to feed the hungry. As soon as Anglo-Saxons feel something, they take action. They discover how to be assertive, and then create assertiveness training for everyone. They can work in groups, they can sometimes demonstrate their love at a mass level.

On the contrary, Latins have the most inhumane institutions. They are in fact, non-existent. But they are very good at the personal level. They will take their own shirt off their backs to give to someone they know personally.

However, because the institutions in North America are so humane the individual has lost a sense of personal responsibility. "Don't come to me for money, go to the bank." "I hear your problem. Here is a list of places where you can find help."

The two cultures have so much to learn from one another. I imagine a world where all the institutions would be very humane, like those in North America, and all the personal interactions would be like those in the Latin culture. We all could have it all.

Planet as School

Our planet is a school. Not only does each of us learn individually, but we learn collectively as well.

For a long time, we have individually and collectively looked outside for answers, like children. The first stages of human growth are projected outwards: being curious, reaching out, grasping and using tools. So we turned our eyes outside ourselves.

We have looked at nature and discovered some principles and laws. We saw materials and created tools. We looked all around and investigated the earth. Having done that, we looked at the moon. Clearly we have gone outwards to see, to explore, to feel, to do everything we could. We have done it so well, we are now at an end of that particular line.

By looking outwards, we have created nuclear bombs and now have the ability to destroy ourselves. We have created the **ultimate negative.** But now, because of that, we can create an **ultimate positive.** By this very process, we have created the greatest possibility ever.

Up to now, history could repeat itself over and over. But now we are in a situation in which if we use what we have created, history will not be able to repeat itself. We have arrived at this point like little children — just by being curious and trying to get answers — which is all good.

We have used the masculine energy within ourselves to arrive at these achievements — the energy that looks out, the energy of outside action.

We have not arrived where we are by design, choice or plan. It just happened. Newton discovered something and one thing led to another — others came and produced other links in the chain. But there was no master plan, no grand design to have a world full of lethal weapons.

Just as children grow up, so does the planet earth and humanity. Planet earth is at the stage of a 40-year-old person. A human being tries one job, then another, one relationship, then another, and by 40 or so stops to take stock of where he is and where he wants to Be. If he is not where he wants to be, he corrects his course of action. If he is, he continues with renewed energy to become a more prominent person in his circle. So at 40 one can say that one becomes a Conscious Being.

In the same way, the world is now becoming conscious of itself. The world is starting to see what it did, where it went and what it has created. The world has grown aware, and is capable of consciously reflecting — looking back and projecting forward.

Since we have brought ourselves to the possibility of total destruction, we have also created the possibility of achieving total Peace for the first time in the history of mankind.

The saying goes: "As above, so below" or "As below, so above." Looking below we see Newton's Third Law, which says, "For every action, there is an equal and opposite reaction."

We know we cannot use the bomb. We cannot dismantle it. We cannot, in fact, do anything with it. So we have only one alternative: we must change the nature of man, we must begin to look within.

To solve the problems, we must complete the process. First we must recognize there are no "problems," just a process taking place. Until now, it has been an outward, unconscious, negative process. We must complete the process by an inward, conscious, positive action. For this we must use the female energy. That is what it's for: to look within, ♀ , and let the female energy in each of us light the way. By so doing, each of us will bring balance to the whole.

Once we understand that we have arrived exactly where we are supposed to be, the fear we all have will evaporate. We can realize and accept how wonderful we are — that we have not blown it — and can start to balance by looking inward. By looking inward, we will bring Peace into ourselves and from within ourselves, to the planet.

The power is in all of us. The energy to change the world is in our hands. We can do it! Thanks to all those who existed before us, we are here. Because they did what they did, they made the world grow to its present point of ripeness. Now it is up to us to thank them and move on to integrate everything. As this occurs, balance is obtained, peace achieved.

HUMAN BEING

First stage:	curious about its environment	: touches, smells, experiments.
Second stage:	observes results	: spills, messes.
Third stage:	questions	: "Do I like this? Do I want this?
Fourth stage:	gets answers	: "Yes, I want milk, but no I don't want to spill it."
Fifth stage:	practices	: picks up, smells and experiments but with fewer and fewer messes.
Sixth stage:	**SUCCESS**	: uses the accumulation of what he learns unconsciously (like speaking, touching, walking, etc.) and begins to utilize it consciously. Success is the stage in which something which was learned unconsciously is applied consciously to obtain a desired result.

HUMANITY

First stage	curious about its environment	: looks at the rivers, the oceans, the land. Let's touch, let's experiment.
Second stage:	observes results	: pollution, a broken ecological system. (messes)
Third stage:	questions	: "Do we like this? Do we want this?"
Fourth stage:	gets answers	: "Yes, I want the rivers, the land, the oceans, but not the pollution."
Fifth stage:	practices	: begins to try to clean up the mess.
Sixth stage:	**SUCCESS**	: THIS IS WHERE WE ARE RIGHT NOW.

You may say, "What do you mean there is no evil? Can't you see the atrocities? Can't you see the violence? Can't you see how it is increasing?" Yes, I can. Precisely because I can see, I look at cause, not consequence.

When I look at a seed, I know what it is. The plant and the flower are consequences of the seed. I do not need to see a book written to know someone is a writer. That would be to know by looking at fruits, at consequences; I look at cause. If there is a seed of a writer, there is a writer, period. Sooner or later the consequence will manifest — when, is irrelevant to me.

Let me tell you an incident involving my son, which happened just the other day. I took a piece of bread to toast, cut a square of cheese and placed it on top. I was happy as a clam. My son looked at it and said, "Wait, I want to do something." Immediately he began to tear the piece of cheese apart. I said, "Robert, listen, I am a person that integrates. Leave that piece of cheese together, I don't like to see it all pulled apart!" He replied, "And I am a person that pulls things apart to make them better than what they were before — see, look!" And he showed me that now, instead of a plain, square, integrated piece of cheese, there was a face formed on the toast. By pulling it apart, he had created something far more beautiful.

So it is with the world. Some of us are working on pulling it apart, so that others can build the pieces into a better picture. All of us are in this together!

The increasing violence is not only an alarm but a seed! Nothing comes from nothing! Each human being is doing exactly what he needs to do.

Those who are working consciously must understand those who are working unconsciously, and the necessity of the service they are providing. See the whole, bring us into one camp, unite us all. Maybe an ant is not aware of the contribution it makes on the earth, how useful it is; but it is useful nevertheless.

Allan, my ex-husband, was not consciously serving me, but he did serve, I was consciously serving him, unconsciously I was serving myself. As I met the unconscious in my "experience" (described in chapter 6), I was able to see how all of us serve each other, how the planet really works.

You see, I came to love this planet by simply not stopping the energy called Love, by putting it out there and allowing it to do its thing. The only control I exercised was to make sure I never took my love away from anyone or anything. The rest happened on its own. Now that I truly love the world, I can see how unaware of the world I was before. Now I know I do not love the galaxy, but I will, as I embark upon expanding my love once more.

Planet earth has come of age. We have begun to act as adults, the process has begun and it will continue. When we arrive at peace we will be able to send our representatives to the galaxies, just as we now send our representatives to the UN. Everything is a microcosm of a macrocosm. We have not made our planet (and therefore the UN) work properly yet, because we have not decided on the **Ideal** of the planet. We have not sat as a body. We have not defined which nation is the "head," which one the "liver," which one the "lungs."

We keep trying to change each other, instead of recognizing that the body **needs** different parts. The body must have the inner functions of each organ working in a different manner. We have lots of seeds. We have taken quite a few steps. We must perfect them now — the UN, for one.

The seed, the cause of peace, resides precisely in the fact that we have created the possibility of total destruction. That is the end of the line for unconscious behavior. But having created this possibility, we can see how people are becoming aware of it and are beginning to act consciously. We will need each and every one of us who are conscious to begin working at the conscious level, to pull the "sock" up. The stitches, who are now unconsciously giving us support by being the alarms, by being down as we pull ourselves up, will be pulled up, too — or become conscious. But we can't make them conscious by talking to them. We can only do it by working on ourselves, by pulling ourselves up.

Then things will follow naturally. If you have an apple in your hand and you open your hand, a law takes over — gravity. It takes over until the apple arrives at its destination, or until you interfere by closing your fingers on it again. The same process is true with us. You have love within you; you can open yourself completely to every human being — it does not matter what they do or who they are — and allow the law of love to take you to its destination. Or you can interfere by closing yourself and delay your arrival. The choice is yours.

The process has begun, the end is inevitable. Peace will come to the planet. Relax, don't panic. Let's work, but with confidence, from a place of security and knowledge, not from being scared like little rabbits!

HUMAN BODY

Composed of:	Sizes	Functions: Each organ has its own way of inner working
Organs	Varied	How do the organs relate to each other? By a system which Unites all organs, without interference with the inner workings of each one of them. The brain has its own inner system. The liver has its own inner system. The heart has its own inner system. And precisely because each organ is different, and has its own inner systems and has a system which unites all of them, we see a body which functions.

RESULT: The strength is given not just by the individual uniqueness of the parts but through its unified system: **ONE is** part of **ALL.**

HUMANITY

Composed of:	Sizes	Functions: Each country has its own way of inner working.
Countries	Varied	How do the countries relate to each other? We have NO system which unites all countries, without interference of their inner workings. Russia has its own inner system. China has its own inner system. U.S. has its own inner system (and so forth). Precisely because each country is different and has its own inner system, we can NOW begin to create a system which will Unite all the countries and we will see a planet which will function. It is not our weakness that each country is different. It is our strength! The addition of this last system will answer the who, what, why at the planetary level and by doing so bring clarity, cohesiveness, completion to the whole.

RESULT: We will then have the **ONE** (country) being part of the **ALL** (planet).

How We Are Whole (And Can Come to Realize It)

Nothing exists that should not. Everything has a purpose, but we may not have learned yet how to use what is there.

Someone said, "Love is letting go of fear." Some ask why hate even exists in the world. But we need everything — including fear and hate — that exists. If we did not need it, it would not be here. So the trick is to look at all the pieces and form the puzzle. In fact, the puzzle is so simple, so obvious, that the solution has eluded us for a long time. But we are now ready to become conscious and begin to choose our pain consciously to arrive at absolute joy, wholeness and ecstasy. Oh — come with me, don't let me experience this extraordinary feeling alone! It is for all of us!

I suggested that there is one energy and two centers. Or one sock and two sides. One center, the Center of Fear, should be used inwardly — to check whether we have brought out as much understanding as we possibly could in each situation; to judge if we brought forth as much love as we could to whomever we found next to us. And I mean literally next to us: that person standing next to us in the supermarket. Did I bring forth a smile? Did I bring forth a kind word when I saw how impatient he/she was about having to wait in line? Was I able to make her feel how wonderful she is? I wasn't? How stupid of me to miss the chance! How many times do I have to go through it to learn to bring out my very best?

That is why we have judgment, that is how frustration must be used — inside ourselves: "I hate it when I keep missing opportunities because I feel shy."

The other center: Center of Love — should be used externally.

Let me share an experience from my life. I began to talk with a person in the supermarket because he looked impatient. He looked at me and said with big, cold eyes, "I don't speak with Latins." A chill was definitely in the air. I looked back and smiled. I did not get angry, I couldn't. I understood by his answer that he was using his Fear Center backwards and by his reply he told me the degree of the fear he felt. I replied, "Yes, I know how you feel. When I came to North America, I felt like you sometimes, when Anglo-Saxons talked to me. It was because I was a bit scared, a bit uncertain, because I did not know them well then."

He was surprised. He had just insulted me, and I had come back by placing myself next to him and sharing something that in my case was not even true! But I always know this technique works to make a person feel OK. That is how I used "lies." Before I knew it, he was speaking to me. He may not change his attitudes about all Latins, but now he knows that he experienced one Latin person whom he was able to enjoy. And I had just become a bit more of who I am — understanding, compassionate, loving.

He gave me the opportunity to be more of who I was — to practice my "Being." To bring out understanding and a smile when they were not expected. In this way he actually was very kind to me.

We can always choose to be the example of what we really are, to use our centers properly. And we can refuse — no matter how anyone may provoke us otherwise — to manifest anything but our true selves. Our inside feelings should correspond to our actions. If they don't, we can practice by acting loving, and later go through the interaction in our minds until we can turn our angry, hurt feelings to those of understanding for that poor person. One day you will be able to thank that person because "difficult" people give you the greatest opportunity to reach fulfillment and happiness.

If you want to learn to read, you must find someone who can teach you. If you want to learn to "Be," you must find people who give you the opportunity to exercise your "Being;" that is the only way to create a "self." You may say you are using that person, but there is a right and a wrong way to use anything. We want to create selves that will grow enough to die — and be born as part of a bigger whole. At that moment you'll learn you know nothing.

Yet here I am trying to show you how I got to know nothing and to knowing that by using our minds, we will arrive at a place beyond mind. We use words and knowledge which will all be discarded when we reach that place. Yet we must do it.

It is like when we all wanted to grow up to marry Mommy or Daddy. No one tried to tell us that was not possible. They understood we were young and did not know better. They let us play with those ideas until, by the process of growing up, we ourselves realized we would not be able (or want) to marry our parents.

So we need to use what we know today until we reach the realization that what we know no longer applies — and then move from there. Until we reach beyond mind, let's use our minds to analyze what we feel. Since we have the map of how to use those "negative" feelings inside in their proper place, we can start looking at one another with a lot more understanding.

We are on our way. Each of us is doing the best we can with the information we have.

Some of us are operating unconsciously — the alarms. As we wake up and train ourselves to Become, we will have a balance of conscious and unconscious examples in the world. When each and every one of us breaks the barriers of his/her own unconscious, it will be easy to agree on anything. It means we will all be manifesting understanding; we will receive information consciously from the one source — by intuition.

When we break the barrier of the unconscious, when we each arrive at true "I am," we will know the purpose of our lives. We will have an incredible drive to express who we know ourselves to be and to do what we will have "heard" we were to do. As each of us does this, each one will fit a little piece into the puzzle of the world and a perfect whole will be formed.

Filling the Void

We all feel a void. We have come to accept that this is the way it is and we keep looking for others to fill that hole. But if we feel a void, it means that at some point there was no void. How else could we know of the feeling of wholeness unless we have been at some time whole? Yes, we have. We used to operate with our centers in the proper place, we used to use ourselves properly.

Since we have been using our Fear Centers outwardly and our Love Centers inwardly, we have felt a void. We will not feel that void if we put the centers to work in their proper places.

Let's imagine that we put a pair of sandals on with each sandal on the wrong foot. We have created a void. Some of our toes are unsupported. If we put on our sandals correctly, there would be no place where our toes would not have support.

This is what happens in our lives, because we have reversed the centers of operation within ourselves. We feel a lack of support, a void produced by the switch.

If we use the two centers as they are meant to be used, we will not need support. We will feel that the pieces of the puzzle fit. We will feel whole. But because we are being natural, we will be supported — not because we need it, not because we ask for it, but because we can't help but support one another.

If we use a vacuum cleaner properly, the way it was intended to be used, it will clean naturally wherever it is used. But if we reverse its use, it will blow out dirt, it will deny its function. You see, there is no evil, there are not two different things. It is all one item, being used either correctly or incorrectly. What we perceive as evil is simply one of the beautiful pieces of the puzzle, being used improperly.

When we see what fear produces when it is used outwardly, we might decide we have to let go of it altogether. The truth is, we can't. We must never let go of anything. We must see what its purpose is. There is nothing in the universe which should not be there!

Once we know why fear is there and how to use both the Fear and Love Centers, we will begin to see fantastic changes in ourselves. Learning to listen is important, but what we must listen to is not only words or actions. We must begin to recognize from which center a person is coming. If someone is coming from the Love Center, we will know it because we will hear understanding, clarity and integration coming out of his or her mouth.

When the opposite is coming out, then the person is operating from his/her fear center. We then have the greatest opportunity to be who we really are with that person and not be shaken. We will not change them and will not want to change them. The more you practice being who you are, the more automatic your response will become. Then anyone will be able to say anything to you and you will not feel pain, hurt or anger, but only understanding for that person and compassion for his/her pain.

So you see, happiness is arrived at by consciously approaching people who will inflict pain upon you and by you then consciously making the metamorphosis within yourself from pain to understanding.

Integration

We must learn to use our centers properly, not only on a personal level, but on an international level as well.

As nations, we must begin to act with our Love Centers out. As nations we must begin to be "vacuum cleaners." Yes, we may have to allow some other country to invade us; we may have to just sit, refuse to cooperate or allow them to kill us — and not respond. In other words, not react, just act. We may have to go through this process before we arrive at real Peace.

We will have to integrate theory into our very Beings. For example, I can read an article about cancer, therefore I **understand** it. A friend comes and tells me she has cancer; I **feel** for her. I go to the doctor and he tells me I have cancer; I **know** about it.

Or it could work another way: I go to the doctor and he tells me I have cancer — I **know** about it. Then I begin to read because I need to **understand.** And, of course, I **feel** it, because I own it, it is mine.

For us to arrive at peace, we have to go through this same process of integrating the understanding, the feeling and the knowing at every point. We are to eat from the Tree of Life — not the Tree of Good and Evil.

As nations, we should ask ourselves, are we willing to refuse to fight? If another country should invade us, are we willing to go hungry but refuse to work? Are we willing, each of us, to die? Are we willing to show we will not tolerate an invasion and yet not manifest negative energy as the other side is doing? Can we simply sit and manifest light? They may not be conscious yet, but **we** are. We understand that light overtakes darkness. Perhaps we may all have to die.

It may take a generation or two, but we are consciously working to manifest what it takes to be the positive, loving human beings that we are. And we must recognize that even if a whole nation disappears from the earth, it is irrelevant. Sometimes a hand has to be cut off for the body to be saved. Which nation on earth can begin to show light? Which of us will begin to show for peace at the international level?

Until now we were acting unconsciously. It was right for it to be so. But now we are beginning the conscious period. We must begin to act, to take conscious steps leading to peace. But the concrete steps must result from an inner awareness of how we have traveled, what we have accomplished and how we have, in fact, been creating our own choices. Once we can see how we have created a choice, we can begin to consciously decide how to behave to accomplish the desired result we have chosen.

The **ideal** we want to accomplish, comes first. Is the ideal peace? Are we motivated enough? Do all of us really want peace? Or is it "Peace, yes, but if this nation moves in we have to move." That is not peace. We must first dwell in our souls to find out how much we are willing to give for peace. We know we are willing to give our lives for war — that is clear! We have done it and we are continuing to do it. Are we as committed to peace? Are we willing to die for peace? Are we willing to go to jail for peace? Are we willing to begin to show en masse our discontent and pay no taxes? Are we willing to put the money for taxes in the hands of the courts to show that we don't want to keep our money, but we also don't want it to be spent on "defense?"

The answers to these questions will give us a good indication of the strength of our desire.

Once we know whether our desire is strong enough, the action will naturally follow. In the case of peace, it means deciding not to fight. It means deciding it does not matter what any other nation does, we will not retaliate.

The action of non-violence will begin: organizing to stop the money flow for defense, raising money to advertise how to create peace within — it can all be worked out. In fact, it has begun, as we can all see. But what we **must also** see is how the process will take us to the most extraordinary place. We will end up in paradise! Each and every person on earth — as each stitch turns itself inside out and the whole sock turns!

We will begin competing to get to peace: "What is the percentage of the nation willing to die for peace? Ah! Another nation is winning. Good for them! We will catch up. Our nation will vote and decide how many of us are willing to sit and die if necessary in case of aggression next month." You may laugh, but wait and see — we will do it! We **will** arrive at peace.

When we look at a child, we all recognize that the sequence of his life, regardless of how much we may love the child, is out of our hands. We cannot decide to make him experience his 30's first, because it is a nicer era, and arrange to have adolescence second, since it is such a hard period. We understand this is impossible, there is only so much within our control.

It is no different with the planet. The sequence of events on our planet is completely out of our hands. The planet, just as a small child, has seemed to have very little choice in where it was going — until now. We know we did not plan to arrive at this polluted, violent, fearful place in which we find ourselves. It happened — as it should.

Just as a child grows up, so did the planet. As a grown human being can make conscious decisions, the planet has the ability to make a choice now also. We have choices because we have created them. Let's look at the choices. We can, just like a human being, commit suicide — total destruction — or we can rejoice in the other choice — peace — and consciously work to bring it about.

I have tried to show the process the world has experienced so far. It all began because we felt we wanted happiness and wholeness. That is why we all remember, at the subconscious level, how it was to be happy. It was once true.

But once we departed from wholeness by switching our center of operation, we just kept going — just as once you have a baby, it keeps growing. Once the decision to switch centers occurred, the process was really out of our hands. And it has taken us all these years to arrive at an awakening point, because it happened in a very unconscious manner.

If we can see the parallels between our lives and the life of the planet, we will be able to see how, in fact, the planet is only half-way along in its process. We'll be able to take heart by looking at where we can consciously go from here. We should heave a big sigh of relief as we realize that if the process had occurred in the opposite direction — first the positive and then the negative — then we would really have cause to worry! But as it stands now, we should see the beauty of what is happening and how we are evolving in the most extraordinary way.

Let's not panic. Let's be grateful for all those beings who were responsible for bringing us to the point of choice. Let's be grateful for all those beings who are now serving as the alarms for the planet. And let us — the ones who are awake — work hard to experience within ourselves the reality of the unity of the planet.

The more people who experience this unity, the closer we are to peace. And the only way to experience it is to work consciously in our own lives.

There is no gloom. There is no evil. There is just work to be done by all of us, wherever we are. Come with me to this extraordinary place of peace! Come experience ecstasy! Go within. Decide consciously how you will act. There are so many ways to act. Choose one. Bring your love — for external use only — and your fear — for internal use only. It is so simple.

How To Do By Not Doing
How To Give By Not Giving

I have nothing to give anyone. Neither does anyone have anything to give to me. I can only Be — that is all. My liver cannot give your liver anything. But each liver, functioning at top performance, becomes one of the many contributors to a body functioning at its finest. The liver is part of a whole. When my liver is not at its best, when it is negating what it is, my body is unhappy.

Earlier, I gave the example of a sock — the sock being the whole, the world, and each of us being a stitch in the sock. As each stitch turns what is now inside, out, it pulls the rest of the sock inside out. When all the stitches have come inside out, the whole sock is inside out. The stitch cannot give the sock anything, it can only turn itself. By the process of turning, the whole turns inside out. But who pulls the end of the sock inwards in the first place? "Miss Intuition" pulls the string.

So you see, there is no giver, no taker, just being. As much as each of us manifests his/her real being, together we will manifest the real world — an understanding, compassionate, loving world. As much as each of us does not do this, we will see a world which negates the reality of our being. But to manifest what we are, we must first become **conscious** of what we are. Only consciously can we turn ourselves inside out. Only when unconscious do we manifest what is not.

When I saw what place I occupied in the "sock," I became painfully aware that for me to be a stitch on the edge of the sock, some other stitch had to be down there occupying a space to give support to the whole. That changes when the whole sock turns itself inside out; but until then, the stitch on top is there only because other stitches are serving it, giving it (me) support by being on the opposite side of the sock — the opposite end of the energy.

When I became aware of this, I gave every penny I had to the being within my circle who had been serving me so faithfully in this way — unconsciously but nevertheless serving me. I could not quite explain at the time why I gave away all my money. But I knew that words could not express my feelings. Thought, Desire, Action: I became aware, I desired to pay back a terrible debt, and **I had to take action in a manner which the person who lives an unconscious life would understand.** Money would express to such a person my love and gratitude for serving me on earth. I give this example to show I am not talking mere theory. I am talking about how I live, how I have applied what I always knew, and succeeded with it. I can truly say I know of a happiness worth any sacrifice in the world — for even just one second of it.

The other day I saw the movie *Victor, Victoria*. The plot involves a beautiful woman who passes herself off as a man, and then pretends to be a female impersonator. We are these beautiful beings who, because we are scared, pretend to be something other than what we are! This is what many of us do in the world. So we see in the world two expressions: the ones who are **not** scared to show what they are — love, compassion, understanding, joy, and the ones who are too scared to show their true selves and so instead show us what they are not.

I am not saying each person always behaves in one way. I am saying we **can** choose to constantly manifest either side. And everyone who comes in contact with us is always manifesting one side or the other.

We must begin to recognize clearly when others are manifesting what they are not, then get closer to them and be our true selves. Not by "helping," but by being who we truly are, we can give the best example. All by themselves they will do the rest: they will see, reason and, after a while, their fear will melt. We will finally see their true selves come out. We must open our eyes and not be fooled by the expressions from fear.

How the Powerless Have Power
And the Powerful are Powerless

We scream at our leaders and ask them to do one thing or another. There is nothing that leaders want to do more than please people. That is why they take polls so often. But until now, they also have operated from their Fear Centers. Think of it. How would you like to have your job depend on the whims of people you don't even know?

These beings have grown, that is why they were placed in a position to make decisions for others. Now we want Peace, but we can't count on the leaders — the leaders will execute the wishes of the masses. It is unfair and unkind to ask these men who work very hard, to be the ones to turn themselves inside out first, to take a great risk by making a decision based on inner strength when we are not doing it ourselves. If each of us — the ones who have little to lose — turn ourselves inside out first, then we can turn to them, and by "US" being a solid block, help them turn themselves around.

They do want to do their best, but it is very scary. They become politicians because they wanted to help. But the Fear Center takes over, and the last thing they want after a while is to change anything, because it might mean they would be out of a job.

Because they can operate from fear and still serve all those thousands of people, they are showing us they have grown inside. But they are showing us what they are not. They will be able to show us who **they** really are when we, all together, show them who **we** really are. Let's not ask them to do what each of us can't do.

How willing are you to refuse to work for defense? Can you really make that decision? Are you willing to pay for the consequence of being out of work because you want peace? Can you refuse to cooperate in the manufacture, sale and transport of any war material? If enough of us do these things, then there will be no question of how Congress will vote. We say we want peace, but how willing are we to take stands in our personal lives which will demonstrate we mean what we say?

In August 1981, I left the U.S. with money in my pocket and a book to write. I came back with zero in my pocket. I said in August that I could not think of anything more important than working for peace; that was easily said since I had money in my pocket. Was I able to carry through my decision without the money? Was I able to stick to it even when everything looked scary? Yes.

Because I have done so, I have the authority to ask **you** that question. If I could not put forward an example from my own life — of anything I say — I would not be an authority. I would have no right to speak! So, let's be kind; let's not point our fingers outward in judgment of our politicians. Let's wake up to the fact that the power to establish world peace is in **our** hands. As each inhabitant of the planet realizes it, the leaders will follow. To be able to lead, one must know how to follow. To be able to follow, we must learn to lead. Riddles . . . riddles . . .

"But what can I do?" you may ask.

You can begin to do something as soon as you can overlook your fears. Use your mind, every minute, to look at what you feel. Look at it until you can bring a concerned, understanding, loving feeling to the situation before you. If you don't feel it, it is because you are not using your mind properly. Two plus two equals four. There is only one right answer: four. In facing any problem, unless you can bring a feeling of understanding, compassion and love, both for yourself and for the other party — regardless of what you think he/she has done to you — you are not coming up with the right answer. As you follow this path, you will attain an inner power such that you will **know** what you can do. It is not for me to tell you **what** to do, it is for you to find out. But I can tell you the guidelines I followed to go to the source and get the answers I was seeking.

Do you think I am any different from you? I am also one of the so-called little people. I am a high school drop-out who can hardly write, and yet I am doing it. What gives me this power? Where does this power, this drive to reach the world, come from? From the source of peace within myself. From the knowledge that as we each arrive there, we will see a world of peace. Each will know what to do.

But to get there, one must work consciously. To kill the self, one must follow certain laws. You don't have to "believe" for the law to work: you don't need to believe in electricity for it to work or for you to be able to use it. Electricity was there long before it was discovered and the more we use it, the more uses we find for it. So we must also learn to use the power within ourselves, discern the center from which we make decisions, and refuse to make any decision based on fear.

All of us, the inhabitants of this planet, are **free** and **equal.** We are free to choose between two paths — peace or total destruction — and we are all equally important in the effort to bring it about. It depends on each and every one of us. Wherever we are, in whatever position, we can work toward peace through personal inner renewal and by consciously bringing order to our own inner disorder. As we bring order inside, the outside will show it!

Are you aware of what you are asking the leaders of the world?

How easy is it for you to balance your cooking, cleaning, driving little John to sports, being the friend and the wife and finding time for yourself every day? How many people depend on you? How often are you scared to make a decision which may alienate the ones you love? . . . Never mind if you have a career?

Or you, sir, how easy is it for you to balance your job, your friendships, your home life? How often do you feel guilty because you feel you have not done your best — or enough? And how many people depend on you? Two, three, ten, a hundred?

How do you think the person feels who has to make decisions every day — lots of them — and pay for the consequences publicly? Wouldn't you be afraid? How would you like to have your mistakes, your stupid, unthinking remarks, blasted all over the newspapers? How do you think you would feel if your children were abducted by terrorists and your government would not lift a finger.

Wouldn't you feel frightened to the point of not wanting to move, in case you might make the wrong move? That is exactly what happens to our leaders. They are not supermen, they are just like you and me — a bit afraid, but trying to do the best they know how in their fear.

Let's understand them and alleviate their fears by proving to ourselves how strong we are within. For example, we could refuse to work in any job which contributes in any form to the military machine. We would quickly arrive at our destination — paradise!

Yes, we will be able to create a paradise here on earth. Why do we yearn for it? Why do we look for it in every Being, in every job? Why do we look so hard to fill a void in ourselves? Because once there was no void. And there is no need for it to be present now either. The void can be filled! We can be fulfilled, whole and complete. I know it because I have experienced it. We just have to stop pretending that we are what we are not! We are not these

343

scared, violent beings. We must learn to see and be what IS.

We can help our leaders now, and they will be able to help us later. The power is in our hands! Let's see this process and relax. Let's realize there is nothing to worry about, the whole organism is working like a clock. Relax doesn't mean don't **do** anything; it **means action based** on faith, on confidence, on **knowledge** that all is well and perfect. Fear is to be used inside ourselves — for **internal** use only.

What do I mean — use fear inside of ourselves? I said before we have two centers, one Love Center, one Fear Center. The results of the Love Center are understanding, compassion, and joy. The results of the Fear Center are judgment, frustration, anger, and violence. Here's an example in action:

You say, "I want to go to the movies." Your partner says, "I don't want to go with you" — for the first, second, third, fourth or hundredth time.

When fear is being used outwardly, you might say, "Why don't you want to come, are you tired? Are you drunk again? I know — you have work to do. Fine! Have it your way, but you'll come back to me and I'll not be there for you when you want me!"

You have expressed judgment, frustration and anger because you have not been able to get the person to do what you want. It has all been directed at the other person.

When love is being used outwardly, you say, "I would like you to come with me, but if not, I will go with someone else." You think, "I don't know exactly why he does not want to come with me, but I know it has nothing to do with me. It is too bad he does not feel free enough to be joyful. I feel like playing and he feels dragged out — poor man — he is worse off than I am. I may want to go out because I feel bad, but I am not so low that I need to hide in work or sleep. He'll feel differently when I come back — or next time."

What you perceive you need, does not have to come from one person; you can receive the same program from many different TV sets. You can receive love from everyone. It all comes through from the same place anyway!

When you return, you might say, "Oh — I had a great time. So and so and I enjoyed the movie; let me tell you about it." You have just brought understanding from yourself to the other person and come back with joy, having done your activity.

You killed your hate — "When he wants something from me, I'll refuse" — by thinking "Someone who is feeling that badly must feel terrible. Could I show him more love next time?"

You killed your frustration — "This always happens, over and over" — by thinking, "If it bothers **me** that he does not want to go anywhere, how terrible it must be for **him**."

You killed your fear — "He does not love me" — by thinking,

"What he does has nothing to do with me, or with him. He is operating from fear now: that is not him, he is not being himself."

You killed your judgment — "He is a workaholic" — by using understanding: "I am lucky that I do not have the problem."

You can use this same process over and over with everyone! If the result of your thinking is not love, compassion and understanding, you are adding the numbers wrong. You are not thinking right.

In the above example, you have brought understanding and joy to the situation and you went deeper into yourself. The more you grow in outer awareness, the greater your outer compassion and understanding for everyone, the deeper you carve into your subconscious. Finally, the door opens, and the two sides — inner and outer — meet. When they do, you speak in riddles, like yin and yang. You love like crazy. It is a madness everyone should feel — everyone!

Returning to the example, that person may turn you down a hundred times or a thousand times, but as long as he or she does not walk away from you, that person is allowing you to bring the best of yourself each time. Whenever the person says, "Yes, dear, I will go wherever you wish," that person is not giving you the opportunity to dig into yourself and bring forth the best of who you are — understanding, compassion and joy. How can you bring understanding out of yourself when someone is being understanding to you all the time!

So, in fact, the more anyone pampers you, the less that person is **really** giving you! The less the person is giving you, the more he is **really** giving you!

One day, that other person will be free enough to give because he or she is full from within and will want to go out and have fun. When everyone is full, we will all be able to give — not because we want something in return, but because we can't help but Be who we are. A full glass can't help but spill over. A leafy, tall tree gives shade, it can't help but give shade. Because it is what it is, there is shade where it stands. Because I love, I am giving love through my words, I can't help it.

The world could never understand why I love Allan. He looked like he was not doing anything for me. But I was just glad he allowed me to express my love for him! He let me place my love somewhere. I was able to buy for him, to think about him. I can not imagine a greater gift he could have given me. He allowed me to Be, to Be who I was — love — to love him, to love other people. For that, I loved, love, and will always love him. He understood who I was when few people could bring forth understanding of such a nature.

How does one fall out of love? I don't know. I know how to

grow in love to such an extent that one feels, "Because I was born the world will be a better place." Everyone is following this route. All of us. There is not a piece of garbage out of place!

We must use this same process to bring forth our best with our leaders. Let's not judge them, let's bring forth compassion for their situation, understanding for their task, and relief and gratitude that we don't have to be in their shoes. When our leaders vote without showing concern for **all** Human Beings of our planet, when diplomatic talks break down, let's remember that they are not being themselves. The puzzle will take shape in only 200 years. It is nothing! We will all live for a long time if we live like this! There is no need to die, you know. We are almost there. In the blink of an eye, we will consciously change the course of our lives and therefore the planet's.

II. To Specific Groups

To You . . .

Do you know to whom I am talking in this book?

I am talking to everyone in the world, but especially to you — the criminal, sitting in your cell, you who have killed how many — one, two, ten? You who rape women of all ages. Yes, I am talking especially to you.

The numbers of how many people you killed or raped are significant to me. They are the barometer of your pain. Yes . . . I know. How do I know? Because I, too, held a gun in my hand and fired it. I know the pain that drove me to do it. Just like you. But I was so terribly lucky, I had people around who did not judge me. They told me I was extraordinary, I was good — it did not matter what I did, they kept telling me how beautiful, kind and loving I was. Even the judges told me so. And I knew that to be true. I realized that when I behaved in any manner which did not show that truth, I was not being myself. You know what I discovered when I felt pain? That it did not belong to me. Yes, that is true!

I imagine you are sitting in your cell being quiet, actually quite peaceful, dreaming about that time you and your lady were laughing together . . . and the guard comes and snaps at you. You feel his words twist like a knife in you and all of a sudden you want to kill him. That pain you felt was not yours. It was the jailer's. He passed it on to you with his outer words. But you took it, you made it yours by believing that what he gave you belonged to you.

If someone gives you a pail of garbage, you don't need to keep it. Throw it back. Within your mind, learn to see that those harsh words, those violent actions belong to him, not to you. Those actions are telling about **his** pain; they have nothing to do with you. Only when someone gives you a bouquet of flowers, do you need to take it.

As you look within yourself, you'll begin to perceive how much pain surrounds you. Your eyes will open, not just to your pain; in fact, you'll begin to see that you experience no pain of your own. When you train yourself to see their pain, you will have transmuted your pain, your fear, into understanding.

People say, "I am a doctor," which of course they ARE not. That is what they **do**, not what they ARE. People never talk about what they ARE: loving, understanding. If someone dares to do so, others get very angry about it. When that happens, observe how much pain they must feel. They may even accuse **you** of being self-serving, but that is all right. It is better to begin to tell the world who you really are than to keep pretending to be who you are not!

To you — all of you — the ones who are being the symptoms, the ones who kill, rape and steal — please know that I am working as hard as I can. I know you are, too. The more of us who are working to be our true selves, the less time you will have to be doing the job of being the alarms. I am sorry for not producing enough "food" for all of you, so that you felt so hungry within, so frustrated that you felt the need to strike out to be heard.

To you, the terrorist . . . I know you want the best for the world. You want to do it your way, and no one pays attention, so you make your statement. They'll have to listen to you now. Yes, we are finally beginning to listen, your violence is waking us up. Each of us will understand what you are trying to tell us. We can be a bit dense sometimes, but just like you, we are doing the best we can. We all are — if we could only realize that and trust that it is so!

I am also talking to you, the one who is out of work. You, who gave 30 years of your life to a company and now feel cheated and abandoned: You have the power to bring world peace. Out of your pain, your fear of failure, you can turn the world around, just by turning yourself. And you thought you had nothing to contribute! Contribute yourself! By turning **yourself** inside out, you'll find peace within yourself. That, no one can take from you. Why bother to work for something that anyone can take away? You already know how that feels. Work for what is invisible; work for what you can control — your love, your Self. No one can take these from you, no one. And if you make them grow, as you can, you are the beneficiary.

When we, the ones who belong to the part of the body which has not manifested its illness, wake up and consciously begin to look at the whole body and take care of it — to realize the need for a wholistic approach — we'll begin to organize and to unite. Be patient with us. We'll be grateful to you for waking us up from a long sleep.

One only commits suicide when one sees no other exit. But we have begun to see, so we will not take the alternative of total destruction, don't worry. When we are all awake, you will not need to be that alarm. You will not feel that pain anymore. Be patient with us.

The energy of the world is turning. We see it in the growth movement, in the changing of emotions, in the concern for the land which is everywhere. So you see the powerless do have the power. We are the ones who have it in us to lead our leaders.

To you young people, to you who did not see the 60's and the yelling for Love and Peace: We have not deserted those values, we are still working on them and they are beginning to sprout. Have faith. Is it hard to find a job? You come from a broken home? You feel lonely and useless? The pain is growing and the drugs are there. On top of it all, when you try to lessen your pain, they judge you?

Now you know how it feels when others judge you. Don't judge them. You have the power to turn it around. Don't contribute to the vicious circle. You do have the power, it's just that you have not yet realized it. That is why this big mommy, the mommy of the world, is writing to all her children: to give you the only thing I developed during 40 years — my love for you all.

You see, you too are being of great help; but just as when we complain of our pains, instead of being grateful to them for telling us to go to the doctor, we are complaining about all of you. We do everything backwards because we operate from fear — but no longer!

When someone tells us we are "bad," we believe it. When someone says we are "good," we don't. When we talk about ourselves, instead of speaking the truth about how tender, how loving we are, we hide under a tough appearance, or an intellectual aloofness. By trying to appear superior and fool others, we end up short-changing ourselves. Trying to protect ourselves, we become prisoners of ourselves — our own jailers! Who can protect us from ourselves? We own only our love — and we have complete control over it. We can give it freely to everyone and grow by it, or we can hide it and diminish ourselves.

To you, assembly line worker: you who are a giant among giants! I know I could not do your work. It requires incredible creativity to be able to stay in one place hour after hour doing exactly the same thing without going crazy. It is certainly much easier for me to do "creative work," immerse myself in it, and feel good afterwards. But what you do takes a stamina I know I don't have! You did not realize the power you have? Wake up!

To you, my dear receptionists and secretaries, you who are the very foundations of companies, who hide what you do, because the world judges you to be worthless, who often deny what you do in order to have a serious conversation: I know your pain; but can you see why this happens to you? It is because the ones who put you down are in so much pain that they need to pull someone else down to feel themselves up! I told you we do everything backwards. We just have to raise ourselves up, and as we move up we will bring everyone with us. I know your pain, but smile and remember that they were not talking about you when they talked down to you. They were talking about how they felt about **themselves**, about their own insecurities. What they say has nothing to do with you!

To you, farmers of the world, you whom no one considers very much, you who feed us all: Without you, we could not live. If you did not produce food, the rest of us would have to! I know your love for your land, and I know your pain, a pain which does not come from hard labor or long hours, but from the way people look at you, judge you to be worthless. Yet, you keep giving us your wares. Thank you. Make your mind your greatest garden, where only good thoughts will grow. Pull the bad ones out, just like weeds. You have the power, take it! We need you. We need each other! We depend upon one another!

My dearest politicians, you know of my love for Roberto. You know I understand you; but can you think of the people who have no contacts, no education, no way of seeing a bigger picture? They may not be able to see the picture at a national level, but can you expand your vision to a global one? It is so easy to see the narrowness of others, to see what others cannot. But can we see **our own** narrowness? Within our own environment, can we stick out, take a stand, gamble on "naivete"? Can we bring the words "love and compassion" to our congresses, senates and assemblies?

I know the agony of trying to pass a bill — to weigh how much one must yield to get what one wants. I know how easy it is to get lost in the forest because of the trees, how easy it is to just follow along, without knowing one is losing one's soul — after so much work, such long hours, all the sacrifices of personal life! I know your pain, too.

I am saying that all of us together have an exit — just one — and we must take it. But, to create peace, our minds must expand enough to see the whole picture: to see that there is no "us" and "them," but just "us" — the inhabitants of this planet. We must come to terms with this and learn to think in a manner which creates a complete unit of **everyone** and **everything** on earth. This picture must incorporate everything from rocks to plants to the animals of which we are but one species. By this vision of unity, we can raise ourselves up so that we do not feel the need to put another species down to make ourselves feel better.

The Gathering:
Seeing the Invisible Cause

We are beginning to gather to proclaim: "We are the Peace-makers." Yes, we all are: even the Hitlers of the world, all of them are peacemakers, too. They are serving us most effectively by showing us the degree of imbalance. But instead of recognizing their useful labor, we are judging them. Let's use those symptoms and work within to bring about the change we want, knowing that as balance is established, the symptoms will go away. Let's make the symptoms an integral part of our work for Peace.

Everything we see in this world is the consequence of the invisible world. You and I exist only because our mothers and fathers felt something; out of that feeling, we Became. The cause of our very existence was "feeling" — an invisible.

If we consider the house we live in — someone had to think of it; then as a consequence of thinking, it was built. The chair you are sitting in to read this book had to be "thought" by someone; then, as a consequence, it was built.

If everything we see resulted from an invisible cause then the only way to bring about peace is to treat the invisible cause of the lack of peace. Cause, as we have seen, is always invisible. So only by consciously transferring energy from the negative into the place where it can be positive, will we be able to see peace in the world. In other words, we must begin to act instead of react. What are "acting" and "reacting"? Acting is but one thing — placing love outwardly. Reacting is placing fear outwardly.

When we act, just like a vacuum cleaner, we clean. We absorb dirt — negative energy — and inside of ourselves we convert the dirt into something useable. By reacting inside, by using the Fear Center inside, we can use our judgment to bring about understanding through reason.

If we do this at the invisible level — at the level of feelings for some people, at the level of energies for others, we will then see on the outside the change that took place on the inside.

But unless there is a metamorphosis from pain to understanding, we won't see a change on the outside. We must work at the level of consciousness, the only possible level at which to bring about peace. The invisible must first be at peace, then we will see peace on the outside.

But we can't shout "Peace!" and at the same time point the finger at another. That very process is divisive. Pointing does not bring integration. Until "we — the peacemakers" stop pointing fingers at "them — the war mongers," there will be more of them: more alarms to help us see how much work we need to do.

We need to consciously reverse our judgment, our fear. As long as we keep judging outwardly, instead of inwardly, we are

350

not creating Peace. In fact, we are responsible for creating more and more war. You can't throw dirty water somewhere and expect it will not affect all the waters. We know that if enough dirt is thrown, all the waters get dirty. This is like the outer manifestation of consciousness. Unless in our minds we can direct our thinking and feeling towards unification, towards seeing how the whole works and how we are one, we will not have peace. Peace is in our hands, but only inasmuch as each of us begins to recognize that by creating peace within ourselves and functioning in an integrated manner, we can affect the whole process.

We have this silly notion that you and I are separate beings. That you have your "private" life and I mine. Nothing could be further from the truth. We know how ecology works, yet somehow we feel we are not part of the same system. It's like saying my toes have a "private life" separate from my hands.

What we think determines the very basis of our world! What we see is the addition of all our thoughts. That is what consciousness is.

So if we want to see a different picture, we must recognize that each of us is responsible for the picture. We can form it by Being who we really are in whatever place we are. Working for peace does not mean, for instance, that you need not attend to your child. It means that you must transmute into understanding the frustration you sometimes feel when taking care of your child. Understand why you are feeling it, and what you have to learn through it. What opportunity is this tiny baby giving you? How is this Being serving you? As you "clean" your inner Being every minute, you are actively working for Peace in the world.

For example, when someone tells you something is ridiculously organized, you might reply by adding some understanding. With a little comment like, "Well, that job may not be easy," you counteract the negative energy out in the collective consciousness. For those who do not understand about consciousness, but know about feelings, you can come back with a good feeling when an unpleasant one is being presented.

We must begin to see that whatever comes to us is the best for us. You might say: "How can having a drunk person sit next to me be the best thing for me?" Let me tell you about Pilar, the lady in Spain. Her husband Manolo used to drink sometimes. She hated to see him drink. But each time he came back drunk, she would look at me and say: "This is not him, this is the alcohol speaking, pay no attention, Beatriz." Of course, with my training, I paid no attention, but she did not know I, too, was operating as she did. She was able to see, to observe and to remember who he truly was. She could act towards him according to who he was, not according to what he was doing. There is a difference between the "who" and the "what."

We must act according to who we are, and toward others according to who they are. We all are Love. But we often react according to what others **do**. When we see others doing something which negates who **they** are, we react by not being who **we** really are.

Often when we feel "bad" about someone, we walk away from that person. We make a change. Yes, we do need a change, but a change of feeling, not a physical change. We can change our feelings because each of us has a brain; if we use our brains properly, they can not only take us to the moon, but to far greater places than that: to ecstasy, to happiness, to a place beyond mind. Yes, by using our minds we will travel beyond mind, to spirit.

The feeling we have of needing distance is a real one. The distance we need is between our minds and our feelings. By putting distance between them, we can see clearly and change the feelings. We don't need to put distance between people.

Beginning and Change

Once we are whole, once we can operate for a long time with the centers in their proper places, we automatically begin to use the system properly at each instance.But at the beginning, of course, it is awkward.

When we begin to type, our fingers do not go to the right keys. It takes practice and hard work to make each finger move to the right place. But after we apply ourselves, we can actually do it automatically.

In the same way, each of us is accustomed to using his/her Fear Center outwardly. When we begin to use them inwardly, our life patterns change. First, when we start using the Center of Love outside, we begin to talk differently. We find ourselves saying nice things about people around us and about ourselves. When was the last time you publicly said, "You are a terrific person!" to your wife or husband or child or friend? When?

You see, we are not expected to say how marvelous our spouses are! — or how terrific people we have known for a long time are. You are supposed to say it just when you fall in love; then it seems as if "reality" sets in. The fact is, what you experience first is reality. Yes, that person you met **is** terrific. What you began to experience later was his or her fear. Don't give reality to that fear by saying how terrible so and so is because of such and such. Remember what you saw, said and thought when you first met. Recognize that the other behavior is just his or her Fear Center acting externally.

When Jose and I talked for the last time, he said to me, "I

352

thought I would drive you away by going with other women, by misbehaving with you. Yet, you stayed — even more loving than ever — why?"

"Because when you began to 'treat me wrong,' you showed me how scared you were. Therefore, I could not help but love you all the more," I replied.

He said, "You are right, I am scared."

I am not saying the road to this incredible inner happiness is easy. In fact, it is very painful. But it is a pain you consciously choose instead of waiting for life to throw pain at you. If I am to experience pain, I want to be able to choose that pain and to know its purpose. For 40 years, I believed that the purpose was to express who I was: I had a need, I followed it. I had no idea I was to arrive at a happiness and love that would encompass the world.

If you knew me, the last word you would use to describe Beatriz is "meek." Yet when Allan did not take care of me while I was pregnant, when he neglected me to such an extent that my friends had to come and take me to their house to bathe and feed me, I did not take my love away. When Jose "cheated" on me, I did not take my love away. When someone says to me with pity, "I would not want to be a secretary" — and I am one — I look at them and understand their insecurities and their pain. I love them all the more for it — that is being "meek."

At the same time, I proclaimed to the world how marvelous I was, how kind and loving, because I felt so. At the time, I did not know I was not the doer. Yet there was no superiority in my statement, because I could truly love everyone. They felt it because of my inner meekness. We do not necessarily wear meekness on the outside; it is something inside to which people respond by accepting — people who are very different from you, who would normally feel uncomfortable with you because according to the world they are supposed to be inferior. When those people accept you as equals, then you know you have really succeeded in loving. If you had felt superior to them, they would have felt it and not accepted you. So there are barometers to show us how we are doing in our conquest of self!

To begin that conquest, we must not respond with anger or hate — especially in our hearts — toward those who judge or hurt us. It becomes easy when you know why anyone is doing what he/she is doing. Each of us is operating out of fear when we are not being loving. How can you be angry when you see someone is afraid?

In the beginning I felt frustrated because sometimes it did not matter how much I tried to show how loving I was or how loving the other person was — my love was not strong enough to turn his/her centers around. Now I know that I can't do anything for anyone. They must do it for themselves. I can only Be the best I can be at the moment. That is all.

No Hope

The other day, I was speaking with a friend. He said, "You were always such an optimist. It's good you're writing to give hope to the world." I went home quite disturbed by this remark. I don't want to bring hope. This is not why I am writing: I am only showing what IS.

I Am a Human Being. I don't hope to be one — I am one. No optimism in the world can make me otherwise. I can't change the fact that I Am a Human Being. I can have an operation and look like a man. But that is changing the package, the outer — what is not. What is NOT can be changed, not what IS.

For example, I can take light and put it anyplace. Light is an IS. When I bring light to a dark room, the darkness changes to light, because darkness is an IS NOT. Light does not change to darkness; we can't take darkness into a room that has light and change it to darkness.

Just as light is an IS so is the energy of the world. I am not presenting this picture of us arriving at total peace out of being an optimist or being hopeful. I don't need to be an optimist anymore. Before I was an optimist — I would look at a glass and recognize only that it was half-full (not half-empty). Now there is no optimism: I see what is. Half the glass is full **because** half is empty. So it is with the world.

Because we have come half-way and are at the point where we can destroy ourselves completely, we have arrived at the possibility of total peace. Because we have come half-way without planning it, the next half **must** be planned. Because the first half was unconscious, the next half **must** be conscious. Let's recognize the conscious process already begun. It is not a matter of hope, optimism, faith or belief. There are laws of Love. If one follows them consciously, one arrives at peace within, War is an IS NOT; Peace is an IS.

Often we get caught up in the externals: we see the "evils." But just like the lighted room, so it is with the world: what we **are not** can't take over what we **are**.

We can also look at the microcosm of matter itself to get a clearer picture of how the whole functions.

There is a universal tendency of all matter to proceed toward a state of maximum randomness, unless compelled by a stronger counter-force to adhere to form. For example, if the cells of my body were not bonded together by connective tissue, I would be an amorphous blob of protoplasm on the floor. The blob itself, unless constricted by external, stronger forces, would rapidly disintegrate, flying apart into smaller, randomly-moving molecular units.

What we have experienced on the planet is precisely this action of proceeding toward a state of maximum randomness. Now this randomness begins to be compelled by a stronger counterforce to adhere to form, to adhere to its destination — peace.

Everything in the visible world tells one how the invisible works. Everything. As below, so above. As above, so below.

It is not a matter of hope that we will arrive at peace. It is a fact. But we must see the facts so that we can move with confidence and trust, not from fear.

Not My Will But Thine

I have had, as you have read, a varied and interesting life. But it has **not** been one in which I did just anything I wanted. You could say I was loving to any Human Being who came close to me, or anyone to whom I went close. But that is **not doing**, that is **Being**.

I began to work because my family needed help. I left the country (as you read in the letters), because my family needed that. I helped Allan study, because he felt he needed it. Clearly, the letters express that I thought he did not need to study. But once he decided that is what he wanted, I pushed to get it done. I purposely became the "legs" of everyone. I was not the legs because I could not be the "head." I knew very well I had a good head on my shoulders. I consciously chose to be the legs. In fact, everyone kept pushing me to "do my own thing." "You are riding on someone else's trip," they told me.

Freedom is the knowledge that you can walk on this path or that one — and choosing one. For example, I was married for 16 years. I never lived in an environment I liked. As soon as I got a divorce, I immediately changed my environment to suit my taste. The fact that I changed it, shows I clearly knew what I liked and could manifest it. The fact that I did it immediately, shows how truly important it was to me. On the other hand, my husband did not like his living environment either; but when alone, he did not create a different environment. In fact, his house now looks and feels like our house used to look and feel. Although he did not like it, he could not bring about a change. Or if he could, he decided it was not important for him. Since he was unhappy with it before and did not change it, he was not free. Freedom is choice. He did not like what he had, but he did not know **what** he liked.

On the other hand, I consciously knew I could change my environment and how I could do it. I even had the money for it, but I kept a tight rein on my desires. It did not matter how trivial the subject, I was training my self to do everyone else's will. Through the training to do everyone's will, I came to know "his" will — that of my higher self.

For a seed to be planted, the soil must be prepared. To learn to multiply, we must first learn the numbers. If we are to align with

Divine Will, we must train consciously to do others' wills. To do that when you could clearly do your own thing is hard. Yet, the rewards I have harvested warrant 1000 times more of relinquishing all my personal wishes. I can't say enough times that I present these examples because I live them; but I know that "I" am not the doer.

If we want to hear the words of our higher selves, we must prepare for it. We must show — in our thoughts, feelings and actions — that we are willing to ignore what we personally want. Not to do what you want because you are not able, is very easy. What counts is not doing when you could — or doing when you think you can't.

This brings us back to peace, of course. If we feel we can't fight because we don't have the equipment, our not fighting is of little value. But when we do have the equipment to fight and know how to use it, but consciously refuse to do so, regardless of the consequences, **that** is strength. That is choice. Then a nation with military strength can say, "I know I can drop an atomic bomb, but my actions will instead be based on moral strength, not material strength. Therefore I proclaim to the world that it does not matter what happens, it does not matter who invades, it does not matter what the provocation. I will not respond in kind."

By following this road, your will and the higher self's will become one. And finally you hear what your inner being, your higher self wants you to do. At this point, the two merge: what your higher self wants and what you want are one and the same. So all your energies are finally pouring out in a single purpose.

I talk about "his" and "higher self" out of convenience. I do believe in God. But of course this is irrelevant. You may say, "I do not, I am an agnostic." Personally, I find the word "God" divisive. And I can let go of anything which gets in the way of integration, of unity, of creating a unit out of all the pieces. "God" is just a word. I do not need to believe in "electricity" for it to work; I do not need to believe in "gravity" to see its effects.

In the same way, if we begin to put distance between our minds and our feelings, so that through logic and reason we can change what we feel, over and over, there is no way we can but see results of extraordinary magnitude.

One Human Being, Gandhi, brought the seed of non-violence right after the creation of atomic power. Now that seed is beginning to sprout. I am not saying he was the first. I am saying he came to remind us of how to behave in this 20th century. We can consciously work with this seed to bring it to full fruition and collect the inevitable harvest — Peace. Peace out of our inner love given from one to another; authentic, freely-chosen, consciously-decided, hard-labored by all of us, for all of us: Peace.

Keeping an Eye on the Eternal

How do we begin to make the changes inside ourselves that will bring us to peace? Let me give you an example from my life:

Dear Beatriz:

I love you. Very much. To the stars and all the worlds beyond, as well as right here on this earth. I feel the pain that you suffered because you were with me and loved me and stood by me when I truly needed you. And I feel the love that led you to do it. Even in my blackest more fearful moments, when I did not like you, or felt you wanted out, I knew you loved me. In my heart of hearts I knew. My sorrow is that I did not show my love for you. It was always qualified, reduced, rarely full and free . . .

This letter shows how much he felt my love. I did not need to spend time with him. We did not need to do things together. We did not need to be a couple. None of it was necessary for him to feel my love. What was necessary was that I kept my eyes fixed on the eternal — with my heart, with my mind, every day.

By keeping my eyes on the eternal, I grew in the eternal. By keeping my eyes on love, I grew in love. By growing in love, we'll conquer death. Conquering death does not mean we won't die; it means we become immortal — like Shakespeare, Dante or Blake. You may say, "We are not all Shakespeare, we can't all produce work like that." But that's looking at it backwards. If you do not look at the eternal, you can not Be eternal. Because we don't think in terms of eternity, we don't grow to be part of it. Because they did, they grew in love and conquered death. We love them — they are not dead. As long as we keep them in our hearts, they have not died.

This is the first step in conquering death. The second one is to reach the place where one does not need to physically age and die. Not all of us can arrive there in one lifetime. But we must know that it can be done. In fact, that is the end of the line.

The process begins with little things. If I pay attention to my ego, "I" want two hours with Allan. When my ego does not get what it wants, "I" withdraw. Then love, the eternal, cannot grow. But if we can keep our eyes on the eternal and keep our love faithful, it will grow; then our egos and their desires gradually become less important.

To be faithful in love does not mean that you never go to bed with someone else. If you take love away, if you say, "I am not available for you," then you are being unfaithful. "Faithful" means unquestionable: you put your love out as a lover, as a friend, as a mother — in whatever role you are called upon as a human being.

If we keep our eyes on love, if we keep our energies concentrated on making sure our love is "faithful" and consistently available, then we are acting for eternity. We will grow for eternity. You don't allow your ego to say to you, "Well, I know she thinks I am full of hogwash — who wants to have a friend like that!" or "I know he thinks anyone who believes in reincarnation is ignorant. Why should I give my love to someone who thinks that?" You don't question. You ignore the voices of the ego, which are many. You keep your love firmly out, faithfully out, for anyone who wants it.

I can assure you, you will experience that for which you are longing — happiness. After years your pain will disappear. Any action contrary to this will continue the roller coaster of pain and pleasure, of elation and disappointment. How do I know? Because I have lived consciously in this way and finally harvested the fruits of it.

Usually we look at another person and ask, "Does he love me? Is he showing **me** love? Is he giving **me** what I want?" But the work necessary for love to grow is our own inner work. Are we allowing love to flow out, regardless of the circumstances presented to us by life? Can we remain loving when those circumstances change?

When I met Jose, he seemed to be rich, healthy and together. I knew that he was not completely balanced, but I did not expect that he would end up broke, in a hospital, with a diagnosis of chronic alcoholism. Some people said to me, "Do you want to do the same thing all over again?" Others said, "You don't want that situation; you can do better than that." I wondered how anyone could do better than having the possibility of loving someone — anyone. To ask, "Do you want that?" would be unfaithful to the laws of love. If he had allowed me to love him, I would have taken care of him and worked as a maid if necessary.

The decision of **whom** to love was never mine. I always knew I was the one looking for a place to park my love. The decision of **where** to park it belonged to the other person. For me it felt like what people go through when they look for a job. They know what they can do. They apply, but the decision of where they end up working is in the hands of the employer. Of course you apply to a company and for a job for which you know you are qualified. In the same way, if you do not apply — if you are not open to love — you will not get "hired." That is why I went from Allan to Jose. Jose needed a great deal more from me than Allan ever did. I also knew by then that I had grown a great deal more, I had a lot more to give.

You must remember, however, that this was when I still saw the world divided between the needy and the giving. I was not aware that my need was to give. I felt only that I could not help myself, I **had** to give. Since I needed to give, after a while I felt dry; then I had to fill up again and give some more. It was futile —

a yo-yo. Now my needs are gone — all satisfied.

At the time, the need to give was like prayer for me. I knelt down — by finding someone who was not, so to speak, finished, established or balanced — and raised my arms up towards the sky, keeping my eyes on eternity. By this process, I activated the eternal patterns instead of the mortal ones.

At no time in my life have I failed, because I was always growing. And I accomplished my mission: to find out who I am, what I am and why I am. We can all arrive at happiness, joy and peace if we follow the laws of love.

"The Kingdom is Within"

What this meant to me is to look at the world and view it in its depth. I have looked at its "within" and by this process lived in a "within" world.

When I went to see the movie *Victor, Victoria*, I did not see a movie about a woman out of work who, out of desperation, became a man, then pretended to be a woman. That point of view had no universality whatsoever for me. What I saw was how we all pretend to be someone we are not. We pretend to be Human when in fact we are Divine. We pretend to be mortals when we can be immortals — as a few Beings have shown us.

To live within does not mean to just sit and go inside ourselves. It means to look in depth, to see the innermost part of every action, every person, every instance. For instance, when I met a salesman who was attentive and helpful, I was happy, not because he was helpful to me, but because I could see he was expressing who he is through his job. He was allowing his real self to flow out. But when I met a salesman who was in a rush, and looked at his watch, who was impatient and couldn't wait until it was time to go home, then I felt uneasy. That is not because he was treating me badly, but because he was treating himself badly. He had not found a way to express who he is through every action. He had not gone within. If he had, he would have all his attention and energy focused on one point. He would be 100% there.

In 1975 I had a spiritual reading done by Marshal L----. He gave me a diet which I followed (as I explained in the chapter "God of Food"). But while I follow it, I watch carefully whether the diet will become a way of life within me — whether I can go back to my previous diet. Because I still like to eat as before, I am still following the diet. But the minute I find myself unable to eat as before, the second I find myself thinking, "I smell a steak — how horrible, I can't ever eat that again," I will let go of the diet and eat meat. It would feel to me as if the diet owned me. One must keep one's eye on the within. The diet must be a framework through which I can progress. If it becomes a habit, it no longer provides exercise. I would be living on "automatic."

I have tried to keep my outside life, active, alive and unscheduled; in fact, it even looks undisciplined. But on the inside, I keep steady, unmoving and disciplined. By unmoving I mean I do not open my heart and close it. I do not say, "I love this person but not that one." Or "I love you today because you gave me what I wanted, but I will remove my love from you if you are not good to me." I do not move within.

On one level I have done outwardly strange things, like going to talk with professors, negotiating raises for my husband, and giving my money away. This behavior looks very unorthodox and unpredictable, yet there was consistency. Everyone knew he/she could come talk with me and invariably feel better. I invariably would feel depleted, because "I" — my ego — was trying to give. I was not connected with the whole, with the Higher Self. Therefore I was getting outside of myself, and in the process of giving my energy, was losing it. I did not understand that I had to remain within, that all I needed was to Be.

There is a "going within" in the outer and a "going within" in the inner. On one level, the outside and the inside are one. So by going within in the outer and in the inner, I live in the inner all the time. It may sound confusing. Look at an example in the physical world: the air is outside of us, yet inside of us as well. We can see how this functions in interaction. The outer is an inner, the inner is an outer. And both are separate and yet interdependent. So the kingdom is within — within me and you. For me to live in the kingdom, I have to be within and only see your within.

That is the first step. The second is experiencing how the outer resulted from the inner. As one experiences this, one can see the whole.

Specialists

We all understand that there are specialists. If we need to build a house, we would find someone who knows how to build houses. When we get together to agree on the Ideal and Purpose of the planet, we will need specialists also. We will need people who understand how to look at a situation and see the cause. These people have what the world calls "insight" — the word itself means to "see inside," to see the invisible.

When a girl sings, we can all see her happiness. When a boy cries, we can easily see his unhappiness. These are clear cases when we all can see the inner through the outer.

But it is not so easy to see the cause in the dealings between nations. Only those who have spent a long time looking at cause in their own lives — and have counteracted those causes — will be able to see clearly what the world calls "problems." For one thing, these people have practice; for another, they function as "outsiders." They have arrived at a personal level of detachment, so they can see everything with a perspective that most people don't have.

Perspective is terribly important. If we enter a concert hall to listen to music, we know we need to sit back a bit. If we want to look at a picture, we know we need to stand back a bit. Everything in the outer tells us of the need to put distance between oneself and what one wants to hear, see or feel.

So if we want to solve the "problems" of the world — which we have established are spiritual — we need people who have put distance between themselves and the world. We will need specialists of the spirit world. Until all of us get there, the specialists can give us "insight" into the problems. This will be a temporary situation for maybe 100 years or so.

Every Human Being on earth must arrive at this knowledge. Everyone must learn to use his/her mind, to change his personal, troubled feelings into calm, compassionate ones of love. But until this happens to **everyone**, we will need to call on the specialists. In our personal lives, we often do go to them. Most people go to someone for help in seeing things more clearly. And usually this person is one to whom many others go for the same reason.

Internationally, we should begin to seek out those people who by their very lives have shown these qualities; we should make them part of the process of peace. These people have no vested interests except their love for the planet.

Here comes Beatriz again with her riddles: "Because I am no longer of this world, I am thoroughly involved with it. Because I see no problems, I can solve problems. Because I am nothing, I can do something. Because I am not the doer, I have the courage and power to do."

What makes a person a specialist? A specialist **breaks the barrier of time** by virtue of his or her knowledge. For example, a gardener can look at a seed now, in the present, and by virtue of special knowledge, tell where it came from — the past. He can also tell us what it will become, if we plant the seed — the future.

If one goes to a doctor, he looks at one's condition — the present — and says, "Did you feel so and so? Do you experience any pain here?" He also goes back to the past to be able to tell the future: if the situation is not corrected, it will develop one way; if it is treated, it will look another way in the future. The fuller the picture he views, the more multidimensional, the greater the possibility of helping you. He may look at your body, but he needs to ask about your work and your homelife. He sees the interconnections, but he begins on the physical level.

These are people who by their special knowledge can see the present, and use it to go forward or backward in time. The gardener decides how the garden will look; the garden does not just happen. The doctor, by looking at today's condition, has a hand in shaping the future. The better the specialist, the greater the ability of that person to produce satisfactory results.

Spiritual specialists work the same way. They can see events long before they happen, simply because they see the seeds of those events. When a gardener plants a rose bush, it is not "hocus-pocus" if he says that in six months we will see a rose. Likewise, when a person looks at a situation and understands the inner laws, that person also can say what each decision will bring about.

In a minor way, we all have a bit of that ability. If **any** of us sees a youngster beginning to slip in school, becoming irresponsible, he/she can see where this behavior will lead if it does not change. The spiritual specialist looks at the outside as a reflection of the inside. Since the seed of the future is now, since he understands what he is looking for, he has control over his life. Life does not just happen to him. He plans life by choosing what seeds he is going to plant.

In my own life, as a child and young person, everyone told me, "Wait, you don't know anything, life will show you that what you want to do is impossible." Later they said, "Wait, once you have children, you will change your mind," or "Wait, you have no idea what it is like to be married." When I got married I clearly stated what I would accomplish with my husband Allan and how I would have to let go of him once the job was done. They all laughed at me; but 17 years later, it happened as I had said it would.

I did wait, and everything I ever said I would do, I did. Life did not throw curves at me. I consciously chose pain. I knew what I wanted to accomplish and did it. At some level, everyone does this. For example, when most people register for college, they decide what they want to learn and register for the courses which will teach them that. One cannot take a course here, a course there and then look back after four years say, "I guess I will be graduating as a lawyer."

There is no room for hindsight when one wishes to control something. In order to accomplish, one must decide: "I will open a restaurant"; "I will be a pianist"; "This is the subject of my book." Everyone understands this process perfectly well. It is not different when our "Being" is in control, except that the "Being" decides — not the emotions, the body or the mind.

The specialist would look at the "problem child" and realize that the child is operating from his Fear Center. He is beginning to show frustration with his work, anger toward his peers, hate toward society — ultimately he'll explode into violence. The initial actions may be minor ones, like throwing rocks at cars. At the group level, we can see the incredible fear which moves 300 individuals to sign a budget for the purchase of arms. This is a clear way of saying: "I am afraid. Someone will attack. I need to defend myself." Clearly this action comes from the Fear Center.

Even if everyone possessed guns, a person operating from the Love Center would not arm himself. One could allow others to kill or hurt, but one would not react. The action would be one of non-action, it would be a statement of inner strength: "I will not be made afraid. I will remain calm, even if you hate me." This has been my action for 40 years, including for 17 years with Allan, until his fear was gone. We have seen the case of Gandhi; this is not a theory, it works!

In the example of the child, the specialist would begin by talking with the child, but not about the fact that he was late to school for one week and should make an effort to be on time. That would be talking about "consequences." The specialist would begin by saying how "frustrated," how "hurt" he (the specialist) remembered he felt when he went to school. The youngster immediately would recognize someone who understands his own feelings — the cause of his behavior.

By looking at the consequences — the grades slipping, the tardiness — the specialist clearly sees the one cause — pain — being manifested at different levels of development. From this point, the specialist takes action. There is only one action: give love to dissolve the fear — not for one day, one month or one year, but for as long as it takes, maybe a lifetime!

The specialist will not pull his love away, no matter what the child does. The specialist **acts**, he will **not react** once he decides on an action. The specialist will only withdraw love when the other person says, "I want to do it on my own," or when the specialist sees the person is operating from his own Love Center. That would mean the person can now make his decisions based on trust, confidence and knowledge. Such a person would be incapable of signing a budget which would be a statement of fear. He or she could never decide, "I can't vote this way, I would lose too many votes," or, "If I take a stand on this subject, I would lose my seat in the Senate." These are decisions based on fear. Notice how we constantly make decisions like this: we are afraid to lose our jobs, lose a friend, lose the people we love, and so forth.

I give examples of politicians because I know this group of people. I respect and love them. Normally, people make decisions based on fear, but the consequences of their actions are paid for by a few. Politicians, on the other hand, have grown inside enough to be put in positions where others are pulled to them and where their actions can affect many others. They are like trees big enough to give shade: it is very easy to lose sight of the forest. The greater the responsibility, the greater the difficulty.

If they really chose to operate out of strength and not consider what they could lose or gain, they could bring about incredible changes. I know they could. Their work is hard, but before the end of this century they will want to see and be part of the change to redirect this planet. We each must act — every one of us!

For a few years, I also turned away from my Being. I believed I had limits. I bought the idea that I could not do something I wanted. At the time, a friend said to me, "Well, it's time you realized that you do have limits." I love her — she was there to tempt me as no other Being could. She is strong and reasonable; it could have been very easy to have fallen for this or other illusions. I am glad she gave me the opportunity to turn away from that illusion within myself. Otherwise, I would not be here writing to the world, loving this extraordinary world and making the world see that right now we do have the seed of an extraordinary future.

I have already seen this future, because I am that type of specialist. It is not that I can see visions, but I was always able to see and direct my own life. I know we can direct this planet to the place we all want it to go.

Here is the history of the seed:

By 1940 we had discovered the atomic bomb. This is the date of our Success, the arrival at the Perfect Negative — the achievement of the capability of Total Destruction. Since then wholly different Human Beings have been born. We can see that by what they did when they were teen-agers. By 1960, the seed had sprouted. In the sixties — for the first time in the history of the world — the youth roamed the world, proclaiming, "Love and Peace! No more with the old!" But at 18 we were not able to implement our desires. Now, we are coming of age. We have not deserted our ideals. The world is not governed by us yet, but we are getting ready. We are coming. We are not just saying "Love and Peace." Lots of us are showing the way. There is an exit from Total Destruction, but only one: Love. And we will take it, because it IS the solution, because it IS practical, because there IS no other exit. There IS but One Way. From 1980 on the planet will continue to grow toward its destination — Peace!

Things do not need to happen to us, we can make them happen consciously. We can plan and bring them about. But we need to understand that things can only be directed at an inner level, at a thought level. If something is dirty, putting perfume over it does not make it clean. The only way to steer a car is by using the steering wheel. We can't steer the car by its motor, body or brakes. Only the driver has the power to make it go where he wants, and only by using the steering wheel.

Likewise, only the Being in each of us has the power to direct. We must train that Being to take control. The director of ourselves is not our minds or bodies, and certainly not our feelings. But taking control will mean to choose pain consciously. A dancer chooses hard, long, exhausting hours of training to discipline his body so that it will be free to express what he wishes. In the same way, by training our Beings through discipline, we too arrive at the freedom to express who we are through everything we do. And each and every one of us on this dear planet is but one thing — Love/Light.

Because we are Light, we can also manifest absence of Light. But that doesn't mean we are darkness. Darkness does not exist. Darkness is an "IS NOT," the negative side of an "IS" — light. There is only one thing, not two. There are no light and darkness — just light and its absence. When we observe lack of light, we are operating from the Fear Center. When we observe light, we are operating from the Love Center.

Looking Ahead

Specialists see the whole picture — past, present and future. If you don't, your judgment will be way off. For example, if one looks at a picture of a two-year-old with a blanket in one hand, sucking her finger, and forgets that this is only one link in a long chain, one might say, "How terrible, is this the best a Human Being can do?"

This would, of course, be unfair: the observer has not taken into account the whole life span. Yet this is precisely what we do with our dear planet. We look at it and say, "With all our intellect, is this the best we can come up with? Nuclear power?"

Humanity began by expressing fear from the very beginning. Fear is an energy that goes out. After we fear for a while, we begin to experience frustration; after the frustration we begin to be angry; after the anger, we are filled with hate, and hate explodes into violence. We can see how the world has gradually followed this line. Fear, taken to its ultimate manifestation of violence — nuclear weapons — has the ability not only to destroy ourselves, but the planet.

Gradually the collective Fear Center has gone outward, developing to its ultimate possibility. This is precisely what we — humanity — are not. But the planet is only half-way along. We began from the center, then we manifested that side of the energy — the natural course. The energy must manifest itself completely, not partially. Can you imagine if we would have begun at the Love Center? We would now have a world of peace, but ultimately we would have to manifest the other side. That would have been something to worry about!

As things now stand, we have collectively manifested fear from the very beginning of time until now. We have arrived at this point in time not by planning, certainly not consciously. No one sat down to decide we were going to have a polluted planet,

365

filled with nuclear waste, dirty waters and so forth. It happened by the process of our living unconsciously, which is precisely how we should operate when we come from the Fear Center.

Now that humanity has traveled to the limits of this side of the energy, we can embark on the manifestation of the other side. Precisely because we have created unconsciously the perfect negative, we'll be able to produce a perfect, conscious, positive picture. This next process will be the opposite of what we have shown so far; it is the expression of love. This side of the process is very conscious, positive and inner.

We know how long it has taken us to come to this point. It will take at least 200 years to see the complete manifestation of the other side. The stages that the Love Center goes through are: understanding, compassion, love and joy. When we get there, we'll know we are there by choice. We will know all about fear, frustration, anger, hate and violence, but consciously and positively we will have chosen to manifest the whole. We will not remain at the half-way mark.

Now can you see how wonderful it is that we are half-way, that we began from the Fear Center? And can you see how these times will be the most exhilarating for all of us? We will be able to bring about the conscious, positive manifestation of the energy on this planet.

Why are you worried then? Why are you sad about all the violence? It is there to tell us something. It is there to direct us, to help us see. Only through the visible can we understand what happens at the real level, the invisible.

Let's look at these "consequences," these symptoms. Let's see them for what they are and be grateful to those beings who make us aware of the need to bring about the balance necessary. If we look at them and make them part of us, part of the whole, then we have an "us" working for peace. We must know that "they" — the symptoms — will go away if we keep on the job. "They" are an integral part of "us."

The inhabitants of this planet who will work consciously and positively, both individually and collectively, to kill our egos — our personal and national selves — will merge as Us — the Unit: Planet Earth.

Let's begin! I can't wait. But what am I saying! It has already begun. At one level there is really very little to do because the direction from which we have come and to which we are going is out of our hands. We give birth to a child (which itself is a miracle); but the process of growth of that child is out of our hands. The different stages that this person will have to go through do not depend on the parents. We can't decide that he should first go through old age, since it is "golden" and last the teen years, since they are the hardest. The process itself is out of our hands. It is as if we are in a predetermined pattern within which we can maneuver. But who is the real "doer"?

We have all experienced having a problem. We think about it for hours with no resolution. Then, while taking a shower or doing something totally unrelated, the answer comes. It has come through our intuition.

Then we go to work and bring the solution. Everyone applauds. "Mr. Smith has done so and so. Bravo!" It becomes known as "Mr. Smith's solution." If Mr. Smith were honest, he would give credit where credit is due — to intuition. Then everyone at the office would be grateful to the real source of the solution, intuition. In this way, we have filled our heads with the names of those to whom Miss Intuition has given information. She is the "doer." She gives us the new ideas and shows the direction towards which we go. Since we have egos, we like to say we think of things ourselves. But the ideas — big or small — are not ours. Intuition gives them to us. We do so enjoy taking credit for what we do, especially if it is a "good" idea. It would clear a lot of room in our minds if we forgot the middle man and remembered the idea — never mind who said it. There is but one source: Miss Intuition.

Top Secret!

In the 16th century, England, France and Portugal kept maps of wind routes top secret. We think this to be silly today. The fact is they kept the information secret because they were afraid that other nations would use it to outmaneuver them in trade or war. Fear made them keep the information secret.

Things have not changed so much. Today, the subject of top secret information is different; the reason is not. It is still fear. It is so very convenient to decide that the other party has the power! If we realize power is in our hands, we may have to **do** something. And the "something" may be the willingness to suffer. The something may be the willingness to die, not for war, but for peace, as so many Indians did in India at the time of Gandhi — not to die out of weakness, as was the case in Germany — there was no choice there — but to die by choice, as was the case in India.

Gandhi showed that the willingness to die for peace, on the part of an unarmed, poor nation, was stronger than the willingness to die for war of an armed, rich nation. Strength does not depend on the other side: "**I will** stop arming, **even if** you don't." "**I will** love you, **even if** you can't yet express your love." Do you want to be strong? That is the formula. Love conquers fear.

Weakness depends on the other side: "**If they** stop arming, **then I will** stop arming." "**If you** give to me, **then I will** give to you." Do you want to be weak? That is the formula: Fear conquers love.

The behavior of a person and the behavior of a nation are comparable. As a person acts, a nation acts. As a person, you can choose to act on either side: fear or love, weakness or strength. As a nation, we face the same choices. Until now we have acted out of fear. Because we fear, we keep secrets. When the reverse comes about, we love and we keep no secrets. There is no "us" and "them," only "us."

When we love, and someone attacks, we can show our love even more by our willingness to die for peace, by not striking back. To fight you need two. It's impossible to have a war in which only one side shows up, and the other calmly sits and does not cooperate. We will send help, not arms. We will send food for the nation which does not fight. We will take sides, yes. We will give support to the one which refuses to fight. We will not sell arms to the aggressor. Can we really be that strong?

Stop Reading

I want you to read this so you will stop reading. Because I don't believe we should read, I am writing for you to read.

Today I was talking to a friend, a Ph.D. psychologist from Harvard. She comes to me for clarity and comfort and brings various books for me to read. I want her to go to the source of knowledge so that she would not have to come to me for comfort. I said to her, "I don't read," which does **not** mean, "I don't know." The world and I are going in opposite directions.

I feel we are all sitting at a table with a beautiful tray full of many types of food in the middle. If you ask, you get the food. Some of us just ask and are served. The rest are waiting patiently while we eat, chew, digest the food and spit it out. That is what a book is — something already eaten and digested. We can get that same knowledge directly. There is no way I like to eat chewed-up food. I never have. But that is what the world wants me to do.

How can I lead the world to eat the "food" first-hand? Yet here I am writing, which is the "spitting-up." I hope this book will lead the world to go and eat the food first hand. I want you to read, so you'll stop! Only then would we all agree on any subject. It is easy for all of us to agree that we see an elephant if we all see the whole elephant. But it is impossible to agree when one sees only the trunk, another only the tail. Neither person is wrong, but neither can recognize what the other sees because he has never experienced it.

When we are frozen in space and time, we can't agree on a common picture. As we acquire freedom within, we can see the whole picture and know whether we are being true to our real selves when we speak. We can see whether we are acting from our Love Center or from our Fear Center.

As I have said, the route to Peace is within and the killing of the self is indispensable to bringing about peace in the world. But going within — meditation — does not mean just sitting alone in silence. When Rubinstein plays the piano, he is lost in it, all his energy is focused — that is meditation. When Pilar — the lady I met in Spain — washed her clothes, she scrubbed them carefully, looked at every single spot of dirt and observed with great pride as the clothes were hung on the line. All of her was involved — that was meditation.

When I sit and talk with a friend and am 100% there, not one stray thought crosses my mind. I am meditating, I am praying. The training of our energy is to stay focused 24 hours a day. That is meditation. As we train in this manner, we grow in power, inner power.

Conscious Thinking: I

We want peace, but how do we obtain it? When a craftsperson wants to build a chair, he first has to think of it, then desire to build it and finally actually construct it. We must follow the same procedure to create peace: thought, desire, action. But the thought, desire and action must come from the Love Center. If we think, desire and act because we are afraid of nuclear power, afraid of what will happen to the world, we can never achieve peace. An action based on the Fear Center can only manifest as frustrating, angry, hateful and violent.

We have all experienced trying to do a job when we felt very nervous or scared. A job done under these conditions never comes out right. Once we are sure we are acting from Love Center, **then** we can be sure that the actions which follow will demonstrate understanding, compassion, love and joy. We want peace because we understand how the planet works, because we understand we had to travel the road that brought us here. Now we begin to recognize the direction in which we should consciously move the planet. We want to be part of the process which, until now, was unconscious.

We know our destination, because we know we have a choice. We want to take the path of peace, knowing we can do it, knowing that because we were able to unconsciously travel the path of fear, we can now consciously travel the path of peace. We will travel with confidence, with knowledge, with our heads up, because we will finally demonstrate to ourselves who we really ARE: loving Human Beings, living on this tiny planet, conscious of how the success of peace depends on each and every one of us, knowing how each of us, each "stitch," is terribly and equally important.

Once we know we are acting from Love Center, from inner strength, **then** we must determine what type of world we want. Yet the action of each person will vary. Suppose 100 persons get together and all decide to go into the restaurant business. Once they all agree they will open restaurants, they can all go their merry ways and each work to bring about a restaurant. Each will be different, but all will be restaurants.

In the same way, we must agree on the purpose of the planet. We will then go about doing it in our own ways. Each country need not conform in any way, shape or form to another in order to work together. In our bodies, each organ does quite well being different, yet cooperation brings about a good result. We do not need to try to change each other — out of fear that unless we are all alike, we can't work together, or that unless the same political system exists all over, we can't trust each other. Imagine the brain talking to the liver, "Unless you function like me, forget it. I will not work with you." Funny? That is exactly what we do with each other.

So what we want to do is direct our thoughts to bring about a world of peace based on our love for the planet and confidence that the whole process is working well for the benefit of the whole body. I did not say for the benefit of one nation, race or creed, but for the benefit, the preservation, of Humanity.

We will survive. We are not the doers. We do not have the power to destroy what we have not created. We are but children. But children do grow up, and as we all know, the process is painful. The world is also now going through a painful growing process, yet an exciting one — one which will lead us to the most fantastic place man has ever seen: peace for all. Not because anyone legislates it, not because there is an army making sure people do not fight, but peace arising out of the true feeling of each and every one of us. We will recognize our own real selves, and through our understanding recognize those of our fellow Humans. Such feelings must be felt out of inner action, the action of consciously changing one feeling: fear, into another: love.

I feel so terribly inadequate to present the picture that I saw beyond mind. Words seem so sterile, yet I seem to use them now all the more.

I said before that the world and I are always going in opposite directions. When the world was peacefully oblivious of nuclear power — in the 50's — I felt I should be doing something to help the world. Yet I waited to see clearly what I was to do. Now, when the world is beginning to mobilize to do something about nuclear power, I know we will survive and I know what I have to do. I just need to show the picture shown to me: "All is well, don't panic. There is but one thing to do. Look at the whole, look within and understand. Out of understanding, out of being confident that all is well, move and act from the Love Center. We must get together and decide the who-what-why-how of the planet earth."

So at a time when the world was calm, I was worried and concerned. Now that the world is terribly concerned, I feel confident, happy and excited. Riddles, more riddles. When I felt I should do something outwardly, I did nothing. Now that I know there is really nothing to do (except to go inward), I am moving outwardly to say, "Go within."

We will survive, we are going to pull it off. Now that we are beginning to become conscious, beginning to wake up, we will be able to do anything. But we must begin to organize, to get together and decide what we want to do at a global level. And how we are going to do it.

Conscious Thinking: II
Making Decisions

When we make decisions, we will have to begin analyzing whether each decision is based on fear — weakness — or on love — strength. What does this mean — weakness and strength? We show weakness whenever we act because we are afraid. The outer manifestation of weakness is negative. We show strength whenever we act without being afraid. The outer manifestations of inner strength are concern, understanding, patience, helpfulness, compassion and joy — in other words, love.

Let's look at our international relations to see from which center we make decisions.

Country A: "We do not want to be the aggressor, let the other nation attack. We will return the attack, otherwise they will wipe us off the face of the earth. Our friends and allies will not help us."

This decision came from weakness, from the fear of being wiped out, the fear of not getting help. If an attack and counter-attack does happen, the result is people dying out of weakness, dying because decisions were made from the fear center.

What is the alternative?

Country A: "We do not want to be the aggressor, let the other nation attack. If we return the attack, a lot of us will die; if we don't, a lot of us will die, too! We will not return the attack. We will be ready to die, but die from strength. We will die showing our belief, our inner strength, by the action of non-action. We will defend our belief with our very lives."

That is strength — the action which shows so much love for the other that you allow him to kill you, yet so much strength that you stand up for what you believe, regardless of the consequences to you. If you are to die, you might as well die being an example of inner strength.

It is hard to allow someone to attack you at any level — mental, verbal, physical or emotional — and remain understanding to see clearly that they do it because they are operating from weakness. Since you are strong, since you know you can operate from the love center, you choose to manifest that side of the energy. You show understanding and compassion toward another because he can only be what he is at that moment.

I have presented an extreme example — the action of non-action at the level of war. We are not confronted with such an extreme example every day. But every day we are continually attacked at different levels (or at least we perceive attacks).

For example, if I tell my friend how kind I am, and although she doesn't say, "I don't believe you," she thinks it, most people would perceive this as an attack and walk away from that "friend." I certainly know when someone thinks kindly of me or not. Walking away would be an action based on fear. But if you stay and keep loving that person within your heart, you are demonstrating that you are what you said yourself to be — kind, loving and understanding. As I mentioned before, we are a stitch in the sock, some ready to pull us inside out, from fear to love, others not yet ready. But each of us is also a mini-sock within the big sock of the world.

It is very easy to be kind to a child 12 months old who can't run yet. You know that one day, with time, he will run. With those who don't think kindly of us, it's the same. One day, when that being grows, he or she will be able to say, "You are perfect." By then, that person will know that any time you did not demonstrate perfection, you were not being your true self. He/she will clearly see the truth of the statement. The reaction of denial now tells you the person's fears, lack of understanding — therefore the center from which that person operates. And, of course, you must move ever closer to the fearful, unless they, only they, kick you away.

When one operates from strength, the ego does not intervene. In strength, there is no ego — no one can hurt you. Your armor is love: you don't lose anything. On the contrary, you gain with each transaction because the other person gives you the opportunity to be, to demonstrate who you really are.

When we look at our Beings it is the same as with the year-old baby. We have to view things over an extended time. Just as when we view the world over the centuries and see how it has evolved and changed, so with our Beings it takes longer than one lifetime to evolve.

Now we may choose to believe this or not. Let's suppose that the whole thing is a hoax. Let's suppose it's all wrong. Wouldn't it make life a lot more compassionate for us all even if the premise were totally wrong? If I am coming from a "wrong" point of view, but the process and the outcome is loving, can the premise be wrong? And if it is, who cares? If a false premise gives me the strength to be more considerate to the bigot, more loving to the criminal, more understanding to animals, more gentle and responsible with my garden, more attentive to the physical needs of my house — because I feel they are all part of the ALL — then I think I will stick with it.

We all deal with the same things every day, but according to how much we have evolved — where we are in the "sock" — we produce different results. Both a child 10 years old and Einstein, worked with the same numbers — 0 through 9. The end products were quite different. So it is with us. We all work with fear, judgment, hate and violence as a negation of who we are; we all work with understanding, compassion, love and joy as a manifestation of our real selves. Each of us obtains quite different results by working with these same raw materials.

You may say, "But Einstein was a great scientist." That is looking at it backwards. Cause is always invisible. Einstein was a great scientist because he was operating from his Love Center, **because** he was a great Being, a Human Being who developed inside. **Because** he turned himself inside out, he was able to receive new knowledge through his intuition. **Because** within himself he became part of the string that pulls the "sock," he was able to pull the world forwards. The new knowledge that he shared — in other words the outside pulling of the sock that we saw — was the result of his inner ability to turn his mind, to change his negative emotions into positive ones. By so doing, he could see order in the world. He saw order in the world because he put himself in order first.

No one can see the whole until he is outside of it. But then of course, you only see the particular "whole" in which you were. One then evolves to become part of a different, bigger whole, and so we continue.

Let's look at the whole and see if we can understand it. One's lifetime may begin by demonstrating negative, unconscious energy, until that is demonstrated to its limit. At that point one will begin to turn inside out and demonstrate positive, conscious energy. We all have seen people whom we thought horrible, all of a sudden become so good. They were not horrible then or good now. They just are. At some point in their travels through time, they had to show what they were not in order to later demonstrate what they really are. If a person in this lifetime has not demonstrated what he/she is not, it only means he has done it before.

Sometimes we say that, as Human Beings, we all begin at the same level. But is this really true? Why are some people more beautiful than others? Are we really all at the same level of physical perfection? Do we really begin at the same level? We know that we begin the process in the same way and we look like we all have roughly the same parts. Intellectually, we are all born with different amounts of what is called "intelligence." Does this also depend on the Being? I would say it does. I know that as my Being grew, my capacity to comprehend and to integrate did also. So I would say they are related.

We begin with different amounts, so it depends on where in the sock we are located. The Being, when it arrives in a body, begins at a point in space and time, and moves from there. There are different starting points and one cannot always judge how developed the Being is by outward appearances. For instance, one Being may choose to come into a deformed body to be able to deal with self alone. Yet there is a road a Being travels to arrive at a destination where it feels absolutely fulfilled, all desires gone, absolute ecstasy. I know, because I have lived it. Like Einstein, I too am an outsider. I have become part of the string which pulls the sock inside out. This is precisely where every one of us has to arrive.

Yet I know only too well I am not the doer. I am just a silly TV set. If I were to take a TV set to the jungles of Brazil and turn it on, people would give me credit for the marvelous moving pictures. I would deny it and they might think, "How modest she is!" But based on knowledge, it is not modesty, it is fact. When I say, "I am not the doer," it is exactly the same — it is not out of modesty, it is a fact.

Negotiations
One of our favorite tricks when we negotiate is to say: "I do this, you do that." It all sounds reasonable, but it is not. Imagine a doctor saying to a patient, "I will give some more medicine once I see all your symptoms gone," or, "Unless this analysis is perfect, I will not authorize the cure." A bit much, but that is what we do!

We view the symptoms of the world and say, "If this symptom stopped, I would do this or that. Since this symptom does not stop, I will not do anything more. Until this problem area is solved, I will not cooperate. We want to solve the problem, we say, but we expect the problem **first** to be corrected.

Imagine the liver saying to the brain, "If you work two hours like me, I will work two hours like you." We generally refuse to acknowledge we have different inner workings and they are as they should be. We do not need each nation to have the same system for all nations to work together. Just as all organs are not — and cannot — be alike for the optimal functioning of the body, we must acknowledge that all of us, the inhabitants of the planet earth, want to and will work together for a common cause: to bring peace to the planet. We do not all need to be alike ı ler the same system or religion to be able to do this.

This behavior exists because we have the illusion t t we are separate entities. We have the illusion that we begin and end at our skin, that we are not part of a whole. It is precisely at this

374

level that we have to correct ourselves. We can only know the unity when we experience it, not before. And the only way to experience it is by going inside of ourselves, by learning who we are. Kill self! Kill the judgments we have made about one another, the frustrations that we feel because we are frightened.

Every member of Humanity has the same power to do this. We have lived under the illusion that others have more power than we do. For example, as children we believed our parents had the power. As we grew we learned that this was not so. Then we believed our teachers had it. Then, for some of us, our spouses had it, or the company that we worked for or the government. We transfer the concept of power to others and to institutions because the responsibilities of power are awesome. By transferring the power on a conceptual level, it is easier to face than as part of ourselves. But it is there! If we realize we have power, we have to do something. But while we persist in this conceptual pretense — that the power is in the hands of others — we expect the others to act.

We must begin to realize that we can truly act from inner strength. This inner strength will take us far into a perfect, positive, conscious, planned future. This attitude will finish us with the cycle. We did what we had to do. We are at the right place of development. It is the start of the completion of the whole cycle — a conscious, positive, inner path. We must look inside to find where we have been, what we have accomplished, where we want to go and how we are to get there.

All of us will be invoved. Each cell, each self, each one of us is essential. If one person has just one little piece of the puzzle and does not put it in, the puzzle is not done. Each of us has a place. Let's consciously realize our places in space and time; let's begin to work for eternity.

We may die, yes, but just because one worker dies, the company does not stop producing. Once we decide how we are going to work together, how we will integrate ourselves to bring about the balance of the planet, the product will endure long after each one of us dies. Since we will be working for eternity, we will have broken the barrier of time.

It is a long way to peace, but a possible one, too!

Why is it that we keep thinking that things are "either/or"? Why can't we see that if something is there it is because we need it?

For example, suppose we organize the planet as a unit.

We could have each country functioning with a free enterprise system of profit. Some of those profits could be directed toward a central office of government. That Central Office, to operate fairly, would have to divide the money equally among all nations according to population. In this manner we will integrate the two systems, world wide.

Let's see: If we have $100 for the world. We could give $20 to a nation which has 20 persons, $25 to the one which has 25 persons, and so on. Certain essentials would be equally distributed.

We don't need to get rid of either system. We can use them both, cooperatively. If something is there, it is there for a purpose; the purpose is **Always** for the benefit of All, if we place the pieces of the puzzle in place. If we don't, we can't have a puzzle. We can't see the whole picture, as long as we think "This piece should not exist." We are so busy trying to change the pieces of the puzzle, we can't see how or where they fit!

I am as strong as an Oak, and as yielding as a Poplar. Why do we think we need to be either/or: Why do we think we need to compromise? I am both. How nice! How profound . . . ! But . . . What does it mean: What is the practical **use** of this discovery? What does this discovery about myself have to do with World Peace?

We have a Capitalist system and a Communist system.

Why do we think we need to have either/or?

Why do we think we need to compromise?

Why do we think they can't live under one roof, Planet Earth?

If we have both, it's because we need both!

Let's look at a home in any place on this planet.

In every house there are certain things, such as underwear, tooth brush, etc., which are owned by an individual in that household, in other words, privately owned, Private Property.

In every house there are certain things, such as dishes, cutlery, etc. which are owned communally, in other words by all, communal ownership, Communism. No one in their right mind argues about how come that for this specific item we use the private property system, or the capitalist system, and for these other items we use the communist system. It is obvious that each system has its place within one household.

In every town on this planet, there are houses which belong to certain families, and there are streets which belong to all.

There is no difference in the world. Except in our own house, we think in terms of Our House; in the Towns, we think in terms of Our Town. But we are not thinking in terms of Our Planet yet, therefore, we seem to have problems seeing that both systems, are important, and that there is room for both.

It is quite clear the capitalist system has created a great standard of living in the United States. It is quite clear that when a family is out of work, more than two or three months, they are kicked out of their home, and they end up living in their car or in tent cities even if they have children. Obviously, there is a piece missing somewhere, which we need in order to remedy this inhumane situation.

376

Let's begin to look at what we have at the Global level and how we can pull it together, instead of trying to get rid of some of the puzzle. We need them all! If we put the pieces together, we will get rid of the so called **mess** in the world, in other words, once we put order in our lives, the symptoms will disappear. But they can't go away until we stop trying to get rid of something, instead of incorporating.

When we are putting together a puzzle, there is always a **mess** next to us while we are trying to form the picture. But the **mess disappears** as soon as we place the last piece of the puzzle in its proper place. Let's not worry about the mess. Let's concentrate on placing the pieces correctly. The picture will form . . . and it will be PEACE!

Freedom: Creating a Choice

From whatever place we start, we must come to see we are part of the whole. If we see clearly the separateness of our individual "cells," we will learn how our cells fit into the whole. If we know we are part of the whole, it is important to know how each of our separate beings is part of the whole.

The feeling I had that the concerns of others were mine too, goes back to my family, where this point of view was practically a tradition. My mother took on the world: she found people on the streets and brought them home for a meal. My grandmother felt the cry of the workers and organized the first labor union in the country. Nothing in my background told me that one could even think: "This is not my problem."

My father was intimately connected with his workers. He talked to them about religion and converted them. He convinced them they should get married. He screamed at them yet they loved him. They knew he cared, they felt his love. He held their paychecks if he felt they would waste it on drink. He budgeted their money so that their wives and children could eat until the end of the month. I remember once a worker came to our home with a gun, furious, trying to get his money, he was mad because father was interferring. Father remained firm. The worker came back after his drunkenness passed and thanked father for being so good. My father always behaved as if the people he hired were part of his life at all levels.

I owe my ability to be free to two people in my life: Sean and Silver. Sean taught me I could say "no." It may seem like a small thing, but I had no concept that if someone said, "Let's go to this restaurant," I could say, "No, I don't want to go." The fact was I did not care. I could love anyone, anyplace, anywhere; it mattered very little to me. Now this seems to say that I was a mouse, quiet and unassuming. Nothing could be further from the truth.

But only after I learned to say "no," could I freely make decisions. Once I knew how to say "no" and used that option, I was able to feel within myself whether I wanted to behave in that manner. I felt what it meant to set limits, and then I knew it was not an option I wanted to execute.

Silver clearly showed me how one can operate with the point of view being "me" — separate from everyone else. She taught me how to think and act in that manner. Once I had learned it, I was then, for the first time in my life, free to choose. I could not choose before because I did not have the ability to see two roads.

When Silver came into my life, I was amazed to see someone who was as strong as I but knew something of which I had no concept. She kept pointing out to me how this or that problem had nothing to do with me — how this problem belonged to Freddy, not me, how that problem belonged to Allan's life, not mine. She taught me how one can say to someone, "I am not available for you now, because I want to do something else." Her behavior gave me, for the first time in my life, the realization that I could in fact be someone separate from the rest of the world. That was a concept totally foreign to me.

Everything in the outer world manifests our inner world and in this case the manifestation was quite clear. The cars I owned when I lived in California only went forward, not backward! After I learned how to be "separate," I finally acquired a car that went both forward and backward. My cars were manifesting by Being. I only knew how to go forward. I had to learn how to go backwards as well, to be free to choose where to go.

I was part of the whole. I had no concept of "I" being a separate Being. Once Silver taught me this, I was able to choose which of two roads I would take. I then followed the one I had felt and lived since childhood — to act as a Being part of the whole. I felt that being separate was an illusion. I had not yet seen — through my 1981 experience — the totality, but at the time I had made a very conscious decision. Without Silver, I could never have arrived at this inner freedom, this inner happiness I felt and want to share.

So we all must learn both sides. Going or coming, we will all eventually experience the unity, the white and the black, the yin and the yang, the power of love, the force — it occurs beyond words.

In the same way, the world until now has acted as "us" and "them," as separate countries. The world has created a choice. Therefore, we are now free to choose. We all know we want but one choice — peace. We are now coming to terms with the illusion of separateness and we are becoming conscious of "us," the planet. As we all do this on the personal level, the national and international levels will follow.

No Choice

We start by creating a choice. When we come to the realization of unity, we find there actually is no choice. There is only peace. Peace does not mean the absence of fighting. Peace means the realization, through knowledge and experience, of our place in the universe. We then see how we interact not only with each other but even with inanimate objects. So what looked like a crazy experience described in Chapter 6, was no more or less than the experience of the ultimate reality, energy.

It is one thing to go to a lab and see how cells interrelate. It is something else to read that "we are all one." It is quite another thing to experience how we interconnect with all there is at the level of energy.

This experience brings one not only humility but an incredible desire to serve. It causes one to realize: there is no choice. Thousands of illusions are shattered, like: "I am not responsible," "It is not my problem," "There is nothing I can do," and "I have no choice."

Nature is going to play great tricks on us, and we'll have to respond to them. What are we going to say? We could say, "It's not my problem that there was a flood and people in Peru are homeless. It's not my country." Or we could say, "It is my problem that there was a flood and people in Peru are homeless. It's happening on our planet. I choose to make it my problem."

The so-called catastrophe can bring us together to break down the false barrier; through pain we will learn to unite. And since it is Nature's doing, it's really out of our hands — or is it?

It is possible that if we consciously begin to behave with the attitude of unity, Nature may not have to teach us in the first place? Is it possible that instead of life happening **to** us, we can **make** life happen? Think about it. You may have more power than you think. But you may have to change your ideas of things. If the whole idea is ridiculous, nothing would happen, the catastrophes would continue. But **what if** by changing our way of thinking, we can change the electrical impulses and affect the electromagnetic field we send to the cosmos? **What if** we can really change the weather just by changing our ideas about things? We could give it a try. If it works, great! If not, we haven't lost anything.

We must remember who the real "doer" is. The rain IS, and because it IS, it wets. It does not try, it does. The moon IS, and because it IS, it shines. It does not try, it does. The sun IS, and because it IS, it heats. A tree IS, and because it IS, it shades. I AM, because I AM, I love. I do not try, I do.

There is no great merit in my love. I could not help loving the people in my life, then or now. It has nothing to do with me; yet it has everything to do with me. The shade of the tree has nothing to do with the tree, yet it has everything to do with the tree. If we are who, what and why we are, none of us has any choice but to love.

As a tree grows, it gives more and more shade. As a Being grows, it gives more and more love. Is it bad that a young tree can't give as much shade as an older one? Then why do you get upset and withhold your love when the person next to you can't give you what you need? If he or she is not doing it, it is because he or she can't. When a Being grows to maturity, it will give to everyone.

The shade is not the tree, the tree is not the shade. Yet we could not have shade without the tree. We need a vehicle through which shade can be created. Love needs a vehicle, a Human Being, through which it can manifest itself. Love is an invisible, it needs a visible vehicle to be seen and complete the whole. Because the shade is an intangible, it needs a tree, a tangible, to complete the whole.

I am the tree, I am the vehicle, the instrument. And yet, I am love, I am shade, therefore I AM that I AM. I am body, I am love — whole. As we become conscious of the two, as we experience I AM that I AM, we graduate and have the right to call ourselves Human Beings. Until then we must know we are Becoming. As we graduate from this stage, we enter a new school where we know nothing and must begin to learn again!

Matching the Energies: I

We clearly understand that if we are hungry, we need food. What we are really doing is satisfying one energy with its matching energy. The body is a physical energy; therefore, the only energy which can satisfy it is a physical energy — food. If you are hungry and someone says, "I love you," you do not stop being hungry. That's because the person has provided you with emotional energy to satisfy a physical energy.

Each energy can only be satisfied by its match. Sadness, an emotional energy, can only be satisfied by another emotional energy. Curiosity, a mental energy, can only be satisfied by another mental energy. If you want to know how something works, which is a question of mental energy, and I answer, "I love you," you would feel frustrated. An answer at the mental level, a piece of knowledge, would satisfy you. Likewise, we can't give knowledge to satisfy someone who is sad. Or satisfy someone's sadness by giving him food. We may do it, but that does not mean it works.

If we want peace, we must consider that peace is an invisible energy. One can only satisfy it with its match. Peace is a result of spirit, just as understanding, compassion and joy are results of the love energy. Since peace is an invisible, spiritual energy, we cannot bring it about or satisfy our desire for it by creating a world filled with cars, magnificent houses, big salaries and plenty of food. That would be trying to satisfy a spiritual energy with a physical one.

Likewise, if we want peace, we can't bring it about by having every human being on earth become a Ph.D. That would be trying to satisfy a spiritual energy with a mental one. If we want peace and use a bomb or rifle to get it, we are again using a physical energy. Bombs are very physical. Therefore they can never produce the result of peace.

How can one satisfy a spiritual energy, then? By learning to use spiritual energy — by becoming aware of what is! If peace is an outcome of spirit, we must learn what spirit is.

Spirit is what one obtains when we use the three different spiritual energies in balance. It is like mixing colors. You begin with certain colors, but by the process of combining them, a new color is created. The same with spirit: we are always using these three different energies, but when used in proper balance and in the proper situations, we experience spirit.

What are these three spiritual energies? The emotional energy is one manifestation; the mental energy is another, and the physical energy is the third. We may think that these are not spiritual — we experience them every day — but they are just different manifestations of spirit.

Let's look at something physical: water. Water can be vapor, solid or liquid. Water has three different ways of behaving, three different manifestations of itself, but is still water. Similarly, spiritual energy also has three different manifestations: the emotional, the mental and the physical.

Spirit governs itself by the law of "Three in One." There are three different manifestations of the energy, but only when the three different manifestations act in absolute balance do they create the one energy which is spirit.

This one energy is just the three components working in balance, each at the service of the others and therefore becoming one. That is spirit: because I am, I know, I feel, think and act; or, I know, I feel, think and act, therefore I am. By uniting the knowing, feeling, thinking and acting at each moment, I become one: the "I am." Only when we arrive at the creation of this "I am," do we become true Human Beings. At that level we can see the different components of the one energy. We can experience it, therefore we know it.

If I think only, I am not a Human Being, I am Becoming one. If I feel only, I am not a Human Being, I am Becoming one. If I think and feel only, I am not a Human Being, I am Becoming one. If I act only, without thinking, I am not a Human Being, I am Becoming one. If I act only because I feel, I am not a Human Being, I am

Becoming one. Only when we can use the three energies together, at all times do we Become — and arrive at peace . . . Peace within.

This planet is a school where we are learning, getting closer to graduation. Let's rejoice in the opportunity!

I can open up an office and say, "I am a lawyer." Does that make me a lawyer? I can buy lots of tools and say, "I am a carpenter." Does that make me one? What would make me a lawyer or carpenter? If I feel I want to be one, if I apply my mind and body to learn either trade, and if I go into the world and use the skills learned, then I could say, "I am a lawyer" or "I am a carpenter." (Of course, that is not **who** you are, that is only **what** you do!)

In the same way, we can claim we are Human Beings. We can print all the books in the world stating how "superior" we are. We can program the most sophisticated system in the greatest of computers to "prove" we are Human Beings. None of it can make us Humans. The only way we will be Human Beings is by Becoming Humane — by feeling, thinking and acting with Humanity at all times, in every aspect of our lives.

Can we sign a budget that allots 30% for defense on one hand and at the same time say we are Humans — that this is a Humane action toward all of us? We are all learning, all Becoming Human Beings. All of us are in Kindergarten; some of us do graduate from this Kindergarten: Buddha, Moses, Jesus, Mohammed, Gandhi, etc. — but each is learning, each is doing his/her very best.

We want peace. Peace is the result of an inner process, the process of Becoming Human Beings by the usage of the three energies in proper balance.

The three energies have two centers: the Love Center (or positive center) and the Fear Center (or negative center). That is why five is the number of man: $3 + 2 = 5$. You can't have a Human Being without those three energies working in balance **and** the two centers working in their proper places: Fear inward, Love outward.

Matching the Energies: II
Common vs. Normal

Let's talk about the difference between common and normal. A normal body is healthy. Commonly people are sick. But just because it is common to be sick or to have a cold, that does not make it normal. Health is normal.

Commonly we find people behaving in an inhuman manner. That is not normal. It is common. When we gently sign a piece of paper which will produce arms to kill other human beings on the planet, we are acting commonly. All nations have budgets that allocate arms to kill other human beings. It is common. It is neither normal nor humane.

We will be normal when we can all feel as Gandhi, when we can feel love for one another, near or far, when the illusion of separation is gone. That is being normal. Until then we must realize we are **Becoming** Human Beings. We are in a process not just of physical evolution but of spiritual evolution as well. The spiritual evolution is something we each have control over. We can all claim our rightful heritage: we can all become Human Beings and arrive at peace. But we must work with the law of 3 in 1 to be able to obtain results. We are all doing it, but at different stages.

First, we must learn one energy well. Perhaps it's the physical energy. Then we go on to learn the mental and the emotional. When we know each one well, we can put them together and know we are spirit. Just as the spiritual energy has three parts — physical, mental and emotional — so each of these has three parts, too: the physical energy has three parts; the mental energy has three parts; the emotional energy has three parts.

Let's look at an example: I am having people over for dinner on Saturday.

First behavior: I feel happy I invited them. I think what they would enjoy eating when they come. I plan the menu. I set the table with care. I prepare the house for the guests. I relax before they come, to be ready for them emotionally. I make sure while they are in my house that the food is good to satisfy their physical energy, that the conversation be stimulating to satisfy their mental energy and that I project myself, my warmth, so that they can feel my caring and in this manner satisfy their emotional energy.

I used the three energies and therefore I created a fourth: all-around well being, the vibration of creation. It has been a conscious effort at all levels in the smallest detail. This is a behavior of 3 in 1 at the physical level: perfect score.

Second behavior: I feel trapped into having people over. I have no time to think about what to cook. I really don't care what I will serve my guests. When they arrive, I say, "Let's go shopping; we'll pick up something." We sit and talk and enjoy each other.

In this case I have not put myself 100% into what I was doing. My emotions were not one with the event: I felt I did not care about the people coming. My mind was not there to plan for it. Yet, they were coming. So I executed an action into which I did not put all of my Being: mental, emotional and physical. That was breaking the law.

Let's take an example on the level of mental activity:

First behavior: I go to school, but I don't want to learn. I am physically in school, but my mind is at the beach. My feelings are

torn — why am I here? I don't want to be in school! All three of
the energies are not working in unison. That is breaking the law.

Second behavior: I sit in school and want to be there. I want to
learn there. I am enjoying the information I am receiving and I
use it. That is working with the law of 3 in 1 at the mental level.

The same can be shown with emotional energy. For example,
someone calls me and is in an emotional crisis. I go over, I am glad
to be there: I am physically there. My mind is alert to the person. I
want to understand, I may bring clarity to them. I feel for what
they are going through. All three energies are working together.
That is working with the law of 3 in 1 at the emotional level for
others.

Or suppose I am in turmoil: I go away. I take myself physically
out to be with myself. I feel my turmoil. I use my mind to
understand why the turmoil is there and what I need to learn
from it. The pain is a symptom, I know it will go away if I learn.
All of me is there for me 100%. That is working with the law of 3
in 1 for me.

Each time we use this law, we feel well, we create. Being
creative does not necessarily mean to paint or write. It means to
use the three energies in balance to form a new dimension, to
create a new feeling. It might be a perfect meal, an enjoyable
lecture or the rewards one harvests when one goes through an
emotional crisis and learns through the pain.

For a Human Being to become conscious of this and able to
work in this manner, takes time — more time than the 90 years
of one life. We must view this the same way as we view biological
evolution. We ignore that we live and die in the few short years
of a lifetime and look beyond it to see how, over a period of
hundreds of thousands of years, evolution occurs. The changes
are too minute to see in the lifetime of one person. So it is with
consciousness, of a Being. One stage of learning may take an
entire lifetime. It is like a person spending one lifetime in first
grade.

When I can perform an activity using the three spiritual
energies and within each one of them use the same three
energies, I have created a vibration of 4 (unity, creation) for each
energy three times: $3 \times 4 = 12$ and $1 + 2 = 3$. That is the essence of
spirit. That is where we all want to go.

How do we start? In simple terms, everything we do, we
should do well — as Mama and Papa have said since the
beginning of time. There is nothing new under the sun! If we
consciously see how it works we can consciously apply it and
observe others with understanding. When a three-month old
child does not do long division, no one gets upset. So why do we
get upset when a Being in the process of Becoming does not do
what it could not possibly have learned yet. To multiply, we must

384

first learn the numbers. To be Human we must first learn the energies. Let's begin to understand where both we and those we meet are in this learning process.

It is not that difficult to learn, but we must begin. If we want to become surgeons, we can't say, "I don't want to cut a person." In the same way, if we want peace we can't continue to feel, think and act in the same way that has brought us to the point of total destruction. We can't arrive at the opposite of total destruction — total peace — by continuing to walk in the direction of total destruction. If we want to achieve the opposite result, we must think and act in the opposite manner. This is not because that way was "wrong," or because we judge "them" wrong, but because we are now at a different stage of development.

Fear is not material, but we are trying to calm it with material energy — money, big houses, cars and the like. Many of us have discovered that this does not work. Since fear is intangible, only an intangible can dissolve it. Enough love dissolves fear, but not a love which is personal. I hear a lot of people say, "I love him, but he did not do this or that for me. Now that he is with someone else, he is doing these things. Why not for me?" There is pain in this statement.

We have the illusion that we end at our skins. We see each other as separate entities and don't seem to understand that, even though a person is not giving to you directly, he is giving to you. Imagine the feet viewing the mouth eating. You see, the mouth is eating, and I'm here getting nothing! That love is going to a common pot from which we all draw. And it is from that common inner pot — not from the outside — that we can draw the love to calm our fears, individually and globally.

The food that our collective body needs, in order to work properly, is love. When any cell makes a decision based on fear instead of love, it depletes the body. Each time any of us makes a decision based on love, it feeds the body. The health of the body depends upon each human being. The burden of our survival is not on our politicians. They are doing their best also. The burden is on each one of us. Every minute, we contribute to bringing about either health or imbalance. Any action must be positive — there is only good. We must simply learn to see, to hear and to learn from each situation life presents to us.

Who Will Be First?

It is all very nice to speak about peace and love. But it is more important to rise to the challenge of acting on those big words. Who is going to show strength? Which nation will it be? Which of you, my children? Yes, my children. I am a mother, I do have an incredible female energy, the energy that nurtures and loves, the energy that will lift the world. That is what female energy is good for — to bring light to the world.

Will it be Argentina, the nation that prides itself on asking not "Where do you come from?" but "Where are you going?" Not "Who were you?" but "Who do you want to be?" Will you, Argentina, be the first to come up with a budget that will represent strength and trust, not fear?

Will it be Canada, the nation that broke away from England peacefully? Are you the country that will lead the world with concrete steps in your national budget to express that you want peace? Will you mark your dollars and cents for peace, not for defense?

Will it be you, the United States of America, the mighty nation who led the world to great dreams? Can you be really strong and lead the world in a show of strength that has never happened before? Can you, my dear United States, be free enough, trusting enough, strong enough within to come out and say to the world: "Because I am strong, because I am free, I will walk where no one has walked before. I know I have the money to spend on war materials, but I will freely **choose** not to spend one cent on them. Instead I will invest in education, old age programs, cleaning the waters of the world, and so forth. I am a young nation and may be naive, but I am for peace. And I will put my money where my mouth is."

Or will it be you, dear Russia? Are you the miraculous nation which in 50 years transformed a population of illiterates into literates? Is it you who will come up to the challenge, you, who did that seemingly impossible task? You, who educated your people, can you now stand up and be counted as the great nation that you are and begin the show for peace?

Or will it be you, Spain? Who have seen so much pain, so much blood that your soil is still damp with it? Will it be you, the nation that is so indomitable that even Napoleon couldn't conquer you?

We should look within ourselves, each country, and discover by ourselves what we can contribute to the whole. What is our purpose as a nation? In what stage of development are we? Let's look at our inner strengths and see which countries have inner knowledge. Can other countries learn from them and exchange what they have, perhaps technology?

In this manner we can deal as equals: one country possessing the product of the outer, technology, which can be used for the betterment of mankind; the other country possessing knowledge of the realms of the inner man, that which can be used to integrate oneself. When each part of the world integrates the outer with the inner, we will have an integrated planet.

As we have seen, peace is no more or less than all energies within us integrated and in balance. When this occurs, we are at peace with ourselves; therefore, the world will be at peace.

Just as a Human Being has different ages, so do countries.

Europe seems to me like the 60-year-old man. It works to live, it doesn't live to work. The U.S. is the teenager of the planet: nothing is impossible. "Do you have a problem, surely I can solve it!" Japan is the 80-year-old man: old enough to know the young have good ideas and to take them; wise enough to know the old must be preserved.

I do not know the whole world; I have not traveled all over. But I will, and as I do, I will be able to feel more the different parts and how we can create a unit which will function harmoniously.

But we can't function harmoniously until we decide the what and why of us, the planet. I suggest we get together and decide the Ideal and Purpose of Earth: We, the inhabitants of this planet (the "who") are going to set up a system to work together for the purpose of achieving world peace (the "what"). We are all going to work together because we want to survive (the "why").

Since peace is an invisible, to bring it about we must understand the laws that govern the "invisible." As mentioned earlier, we perceive the world as three dimensional. Nothing could be more wrong. We have been told through fictional stories like "The Lord of the Rings" that with three rings — three dimensions — a fourth is created. We are constantly creating. We are co-creators, but unconscious ones until now. What does this mean? It means that if we use the law of 3 in 1, we create a world that has a fourth dimension.

Here's an example of a conversation in a three-dimensional world and the same as viewed in four dimensions.

Beatriz: "You should run, it is good for you, John."

John: "I like walking. Will you walk with me?"

This looks like two individuals speaking to each other and a message being communicated. Two people plus one message equals three items — a three-dimensional view. That is one way of perceiving reality, but it is not complete. Beatriz is talking to John, but she is also talking to herself. She is telling herself that she should run, too. So now we have the fourth dimension. The message sounds as if it is going out, yet it is also going in.

This is a tiny example of omnipresence. We can see how something can travel faster than light, in fact instantaneously. At the same time Beatriz is telling Beatriz. To John through a "wave," to Beatriz as a "particle." These are the two ways that scientists now describe the nature of light. It looks like a paradox, yet it is not. It moves yet it stays put, a wave and a particle. It is here and there all at once.

This is a very crude way to explain how the barrier of time is broken. It happens all the time, but our ideas of things do not permit us to see it. For us to be conscious of this reality, we have to become observers of ourselves. We must be one step removed to be able to hear ourselves as we talk to others. If we do this, we will hear our higher selves talking to ourselves. No one is higher than you. As you talk to others, listen to yourself and you will know what to do. We do not need to go outside of ourselves to get answers. But we must each learn to listen to his/her own "voice." And the outside voice is not different from the inner voice, since the outer and the inner are one and the same.

Let's look at an international example:

Russia to the U.S.: "I want you to stop arming. If and when you do it, I will do it, too." The message "I want you to stop arming" is the voice of Russia to the U.S., but also of Russia to Russia: "I must stop arming. That I must do." That is power. But then comes the rest: "If and when you do it, I will do it, too." That is giving the power away. What I can do is diminished if I make it depend on what you do. That is acting out of weakness. In strength, there are no conditions:

"I want you to stop arming." I state what I want. "I will stop arming myself regardless of what you decide to do." That is, I will act according to what I think is right, regardless of what you do. That is being powerful.

More examples: "Allan, I want time with you." I state what I want. "I will love you regardless of what you decide to do." That is, I will act according to what I think is right, regardless of what you do. This is being powerful — one does not compromise.

"I will spend my capital towards building, not destroying, regardless of what you do." This is power.

"You can count on one percent of my budget for whatever purpose you feel you need, regardless of what you do." This is power.

Power is deciding what to do and doing it. To be able to accomplish this, one can never add conditions from the outside. If one does, then the outside can block your actions. But if you decide what to do regardless of what the other side decides to do, no one can stop you.

Do you think Russia would stop the U.S. if the States decided to share part of its budget? Would this action encourage the other nation to stop allocating money toward defense? I would say so. The weak listen to words. The strong see action. Actions speak louder than words, and for the integrated person or nation, words and actions are one and the same.

We are acting like a bunch of weaklings. "I want to bring peace, but I can't." "I can't because he does not let me." "He does not stop fighting, so I have to fight." How long are we going to be weak? For how long will we give our power to the other side?

Can we take control immediately by acting as "we" — the whole planet? "We" is peace.

The World in Four Dimensions

Nothing is being said to you that has no bearing for you. We may not quite understand how it fits, we may not see why we are listening to it, but if we hear it, we need it! That is what it means to be open to all.

When we arrive at this openness, we can see the inter-connection of the human and non-human levels. At that stage since there is but one energy vibrating at different levels, one can't ignore the world, because one has experienced the Oneness, not only of humanity but of the universe. We must all walk towards this experience of Oneness. Only through it can we become consciously one unit, working together.

If we perceive two people speaking like this, we have a diagram which is four dimensional:

$$\text{Inner} + \text{Outer} = \text{Conscious} + \text{Unconscious}$$
$$\text{Outer} + \text{Inner} = \text{Conscious} + \text{Unconscious}$$

Each message is going both ways: in and out. This equals one, complete, balanced and conscious interaction per person. Such an interaction shows no waste. Energy has been used in balance, in opposition; through this balance something new was created. Through the balance and movement of energy, we can see the stability — the "conversation." So the real world is far from three dimensional. The interaction at the energy level will depend on the energy being used: physical, mental, emotional or the three in balance — universal love.

We could see this clearly if we could look at matter at the atomic and subatomic level. When we begin to study the use of the four different vibrations of the one energy, we will begin to see that what we call probabilities are not probabilities. There are real bases for those probabilities to be so. If we begin to see that in "awareness" of the uses of the different energies resides the probabilities, we will discover new physical laws. But we have to understand that the physical is only manifesting the invisible. Then we will begin to see the patterns and begin to understand how we are, what we are and why we are.

The world is our creation — at one level. What we think, it becomes. It is as if the universe is just thought. I thought about the health food store in Nerja, La Feria, the pizza place — and they appeared. My weird experience may have been weird, but it does not mean it was not so. I have arrived at these conclusions of the universe through the weird experience. I am sure science will arrive at the same place. From within or without, we will come to see the whole.

In one sense, I had already arrived at these conclusions before my experience, but the experience confirmed to me what I had thought my entire life. On another level, although we are constantly creating, we are only the brushes, the instrument. The universe is the picture, the Love Force is the artist. But the picture is far from complete. When the planet and every human being arrives at peace, then the picture will be finished (to be continued, of course, at a different level). Mind and matter are in fact one and the same. One is the manifestation of the other. But the purpose, the intention of mind is what determines the pattern of matter. We can activate certain patterns — physical ones, mental ones, emotional ones or divine ones.

Let's take a practical example: we have the idea there is a limited amount of oil and other natural resources. What we don't understand is that the scarcity exists because we are wasting invisible energy. If we become aware and conscious of this energy, if we begin to use it at the invisible level, we will begin to create whatever resources we need. The material — matter — comes from thought. If we become aware of how to activate the invisible patterns, we will be creating the raw materials or matter that we need. We will conquer matter with anti-matter.

So it is true that we are wasting resources, but the waste is not at the physical level, it is at the consciousness level, at the love level. If we use that energy — love energy, divine energy, whatever you want to call it — we will really multiply the loaves and fishes!

But to be able to do it, we have to spiritualize matter; in other words, we must make ourselves Conscious Beings. We must become people who can control our own lives. We must see that in the measure we control our own lives, we control the direction of the planet.

Control is truly important. Yet, we try to control others. We have the illusion if we control others, we have power. The fact is that if we can control ourselves, we are powerful. When we want to control others, we are showing how weak we are.

We think the ecological system is damaged, but the real ecological system is not just physical. There is an ecological system at the invisible level also. The visible and invisible are two parts of one ecological system.

Any doctor can tell you that all the medicine in the world would not help the person who has lost the "will to live." There is an invisible — spirit.

If we look at water, we can see solid, liquid and gas all working together in the universe as one system. There exists another system which, through the use of universal love, activates the energy which produces what is needed. So we have the invisible creating the visible, and the visible, upon spiritualizing, becomes invisible. Different, yet the same. Spirit, yet matter. Matter, yet spirit.

Imagine the water saying, "Well, I am not essential, the world can do without me." Or the plants saying, "I am not essential, the rest of the planet can exist without me." Only man, in his ignorance and inability to see his place, thinks of himself as apart and disconnected, as something which nature can do without. This shows how powerful we are! Love is the Creative principle. Through lack of its use, we have created scarcity. Through its conscious tapping, we will create great abundance.

Until now, we have used love in a selfish way and broken the ecological chain. We can connect again through living with Divine Love in mind. We must be "Other-fish," not "Self-fish." The "fish" must not be used for self, but for others; by so doing, we consciously create. We are Gods! Both conscious and unconscious. Unconsciously, we have created for our own destruction 1/2 ☽ . Consciously, we will create and complete the cycle; we will arrive at our final destination — peace: ☽ , one whole.

If you saw me before the experience and compared me with the rest of the world, I was always happier. That's because I sacrificed, I made each action in my life a "sacri- (sacred) fice (something made)." I sacrificed constantly. That doesn't mean I was a person who went around depressed. I lived the "sacred fish." That is how I arrived at the Aquarian Age, by living the Piscean Age in my own life. If we want to move forward toward the Aquarian Age, we must do it by using the "fish" for others.

If we look at our life, we can see how we start by belonging to a family. As we grow, the circle expands. We go to school; as we mature more, we create yet another family, and as our family matures, we become part of their families as well.

The planet is the same. The planet is our family, and we are now about to extend ourselves from the inner circle of mommy and daddy into kindergarten, from national into global. Once we are mature enough, we will graduate from that school and have our planet in order. We will be ready to start our own planetary family at that moment of maturity. Then we will begin to participate with other civilizations in the cosmos.

Right now, we are in the stage of "thinking" or "creating" this future reality. When we are ready, we will "discover" civilizations from other planets. Then we will wonder why we never "saw" them before. It is because as we think, so we create our reality. And as we are reading, we advance. Science and spirit are one. We cannot have matter without spirit.

So you see, talking about love is not just "nice," it is downright practical. If we want the material problems of the world to be solved, we had better begin to understand how we can grow in love. How this energy called love works.

Love produces results. Have you ever seen anyone who loves

who is unwilling to do something for his or her beloved? Have you ever seen someone who loves who is unwilling to sacrifice for the object of his or her love? Unwilling to share her money, her food, her being?

If we look at war, we can see this clearly. During war — the most inhuman of situations — the people involved discovered their deepest humanity. The inhuman situation gave them the possibility of being truly human: to care for the other, to risk for the other, to feel how they are available for one another. They feel the interconnection which in "normal" life they did not allow themselves to feel and which, unfortunately, they do not know how to translate into their everyday lives once the war is over. Let's learn the lesson that war has for us. Let's take the gold that the pain of war has given us and apply the knowledge gained from it.

We do not need to be forced into that situation. We can consciously choose to sacrifice ourselves for another, and through it experience our humanity. We do not need to use the fish for "self." Thought is the basis of the universe, but the intention behind the thought gives the direction — or probability, as science calls it. But this is really not probability — love is as exact as geometry, math and music. While working consciously for others, we work for ourselves. But when we want to take from others to give to ourselves, we don't only take from them, we rob ourselves also.

In the first instance, we create abundance; in the second we create scarcity. Which of the two paths is wiser? Do we want to rob ourselves? Do we have a choice? There is but one road — love. Just one choice.

Planetary Sales and Communication

By now we are aware that anyone can sell anything through advertising. We know that a company can put an idea in your head, tend to it, repeat it, and through it create a desire. The desire takes over and makes you go purchase "McDonald" or "Tide." An idea which has come from the outside is controlling you.

We know that this extraordinary method works. But do we, the people of the world, want this method to be used for these purposes? Or do we want to grab it and use it to bring about peace?

We do not need a company to put an idea into our minds. We can put forth our own ideas, such as, "What are we doing on this planet? How can all of us work together?" We tend to this idea as it grows, and we can take action on it. But this time, the one who will act will be you, the "Being," not you, the "body."

Can you see, my dear world? Why are you so sad, my dear

world? Why are all your newspapers talking about doom? If any company can sell anything, we too can bring about what all of us in the world want. We can! Let's see what is there — television, movies, magazines. Let's start mobilizing at the international level. Let's use the media in a positive way. We can begin by talking about the planet, not specific regions — about humanity, not specific groups.

In the 60's, young people around the world proclaimed: "Love and Peace!" They travelled around, seemingly "doing nothing." They were "thinking," giving energy. The drug culture came and brought the same information to many people. After that we saw the revolution of computers, which also meant the same information becoming available to a large number of people — the whole hooking itself to one source.

As we see the physical world centralizing, becoming smaller through communication, information traveling from anywhere to anywhere, we can see also that more and more people are hooking themselves to the higher self. This again brings the same information from above to everyone.

What you see in the material world is a reflection of what is happening in the invisible world. The invisible in fact is more real, since the invisible is the cause.

We must pause to contemplate. We must take no action until what we must do surfaces from within. Then we may act. To "contemplate" is not the opposite of to "act." There are no opposites; one thing always merges into another if done in the proper order. If done out of order, instead of synchronicity, we have a-synchronicity; instead of order, we have disorder; instead of peace, we have war; instead of building, we destroy; instead of abundance, we have scarcity. So simple.

If we want to go right, we must go right. We can't go right by walking left. There is no choice. To go to peace, you go to balance — not left, not right. Not contemplation without action or action without contemplation. But action which comes from contemplation; from looking at the invisible, we can bring the result of thought into the visible world.

If we look at nature, we can see everything we need. When we observe a dog or horse walking, trotting or running, we will see that first, pairs of feet fall together. Then, as it increases in speed, there are three steps — two legs together and one alone. Only when it is running at top speed do we see each leg working separately to bring forth as much power as possible and therefore run as fast as possible. Separate, yet together — that produces maximum performance.

Our being and its energies are the same. If we really look at nature, we will know what to do with ourselves.

The same with our organs. Each organ works separately, yet

together. And so with the planet. We must define each organ, each country and accept that the inner working of each part is different from any other. We must accept that we can work separately to bring maximum performance to the whole. Let's stop fearing that our differences are a threat. On the contrary, our differences are our contributions to one another. Half the world understands the invisible (or spirit) world. They have that to offer to the other half. The other half understands the visible, material part. They have that to offer to the first half. As each half learns what the other half knows, the whole becomes Whole.

III. To My Children

Life Summary/World Summary
This is the way I functioned: (1945-1972)
I **WILL** live to prove there is no evil (age 4) (Love)
I **WILL** give myself to everyone at every level **EVEN IF** the world disapproves, and it hurts. (Love, Sexual, Emotional, Intellectual Freedom)
I **WILL** go to Canada **EVEN IF** I don't know how yet (age 22) (Economic Freedom, Personal Power)
I **WILL** send the money back **EVEN IF** I don't know how yet. (Economic Freedom)
I **WILL** pass Immigration **EVEN IF** I don't know how yet. (Political Freedom)
I **WILL** get married by March, **EVEN IF** I don't know to whom yet. (Personal Peace and Personal Power)
WE WILL go to Columbia University **EVEN IF** I don't know how to pay yet. (Economic Freedom)
WE WILL buy a house where we want **EVEN IF** we don't know how to pay yet. (Economic Freedom)
I **WILL** stay in Europe **EVEN IF** I don't have all the money yet. (Economic Freedom)
I **WILL** love Sean **EVEN IF** he judges me, and it hurts. (Love, Social Freedom)
I **WILL** love Silver **EVEN IF** she thinks I am not pure, and it hurts. (Love, Social Freedom)
I **WILL** love Andrea **EVEN IF** she thinks my ideas are those of ignorant people, and it hurts. (Love and Peace)
I **WILL** love Allan **EVEN IF** he blames me, and it hurts (Love, Personal Power)

This is the way I functioned: (1972-1978)
In California, the Freedom State — my "boxed-in" state.
If you call on the phone **THEN I will** call you (Emotional Slavery)
If I buy a house I want and am alone, **THEN I will** not be able to keep it. (Economic Slavery)
IF Allan does not come to take care of the baby, **THEN I will** be stuck. (Physical Slavery)
IF Allan does not make love to me, **THEN I will** die. (Sexual Slavery)
IF the pain stops hurting, **THEN I will** give my all and keep calling you. (Emotional Slavery)
If I had degrees, **THEN I could** contribute to the world. (Intellectual Slavery)
This is a life of failure, weakness, slavery, pain, war within.
We both had pain, Allan and I.
My formula ends the pain through love, which leads to peace, which leads to life.
Your formula ends the pain through violence, which leads to war, which leads to death.
If we both are going to have pain anyway, why not choose conscious pain. Why not walk towards pain with open eyes? In every other aspect of life we do!
We choose hard universities to train our minds (painful), and it works.
We choose to sweat to train our bodies (painful) and it works.
Why don't we choose emotional pain? It works, too. The ability to choose is a quality of humans. Finally, we will be beyond choice. There is only one direction to go — towards life.
Funny, I spent my life showing people they have choices while I led mostly a life of no choice.

This is the way I have functioned: (1978-1980)
I will call you **EVEN IF** you don't ever call me, and it hurts. (Emotional Freedom)
I WILL buy a house I want **EVEN IF** I don't have all the money myself yet. (Economic Freedom)
I WILL do what I want **EVEN IF** I have to leave Robert alone, and it hurts. (Physical Freedom)
I WILL satisfy myself **EVEN IF** Allan does not satisfy me, and it hurts. (Sexual Freedom)
I WILL give my all **EVEN IF** I keep feeling this horrible pain, each day even more. (Emotional Freedom)
I WILL love Jose **EVEN IF** he is broke, sick, drinks, gambles and goes with other women, and it hurts. (Love, and Social Freedom)
I WILL leave Allan **EVEN IF** I love him, and it hurts.

I WILL love everyone **EVEN IF** it hurts and the pain kills me. It did — the pain killed the ego. The ego was my pain. (Personal Peace)

I did and I do love everyone, because I understand why they do what they do. They feel pain. What else can I do? Forgive? No! There is nothing to forgive. How can you forgive someone in pain! I can only soothe the pain — and I did because I knew.

This is the way I functioned: (1980-present)

I WILL contribute to the world **EVEN IF** I don't have any degrees. (Intellectual Freedom)

I WILL write **EVEN IF** I don't see the money coming yet. (Intellectual, Emotional and Economic Freedom)

I WILL write this book **EVEN IF** I don't know how to write, because I don't hurt anymore!

I WILL spend my last cent for this book **EVEN IF** I don't know the world will accept it, because I don't hurt anymore!

I WILL learn to write, to reach the world **EVEN IF** I don't know what you, my dear world, will do with me . . . such a strange duck . . . because I don't hurt anymore, and I want to heal you.

I WILL get up **EVEN IF** I fall down a thousand times; the failure is in not trying, in giving up, in settling for unrealized dreams.

I WILL not fail, **EVEN IF** I don't know what you will do.

Thus the circle was completed — from freedom to slavery to freedom.

From freedom with personal pain to slavery with even worse pain to freedom without personal pain. If I fill the need of others, then my needs will be fulfilled. From: **I WILL** . . . **EVEN IF** they. To: **IF I** . . . **THEN MY** . . .

In 1945 I decided I would live to prove there is no evil.

In 1981 I write this book to explain why there is no evil.

I call this a conscious life, because I have experienced both sides of the coin:

Self-conscious: 1945-1972
Un-conscious: 1972-1978
Self-conscious: 1978-1980
Cosmic conscious: 1980-

This is a life of success, power, freedom, love and peace within! I know it is not done. Who cares if it is done or not? The point is: Do we want to behave in this manner or not?

Why do we need to continue being sheep?

Can we show real leadership?

Can we stand up and try the untried? Do the undone?

WE CAN and WE WILL!

This is the way the world functions now:

IF they stop arming, **THEN WE Will** stop arming ourselves. (Military Slavery)

IF they attack us, **THEN WE Will** attack them. (Military Slavery and War)

IF they criticize us, **THEN WE Will** stop trading with them. (Economic Slavery, Psychological Slavery)

IF you stop trading with so and so, **THEN WE Will** trade. (Economic Slavery)

IF you stop thinking this way, **THEN WE Will** be able to negotiate with you. (Ideological Slavery)

IF you stop being a Communist, **THEN WE Will** be able to trust you.

IF you stop being a Capitalist, **THEN WE Will** be able to trust you. (Ideological Slavery)

IF you freeze nuclear military development, **THEN WE Will** do it also. (Nuclear Slavery)

From the Times Tribune (April 9, 1983, page 10)

Russia expelled two Britons in apparent retaliation for the ouster of three Russians from London.

The Press is to blame for recent setbacks to the president's defense program, a White House aide said.

If you expelled . . . **THEN I Will** expell . . .

If the Press . . . **THEN** the President will . . .

If you give me your peanut butter sandwich, **THEN I Will** give you my tuna sandwich (Sandwich Slavery)

How long are we going to continue to act as third grade school children. It is true, we are in school. The world is our school and we are all learning. But can we pass to the next grade? This is a life of failure, weakness, slavery, war.

Come with me, let's go together, I know we can.

And Beatriz always knows — that is why she does not know anything! I am right, and because I am right, we will all win!

This is the way the world **could** function:

I, Russia, **WILL** stop arming **EVEN IF** the U.S. has not stopped arming yet.

I, the U.S., **WILL** stop arming **EVEN IF** Russia has not stopped arming yet.

I, El Salvador, **WILL** spend all its money for the poor, the uneducated, **EVEN IF** no one else has done it yet.

WE WILL behave humanely towards them, **EVEN IF** they don't behave humanely towards us.

WE WILL show them we care, **EVEN IF** they don't care for us yet.

WE WILL show the world who we are, EVEN IF they don't know yet.

WE WILL and WE CAN, because no one can stop us from behaving in a humane manner.

Which nations will be "the chosen"? The ones who will choose to act in a humane manner. We are all "chosen" if we choose to be human. Until now, none of us has chosen to be "the chosen." This is a planet of success, power, freedom, love and peace. I know it is not done. Who cares if it is done or not? The point is: Do we want to behave in this manner? Or not? Why do we need to continue being sheep?

Can we show real leadership?

Can we stand up and try the untried? Do the undone?

WE CAN and WE WILL!

"I wish to have the serenity to accept the things I cannot change, the courage to change the things I can and the wisdom to know the difference."

These are nice words, but what do they mean?

Things that we cannot change: others.

Things that we can change: ourselves.

I am responsible for being such an example that whoever is die or be negative.

I am responsible for being an example such that whoever is around me will decide to change, because he can see it pays off to do so — at the personal, city, state and country level.

It is not a matter of belief. It is a matter of Doing it.

I may feel scared of electricity. I may feel I can get electrocuted if I plug in a switch, but IF I do it, I will be pleasantly surprised that the bulb lights up **even if**, I am scared, **even if** I don't believe in electricity. If I wanted someone to try to prove electricity, I would choose a person who does not believe in electricity.

The same is true with my formula. It is not a matter of belief. The formula works.

Let's take another example:

One person rapes another. What is the right response? What is the wrong?

I feel sorry for the victim. I would not want to have that happen to me. That person must feel terrible.

= understanding and compassion for victim.

I could say the person who rapes should be put away. That person does not deserve to be around others. That person is evil.

= lack of understanding and lack of compassion for rapist.

This adds up to:

For one party — understanding and compassion

For second party — lack of understanding and compassion.

Wrong Answer — UNBALANCE: 2 + 2 = 5
*****
I feel sorry for the victim. I would not want to have that happen to me. The person must feel terrible.
= understanding and compassion for victim
I could say, how much pain, anger, frustration, isolation this human being must have felt to strike out in such a brutal manner!
= understanding and compassion for rapist
This adds up to:
For both parties — understanding and compassion
Right Answer — BALANCE: 2 + 2 = 4
Why is 2 + 2 = 5 wrong? Because if you build a house based on the result of that calculation, the house would not stand very long. Why is 2 + 2 = 4 right? Because if you build a house based on the result of that calculation, the house would remain standing.

Wrong calculation gives wrong results. 2 + 2 = 5. The house falls down = WAR.

Right calculation gives right results. 2 + 2 = 4. The house remains standing = PEACE.

Wrong thinking gives wrong results = anger, frustration, hate = WAR.

Right thinking gives right results = understanding, compassion = PEACE.

Why in the first example is the answer wrong?

Because the person who is using this method of thinking is arriving at a result which does not unite, but separates. There is understanding for one party and anger towards the other party. Thus, there is a split in the Self. This split equals WAR, lack of unity was created. Because the person split between UNDERSTANDING and ANGER, the answer is wrong.

Why do we arrive at a split result?

Because we began with the premise that the rapist is different from ourselves. We have placed him apart from us. The premise itself is split. He is evil, and of course we are not!

Why in the second example is the answer right?

Because the person who is using this method of thinking is arriving at a result which unites. There is a unity in the Self. There is understanding, compassion and love for both parties involved. This unity equals PEACE. Peace was created by integrating all the parts in the Self. Because the person is able to unify with UNDERSTANDING, COMPASSION and LOVE to both parties, the answer is right.

Why do we arrive at a unified result?

Because we begin with the premise that the rapist is no different from ourselves. That his actions are a consequence of inner pain. Because we can see in ourselves that when we are in pain, we too strike out. And with this knowledge, we can project

399

how far along the path of pain this human being must have gone to have struck with such brutality. The premise itself is unified.

If we have any situation of 2, 5, 10, 100 or the whole planet, and cannot come up with an answer which brings understanding and compassion to all involved, we must know, we have not arrived at the right answer. We must keep thinking until we do! Brains are for thinking and thinking brings results.

CONCLUSION: UNDERSTANDING, COMPASSION AND LOVE FOR ALL PARTIES INVOLVED IN ANY SITUATION IS THE RIGHT ANSWER.

There is but one right answer in math. There is but one right answer in life.

However . . . if we want the planet to die, the wrong answer is the right answer = SPLIT = WAR.

If we want the planet to live, the right answer is the right answer — UNITY = PEACE.

For the formula to work, the intentions must be PURE. Which means, the intention must be for others: FILL A NEED. If the need of others is filled, then your needs will be filled.

Pure intentions fill a need.

Impure intentions create a need.

Intentions for others:

Pure intentions: Allan will need me only until he finds his own strength.

Impure intentions: Allan will always need me.

The first leads to freedom not just for others but for yourself. The second leads to slavery not just for others but for yourself.

Intentions for self:

Pure intentions: I will do _____ , even if _____ .

Impure intentions: I can't do, because _____ .

How Personal Experiences Relate to World Peace

Personal Situation:

Allan makes a date with Beatriz for 10 a.m.

Allan arrives twelve hours later at 10 p.m.

World Situation:

Argentina attacks Falkland Islands.

Britain is hurt.

Normal Response to Personal Situation:

She: "How dare he treat me like this! To hell with him!" (Due to her anger, she rejects him.)

He: feels the rejection, becomes even more scared and goes deeper into himself.

Normal Response to World Situation:
Britain: "How dare Argentina treat us like this! We'll show them!" (Due to their anger, they reject peace.)
Argentina: becomes scared, arms itself for war.
In this interaction, the mind of each nation has not been used to transform feelings of hurt, injured pride and anger into understanding, compassion and love.

Actual Response to Personal Situation:
Beatriz: sits for twelve hours, puts emotions aside and uses her mind to bring understanding to situation. "Now, why is he late? What is the cause?" Beatriz knows that cause is always an "invisible." No one acts to hurt. No one. "He asked me out. He is interested in me. He called at 8:30 to apologize. Why would anyone act like this?"
Then, at 9:30, the answer comes: "Ah, he is a person who is terribly frightened. His inner being is operating on fear."
The result: her mind brought light to the situation, therefore her feelings are calm because she realizes that what he does has nothing to do with her.
The next step: "What can I do?" she asks herself, "I know who I am, I am love. I know how to love. I will put my love out to him until I see that he no longer feels fear. I accept this as my job and I will continue to do it until my goal is accomplished. Seventeen years later, I have melted his fear with my love. My job is done."

Possible Response to World Situation:
Britain uses mind to bring understanding, puts feelings aside. "Now, why did Argentina invade us? What is the cause? All of us here in Parliament know that no one acts to hurt. No one!"
Then the answer comes: "Ah . . . they had 150% inflation. Their people are beginning to riot because of the economic situation. A foreign country wants to look for oil deposits near the islands. They could use the money from any oil found. They are frightened. They saw no other way out of their economic mess except to invade the Falklands.
"Now, why are they in such an economic disaster? Has this nation been at war for several years? Is the soil no longer any good? Are all of the inhabitants illiterate? Do they have no one capable of constructing appropriate economic plans?"
To answer these questions, the Parliament divides the questions into three sections: material, intellectual, spiritual.
Their conclusion: "No, it is not a material problem. They have good soil as well as all the other materials that they need.
"And no, it is not an intellecctual problem — they do have intelligent, capable people.
Then . . . ah! . . . it is possible that the situation in which Argentina finds itself is a spiritual problem? That their troubles have been brought about by pain?"

Having resolved the question, Britain approaches Argentina: "We've gotten together in Parliament and this is what we've decided . . ." (explains to them Parliament's thinking process). "Now, is there any way we can help you bring pain under control? Is there some way that we can work together to use these resources for the benefit of everyone?"

At this point, Britain acts by putting herself next to the other country and, in this manner, creates a unity, instead of an adversary situation. Integration occurs instead of opposition, peace instead of war.

Last Chapter: What Does it All Mean?

Here we are on the last chapter. After all these weird experiences, what does all this mean?

Let's imagine that you have believed since you were a child that there were little tiny invisible "somethings" in the air and based on that belief, you begin to always wash your hands before meals. Later, you become a doctor and, based on your earlier beliefs, keep washing your hands and begin to observe how it really makes a difference with your patients.

You cannot prove what you believe, but you can see that there are less infections by doing so. Then someone invents a microscope and gives it to you. Now you can finally see that all your beliefs, all the experiments you did, had a real basis in fact. Through the microscope, you can see that it is so.

This is exactly what happened to me. My belief of the law of 3 in 1 is no longer a belief. I saw the law. I know the law. I used the law. And I am here to show how we can all use it at the personal, national and international level. In the measure we use it, we will see the results of peace: which is the goal every human being on earth wants.

Just as in our genes we carry the blueprint of our physical being, so our own bodies make up the blueprint of the planet. The planet is an organism, just like our body. Each country is an organ, each human being is a cell. And just like a human being, the planet has stages it goes through.

As with the organs of the body, each nation has different inner workings. But until now, because we have operated from the fear center, we tried to change each other out of being scared. We felt that if someone was not like us, he was against us. Thus "us" and "them" were created.

It was as it should be, because we were manifesting the negative side of the energy, we were creating a choice. We have travelled to this point to create an unconscious, negative picture. Of course, we needed to distrust. Of course, we were trying to change each other. And of course, we resisted with all our might. That was the perfect way to arrive at this point: the possibility of total destruction.

402

Now we have arrived. We have done it! We have created the choice, and it is clear that everyone wants to select the choice of peace. For that, we must begin to operate in precisely the opposite manner we have done so far. What the TV was telling me in my experience was correct. Right is left. Left is right. You is me. Me is you.

I am calling all my children — the nations of the world — to act. That is good and fine. But what is the work to be done? Let me tell you. In my culture, I grew up with a myth called "Snow White and the Seven Dwarfs." It goes like this: there was a Bad Queen. She wants to be Number One. She looks at a mirror which does not lie and asks, "Who is the fairest one of all?" The mirror tells her that Snow White is Number One. The Bad Queen gives Number One a poisoned apple and puts her to sleep. For a long time, the dwarfs look after Snow White. As they do so, the dwarfs learn to work together and become known as the Seven Dwarfs. Finally, the Kiss of Love wakes Snow White up.

What does all this mean? The Bad Queen is the national ego, which wants to be Number One: "I — I am better than you! I am stronger than you! I . . . I . . . I." The mirror is our consciousness. We are beginning to ask the mirror. The mirror never lies. Snow White, who has been sleeping, is our moral nature. It is our action based on moral judgments, our very being, pure as crystal. The one who can be human and compassionate, the one that can sit next to another nation in harmony instead of in an adversary position. The Seven Dwarfs are the parts of us which must work at the service of our moral values, which must get up and take action even when we don't feel like it or are afraid to. The parts which must share what we have or even play dumb or allow someone else to insult us, knowing that they are doing it because they are using the ego, the Bad Queen. If we use our Seven Dwarfs (our seven chakras, our seven senses?), the white, pure crystal Self rises. Finally, she gets up!

Because of the Bad Queen, the Seven Dwarfs unite and work as a block. All of them together look after Snow White. It is thanks to the Bad Queen that unity occurred. Now we must finish our myth. Snow White will get up. She will thank the Bad Queen, just as Mommy Beatriz thanked Allan for all the pain. We are learning to work as a block in the world, too. We are becoming aware of our mutual desire for peace.

This is what we are about to start doing. We are consciously going to begin to work together to wake up that Snow White in each nation. The Bad Queen has governed for a long time. She has had her time, she has succeeded in her task: the block is created — we all want peace. The egos are out, but now is the time for Snow White to wake up.

We will wake her by exercising our strength. Not an "apple" strength, which is physical (like bombs), but an invisible, moral strength — the Kiss of Love. We have evolved now. This is a new stage of the game. As we recognize it, we can turn 180 degrees without losing face. We can say, "Yes, before I behaved in that manner, it was right. Now there is no need. Now, because we are going toward world peace, because we are waking up Snow White, because moral values are the ones by which we will live, this old behavior will not do."

My father used to tell me this story: a man was in the middle of the desert. He was very thirsty; in fact, he was dying of thirst. A person went by and gave him some water. He drank and revived. He was very grateful. Then he received more water, he bathed, he felt refreshed. Then he began to swim. But the water kept coming and he drowned in it. The same water which saved his life also ended it.

We have behaved admirably to arrive at this point in history, but too much can kill us. We must know when to turn this behavior off. Let's realize our success and consciously come together to organize ourselves as "us" for peace — the opposite of "us" and "them." We all want peace.

Which of my children will it be? Who will take the first step to say, "No longer will our ego govern, no longer the Bad Queen. Let's dispose of the poison apples!"

Numbers do speak. In ancient times, numerology used to tell the story of the person or nation. Even today, we can use the old numerology. But in this 20th century, we have a new numerology. We call it "budgets" and "the economy." Today our budgets tell the story of how frightened we are. The allocation of bigger and bigger percentages for defense and weapons shows it.

Which one of my children will come up with a budget next year which shows that Snow White has awakened? I am waiting for your answer.

Mama Beatriz

WORLD

Only by choice ← does not destroy → has no choice

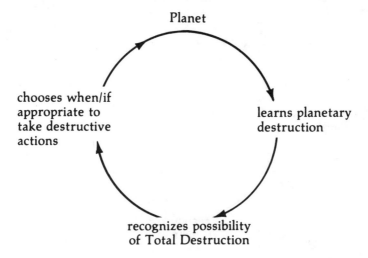

Planet

chooses when/if
appropriate to
take destructive
actions

learns planetary
destruction

recognizes possibility
of Total Destruction

Only by choice ← does not pollute → has no choice

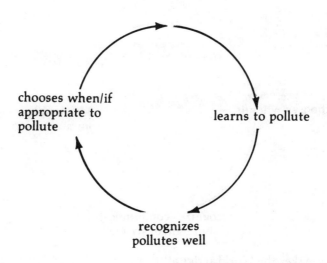

chooses when/if
appropriate to
pollute

learns to pollute

recognizes
pollutes well

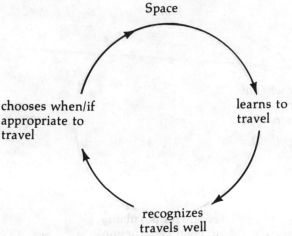

Only by choice ◀— does not travel —▶ has no choice
by air/water/land
Space

chooses when/if
appropriate to
travel

learns to
travel

recognizes
travels well

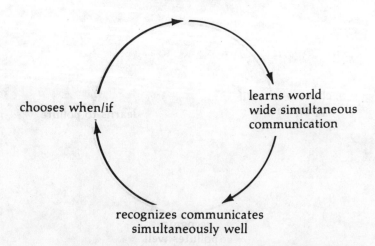

Only by choice ◀— does not communicate —▶ has no choice
worldwide simultaneously

chooses when/if

learns world
wide simultaneous
communication

recognizes communicates
simultaneously well

What makes the World arrive at the point of choice? SUCCESS.
A skill is learned and then we can choose **if/when/never** to use it.

IV. Conclusion: Let's Move On. We Have SUCCEEDED!

I wish to go camping but you won't go with me so I can't.
I wish to work but you will not hire me so I can't.
I wish to be open but you don't let me show my anger so I can't.
I wish to see the bathtub clean but you don't let me hire someone so I can't.

People with wishes don't have wills. To develop will one must live by:

I will go camping **even if** you don't go with me.
I will work **even if** I have to do it for free.
I will be open **even if** you don't approve of me.
I will hire someone to clean **even if** you don't want me to, unless you do it yourself.
I will open up a restaurant **even if** I know nothing about it yet.
When one lives by I WILL, one develops Will.

Great souls have wills; feeble ones have only wishes — Chinese proberb.

Great souls are developed like anything else. The soul, to be developed, must be exercised. I have presented the formula for developing our souls. It is up to each one of us. No one can do it for you! But we can certainly support one another in our journeys toward the development of our souls.

Countries have souls as well.

I wish to live in Peace but I can't because Russia does not let me.
I wish to live in Peace but I can't because the U.S. does not let me.
I wish to live in Peace but I can't because Israel does not let me.
I wish to live in Peace but I can't because the Arab nations don't let me.
I wish to live in Peace but I can't because the Protestants don't let me.
I wish to live in Peace but I can't because the Catholics don't let me.
I wish to live in Peace but I can't because England does not let me.
I wish to live in Peace but I can't because Argentina does not let me.

If you fly over my territory **THEN I WILL** shoot you down.
If you shoot me down, **THEN I WILL** boycott your vodka.

Oh . . . my children . . . until when . . . until when?

We **Have** Succeeded! Let's move on!

INDEX

INTERNATIONAL PRESS REVIEW

There are books which are like a glass of water to the thirsty, a chair for the tired or a friendly hand for the lonely: Beatriz achieves all these and much more with her book, "Beatriz — A Manual for Peace."

This book is like both high noon and sunset — high noon, because it appears as revelation from above, and sunset because the experience of a human life is vivid and raw. High noon disorients; sunset impassions.

"Beatriz — A Manual for Peace" is not a book, it is several. In one the seed seems to die, to fruit in the next. Like the ear of wheat which ripens because "The sun illuminates it," Beatriz can feel herself mother of all children and dispense bread to Planet Earth. Human and shaken by life, she finds her way, and brings smiles to all who cross her path with tearful eyes. Peace is possible when we know and live Love.

Jorge Brignole
San Francisco, Nov. 30, 1983

Jorge Brignole Corrales is a Chilean journalist correspondent for Italian News Agency (ANSA) in California, where he is a radio commentator as well. He also writes for newspapers in Spanish on the American continent. His career began with the Berlin Wall in 1961, and his first interview was with German Chancellor Konrad Adenauer. In Chile he had a television program (Channel 13) for two years before he was sent to cover the Ecumenical Council, Vatican II. He was part of the group of journalists which accompanied Chilean President Eduardo Frei on a visit to Europe in 1965. He declined the position of Cultural and Press attache in Italy to keep his objectivity and journalistic impartiality.

CRITICA DE LA PRENSA INTERNACIONAL

Hay libros que son como un vaso de agua para el sediento, una silla para el cansado o la mano amiga para el solitario: Beatriz logra esto y mucho mas con "Beatriz — A Manual for Peace." Su libro es como el zenit y el ocaso, el zenit, porque verticalmente pareciera revelado, el ocaso, porque horizontal, es la experiencia de una vida humana cruda y viva. El zenit desconcierta, el ocaso apasiona.

"Beatriz — ..." no es un libro, son varios en uno solo donde la semilla parece morir en el primero para dar fruto en el que sigue. De la espiga que madura por "El sol que la ilumina," es que Beatriz puede sentirse madre de todos los ninos y repartir el pan en el Planeta Tierra. Humana y sacudida por la vida, ella encuentra el camino para si misma y para todos en las manos que se cruzan, en los ojos humedos, para hacerlos sonreir. La paz le es posible cuando conozcamos y vivamos el amor.

Jorge Brignole
San Francisco, 30 noviembre, 1983

Jorge Brignole Corrales es un periodista chileno corresponsal de la Agencia Italiana de Noticias ANSA en California donde ademas es comentarista radial. Escribe para periodicos en castellano del Continente Americano. Su carrera periodistica nacio con el muro de Berlin en 1961 y su primera entrevista fue al entonces canciller aleman Konrad Adenauer. En su pais, Chile, tuvo un programa televisivo (Canal 13) periodistico-cultural que duro 2 anos antes de ser enviado a Roma para cubrir el Concilio Ecumenico Vaticano II. Formo parte de la comitiva periodistica que llevo el presidente de Chile, Eduardo Frei cuando visito Europea en 1965. Reuncio al cargo de Agregado Cultural y de Prensa en Italia para mantener su objetividad e imparcialidad periodistia.

ORDER FORM

Please send _____ cop(y)(ies) of

BEATRIZ A Manual for Peace by Beatriz G. Prentice

to me at $9.95 per copy plus postage, handling, and sales tax (see below).

Name _____

Mailing Address _____
                        (street address)

                    _____
                    (city)   (state)   (zip)

_____ book(s) at $9.95 per book = _____

Postage and handling: Add   _____
$1.00 for 1 to 3 books;
$ for   to   books
$ per book for over
   books

Sales tax: NY residents, add   _____
8¼% to cost of books

               TOTAL   _____

Please make check or money order for the total amount to "Coleman Publishing" and send to
                Coleman Publishing
                99 Milbar Boulevard
                Farmingdale, NY 11735

ORDER FORM

Por que quiero el mundo is a book of verse in Spanish compiled by Beatriz G. Prentice.

Use this form to order copies at $4.95 each plus postage, handling, and sales tax (see below).

Name _____

Mailing address   (street address)

_____
                    (city)   (state)   (zip)

_____ copies of *Por que quiero*
el mundo at $4.95 per copy = _____

Postage and handling: _____
Add $1.00 for 1 to 3 books

Sales tax: California   _____
residents, add 6/6.5%
to cost of books

          TOTAL   _____

Please make check or money order for the total amount to "World Purpose Foundation" and send to

World Purpose Foundation
140 University Ave., Suite 4
Palo Alto, CA 94301

Coleman Publishing
99 Milbar Boulevard
Farmingdale, New York 11735
(516) 293-0383-84